REFORM ZIONISM

REFORM ZIONISM

AN EDUCATOR'S PERSPECTIVE

MICHAEL LIVNI (LANGER)

gefen
publishing house בית הוצאה לאור

JERUSALEM ◆ NEW YORK

Copyright © Gefen Publishing House
Jerusalem 1999/5759

Typesetting: Marzel A.S. -- Jerusalem
Cover Design: Studio Paz, Jerusalem

**The author and the publisher thank the following for granting permission
to use material included in this book: ARZENU, The Jerusalem Post,
Judaism, Reform Judaism, UAHC.**

Edition 9 8 7 6 5 4 3 2 1

Gefen Publishing House
POB 36004
Jerusalem 91360, Israel
972-2-538-0247
isragefen@netmedia.net.il

Gefen Books
12 New Street
Hewlett, NY 11557, USA
516-295-2805
gefenbooks@compuserve.com

www.israelbooks.com

Printed in Israel

Send for our free catalogue

Library of Congress Cataloging-in-Publication Data
Livni, Michael, 1935-
Reform Zionism: Twenty Years, An Educator's Perspective / Michael Livni (Langer)
      p.   cm.

ISBN: 965 229 206 0

1. Reform Judaism. 2. Zionism and Judaism. 3. Reform Judaism—Israel.
4. Jewish youth—Education. I. Title.
BM197.L58 1999
296.8'34—dc21

                    99-31958
                    CIP

Table of Contents

I BELIEVE

אֲנִי מַאֲמִין

Laugh, laugh, at all the dreams,
It is I the dreamer who speaks.
Laugh, for I still believe in man,
For I still believe in you.

שַׂחֲקִי, שַׂחֲקִי עַל הַחֲלוֹמוֹת,
זוּ אֲנִי הַחוֹלֵם שָׂח.
שַׂחֲקִי כִּי בָאָדָם אַאֲמִין,
כִּי עוֹדֶנִּי מַאֲמִין בָּךְ.

For my soul still longs for liberty,
I have not sold out to the golden calf,
For I still believe in man,
In his spirit — firm and strong.

כִּי עוֹד נַפְשִׁי דְרוֹר שׁוֹאֶפֶת,
לֹא מְכַרְתִּיהָ לְעֵגֶל-פָּז,
כִּי עוֹד אַאֲמִין גַּם בָּאָדָם,
גַּם בְּרוּחוֹ, רוּחַ עָז.

Shaul Tchernichovsky   (1894)   שאול טשרניחובסקי

And it shall come to pass afterwards, that I will pour out my spirit upon all flesh; and your sons and your daughters shall prophesy; your old men shall dream dreams, your young men shall see visions:

Joel 3:1

וְהָיָה אַחֲרֵי-כֵן אֶשְׁפּוֹךְ אֶת-רוּחִי עַל-
כָּל-בָּשָׂר וְנִבְּאוּ בְּנֵיכֶם וּבְנֹתֵיכֶם זִקְנֵיכֶם חֲלֹמוֹת יַחֲלֹמוּן
בַּחוּרֵיכֶם חֶזְיֹנוֹת יִרְאוּ:

יואל ג:1

*This book is dedicated
to those who would
realize the vision of
Reform Zionism*

FOREWORD

I recall that as a youngster, my favorite section of *The Reader's Digest* was a monthly feature entitled "The Most Unforgettable Character I've Known." I think that if I were writing such an essay, it would describe Michael Livni (Langer).

I first heard of him in 1974. Prior to an orientation meeting he had prepared at Kibbutz Gesher Haziv to meet with the adult leaders of American Reform Judaism's Youth Division and their counterparts in the Ichud HaKvutzot Kibbutz movement, I asked a respected friend who had been a national Habonim leader if he knew Livni (then Langer).

"Know him. I was a Langerite!" he exclaimed. He was the first of many disciples of this charismatic leader whom I would meet over the years — and I would like to compliment myself that in some ways I also became one of Michael's students and devotees.

We expected that this introductory meeting would be a perfunctory formality, an exercise in etiquette. How wrong we were. We were not the examiners but the examinees. Livni had charts and blackboards filled and quizzed us on our philosophy. He asked us questions which frankly we should have asked ourselves long before. He persisted in forcing us to think and clarify our basic and driving values.

Almost single-handedly Livni laid the groundwork for practical Reform Zionism. He was a midwife for the birth of ARZA, the Association of Reform Zionists of America, the father of Garin Arava, the first American Reform Garin (settlement nucleus) and, following his return to Israel, the architect of Tsofei Telem, the Israeli Reform scout unit. He was instrumental in the founding of the Reform kibbutzim Yahel and Lotan and in middle age left the established Gesher Haziv to pioneer once again as a member of Kibbutz Lotan in the Arava desert.

Like so many worthwhile things in life, Livni's success is in his contradictions and creative tensions. He is, in Achad Ha'am's terminology, both a *cohen* (priest) and *navi* (prophet). He is a stubborn ideologue and a flexible pragmatist, energetic and contemplative. He takes his mission seriously but not himself when it comes to seeking praise and credit. Not shrinking from the controversial and unpopular, he is courageous and compassionate. He is at home in the halls of academia and washing dishes in the kibbutz.

A Renaissance man, he was trained as a physician concentrating in the field of social psychiatry. His personal youth movement experience, buttressed by an academic understanding of youth movement process, is a key to understanding his proficiency in youth work. In Israel he became an active educator (formal and informal) and an agriculturist specializing in turkey husbandry. He is an energetic administrator, a gifted intellect and, as you, the reader, will see, an original, creative and synthetic thinker.

Livni has been accused of being a Don Quixote, but the success of his projects stands in stark contrast to the cynical detractions. He has been criticized as being anachronistic, but much of what he has spoken and written is timely, bordering on the eternal.

This collection of essays and articles, written over more than a score of years, provides a rare insight into classical Zionist thought as it dialectically intersects and synthesizes with its onetime adversary, Reform Judaism. Both basic philosophy and practical applications are dealt with in these works whose insights incite.

The Reader has a rare opportunity to be challenged and enlightened by meeting a gifted, seminal thinker and an effective doer.

— *Rabbi Henry F. Skirball*

INTRODUCTORY PREFACE

A Summary of Personal Involvement

The articles and essays collected in this volume reflect twenty years of involvement with Reform Zionism. During these years the organizational locus of that involvement has varied. The different organizational foci also represent different target audiences. This is reflected in some but not all of my writing. Hence, a thumbnail sketch of my involvement is necessary.

My organizational involvement with Reform Zionism began with Rabbi Stephen Schafer, the then Director of the Union of American Hebrew Congregations' Youth Division, recruiting me as the first *shaliach* (emissary) from the kibbutz movement to the North American Reform movement — 1975-1977. My work, in tandem with Rabbi Schafer, involved advocacy for long term Reform programs for youth in Israel, organizing a *garin* (settlement group) of American Reform youth for the movement's first kibbutz (Yahel), and integrating the idea of Israel in all the Youth Division's departments. The fact that the Reform movement was without political leverage in the World Zionist Organization (WZO), and hence not a recipient of WZO funds in a measure commensurate with the scope of its Israel oriented youth work, made me a behind-the-scenes advocate for the establishment of ARZA, the Association of Reform Zionists of America.

During the term of my *shlichut*, I edited REFORM ZIONIST PERSPECTIVE: JEWISH COMMUNITY in the MODERN AGE. It was my first attempt to develop a comprehensive ideological synthesis between Reform Judaism and Zionism — in particular Labor Zionism.

My experience in America convinced me that if a blend of Reform Judaism and Reconstructionism could find a suitable venue within Israeli society, an alternative to the secular-Orthodox polarity extant in Israel could evolve. In the late Seventies it was still possible to believe that the Kibbutz movement could have a major role in pioneering such an innovation (see Section Seven).

In 1979 the World Union for Progressive Judaism (WUPJ) requested the Kibbutz movement to recruit me in order to serve as Coordinator of Reform outreach to Israeli youth with the purpose of creating an autonomous youth movement for the Israel Movement for Progressive Judaism.

In fact, the decision to recruit me again was a coordinated decision between the UKM,[1] responsible for the logistics of the Reform kibbutz, the WUPJ director, Rabbi Richard Asher Hirsch and the UAHC Youth Division. It was the UAHC Youth Division Staff in Israel (Rabbis Henry Skirball and Allan Eliyahu Levine), backed by Rabbi Schafer that were initially responsible for recruiting Israeli *Garinim* (settlement groups). The IMPJ was only marginally involved.

There was another fortuitous connection between my *shlichut* in America and my new task as coordinator of Telem Noar.[2] While in America I had worked with the 16-year-old Israeli participants in the Eisendrath International Exchange (EIE) program. This program, organized by the UAHC Youth Division at the time, brought Israeli youth to America for six months to attend UAHC Camps and to be adopted into Reform congregations. Some were from the few IMPJ congregations that existed and some joined IMPJ *garinim*. In the years 1980-1982, my previous contact with these young people enabled me to recruit a number of them to form the nucleus of the youth movement leadership group. Without them it would probably not have been possible to start the movement. However, their young age and hence their inability to commit themselves to more than one or two years, remained a flaw that was never really overcome.

I remained as coordinator of Telem Noar (which became Tzofei Telem) until 1983. This period of intensive personal involvement sharpened my perspective both on Zionist Jewish education and on the Israel Movement for Progressive Judaism.

In December 1986 I moved from Kibbutz Gesher Haziv where I had lived for 23 years to Kibbutz Lotan, the second Reform kibbutz (established in 1983) first as adviser and later as member.

As a result of the elections to the 31st Zionist Congress in December 1987, the chairpersonship of the Department of Jewish Education and Culture in the Diaspora was apportioned to ARZENU, the international federation of the Reform Zionist movement. ARZENU appointed Rabbi Henry Skirball to chair the department. In 1989, Rabbi Skirball recruited me from Kibbutz Lotan to serve first as adviser and then as executive director of the department. I served in this capacity until after the 32nd Zionist Congress (1992).

In 1994 I was elected to the Executive of the Israel Movement for Progressive

---

1. United Kibbutz Movement.
2. IMPJ youth.

Judaism. After completing a two-year term, I resigned from the Executive because of disagreement with the policies being pursued.

As noted above, there is some correlation between my writing and the focus of my personal involvement at a given time. However, the issues facing Reform Zionism are interrelated and hence I have dealt with them at various times in response to circumstances within the Reform movement and the Zionist polity in general.

The nature of my involvement has never permitted a "pure" delineation of various aspects of Reform Zionism. Many Zionist activists have been faced with a similar problem in delineating the foci of their endeavors. Nevertheless, I have seen fit to arrange this books in sections. Each section of this book deals mainly with a particular issue or a particular aspect of an issue within Reform Zionism. The essays and articles dealing with that issue are presented chronologically within each section. The introduction to each section chronicles the circumstances which led me to write particular articles at a particular time. Hence, there is an element of intellectual autobiography in the introductions which may shed light on the development of my ideas. The central issues raised in each section are briefly summarized below.

Reform Pro-Israelism vs. Reform Zionism

The core issue for Reform Zionism, in the Diaspora and Israel, is the differentiation between pro-Israelism and Zionism. The ongoing attempt to define Reform Zionism, both ideologically and by a distinct action program, is the focus of Section One. The implications for Reform Judaism in Israel are the focus of Section Two.

For Reform Jews in the Diaspora, pro-Israelism means mainly financial support for the State of Israel and, in particular, advocacy of Reform rights and support of Reform institutions. Secondarily, it means utilizing Israel as an educational tool for strengthening the Jewish identity of Diaspora Reform Jewish youth. Within this basically non-ideological framework there is no particular vision for Reform Zionism in Israel — there are merely Congregations of Reform Jews currently fighting for their democratic rights.

Reform Zionism implies a certain vision regarding the nature of the Jewish State, the Diaspora, and the relationship between them. Any Zionist vision must be rooted in a rationale relating to general and Jewish history and Jewish values. Ultimately, the question is: What is the creative significance and purpose of Jewish Peoplehood in our times?

Reform Zionism necessitates an action program outlining the path (or paths) to be followed in realizing its vision. Perforce, such an action program must create instrumentalities necessary for furthering the actualization of the program. The instrumentalities are those within the Reform movement and those encompassing the Jewish polity without (e.g., the Jewish Federations, the Jewish Agency, the WZO).

Every Zionist movement has had its vision of the Jewish State (and of the Jewish People) which it attempted to realize. What is the vision of Reform Zionism?

Pro-Israelism vs. Zionism Within the Israel Movement for Progressive Judaism

Section Two deals with this question as I have interfaced with it over a period of twenty years.

The Israel Movement for Progressive Judaism (IMPJ) was and is mired in a double conflict. The first conflict, a core conflict, is at the conceptual level. Is the IMPJ the expression of Reform Zionism as a movement impacting on the emerging nature of the Jewish State in Israel or is the IMPJ an organization for furthering the establishment of Reform congregations in the State of Israel and ensuring their rights? The Reform Zionist option surely includes the congregational option even if it is not coextensive with it. However, the congregational option does not necessarily imply a Reform Zionist rationale.

The second conflict stems naturally from the first. It has centered on the priority (as measured in budgetary terms) given to Reform education, formal and informal, as distinct from congregational development. During the years 1995-1996, the IMPJ spent more than twice as much on congregations as on formal and informal education combined.

A related aspect of the conflict has to do with the question of leadership. Will the IMPJ be built by professional (in particular rabbinic) leadership on the Diaspora model or should Reform Zionism in Israel seek to be a popular, humanistic movement of numbers with lay leadership utilizing rabbinic leadership as leavening? If Reform Zionism replicates the authority structure of Orthodoxy, can it still maintain its ideological integrity and its potential for projecting an alternative to a secular public?

What might be a practical path for synthesizing between the above polarities?

A Reform Zionist Approach to Jewish-Zionist Politics

Section Three deals with another major issue — A Reform Zionist approach to

Jewish-Zionist Politics. From the moment that ARZA became a part of the World Zionist Organization, I felt that Reform Zionism had a central role to play in the democratization of the Jewish politics as a basis for Israel-Diaspora relations of the future. Reform Zionism has, indeed, actively fought for democratic Zionist elections in the Diaspora. However the movement has refrained from initiating attempts to democratize the Federations. Nor has the movement aggressively pursued the demand for separate elections in Israel to a world Zionist-Jewish body. Such a democratic body could be a unique contribution of Reform Zionism to the renewal of a feeling of mutual engagement and, hopefully, partnership in Israel-Diaspora relations.

Pro-Israel Jewish Education or Zionist Education?

Sections Four and Five deal with Zionist Jewish Education. Without making education a cardinal *Mitzva* (commandment) Judaism would not have survived. Today we have expanded the Torah commandment "*Ve higadeta L'bincha*" (You will say unto your son) to include the daughter as well.

Jewish education has always had an element of the explicit and has not relied on the implicit alone. How does one balance the authoritarian explicit with the humanistic-democratic implicit? This is the challenge for Reform Zionist education — a path melding the religious and secular humanistic approach.

All Zionist education is Jewish pro-Israel education. However, not all Jewish pro-Israel education is Zionist education. Jewish pro-Israel education conforms to current norms in existing Jewish society. Zionist education means education to norms that are not yet. Hence, by definition, Zionist education seeks to inculcate norms at deviance with those of existing society. Therefore, both formal and informal Zionist education require an educational rationale distinct from pro-Israel Jewish education. This is the burden of Section Four. Much of Section Four is the outcome of the 3½ years (1989-1992) that I spent in the Department of Jewish Education and Culture.

The question of pro-Israel as distinct from Zionist education is not solely a Diaspora issue. Quite the opposite. Ironically, the dismantling of the Labor Zionist school system in 1953 left Israel with a State system without any specific Zionist ideology. Without doubt, this decision was a factor in Labor's passing from power a generation later. The State system is, in fact, "pro-Israel" education. The Religious Zionist educational system was not dismantled. The asymmetric result has been that the State finances only one variety of Zionist ideology — the Orthodox Zionist. The last decade has also witnessed the growth (with State financing) of the ultra-Orthodox, non-Zionist independent school system. This vacuum calls for a Reform Zionist response.

Historically, formal Zionist education was supplemented by a framework of informal education — the autonomous youth movement. The youth movement existed in tandem and yet in tension with the system of formal education. The diminution of the secular youth movements' role is a result both of the radical changes in youth culture as well as the decline of the "anachronistic" norms of pioneering Zionism.

Zionism needs a Reform Zionist response to the vacuum existing between sterile pro-Israelism and authoritarian Orthodox Zionism (and non-Zionist ultra-Orthodoxy). Such a response will come about only by educating to Reform Zionism in the Reform congregational world outside of Israel (Section Five) as well as developing formal and informal Reform Zionist education in Israel. (Section Two and Section Six).

Reform Zionist Youth Movement in Israel

Theory would dictate that a Reform Zionist Youth movement would follow logically from a Reform Zionist IMPJ program. In fact, the Reform Zionist initiative for transforming a loosely knit network of congregational youth groups and *garinim* (settlement groups) came from outside the IMPJ. The United Kibbutz Movement (UKM) convinced the World Union for Progressive Judaism (WUPJ) that a Reform Zionist youth movement was necessary in order to ensure settlement groups for the Reform kibbutzim and in order to create committed leadership for the IMPJ of the future. In 1980 Tzofei Telem became a joint venture of the UKM and WUPJ, financially and ideologically. The UKM brokered the entrance of Telem-Noar (IMPJ Youth) into the *"Tzofim"* (the Israeli Scouts). Telem-Noar became Tzofei Telem.

The articles and essays in Section Six detail issues that arose during the years that I served as coordinator of the movement (1979-1983). The interested reader is referred to the introduction to that section. Most of the issues in the previous sections markedly influenced my work with Tzofei Telem as a Reform Zionist Youth movement. A central question with which Tzofei Telem had to contend was Zionist education as distinct from pro-Israel education. The ongoing attempt to formulate and implement patterns of Reform Zionist community defined the Tzofei Telem educational enterprise.

Ultimately, in the absence of a Reform Zionist oriented educational system, Tzofei Telem did not have the leadership resources to maintain itself as an autonomous "island" of informal Reform Zionist education in the surrounding sea of "pro-Israel" educational pressures of the Israel Scouts on the one hand and the IMPJ on the other hand.

The financial and ideological crisis within the Kibbutz movement which came to a head in the mid-Eighties resulted in the withdrawal of financial and political support needed to maintain an autonomous youth movement. Tzofei Telem became totally dependent financially on the IMPJ.

Tzofei Telem survived as a Reform Zionist youth movement for fifteen years mainly because of the support of the Reform kibbutzim, which were in turn supported by the UKM. For six years Kibbutz Lotan supplied central staff for the youth movement. When it was no longer able to do so, Tzofei-Telem reverted to a youth organization — Noar Telem.

The Reform Kibbutzim

The Reform kibbutzim (Section Seven) were founded as a result of the initiative of individual Reform Zionist activists within the pro-Israel climate of the Union of American Hebrew Congregations after the Six Day War and the Yom Kippur War. As described in the beginning of the preface, "This is where I came in." The Yom Kippur War also had an impact on Israeli youth which made it possible to recruit Israeli *garinim* (settlement groups) as well. The Reform kibbutzim have become a symbol of Zionist involvement for the Reform movement outside of Israel. The mutual relationship between the IMPJ and the kibbutzim has been ambivalent.

It is the kibbutzim that have had to contend with the question: "What happens in terms of Reform Zionism after the youth movement?" A community of Reform Zionist commitment is the "natural" outcome of a Reform Zionist youth movement. The kibbutz is theoretically an ideal framework. The Reform kibbutzim have shown themselves to be somewhat of a "pilot plant" for Reform Zionism. However, additional (non-kibbutz) forms of Reform Zionist community have not emerged. The kibbutzim are the first to be aware of the necessity for additional forms of Reform Zionist community.

The failure of Reform Zionism to adequately support the Reform kibbutzim (especially with additional committed candidates for membership) is indicative of Reform Zionism's functioning as a pro-Reform Judaism in Israel organization rather than as a Reform Zionist movement. The kibbutzim have been left to their own internal resources to achieve a minimal critical mass.

A Few Acknowledgments

Rabbi Henry "Hank" Skirball not only agreed to write the foreword for this book — he has been a continuous source of encouragement and he has helped me with numerous suggestions regarding its format.

Brenda (Naomi) Herzberg has given me her full support as I dedicated time which should have been ours to this compilation.

My thanks to Shaul Vardi, a graduate of RSY Netzer (UK), who helped translate nearly all of those articles in this book, which were originally written in Hebrew, into English.

Finally, my home — Kibbutz Lotan. Imperfect. Struggling economically and socially. Very alone with too few members. Not afraid to see itself as a Reform Zionist community in ongoing tension with its ever evolving identity. This book was almost not written because of the pressures and the distractions of life on Lotan. This book could not have been written anywhere else.

Reform Judaism and Zionism

* ARZENU — International Federation of Reform and Progressive Religious Zionists

Synopsis of the Section

The articles deal with the interface between Reform Judaism and Zionism and the formulation of a Reform Zionist ideology and action program. They reflect the development of the author's thought within the framework of his personal involvement during twenty years.

In 1975, as the first *shaliach* (emissary) of the Kibbutz movement (and in fact, of the World Zionist Organization) to the Union of American Hebrew Congregations, I was faced with the challenge of defining the interface between the two movements. In effect, this meant defining an ideological stance.

Defining the Synthesis

Since my late teens, I have defined myself as a Cultural Zionist. Growing up in Canada, I saw no relevance in the "negation of the Diaspora" doctrine. My Zionist approach was shaped by the ideas of *Achad Ha'am* as interpreted by the English-American writer, Maurice Samuel (1895-1972). After over a decade in Israel, I had become aware of the sterility, from a Jewish point of view, of much in secular Israeli culture. In conversations preliminary to my recruitment as *shaliach*, Rabbi Stephen Schafer, the Director of the Youth Division of the UAHC at that time, and I reached a consensus that our challenge was to create frameworks within which Reform youth could relate creatively to Jewish community. Both Rabbi Schafer and I were fully aware of the effect of modernity in undermining commitment to Jewish community. The idea of linking Kibbutz community with Reform Judaism had arisen in the framework of dialogues between Reform Rabbis and Kibbutz educators in the early Seventies. The challenge of linking Reform Judaism and in particular Jewish Youth in America with this vision was both ideological and organizational.

REFORM JUDAISM AND ZIONISM AS JEWISH RESPONSES TO THE MODERN AGE was the ideological statement developed during my first year as *shaliach* as a rationale for my work. The central thesis proposed in this essay was that both Zionism (and in particular Labor Zionism) as well as Reform Judaism were movements of reform, responses by the Jewish people to the impact of modernity, influenced by prophetic Judaism. Our challenge was the synthesis of the Reform in religion with the ongoing reform in Israeli society. A Reform kibbutz could become the symbol of such a synthesis. Section 7 expands on this theme in greater detail. This essay appeared as the introductory essay in REFORM ZIONIST PERSPECTIVE which appeared in print shortly after my return to Israel in the fall of 1977. At the same time, the Biennial of the UAHC meeting in San Francisco approved the establishment of ARZA, the Association of Reform Zionists of America.

The Progress of Reform Zionism

The constitution of the World Zionist Organization (WZO) requires five national bodies in order to constitute a federation within the WZO framework. In 1980, ARZENU was established as the international confederation of Reform Zionist movements. My memo, REFORM ZIONISM: STATEMENT OF POSITION AND AIMS, was submitted in this context. In 1983, the first printing of REFORM ZIONIST PERSPECTIVE ran out. The UAHC Youth Division agreed to sponsor a second printing. I felt unable to revise the book but agreed to write an updated introductory essay. At this time I was already heavily involved in the Israel Movement for Progressive Judaism (IMPJ) as coordinator of *Tzofei Telem* (see Section 6). REFORM ZIONISM: PROBLEMS AND PROGRESS presents an overview much of which is still timely, in my opinion, fifteen years later.

In 1987, Rabbi Henry Skirball was appointed by ARZENU as its representative on the WZO Executive and became the chairperson of the Department of Jewish Education and Culture of the WZO. In 1989 he asked me to join him as his Executive Director. I did so as an "outside worker" from Kibbutz Lotan. Perforce, this position led to my becoming a part of the "ARZENU team" in the WZO. In addition to the major focus of my activity and thinking on Zionist Jewish education reflected in Section 4, I became involved in the ARZENU-WZO connection. THE ARZENU PROGRAM: (Letter To Rabbi Michael Stroh), and ARZENU-WHAT NOW? (Letter to Rabbi David Lilienthal) reflect my positions on ARZENU policy.

In 1992, ARZENU withdrew from the coalition with the Labor Zionist movement in the WZO because of the latter's refusal to promote democratic elections in the Diaspora for the 32nd World Zionist Congress. This ended Rabbi Skirball's and my tenure in the Department of Jewish Education and Culture. However, I continued to serve on the Israel advisory committee of ARZENU as well as deputy member for ARZENU on the Zionist Actions committee.

My disagreement with the ARZENU Executive's decision to remain on the WZO Executive, essentially an unelected body, is expressed in my letter to Rabbi David Lilienthal, the Chairperson of ARZENU at the time.

There were two reasons for my memo to Rabbi Lilienthal in 1994 on AFFIR-MATIVE ACTION FOR REFORM ZIONIST ALIYAH. First of all, my involvement with the IMPJ convinced me that the *Aliyah* of even one hundred truly committed Reform Zionists could have a significant impact on the passive, largely professionally led IMPJ. Secondly, the almost exclusive concern of ARZENU with Zionist politics while ignoring practical Zionist work, seemed to me an incorrect strategy. But advocacy of Reform Zionist *Aliyah* was only one point in an overall strategy of what Reform Zionism should be doing. A RATIONALE AND PROGRAM FOR REFORM ZIONISM is essentially a statement of my basic ideological approach to Reform Zionism as the year 2000 approaches. As such it stands in evolutionary relationship to the first essay in this section, REFORM JUDAISM AND ZIONISM AS JEWISH RESPONSES TO THE MODERN AGE, written almost twenty years earlier.

Perspectives for an Action Program: Reform Judaism and Zionism as Jewish Responses to the Modern Age[1]

The Modern Age and Human Evolution

Reform Judaism and Zionism have been in the past and continue to be in the present responses of the Jewish people to the challenge of what we may broadly described as the Modern Age. The coming of the Modern Age probably constitutes the greatest discontinuity not only in the 6,000-year recorded history of mankind, but also in the three to four million year evolutionary history of the genus *Homo*. The challenges that the Modern Age posed (and poses) for the Jewish people are really secondary to this major discontinuity that the Modern Age constitutes for all mankind.

As Rene Dubois has pointed out in his book "The God Within,"[2] during the millions of years since humans first made their appearance, the normative social environment was the small group or band. During the last 5,000 to 10,000 years when we gradually developed sedentary habits, the normative community became the village. In either case, the social basis was a relatively small group, generally an extended family group or perhaps a group of extended families which formed a community. The ecology of the group was a rural one. The social cohesion of such communities was maintained by a framework of implicit mutual obligations between members. At a later stage (corresponding to the beginnings of recorded history), such mutual obligations became more explicit. Such an evolution from the implicit to the explicit is clearly traceable in the development of Jewish traditions.

One hundred and fifty thousand generations developed within a social milieu of a certain common communal quality. It would be reasonable to assume that such a period of time was adequate to allow for some selection of the species in this direction. In other words, in terms of biological endowment the communal-

---

1. Published in part: *CCAR Yearbook*, Vol. 85, 1976; *Midstream*, April 1977. Published in full — 1977 in: Langer, Michael, ed., *A Reform Zionist Perspective*, UAHC Youth Division, New York, 1977.
2. Rene Dubois, *The God Within*, Charles Scribner, 1972. See esp. ch. 3 & ch. 13.

extended family framework with inter-personal relationship based on mutual
obligations is the normative one for *Homo Sapiens*. The generalization can be
made without gainsaying the tremendous variety of such frameworks that did
develop.

The Traditional Order Breaks Down

It is the last five to ten generations which have witnessed the breaking down of
the traditional order in its many forms, thus bringing about the major discontinuity in our evolutionary history. Such a period is equivalent to perhaps one
twenty-thousandth of our existence, or one day in the life of a fifty-year-old adult.

The dynamics of the passing of the traditional order can be briefly sketched.
The Renaissance and the Enlightenment of the 16th, 17th and 18th centuries
sundered medieval philosophy into natural science, political philosophy (political
science), theology and metaphysics. The religio-philosophical base of human
existence which related man through community to the cosmic was undermined
by Copernicus and Galileo. An age of discovery, both scientific and geographic,
was initiated. The economic and technological changes stemming therefrom led
straight to the Industrial Revolution.

The political philosopher, John Locke, posited a political state whose purpose
was to ensure "the rights of the individual" as against defining the obligations of
the individual to his community. The cumulative result of these processes was the
disintegration of the organic community and its world outlook. The Age of
Discovery provided the opportunity of founding new communities unfettered by
traditional ties. New wealth flowed into the hands of new classes who had no
place in the traditional order. Most important of all, the rural ecology on which
traditional society was based broke down as the Industrial Revolution
progressed.[1]

The dislocation of the rural population to an urban setting was characterized
by the transformation of the extended family village unit to the fragmented urban
nuclear family. Within the city itself, new modes of production broke up the
network of guilds and fraternities — the medieval urban equivalent of the village
socio-economic framework.

In summary, the Modern Age made traditional ways of understanding and
looking at the world meaningless and social frameworks and established norms
lost their relevance. Perhaps the most unsettling aspect of these epochal changes

---

1. See for this perspective Stanley Meron, "The Individual and Society," Ichud HaKvutzot
   VeHaKibbutzim, 1966. (English translation in Langer, Michael, ed., *A Reform Zionist Perspective*, UAHC
   Youth Division, New York, 1977, pp. 38-48.)

was (and is) that they constituted not a one-time discontinuity to which humans could adjust, but rather a continuing and continually accelerating discontinuity as a "constant" factor in one's life.

Secondary Effects on the Jewish Community

The erosion of the medieval community's organic order, both temporally and spiritually, was bound to have effects on its various components — including the Jewish community. For a correct analysis of the Jewish response to the modern age, it is most useful to distinguish between the primary impact of the modern age on the Jewish community itself as against the secondary effects on the Jewish community of the breakdown of the traditional order among the peoples in whose midst Jews lived. Two such *secondary* effects were the Emancipation of the Jews and the rise of modern anti-Semitism.

As Arthur Hertzberg has pointed out,[1] the Edict of Emancipation was not primarily altruistic. Rather it was a grudging conclusion reached by Rationalists who identified organic Jewish community with the feudal order. In order to eradicate every vestige of medieval community and communal authority, the Jews too would have to forgo their communal autonomy and become individual citizens in the nation-state. The political philosophy of the French Revolution would not permit the existence of communal frameworks as intermediaries between the citizen and the state.

A more ominous secondary effect on the Jewish people stemmed from the compensatory reactions within some nations to the loss of organic community. The dislocation and frustrations engendered by this breakdown of traditional society resulted in some cases in a process of substituting the nation as "organic community." The end result of that process for Jews was modern anti-Semitism, as a result of which Jewish existence became increasingly non-viable in Central and Eastern Europe. Thus we have the birth of the problem of the Jews. Hence the "problem of the Jews" was a secondary effect of the impact of the Modern Age on certain host-societies within which Jews lived.[2]

---

1. Arthur Hertzberg, *The French Enlightenment and the Jews*, Jewish Publication Society, 1968.
2. An incisive analysis of the peculiar vulnerability of the Jews to the disaffection of those dislocated by the transition from the medieval order to the political nation-state will be found in Hannah Arendt, *The Origins of Totalitarianism*, World Publishing, Meridian Books, Cleveland, Second Edition 1958.

THE MODERN MANIFESTATION OF THE PROBLEM OF JUDAISM

But the focus of our discussion is the effect that the onset of the Enlightenment had on Judaism itself. Our concern is the impact of the Modern Age on the traditional Jewish community, bound together as it was by its network of explicit and implicit mutual obligations, communally accepted as binding norms, and a way of life — its *Halacha*.

Towards the end of the eighteenth century many Western European Jews came to feel that operative Judaism as defined by traditional Halacha, and Judaism as a form of community and expression of Peoplehood, were non-relevant in the emerging modern world. Traditional Jewish community was seen to be as dated as medieval society itself. This became the problem of Judaism — i.e., the question of the contemporary viability of Jewish organic community based on the norms of Rabbinic Judaism. Both the problem of the Jews (or modern anti-Semitism, depending on which side of the coin you want to look) and the *problem of Judaism* reflect for us as Jews in different ways the results of that major continuing discontinuity in human evolution and history introduced by the advent of the Modern Age.

The Response of Reform Judaism

In Western Europe the first major response to this challenge was Reform Judaism. The founders of Reform Judaism in the first half of the nineteenth century correctly divined that the far-reaching political, social and economic changes taking place in the Western world heralded a new epoch in history. If the social order presaging an organic community was being replaced by a new form, the nation-state, then Judaism would have to reflect (indeed it was its duty to reflect) in its own way the radically changing historical conditions.

At first the early Reformers reacted by an attempt to formulate new norms — a new Halacha. Gunther Plaut has pointed out that Reform's abandonment of traditional Halacha (Jewish Law) did not necessarily imply negation of Halacha as such.[1] Rather, this reflected a determination to reform the Halacha and define new forms of observance and commitment based on what were understood to be the ethical and moral teachings of Jewish tradition. That tradition, when scrutinized by the "Wissenschaft des Judentums" (the Science of Judaism), was in any case seen to have evolved considerably due to changing historical circumstances during the three millennia that had passed since the seminal experience of the

---

1. Gunther Plaut, "Is Reform Ambiguous?," *Reform Judaism*, October 1974.

Israelite tribes in the Sinai Desert. Was the Jewish "body" (the particularistic people-community) still a necessary vehicle for the Jewish spiritual heritage? Abraham Geiger thought that it was not.

Perhaps it was because of the fact that the social sciences and behavioral sciences were among the last to develop, that a fatal flaw came about in the analysis made by the "Wissenschaft des Judentums" at this stage. It failed to see (from a theoretical point of view) that *because of the breakdown of community the social basis for achieving a consensus on new and binding Jewish norms (a new Halacha) was absent.*

The failure to perceive fully the role of community and the role of "community of communities," i.e., peoplehood, led the founders of Reform Judaism to abrogate Judaism's tie to the land of Israel. The basis of this annulment of God's contract with Abraham was the negation of the particularistic in Jewish peoplehood and the affirmation of Israel's universal mission of disseminating a special ethic — in particular the prophetic ideals of social justice — to all humanity. Judaism was to be a religion of universal significance but not a particularistic nation community intolerable to the modern nation-state.

The stance of classical Reform was in keeping with much of the optimistic outlook of most of the nineteenth century, which interpreted contemporary events as heralding mankind's evolution from particularistic to universalistic frameworks. We will recall that Abraham Geiger, in his de-emphasis of the particularistic within Judaism, was a moderate when compared to a contemporary of his, another German born into the Mosaic persuasion, who negated all religion and especially Judaism in the name of a universalistic outlook which posited economic class as the true and ultimate determinant of community of interest in human history.

World War I and the resulting collapse of the Second International exposed the fallacy of the Marxist assumption that class interest would take precedence over identification with nation-community. The pathological culmination of the concept of organic "nation-community-race" in the land of Reform Judaism's birth called for serious re-evaluation of Judaism's universal mission and made the negation of Jewish national particularism (peoplehood and a national home) untenable.

Both Marxist Socialism and Classical Reform, in spite of their major differences, can be seen today as quintessentially products of the nineteenth century — products of political and social forces whose immediate political progenitor was the French Revolution. But in a wider sense, these forces represented initial nineteenth-century responses to the passing of traditional society and the problematic onset of a new epoch.

The Response of Zionism

Modern Zionism emerged towards the very end of the nineteenth century, almost two generations after Reform Judaism and a generation after the East European Haskala. From the vantage point of the cumulative post-Emancipatory experience of the Jewish people during the nineteenth century the Zionist movement drew two conclusions:

1. In most cases the modern political state constituted a new type of particularistic polity inimical in varying degrees to Jews as such. Only within a sovereign state of their own could the Jews find a place where they would be fully free and equal. Such was the political solution posited for the Problem of the Jews by Herzlian Zionism.

2. The dynamic historical bond between the Jewish people, the land of Israel and their religion made Eretz Israel not only the mandatory focus of their national aspirations, but also the most likely place where a Jewish community might evolve norms of living and a contemporary Hebrew culture which could ultimately be relevant for Jews everywhere. This then was the orientation of Achad Ha-Amist or Cultural Zionism in confronting the Problem of Judaism.

The Outlook of Labor Zionist Chalutziut

It was the synthesis of a medley of socialisms — Marxist, anarchist, social democratic, populist and moral (religious) — with Zionism (especially Cultural Zionism) that engendered the most radical of the Zionist responses to the Modern Age. This was the Labor Zionist response and in particular the response of its pioneering (chalutzic) element.

The Labor Zionist trend accepted in principle a synthesis of political and cultural Zionism. In particular, Labor Zionism espoused the Hebrew revival. But the chalutzic (pioneering) movement within Labor Zionism went much further in terms of practical interpretation and in its religious demand of personal self-realization and commitment.

Political Zionism was perceived as being only a means for enabling the chalutzim to contend with the total challenge of the Modern Age. In this context, first priority was to be given to reconstituting the Jewish community by radical reforms in its ecology:

1. At least in part there was to be a revival of a communal village framework. Personal relationships were to be defined by the mutual obligations of members of the community to each other and to the community as a whole. The idea of extended family was to be interpreted anew by the egalitarian kibbutz-commune chavura.[1] Physical labor and "return to the soil" were the cardinal tenets of the chalutzim in their determination to revive a rural ecology for the Jewish people in its National Home.

2. The artisan skills and service professions were to be organized in their own trade unions. However, these were to be somewhat similar to the medieval guild-communities in their all-encompassing concern with the social, cultural and even religious (now transposed to political) aspects of their members' lives.

3. An umbrella organization (Histadrut) of these frameworks for mutual responsibility — both agricultural collectives on the land and guild-unions in the cities — would provide initiative for economic development. Thus the dichotomy between the innovating capitalist class and the exploited laboring class was to be resolved, at least in part, by creating a significant sector of the economy in the Jewish National Home where both functions were modulated by the same over-arching workers' community ("chevrat haovdim").

    It is to be emphasized that such a concept assumed a national network for community based on the acceptance of mutual obligation, not only between members of a given community for each other, but also of all communities for each other.

4. The vision of a new Hebrew society, freed from the constraints of a rabbinic Halacha more or less in alliance with the undemocratic authority structure of shtetl society (parnasim[2]), provided the motivational amalgam for the Labor Zionist conception. Certainly the level of social idealism expressed in the shtetl community was seen as falling short of and often perverting the prophetic ideals of social justice.

Hence Labor Zionism was a particular interpretation of Cultural Zionism — of the new Hebrew society. It saw itself as a do-it-yourself Cultural Zionism which emphasized the concept of community (a Hebrew laboring class community) in the Jewish National Home as being a prerequisite for a renaissance of the Jewish

---

1. Chavura — fellowship based on shared ideals.
2. Parnasim — the providers of funds (the 'big givers').

People. The Halacha for such a community was to be adapted from contemporary schools of socialist thought which were seen as being of universal significance and as constituting the carriers of Jewish ideals of social justice. As already noted, Rabbinic Judaism and its 613 mitzvot were further discredited by their association with the social conservatism of the shtetl's power elite.

A PARALLEL BETWEEN REFORM AND LABOR ZIONISM

It is of some interest to note a fascinating parallel between classical Reform and classical Labor Zionism. Classical Reform (and radical Reform to an even greater extent) believed optimistically, and perhaps naively, that the age of universal enlightenment would be a guarantor of their civil rights and status everywhere. Events interpreted by the Zionists as harbingers of worse yet to come were seen as local and passing aberrations on the highway of human progress. Indeed, as carriers of the ethical and moral values of Judaism, as free and equal citizens of the political state, Reform Jews saw themselves as active promoters, wherever they might be, of the universal enlightenment which seemed so congruent with universalist Jewish values. Those values were no longer in need of nurture by a particular Jewish polity.

On the other hand, the Labor Zionists (in particular the Marxistically oriented wing) identified so strongly with the "Progressive Socialist" regimes that in some cases they conceived of the Jewish National Home as only an intermediate step to a universalistic socialist utopia. The Soviet Union as the "Mother of Socialism" was almost beyond criticism, even when left-wing Labor Zionists were being actively persecuted. Labor Zionism would "prove" ultimately that it was all a mistake — the emerging Jewish Workers Society would finally be found to be deserving of Soviet Russia's approbation.

The rejection of the universalist Reform outlook by German nationalism was traumatic and total. In America the universalist outlook was expressed through social action. The ambiguous relationship of the Jews to the Negro struggle for civil rights, the Vietnam War, the Six Day War and the Yom Kippur War have all served to bring about a new perspective and a new balance between Jewish particularism and universalism within American Reform.

It was not until the 1950s that the Soviet Union's uncompromising attitude — both in internal and external politics — forced even the radical Labor Zionist left wing to divest itself of its illusions regarding its socialist "mentor." The ideological crises within Labor Zionism (and in the kibbutz movement) in the two decades between 1940 and 1960 with regard to the orientation to socialism were surely more acute than the controversy with regard to Zionism that was taking place within Reform Judaism.

Let us summarize up to this point. The advent of the Modern Age posed and is posing the greatest challenge that Judaism has ever faced. The viability of Jewish community was and is problematic. Without a communal framework, within which there are communally accepted and binding norms, there can be no basis for the development of Halacha and there can be no firm foundation for a Jewish way of life.

The classic response of Reform was affirmation of tradition but with radical change (reform) by renewed interpretation and by new legislation, with respect to Halachic norms. Jewish community and the community of communities (peoplehood) were largely negated in favor of integration ("self-effacement," Achad Ha-Am called it) in the newly formed nation-states and the fulfillment of a universal mission within them. Jewish particularism was to be expressed in a brotherhood of the spirit alone.

The response of Labor Zionism and in particular the kibbutz movement was affirmation of Jewish peoplehood and Jewish community, but with radical change (reform) in their structure and ecology. On the other hand, Labor Zionism negated the particularistic Jewish Halacha tradition in favor of adaptation to various streams of universalist socialist ideology.

Hence, these responses, the Labor Zionist response and the Reform response, were mirror images of each other. Neither response related to the problem of "flesh *and* spirit," Judaism in its totality. Neither response related to the double challenge of the creation of an organic Jewish community, committed by virtue of its being a Jewish community, to evolving a Jewish way of life (Halacha) compatible with the Modern Age.

Both Reform and Labor Zionism were motivated by concern with social justice arising from the impact of the Modern Age. Labor Zionism approached the question from a particularistic stance but with a universalistic ideology. Socialism was its "religion." Reform Judaism's point of departure was universalistic — rejecting Jewish particularity — but its "ideology" was Judaism.

It behooves us to examine, at least briefly, the historical processes by which we are arriving at a synthesis between the response of Reform Judaism and Zionism and especially Labor Zionism.

The Evolution Within Reform Judaism

It is, of course, true that a strong and articulate minority within the Reform Movement always identified with Zionism. Stephen S. Wise, Judah Magnes, Abba Hillel Silver, Gustav and Richard Gottheil, and James Heller (a Labor Zionist) were central figures within American Zionism. Indisputably their Cultural Zionism was a central motif in their personal Zionist commitment. But historical circumstances were to determine that the focus of their activity was largely the political struggle for the establishment of the Jewish State. The question of Liberal Judaism shaping a new Jewish way of life in the emergent Jewish National Home could not be a major focus for them. They were Reform Jews who were Zionists. An ideological synthesis between Reform Judaism and Zionism was latent in much of what they said and did, but they were not perceived as promulgators of a distinct "Reform Zionism" as such.

The rise of Nazi Germany made anti-Zionism (in its political sense as a movement opposed to the creation of a sovereign Jewish State in Palestine) almost untenable in the American Jewish community, including its Reform wing.

Two additional factors prepared Reform Judaism for the Columbus Platform and a future synthesis with Zionism. First, Reform Judaism became increasingly a movement of the descendants of East European Jews less ambivalent in their relationship to Jewish Peoplehood than the members of "Our Crowd."[1] Secondly, the approach to Jewish Peoplehood, posited in Mordecai Kaplan's Reconstructionist Judaism as an evolving religious civilization, had been anticipated by Classical Reform (Geiger) almost a century before the publication of "Judaism as a Religious Civilization." But Kaplan's thesis of reconstructing the Jewish community was predicated on the indissoluble link between religion and peoplehood, which Classical Reform negated.

The Maturing of Israeli Zionism and Labor Zionism

Let us recall that, although Zionism was born in response both to the problem of the Jews *and* the problem of Judaism, the pressure of historical events demanded an emphasis on the immediate and practical. Zionism concerned itself with the establishment of a secure political framework which could solve the problem of the Jews. Diaspora Zionism concerned itself with fund-raising and political work. Until 1948, Israeli Zionism concerned itself mainly with the actual struggle involved in the creation of the State of Israel. In the period immediately after the

---

1. Stephen Birmingham, *Our Crowd*, Harper & Row, 1967. Saga of New York's German-Jewish families.

establishment of the State, the central concern became the defense of the State and the absorption of hundreds of thousands of new, disadvantaged immigrants.

Almost from the time of the initial confrontation between cultural and political Zionism at the beginning of the century, and until well after the establishment of Israel, questions of survival simply shunted aside any serious discussion on cultural Zionism — i.e., the significance of the State as a means for ensuring a viable Jewish response to the Modern Age.

Developments within the kibbutz movement and the relationship between the "Labor Zionist elite" and the Zionist movement as a whole illustrate the process which took place.

Labor Zionism had always been a particular variant of Cultural Zionism. Its socialist vision of the new Jewish society was not shared by the Zionist "establishment" as a whole. But within the practical realities of upbuilding the National Home, the kibbutz movement was a useful — perhaps indispensable — partner. Kibbutzim represented the most economic way to settle the land for the chronically under-financed Zionist movement. The relatively high intellectual level of kibbutz members and the principle of collectively farming large areas made the kibbutzim the logical vehicle for the rapid introduction of a modern agriculture for the growing Jewish urban population. In the 1920s and 1930s the kibbutzim constituted an important framework for the absorption and training of immigrants. From the late 1930s and until the early 1950s the kibbutzim were the most feasible and flexible way of establishing Jewish settlement in the face of growing Arab and British hostility. It would be difficult to imagine what the armistice lines of 1949 would have been were it not for the role of the kibbutzim, direct and indirect, in the struggle for statehood.

All of this had little to do with the kibbutz's relationship to Cultural Zionism. Many kibbutz members, too, came to see their role as that of a means to the end of creating the Jewish State. Through the 1950s the kibbutz movement went through a major crisis of purpose. Many kibbutz members felt that it was hardly relevant to remain on the kibbutz. The climax had been reached and passed.

The crisis of purpose and identity was sublimated, institutionally, in a bitter and destructive ideological battle on the nature of the kibbutz's (and Zionism's) relation to socialism. It was the "Mother of Socialism" herself who put an end to the strife by unambiguously and traumatically disowning the Socialist Zionists who had blindly sworn fealty to her.

It was not until the relative calm of the early 1960s that many thinking Israelis and kibbutz members began to ask themselves: "Now that we have a Jewish State — what do we do with it?" Of special interest has been the evolution of the thinking of younger Israelis on the subject of their Jewish identity. The impact of the Eichmann trial in 1961 and Yigael Yadin's Masada "dig" in 1964 were early, well-publicized manifestations of young Israelis' concern with their identity.

The proliferation of "Circles of Searchers for the Way" (Chugim L'Mechapsei Haderech), the establishment of an intellectual and literary journal, *Shdemot*, by and for the young kibbutz members, the establishment of the first Progressive Jewish congregations and the Leo Baeck School, were less apparent signs of a return to the concept of Cultural Zionism — a search for the Jewish meaning of the Jewish State. The Six Day War and the Yom Kippur War were decisive in demonstrating to Israeli youth their Jewish identity. It became clear to them that only the Jewish People were really committed to Israel's survival. The Jewish bond is now perceived by many young Israelis to be functional for that survival. "Zioniut," once a term of disparagement, has again become respectable.

Within the kibbutz movement itself, a definite shift has taken place in the kibbutz's self-image. The kibbutz sees itself more and more as a society (albeit "secular"), living according to Jewish values. The socialistic rhetoric is becoming muted. Concern for Jewish content is on the rise. Most significantly, the kibbutz is coming to be seen as one possible expression of the Jewish significance of the Jewish State, both by those within it and by many thinking Israelis without.[1]

The Synthesis Between Reform and Labor Zionism

It was in the period between the Six Day War and the Yom Kippur War that the Reform Movement began to seriously think in terms of its impact on the Jewish State. In order to confront the political and religious reality, it was clear that a Progressive Jewish presence would have to be established. The World Union for Progressive Judaism moved its headquarters to Jerusalem. The Hebrew Union College established a campus in Jerusalem and made a year of study there mandatory for ordination in the Reform rabbinate. A group of rabbis from the Central Conference of American Rabbis initiated a series of dialogues with leaders of the kibbutz movement and the idea of a Reform kibbutz was born. The idea, however, had to await realization until the youth groups of the tiny Israeli Reform Movement matured sufficiently to attempt to realize it. A real Reform kibbutz movement also depends on the evolution of a pioneering Reform youth movement in North America.

---

1. In his thesis for the Doctor of Hebrew Literature at Hebrew Union College, Rabbi Shalom Lilker, today a member of Kibbutz Kfar Hamaccabi, claims that the kibbutzim have been a religious phenomenon all along. Lilker's thesis, *Kibbutz Judaism: A New Tradition in the Making*, was published by the Herzl Press, New York, 1982. Lilker's analysis is partly based on and was anticipated by Martin Buber a generation ago in his essay, "The Experiment That Did Not Fail," in *Paths to Utopia*, Beacon Press, 1958.

In January 1976, the World Union for Progressive Judaism formally affiliated with the World Zionist Organization and its Jerusalem based director, Rabbi Richard G. Hirsch, became a member of the WZO Executive. At the Biennial of the Union of American Hebrew Congregations, in November 1975, Rabbi Alexander Schindler, the UAHC President, responded to the challenge of the UN Resolution equating Zionism with racism, by declaring:

> "We are all of us Jews and whether we use the small z or the large Z, we are all of us Zionists. The land of Israel which is Zion, and the children of Israel who constitute the Jewish people, and the God of Israel are all bound together in a triple covenant. At no time in our history have we ever stopped praying or longing or working for Zion."

Heady stuff for a movement that harbored within it the most vocal Jewish anti-Zionist element — The American Council for Judaism. Nor should one underestimate the ambivalence felt towards the "establishment" in Israel by prominent circles within Reform — because of the "dovish" proclivities with regard to Israel's foreign policy, because of the Orthodox stranglehold on established religious expression, and lastly, because of the demand for increased funding for Judaism in America.

Hence it would be incorrect to assume that Reform Zionism will imply uncritical support of the State of Israel. Its central thrust will probably be a socially concerned Cultural Zionism, with particular emphasis on the development of a Progressive Judaism in Israel.

The synthesis between Reform Judaism and Zionism, in particular Labor Zionism, is a resolution of opposite and sometimes opposing but fundamentally complementary responses. The cataclysmic events of the last sixty years of Jewish history were the dynamic which at times hindered and are finally militating in favor of such a synthesis.

Such a synthesis is based on Reform's acceptance of the "triple covenant," as posited by Rabbi Schindler. Jewish tradition is inseparable from Jewish Peoplehood. Likewise, there can be no meaningful Jewish Peoplehood without an affirmative relationship to Jewish "religious civilization." Ongoing Reform ("Reconstruction") is a necessity both for Jewish tradition and for the Jewish People as community, wherever they may be.

It seems to me that we have arrived at a point where we must assume a Reform-Zionist synthesis in order to deal effectively with the problem of Judaism. Hence, we pass from the realm of historical analysis to a tentative statement based on such a Reform or Progressive Zionist synthesis, and an ensuing proposal for an action program with regard to Progressive Jewish education and Reform-Zionist Aliyah.

BASIC THESES FOR A REFORM ZIONISM

In my opinion, our chief concern today, in our confrontation with the Modern Age, is the continued creative survival of the Jewish People, be it in the Diaspora or in Israel. This definition of concern in no way detracts from the focal importance of Israel, whether immanent or actual, as the National Home and center of the Jewish People. But the concept "Eretz Israel" is relevant only within the context of Am Israel and hence, we are bound to accept Eli Wiesel's words to the Jewish Agency assembly in June 1974: "Whatever our geographical or economical differences may be, it is my absolute conviction that the oneness of our people is of an ontological nature. Whoever chooses one against the other cannot be defined as truly Jewish. Whoever attempts to oppose Israel to the Diaspora or vice versa will inevitably betray both in the end."

The Meaning of Reform Zionist Commitment

In order to realize our commitment to deal with the continued survival of the Jewish People, we must reject the views of those, be they Israeli or American, whose point of departure is the dichotomy between Israel and the Diaspora. There can be no Jewish "agenda" which does not base itself on both Diaspora and Israel, if we do indeed affirm the oneness of the Jewish People and its common historical destiny. The Jewish State cannot be seen as an end in itself. We must not deprecate the important role that Israel has played and may still continue to play as a physical haven for Jews in need. But ultimately, as Achad Ha-Am foresaw, the political state of Israel is only a means to the end of making contemporary Judaism viable in all free societies.

Such an orientation is a prerequisite to a Zionist commitment today, whether for an Israeli Jew or an American Jew. The presence of a Jew in Israel does not automatically make him a Zionist. Nor can we accept the concept of Aliyah as an isolated act constituting the end-all of Zionist commitment. True, Aliyah will always be considered a valued act within Jewish tradition, but as an ideal act within the Zionist context it is of significance only insofar as it expresses an abiding commitment to action — a continuing sense of "cavanah."

A suitable *modus* must be found for Diaspora Zionists to express concern in matters affecting the Zionist nature of the State of Israel. Similarly, the question of Zionist orientation in the Diaspora must be seen as a legitimate subject of concern for Israeli Zionists.

A Reform Zionist commitment implies a readiness to innovate in utilizing and interpreting the Jewish heritage and communal institutions both in the Diaspora and in Israel. Such creative innovation by those firmly rooted in their identification with the Jewish group (Jewish Peoplehood) should result in a vital and dynamic Judaism with its own unique contributions to an ever-changing world. Such a Judaism would, hopefully, impart greater significance and meaning to the individuals who identify with it, and through it.

To achieve maximal self-realization Reform Zionism presumes ongoing inter-action between a Progressive Judaism in Israel and the various Liberal Jewish communities in the Diaspora.

An Action Program for Education

The time is ripe for Jewish educators and youth workers in America to confront, coherently, the question of motivating the next generation to involve itself in and to identify with the Jewish People, be it in the Diaspora or in Israel. The histori-cally innovative stance of Reform Judaism makes it a natural candidate for new approaches to Jewish education.

Motivation toward and identification with the Jewish People implies an affective relationship. In the past, an affective relationship to and identification with Judaism was effected through the medium of the organic Jewish community. It was the community and the extended family that provided the social setting and the experiential situation within which education took place. Such an organic community is no more.

It was Martin Buber who pursued the problematics of the breakdown of community and in particular, Jewish community, as a result of the advent of the Modern Age. The ramifications are many — absence of community means absence of dialogue between individuals, it means the alienation of the individual from the group. In Buber's eyes, only through organic community could the individual relate to God. This led Buber to the position that *without authentic Jewish community there can be no authentic Jewish experience.*

Hence, the basic educational problem both in Israel and in the Diaspora is: How do we create an environment of Jewish community within which we can educate our children and youth? Let no one think that this is not a real problem even in Israel. But it is a much greater problem in the Diaspora.

Building a Progression of Experiential Education

The question of Jewish day schools as a learning community is one that the Reform Movement has already begun to contend with, but it remains problematic for the Movement. The trend toward some ethnic retrenchment in America may well prove to be a factor that will hasten American Reform's re-evaluation of its traditional stand on this issue.

Without any doubt, the Jewish camping movement is the bright spot in the educational picture for youth here. Not all Jewish camps are utilizing their potential, but it seems that the Reform Movement, fortunately, has a group of rabbis and educators committed to using the camp setting to create community, to create *chavura*, to acculturate the child and adolescent to certain values, attitudes, and identifications. The availability and utilization of camp as an educational resource for Reform Jewish youth should be a major item on the Reform Movement's agenda. The camp experience should be a stimulus for a creative temple youth group. In part, the content of the camps' educational program is an outstanding example of creative adaptation from the nascent ethos of the Jewish State.

The Role of Israel in the Educational Progression

For the older adolescent (let us not forget that in this society, adolescence as a social and psychological phenomenon, extends well into one's twenties) the question of Jewish identification becomes an acute one. The more developed emotional and intellectual capacity necessitates an additional dimension of experience, of *chavaya* (the experience), to stimulate and enrich the concept of Jewish Peoplehood and to evolve a mature identification with Jewish history. A properly structured Israel experience or series of Israel experiences are the best educational resource at our disposal for ensuring that the Zionist commitment will be one of the components in the crystallizing personality of the older adolescent.

Clearly, the Israel programs of the Reform Movement must be planned and administered in such a way as to integrate Progressive Judaism as part of the *chavaya* (the experience). There must also be advance planning at the congregational level (religious school, junior youth group, senior youth group) with regard to the integration of youth returning from the Israel experience. Part of the programmatic content of that experience should be devoted to the participants' role in their home communities.

A positive Israel experience should also motivate Jewish youth to continue upgrading their general level of Jewish literacy during college. It should engender the desire to live in Jewish community. The graduates of the UAHC camps and Israel programs constitute the future lay and rabbinic leadership of American Reform, perhaps even more by virtue of common bonds and *chavura*[1] experience than because of intellectual convictions.

A Reform Zionist Jewish Identity

Within this perspective on the development of a positive Jewish identity, it is more than legitimate for the Reform Movement to be concerned with the particular role of a dynamic Liberal Judaism in determining its shape.

We return for a moment to our historical analysis:

The Classical Reform position is that Liberal Judaism sees itself as being concerned with the attempt to reform *Halacha* so that Judaism might, in the words of the Augsburg Synod, "unfold itself in the spirit of the new age." Let us not be confused by the fact that the events of the past century have necessitated a rather more somber interpretation of the spirit of that "new age." It is a Zionist thesis that such an "unfolding of Judaism" is maximally possible only if Jewish experience and existence can be expressed autonomously at all levels of social and political organization normative to a given age. Only thus can Judaism potentially confront over a period of generations the possibility of reforming the gamut of *Halacha* whether by interpretation, legislation or both. Therefore, a Reform Zionist outlook must concern itself with the significant augmentation of the Progressive Jewish presence in Israel. It is a primary need for the sake of continued dynamic development of Reform in the Diaspora.

The projected Reform (Progressive Jewish) kibbutz, hopefully the first of a number, is surely the most concrete symbol of the rapprochement between Reform Judaism and Zionism in general and the synthesis between Progressive Judaism and Labor Zionism in particular. The avowed purpose of this kibbutz will be to serve as a proving ground for Progressive Judaism within an authentic community. For a small number of young people, in Israel and in the Diaspora, who will seek a very special type of personal commitment to the ideals of Progressive Judaism, such a kibbutz may provide the path of self-realization. Clearly the existence of Progressive Jewish communities in Israel is of decisive importance for the nature of the educational potential that Israel has for Reform Jewish youth from the Diaspora.

---

1. *Chavura — Gemeinschaft* (fellowship) orientation.

The Need for a Reform-Zionist Aliyah Movement

But this is not enough. If Reform Judaism perceives the political entity of the State of Israel as a framework, as a means for the continued evolution of Jewish law and tradition, then it will concern itself with having a broader impact on the social and religious fabric of the society developing there. The affiliation of the World Union for Progressive Judaism with the World Zionist Organization is quite logical, but in and of itself such an affiliation does not ensure for Reform the role which it desires. Indeed, without a Reform-Zionist Aliyah movement, such an affiliation will lack practical consummation. I say a *Reform-Zionist Aliyah movement*, not merely the Aliyah of individuals who are Reform Jews, even though the Aliyah of such individuals is surely of great significance to themselves and to the ties between America and Israel.

A Reform-Zionist Aliyah movement must organize itself in such a way that it will have specific impact identifiable with its orientation to Progressive Judaism. That means group Aliyah — for example to the same development town or neighborhood in an urban area. It means Aliyah to a locale where the sense of community and the sense of "shlichut" (to the idea of Progressive Judaism) might be more easily maintained against the pressures of everyday life. It might mean Aliyah which would focus on new potential projects for Reform in Israel — e.g., educators who would establish new options in education similar to the Leo Baeck School in Haifa and in other parts of the country.

A COMPLEMENTARY RELATIONSHIP

It will be of importance and significance to Israel and Israeli society if American Jewish youth experience Israel as a norm in their Jewish education. In the opinion of many Israelis, it would be most desirable if a more significant Progressive Jewish presence were established in Israel through a consciously Reform-Zionist Aliyah. *But the decisive importance of these phenomena will be in the vitalizing feedback to American Reform Judaism itself and in ensuring its capability of responding to the challenge of our times with a viable Judaism.* This is the nature of the complementary relationship between Zionism and Reform Judaism as I see it today.

Reform Zionism
Statement of Position and Aims[1]

Reform Zionism is a response of Reform Judaism to the impact of the modern age and the resultant mass secularization of the Jewish People both in Israel and the Diaspora.

In order to confront secularization, our commitment to Judaism must find its expression in ongoing reform and renewal, both in questions of belief and halacha, as well as in matters pertaining to Jewish Community and Society at large. The attempt to "normalize" the Jewish People — whether by relating to Judaism in the Diaspora as merely a religious denomination, or whether relating to the Jewish National Home "like all the nations" — must inevitably lead to our cultural and physical assimilation.

Reform Zionism's identification with klal Israel and the Jerusalem Platform[2] commits it to ensuring the continued creative survival of the Jewish People wherever it may be. Reform Zionism believes that such creative survival, both in Israel and in the Diaspora, will necessarily be dependent on generating democratic process within true community (kehila) capable of renewal, interpretation of the accumulated body of Jewish tradition and sources as well as innovations necessitated by modernity.

A. Pluralism and Democracy in Judaism

Both democracy and pluralism are necessary for the evolution of a modern dynamic Judaism. Therefore, our ongoing interpretations of Judaism will be the result of democratic process. While differing with Orthodox Judaism regarding source of principles governing the expression of authority within Judaism, we recognize and respect the right of those who continue to believe that exclusive authority is vested in the Divine Revelation on Sinai as reflected in the Torah and its oral tradition. We expect reciprocal recognition and respect from Orthodox Judaism in our belief that Revelation is ongoing and to be modulated by

---

1. 1980. Mimeo, unpublished.
2. Jerusalem Platform of the World Zionist Organization, 1968.

democratic process in community. We leave to history the ultimate judgement regarding the path in our struggle against secularization and assimilation.

Pursuant to the above we demand:

1) Equal rights for all trends in Judaism, within the World Zionist Organization and in the State of Israel.
    1. ARZENU calls for the implementation of the previous Congress resolution on equality for all trends in Judaism.
    2. Within the State of Israel, as the National home of *all* the Jewish people, ARZENU demands equal rights for all trends within Judaism.
2) Reinforcement of the Democratic process within the World Zionist Organization, by implementing the following changes in the World Zionist Organization constitution.

B. Changing the Status of the World Zionist Organization

The State of Israel constitutes a political framework essential to our survival in the modern age. However, the State of Israel and our national existence are not aims in themselves. They are means for furthering the mission of the Jewish people — the realization of the Kingdom of the Almighty on Earth. Therefore, both in Israel and in the Diaspora, Reform Zionism educates towards a recognition of the unique nature and responsibility of the Jewish people.

The means by which Reform Zionism seeks to propagate its ideas are:
1) Education (in particular by means of Netzer Olami[1]).
2) Publications and Dissemination of information by other means.
3) Developing forms of community, whose commitment and way of life will reflect the ideas of Reform Judaism in general.

We will attempt to raise issues that reflect, in and of themselves, our outlook and will also initiate public discussion both in Israel and in the Diaspora, regarding the nature and purpose of Zionism, and the Jewish National Home.

C. Reform Zionism and the World Zionist Organization

Currently the World Zionist Organization has little relevance or impact on the Jewish community in the Diaspora and almost none in Israel. Constitutional changes are required, which will achieve the following aims:

1) Democratization of the World Zionist Organization.

---

1. Netzer Olami — World Reform Zionist Youth (Noar Zioni Reformi).

2) More significant involvement of Jewish publics in the World Zionist Organization, both in Israel and the Diaspora. Specifically:
   1) ARZENU demands elections before every Zionist Congress; inter-party arrangements, regarding distribution of voting blocs, are to be pronounced unconstitutional.
   2) Elections to the World Zionist Organization in Israel are to be separated from the elections to the Knesset. (Currently there are no elections in Israel; the Israeli delegation to the Congress is a direct multiple [x2] of the Knesset representation.)

The immediate result of this constitutional change will be to focus the attention of the Israeli public on questions of Zionist content and questions concerning the Jewish people as a whole, transcending the problems of day-to-day existence which characterize much of the agenda of public discussion in Israel.

Worldwide (including Israel) democratic elections to the World Zionist Congress will inevitably break down the current Israel-Diaspora polarity by creating common ground for worldwide Jewish discussion.

Clearly, within the Israeli Zionist framework, Israeli Reform Judaism will also be able to present its view.

D. Immigration and Absorption (Aliyah and Klita)

Aliyah from all the countries in the Diaspora and the successful absorption of Olim is essential to the vitality of the Jewish State and heightening its Zionist consciousness. A central task of Reform Zionism is to promote organized Aliyah of Reform Jews. Education and properly structured Israel experiences for youth (preference to long-term programs of 6 months to a year) under a Reform aegis are a primary means to this end. Only on the basis of a significant Israel experience can the young Jew of today confront the question of where and how to realize his Reform Judaism.

In our view, immigration and absorption can be furthered by:

1) Implementing the main conclusions of the Horeb report (unification of Aliyah and Absorption under one authority within the framework of the World Zionist Organization).
2) Granting official status within the new authority to the various immigrant aid groups (AACI, etc.).[1]

---

1. AACI — Association of Americans and Canadians in Israel.

3) Upgrading support and subsidies for long-term Israel programs for youth (Youth and Hechalutz Department).
4) Planning and execution of special projects to attract and successfully absorb young couples and singles.
5) Ensuring a settlement policy (balance between both sides of the green line) which will make it politically feasible to recruit settlers regardless of their view regarding eventual boundaries of the State.

Reform Zionism: Problems & Progress[1]

At first glance, the progress of Reform Zionism during the past six years would appear to be impressive. Indeed, it is impressive when we recall that barely seven years have passed since Reform Zionism as such was but a nascent idea.

1. Organizationally, a worldwide Reform Zionist movement has been established. ARZENU as of this writing includes:
   • ARZA — The Association of Reform Zionists of America. In preparation for the 30th Zionist Congress, ARZA succeeded in registering a membership of some 60,000 members.
   • KADIMA — the Canadian equivalent of ARZA.
   • DZA — Democratic Zionist Association of South Africa.
   • ARZI — The Reform Zionist movement of Australia.
   • PRO-ZION — The Progressive Zionist Movement of Britain
   • LIBERAL JOODE ZIONISTEN — Holland.

At its initial appearance at the 29th Congress in 1978, the Reform Zionist Movement succeeded in mobilizing support for an in principle resolution on the equality of all trends within Judaism within the World Zionist Organization.

RESOLUTION ON RELIGIOUS PLURALISM

"This 29th Zionist Congress affirms that in order to encourage Aliyah from all segments of world Jewry, all World Zionist Organization Departments, instrumentalities and programs shall be administered in accord with the principle of equal standing and equal treatment for every religious movement within its ranks and for every Jew, regardless of origin or of religious and ideological identification. Programs of a religious and educational character should reflect the pluralism of Jewish life throughout the world.

---

1. April 1983. Published in Second Edition, *Reform Zionist Perspective*, UAHC Youth Division (offset).

> This Zionist Congress calls on the State of Israel as the homeland of the Jewish People to implement fully the principle of guaranteed religious rights, including equal recognition of religious authorities and equal governmental support for all religious movements within Judaism."

Significantly, the final paragraph of the proposed resolution was deleted.

> "This Zionist Congress calls on the State of Israel to devise procedures whereby religious rites performed by Jewish religious authorities abroad will be recognized as valid under the laws of the State of Israel."

Clearly, this outlines a possible political aim at a future Zionist Congress.

ARZA, which had been founded a bare three months before the 29th Congress, succeeded in mobilizing support for the resolution in spite of the small size of its delegation (1). There is no doubt that by successfully avoiding elections most Zionist Federations — in particular the American Zionist Federation — prevented the Reform Zionist Movement from translating organizational strength (60,000 registered ARZA members in the USA) into significant political clout at the 30th Congress.

2. Kibbutz Yahel stands as a symbol of the Reform Zionist vision of comprehensive community committed to ongoing Tikkun (Reform) as a life-long vocation (mission, shlichut). Kibbutz Lotan established this year some 12 kilometers south of Yahel means that a Reform Kibbutz movement may emerge.

3. A world youth movement — in embryo — is developing. Netzer Artzi (NFTY graduates in America), Maginim (South Africa), Netzer (Australia), Reform Synagogue Youth-Netzer (Britain) are all in various stages of organizational crystallization.

4. The development of an autonomous youth movement in Israel, Tzofei-Telem, partially integrated within the Israeli scouting movement, is of particular significance. The establishment of a youth movement framework which enables acculturation to Reform Zionist ideals to take place from elementary school age, by means of Nachal[1] through army age and possibly beyond has

---

1. Nachal — "Pioneering Army Youth" — within the Israeli Defense Forces, the Nachal Corps are organized on the basis of "garinim" — potential settlement groups. The defining characteristic is that Nachal units are organized on the basis of movement background and commitment, men and women together. About one-third of the army period is spent together either in agricultural-military outposts or on kibbutzim. The men undergo regular military training during the balance of their service. The women are involved in servicing border outposts and/or future settlement sites.

potentially far-reaching implications — not only for the Reform Kibbutz movement but for Reform Judaism in Israel as a whole.

A CRISIS OF CONTENT: A TENTATIVE APPRAISAL

The undoubted organizational progress that has been made is nevertheless tentative. Its tentative nature stems from the discrepancy at this stage between organizational and institutional existence and the energy invested in that existence on the one hand and the paucity of expression in the realm of ideas and ideals on the other hand.

Neither ARZENU nor NETZER has yet come to grips with the question of translating organizational achievements into action programs.

Within ARZENU it would seem that the registration of large numbers of members has not been accompanied by a program of commitment. This is particularly true of ARZA which quite naturally is the dominant component of ARZENU. There is as yet no vision of ARZA chapters as Reform Zionist fellowships (chavruta) of joint commitment to an endeavor of learning together and doing together. The question of how is Reform Zionist affiliation affecting the lives of members, to what extent is it making them an intentional community remains unanswered (2). The ability of ARZA to maintain its membership in non-Congress years has yet to be tested.

At the level of the World Zionist Organization and the Zionist Federations there would appear to be an overemphasis on the attempt to achieve political power without an adequate rationale for doing so once power is achieved.

In effect, Reform Zionism is in danger of falling into the trap of Political Zionism and foregoing its mandate to pioneer paths of cultural Zionist expression (3).

A similar criticism can be voiced regarding the Israel Movement for Progressive Judaism. Although the Movement has begun to take initiative via Israeli Courts to establish its legitimacy, it has hardly succeeded in projecting itself onto the Israeli public as a spiritual-cultural alternative to secularism and orthodoxy (4).

The above remarks are not meant in any way to deprecate the movement's efforts to achieve political status and legitimacy. The criticism is directed at the lack of balance between organizational-political effort and development of qualitative content commensurate with and as an essential complement to the organizational-political and legal initiatives.

So far, the developments in Reform Zionism have had minimal impact on the

Israel Movement for Progressive Judaism, consisting of some 12 congregations heavily subsidized by the World Union for Progressive Judaism. Less than 1,000 families are affiliated and their activity is limited to religious worship. In Israel, some 3,000 to 4,000 people are involved in Reform Judaism — including the youth movement and the kibbutzim. Another few thousand are on the periphery.

Finally, organized Reform Zionism has not as yet shown itself to be a catalyst for a Reform Jewish Aliyah movement. This criticism is made within the context of Aliyah as a central tenet (as distinct from *the* central tenet) of Reform Zionism. Nor has the number of participants in Reform Zionist Israel Programs, particularly from America, increased appreciably.

The lack of Reform Aliyah in general, and of purposive Reform Zionist Aliyah in particular, is the most serious impediment to the dynamic development of Reform Judaism in Israel regardless of settlement (5).

The Reform Kibbutzim — Symbol and Content

The Reform Kibbutzim, Yahel and Lotan, are in a race against time. They number, together, some 80 members the ages of 20-30. Annual turnover is 10-20%. The enthusiasm of youthful commitment to creating a Reform community which will make the desert bloom physically and spiritually is under considerable strain.

The founding members of Yahel and Lotan, in particular the Israelis, hardly grasped the implications of their participation in the prototype of the synthesis between Reform Judaism and Pioneering Zionism. The institutional initiators of the Reform Kibbutzim (UAHC Youth Division, the World Union for Progressive Judaism, the United Kibbutz Movement) soon realized that staying power for participation in such an enterprise could only be acquired by a lengthy process of movement education. Retrospectively, there was no choice. The pressure to create Tzofei-Telem and Netzer Olami could never have come about if Yahel and Lotan were not already there. Yahel and Lotan had to be founded before a true movement existed to ensure their creative continuity. The chicken had to precede the egg. Having skipped most of the stages of normative development has resulted in many problems — social, economic, and ideological. The alternative was — no problems and no kibbutzim. Historically, a similar crisis of continuity was faced by the early kibbutz movement in the 1920s. The Second Aliyah (1904-14) was not primarily a movement Aliyah. It was not until the 1920s that youth movements were founded to ensure the continuity of the tentative experimental framework which is what the first kvutzot (small kibbutzim) in fact were in the initial stages.

Will the youth movement process catch up to the process of attrition amongst the founding members? It is not a question of the continued existence of Yahel and Lotan. The United Kibbutz Movement is committed to their physical maintenance. However, the future Reform Zionist nature of the kibbutzim remains an open question.

It should be emphasized that the process of attrition in Yahel and Lotan is less than in many or even most other new kibbutzim. Indeed, in the long run, if the attrition is amongst those with less movement commitment, then perhaps such attrition serves a positive purpose as well. However, the current social instability and the lack of continuity make it difficult to stabilize the kibbutzim economically and ideologically and sap the energy of the young leadership. Under these circumstances it is difficult to undertake and carry through Reform Zionist initiatives within the kibbutzim. Mobilizing them for Reform Zionist activity outside the kibbutzim is even more problematic. And yet, mobilize they must — at least at the level of Reform Zionist recruitment within Netzer and Telem Noar — if there is to be Reform Zionist continuity.

Indigenous Leadership

It is an open secret that much of the initiative and leadership, organized and ideological, for Reform Zionism, in particular pioneering Reform Zionism, has stemmed from individuals acting in the name of the movement but hardly on the basis of policy emanating from movement decisions. The initiatives of the Youth Division of the UAHC and individuals within the World Union for Progressive Judaism were initially tolerated but only afterwards partially endorsed by the Reform establishment. A number of kibbutz members, who while identifying with Reform Judaism ideologically, have had no previous organizational connection with Reform, have played a central role in the Reform Zionist enterprise. Circumstances have dictated that their role has extended far beyond the original assumption of "technical assistance" of the Kibbutz Movement to the Reform Movement. This "stop gap" Reform Zionist leadership has inherent limitations.

Hence, the process of developing an indigenous Reform Zionist leadership is a central concern. Clearly, the next five to ten years will be difficult. They will be less difficult if the question is confronted consciously.

There would appear to be a distinct need to intensify education — both in Israel and the Diaspora — amongst those who already have a Reform Zionist outlook. Their outreach is currently not dynamic enough. This would appear to be one of the reasons that Reform Aliyah and Reform Zionist Pioneering Aliyah have not developed as quickly as might have been hoped. This statement is made in full awareness of all the general factors, political and social in Israel and in the Diaspora, which have had a negative influence on Zionist commitment amongst young people in the last few years.

Particular care must be exercised regarding the role of shlichim to the Reform Zionist Youth Movement. Both in Israel and the Diaspora the excessive and incorrect use of shlichim has stifled the development of indigenous leadership in the classical Zionist Youth Movements (6).

Special mention must be made of the role (lack of role) of indigenous rabbinic leadership within the leadership of Reform Zionist youth. Currently, there is almost total insulation of Rabbinic students from Reform Zionist reality — in particular during their year-long stay in Israel. This has negative implications both for developing a relevant perspective as a Reform Rabbi in America as well as providing an experiential basis for rabbinic students weighing the option of Reform Zionist commitment in Israel.

The fact that in the first five years of Yahel's existence no Reform Rabbi or Rabbinical students have felt a call to commit themselves personally to total Reform Zionist community, not necessarily as Rabbis, reflects an over-emphasis on the individual serving individuals within communities of ritual from the pulpit and furthering his/her career as distinct from building comprehensive Reform Jewish community — whether in Israel or America (7).

Indigenous Leadership in Israel

Indigenous leadership in Israel is a core problem of Reform Zionism. It has become evident that the Reform congregations in Israel are unable to generate leadership because of their small numbers and their relative lack of young members. Nor is there an economic base (or ideological rationale) for hiring professional leadership for exclusive activity within the Reform movement. It appears that leadership can be mobilized only from those communities where the ideological infrastructure permits the separation of economic recompense from movement activity. In the case of *Tzofei-Telem* this has meant mobilizing leadership from the Kibbutz movement, including Yahel and Lotan and the settlement groups (garinim) to these kibbutzim. Because of the principle of kibbutz democracy which has been adopted by the Youth Movement, some Rabbis have found it difficult to work with the Youth Movement. However, the problem is not just a question of Rabbis. It is a question of full-time youth leaders who will not only work with children and youth but also create total program-ming from Grade 5 to Grade 12.

Recruiting leadership that can commit itself totally has been and is a central problem. So far, only the Kibbutz movement is organized for doing so. It seems that comprehensive Reform community as a basis of Reform Movement in Israel whether urban or rural will necessitate the establishment of norms of semi-voluntary leadership and movement commitment of that leadership which have no precedent either in Israel or the Diaspora. *Paradoxically, at the present stage, to create a true movement in the cities means strengthening the kibbutzim so that they can release members to create a larger movement which can then evolve viable urban forms of comprehensive Reform Community.*

THE FUTURE IDEOLOGICAL FOCI OF REFORM ZIONIST DEVELOPMENT

Notwithstanding all the aforementioned limitations, the practical work of the past five years has bared foci of confrontation which will doubtless play a major role in shaping Reform Zionism — and perhaps more particularly Reform Judaism in Israel — in the years to come.

The common ideological denominator of these foci of confrontation stems from the separation that has developed between religious worship and social-political norms, values and activity among emancipated Jews, during the past 200 years. For non-orthodox Jews, the tradition of separation between church and state has been necessary for ensuring autonomy in the area of religious worship. Religious worship provided legitimation and a rationale for Jewish particularism in the modern nation state. The disappearance of comprehensive Jewish community which accompanied emancipation and the corollary of church-state separation partially concealed the emerging dichotomy between religious ritual and social behavior (8). The very concept of comprehensive community is scarcely compatible with a classical Reform Judaism, based on the liberal idea of individual freedom of conscience without any accompanying collective social responsibility. The recreation of community means confronting both the liberal apotheosis of individual rights (9) as well as the classical Reform tradition of a Judaism restricted in practice to *Kultusgemeinde* (a community of ritual) (10).

A Reform Judaism of Social Action Means Political Action

Social action and social justice have been watchwords of Reform Judaism from its inception and in the American reality of the post World War II generation the social involvement of American Reform Judaism became a reality.

However, in Israel the Israel Movement for Progressive Judaism has in principle never involved itself in political action outside of the national Israeli consensus. Even on the issue of rights for Reform Rabbis it has been diffident, until lately, in aggressively pushing for equality of rights.

It is now becoming clear (in particular against the backdrop of the Israeli political-social-religious scene) that the movement in Israel will have to become political. This does not mean that Reform Judaism will identify in principle with an Israeli political party or found an Israeli political party. However, the 30th Zionist Congress demonstrated that the natural proclivities of Reform Zionism tend to be "progressive." The involvement of ARZENU and NETZER in the World Zionist Organization will doubtless catalyze this process.

Democracy in Judaism

No focus of ideological conflict has more far-reaching implications for the authority structure of Judaism than the emerging tendency in the Israeli Youth Movement and in the kibbutzim of applying principles of democratic community (adopted from the kibbutz movement) to the area of cultural and spiritual concerns.

The principle of ultimate authority vested in the community or congregation is a direct challenge to the contemporary manifestation of the principle of Rabbinical authority and status in Judaism — whether Orthodox, Conservative or Reform. In Democratic Judaism the Rabbi becomes a teacher and spiritual leadership devolves on those who by personal example achieve such status on an informal basis. In effect, the community becomes the arbiter of Halacha, in terms of the image that Israeli Progressive Judaism wishes to project. In part, such was the nature of many of the medieval Jewish communities where a community council had the right to issue regulations in many areas (Takanot Hakahal) while depending on *chachamim* to decide on issues allowed or forbidden according to Jewish law.

Zealous application of the principle of democracy within the various Zionist Federations and the World Zionist Organization will undoubtedly be a focus for internal confrontations within Reform Zionism as well since practical power politics will militate in the direction of compromise on issues of this nature.

A Reform Judaism of Community and Commitment

It is not surprising that the concept of comprehensive Reform Judaism, while acceptable in theory, has encountered some resistance — particularly in Israel — from the existing Reform congregations.

In particular the evolution of a youth movement committed to comprehensive community, whether in the city or on the kibbutz has meant that congregations based on the Diaspora pattern of a community or worship are irrelevant as models of emulation and identification. What is sought is the community of communities based on the realization of I-thou relationships best realized in communal living. This is what Buber has called the *consociatio consociationum* (11).

The question of commitment in and of itself constitutes an additional focus of ideological conflict. The emergence of norms in a youth movement which encourage total involvement in order to "change the world" are bringing about a confrontation with normative society (including the Israeli Reform Movement) with its emphasis on individual achievement. But it is doubtful that anything less than total commitment (which needs the support of community) can make an impact on the social and political reality of Israel.

It would seem that educational projects such as the Leo Baeck School in Haifa could be a focus for urban comprehensive community. However, if urban comprehensive Reform community awaits the development of a larger "critical mass" of indigenous leadership then this development may still be half a generation away.

The end result cannot be in doubt. Reform Judaism in Israel will eventually be defined in terms of committed comprehensive community or it will not be at all.

Religious Worship — An "Anti-focus"

The nature of religious worship in the comprehensive community will have to bridge sensibilities of "believers" and "non-believers." It will be disjunctive for the movement if "theological" questions (nature of God, centrality of Israel) become foci of conflict.

In the past prayerbook and ritual Reform has been the central expression of the Reform in Reform Judaism. There could hardly be any other expression within a community whose limited togetherness was for religious worship only.

But an intentional community bent on social and cultural (of which religious ritual is only part) Reform will not define itself on the basis of common prayerbook, even if one should emerge. Rather, a need will arise (it is already in evidence in *Tzofei-Telem*) to develop forms of Jewish togetherness which transcend the question of theological belief but will give expression to a common commitment of purposive togetherness in order to creatively relate to the Jewish heritage as a central feature of meaningful contemporary Jewish community of identity and existence.

◆ ◆ ◆

It is in actively relating to the above areas of ideological confrontation, political, social and cultural, that Reform Zionism will emerge as a distinct interpretation of Cultural Zionism and as a movement which seeks to shape Jewish polity and policy both in Israel and in the Diaspora.

Notes

(1)   See: "Changing the Structure of the World Zionist Organization," also appeared in *Midstream*, Feb. 1978. (See Section 3:1.)

(2)   See in Langer, Michael, ed., *Reform Zionist Perspective* (RZP), UAHC Youth Division, New York, 1977, Uriel Tal, p. 304, Jakob Petuchowski, p. 307 for a discussion of intentional community..

(3)   Ibid. See Introduction to Section 3 (p. 71) and Section 4 (p. 85).

(4)   See Tabory et al.: "Reform and Conservative Judaism in Israel Today and Tomorrow," *Judaism*, Fall 1982, Vol. 31:4.

(5)   See Section 1:1 — pp. 35-36 and Section 1:6.

(6)   See *Shdemot* (English) #25, 1986, Langer, Michael, *Zionist Youth Movements in the West*.

(7)   "More than Religious Worship is Needed," in *Judaism*, note 4 above.

(8)   See Section 1:5 pp. 20-21 ff.

(9)   See Stanley Meron, "The Individual and Society," p. 38, RZP.

(10) See Note 7.

(11) Martin Buber, *Paths to Utopia* (an experiment that did not fail), Beacon Press, Boston, 1958, p. 159. Also RZP, p. 33. See also Maurice Friedman, *Martin Buber: The Life of Dialogue*, University of Chicago Press, Chicago, 1955, pp. 43-47. Also RZP, p. 317.

The ARZENU[1] Program

LETTER TO RABBI MICHAEL STROH[2]

9 July 1990

Rabbi Michael Stroh
Chairperson, ARZENU
Ben Tabai 4/22, Jerusalem

Dear Michael,

As the dust settles after two hectic weeks, I would like to relate to a number of points raised by you in the ARZENU Executive, as well as to others arising from the Vaad Hapoel and the Assembly.[3]

Perhaps a central concern should be that ARZENU and its individual affiliates have so far not developed an "in depth" long-term political process. This overarching question will affect ARZENU deleteriously as it attempts to relate to specific ad hoc issues.

You have raised the question as to whether ARZENU is a one-issue movement. Certainly that was the image we projected at the Vaad Hapoel and the Assembly. I do believe that the question of religious pluralism in the WZO and in Israel will continue to be a central concern of ours for some time to come. However, the fact that we negate the negation of ourselves does not indicate what our positive program is or should be.

ARZENU and Education

I think that the main thrust of an ARZENU action program should be through the modality of education. At the local and national level, through federations and the Reform movement, ARZENU should be for activists for Zionist-Jewish education in particular. This is not always *hoch-politik*. A lot of it is nuts and bolts, bucking for educational priorities. In particular, Reform Zionists could use their leverage

---

1. ARZENU — International Federation of Reform and Progressive Religious Zionists.
2. Unpublished letter written in 1990. Rabbi Stroh was on a sabbatical in Jerusalem.
3. Jewish Agency Assembly, June 1990.

in communities to initiate a model community for Zionist-Jewish education (draft proposal appended).[1] The British Liberal community has been the first to enter into the process of crystallizing such a program. We will try to get incentive funding from the Joint Fund.[2]

Let me give some additional examples of Reform Zionist activity within the Reform Jewish educational structure. Reform day schools should have WZO shlichim. Please do not misunderstand. I am not talking about flooding schools with shlichim, but rather of a policy that among a staff of 20 teachers, one or two should be Israeli Zionists open to Reform in order to project a total spectrum of possible Zionist-Jewish identity, both to pupils and the rest of the staff. Clearly, the current Department of Education and Culture in the Diaspora (pending name change) would be prepared to integrate Reform elements for those teacher-shlichim who would be going to our schools. This means nuts and bolts work in the education committee of every school. An excellent example is that of Shoshana and Yaakov Azulas, who were recruited through our department to serve in the Talmud Torah in Edmonton. They are very close to the Reform movement.

At the federation level, ARZENU members should gravitate to the education committees of the federation. In many communities there are day high schools (Toronto is an excellent example) where pluralism is not the practice. Pluralism means that those schools should have teachers and teacher-shlichim who are not only Orthodox. Why should graduates of the Leo Baeck Day School in Toronto be forced to go to an Orthodox day school after Grade 8? Is this fight going to be divisive in the community? The answer is yes. For the sake of "shalom bayit" in the community, members of ARZENU would probably be diffident in raising this issue. But by what moral right is ARZENU prepared to conduct the battle for pluralism in the WZO and the Assembly without conducting it in the backyards of its own affiliate organizations?

Another area of ARZENU educational activity should be the backing of the Reform Zionist youth movement process. In fact, Netzer in Australia, England and South Africa are already strong movements, though it is questionable that the credits for this accrue to ARZENU. I would even say that in those countries, Netzer has to reach a level of political sophistication and understanding that they must be ARZENU activists as well. However, the real problem exists in North America where Reform Zionist youth movement process will probably have to take a different route than the "classical" youth movement process currently

---

1. See Section 4:4.
2. Joint Fund for special education projects — Jewish Agency and WZO.

embodied by Netzer. The role of ARZA[1] and Kadima[2] would be to influence congregations to give partial scholarships to long-term Reform Zionist programs in Israel, with the understanding that the young people involved would be committed to be active when they return in whatever community they find themselves. A central problem within the Reform movement in America has been that for the last ten years no NFTY[3] contingent has been sent to the Machon LeMadrichei Chutz L'Aretz;[4] thus ten years of generating Reform Zionist youth movement process have been lost. If the British and Australian Reform movements are capable of each sending 10-15 youngsters every year — so is North America. Kadima and Arza should pick top NFTY (Temple youth group) leadership as participants and offer them scholarships. I do not believe that the Youth Division of the UAHC is equipped to work at the level of congregational or regional initiative. ARZA-Kadima will have to deal with the questions of turf. In my opinion, knowing some of the people involved, a modus operandi with the Youth Division is possible, and it might even welcome such an initiative.

Of course the ARZENU position all over the world should be that Jewish schools must be open to youth movements. Again, here there is an issue where federation funded community high schools restrict access to youth movements or permit access only to Bnei Akiva.[5] All of this means that local ARZENU chapters must be knowledgeable with regards to local federation educational politics.

The emphases here proposed for Reform Zionist educational activity should be reflected in the program of ARZENU chapters. I envisage a monthly evening program comprising about 25% business and the rest Zionist-Jewish "tarbut," of which a significant portion would be self-education. I think format is important, especially in a religious Zionist movement: an opening five-minute program of appropriate readings (maybe a song); the bracha before the refreshments. The mazkirut[6] of the chapter would also meet once a month and would constitute the activist nucleus of the chapter.

The Politics of Education in the WZO

The ARZENU leadership must become more aware of and involved in the politics of education in the WZO. The basic situation is that our department is politically tied into parity with the Department of Torah Education in terms of budget. This

---

1. ARZA — Associations of Reform Zionists of America.
2. Kadima — Reform Zionist movement in Canada (now ARZA-Canada).
3. NFTY — National Federation of Temple Youth (UAHC).
4. Youth Leadership Training Institute — Jerusalem.
5. Orthodox Zionist Youth Movement.
6. Secretariat.

is in spite of the fact that only 15% of Jewish children are Orthodox. The argument used that Orthodox children comprise the majority of the day school population, and therefore of formal education, is specious. After all, formal education also exists in afternoon and Saturday-Sunday schools. In addition, formal Zionist-Jewish education might well be purveyed by having professional educators (shlichim) as part of the staff of major bureaus of Jewish education and the education departments of the UAHC and the United Synagogue. (Again, in Toronto, this is what the Torah Education Department does.) For lack of funds, we cannot even suggest a matching cost arrangement with bureaus of Jewish education or education departments of UAHC and United Synagogue. ARZENU support (together with Mercaz[1]) on the Joint Authority[2] will be critical to achieve a significant change in this area. The political heat that it will generate will be no less than the symbolic battle over the department's name. However, the benefits will be substantive and not only symbolic. Right now, even without a victory regarding the name of the department, we do not have the money to do anything with the mandate we theoretically have (this was an issue discussed with the subcommittee you assigned to meet with Hank and myself — I must say I was disappointed that you did not see fit to include North American ARZENU representation in that meeting).

On another level — if indeed the Joint Authority will have an executive of 12 — we should demand that on the JAFI[3] side a Reform and Conservative educator-representative be included. I have no idea what the JAFI process will be for picking its executive members, but ARZENU should pursue the matter. The importance of ensuring Reform and Conservative input into the regional advisory bodies, both on the Zionist side and on the denominational side is obvious to us all.

ARZENU-Telem

You raised a number of other issues at the ARZENU executive meeting, but I shall conclude this letter by referring to the question of how ARZENU relates to the Israel Movement. Support for the field of education (formal and informal) as well as the Center for Pluralism and Democracy are good stop-gap measures. I also believe that Reform settlements must be supported because of their unique contribution.

However, it has been my opinion for a number of years that separate elections

---

1. Conservative (United Synagogue) Zionist movement.
2. Joint Authority (WZO and Jewish Agency) for Jewish Zionist Education.
3. JAFI — Jewish Agency for Israel.

for the Congress in Israel would give a tremendous boost to the movement. Not only would elections focus the issue of Zionism in general for the Israeli public, it would also provide a framework for us to purvey our ideological and educational wares. Commitment of the major parties (Likud and Labor) for a constitutional change in the WZO to permit this should be one of our immediate goals.

There are other aspects to the ARZENU-Telem relationship. I do not think that ARZENU can be involved in the internal politics of Telem. However, I do think that ARZENU has to be cognizant of the issues within Telem — e.g., rabbinic vs. congregational authority; professional vs. lay leadership; community outreach vs. educational outreach; political involvements vs. political neutrality. The questions relating to "whither" Reform Judaism and/or Reform Zionism in Israel should be one of the foci in an ARZENU educational program for its members.

I would be happy to discuss the above further with you and others in ARZENU and, of course, to be of help whenever possible.

Sincerely,
Dr. Michael Livni

cc: ARZENU Executive,
    Rabbi Richard Hirsch,
    Rabbi Alexander Schindler,
    Rabbi Henry F. Skirball.

ARZENU — What Now?[1]

26 Cheshvan 5753
November 22, 1992

To: Rabbi David Lilienthal
cc: ARZENU Executive, ARZENU — Vaad Hapoel, ARZENU Negotiators

From: Dr. Michael Livni

Dear David,

Subject: ARZENU — What Now?[2]

Further to our conversation at the Jewish Agency Assembly last month, I am submitting this memo to you and the ARZENU Executive on the above subject.

This memo is being written without information regarding negotiations that may or may not be taking place in New York during November. I do assume that such negotiations can only be concluded in Israel for reasons both of principle and because of the necessity of concluding any agreements with our faction as a whole.

In fact, it would appear that meaningful negotiations are at a dead end. In my opinion, we must review our tactics in the light of our strategic aims — assuming we still have a consensus in this area.

On the issue of democracy we have not progressed beyond what we have received from the Zionist court — a fragile achievement which could be eroded by further political machinations. Nor have we progressed on the portfolio issue (including Deputy Chairperson of the Joint Authority[3] with adequately defined powers). We have not even received satisfaction with regard to what should have been pre-conditions to negotiations. We have not yet received monies owed to us from the Education Departments and, in particular, we have not received recognition (and a budget) for TAMAR, Tnuat Magshimim Reformim.

---

1. Unpublished, 1992. Rabbi Lilienthal was Chairperson of ARZENU.
2. Following the breakdown of the WZO Coalition between ARZENU and the World Labor Zionist Movement.
3. Joint Authority (Jewish Agency & WZO) for Jewish Zionist Education.

In the area of Jewish Zionist education the resolutions we submitted to the Jewish Agency Assembly were disqualified on the technical ground that the Assembly is not empowered to discuss educational matters. We had introduced resolutions similar to those introduced by us at the 32nd WZO Congress on allocating funds for both formal and informal Jewish-Zionist education according to criteria such as size and character of target populations (including outreach to mixed marriages). These resolutions are now supposed to be submitted to the Joint Authority for Jewish-Zionist education.

In the light of the foregoing, the purpose of this memo is to submit TACTICAL SUGGESTIONS in order to further the STRATEGIC AIMS of ARZENU as initially proposed by me in my memo to Paula Edelstein of August 10, 1992, which is appended herewith for your convenience.

Strategic Aims:

1. Replacement of the WZO/JAFI structure with a new world Jewish-Zionist body based on a minimum contribution to the Keren Hayesod/United Israel Appeal to be determined for every country. The cost of elections would be borne by the various National appeals. Election lists could be on the basis of parties, regional lists, independents — in fact whatever the public or a significant portion thereof wants. The appropriate target date for convening the new body and officially phasing out the WZO/JAFI structure would be 1997, the 100th anniversary of the WZO.

2. Elections in Israel to the world Jewish-Zionist body separate from Knesset elections. This would tie in with a movement strategy in Israel of promoting educational awareness among Israeli Jews of the Diaspora in general and the pluralistic nature of the Jewish people and the Zionist commitment to the Jewish National Home. Technically this might be accomplished by separate polling boxes at election time with appropriate arrangements for interested temporary residents to participate.

3. Funding of Jewish Zionist education concomitant with its place as the second priority (after *Aliyah*) of the Jewish Agency. This is necessary in order to ensure not only Jewish identity but also active commitment on the part of the coming generation of Diaspora Jews. This means allocating more resources in general as well as allocating them in line with the size and character of target populations as well as with the degree of their distress. (The question of what constitutes "distress" is also an open issue.)

4. We should remain alert to at least two additional areas in which we have

strategic interests and with which this memo does not deal in detail. We have an interest in *Aliyah* and the successful *Klitah*[1] of members of our own constituency. We also have a strategic concern in strengthening our *Hityashvut*.[2]

Furthering our strategic aims requires a tactical operational program in order to further those aims. It is hereby proposed that the tactical program below (or parts thereof) constitute directives to our executive arm between now and 6/93.

Current Tactical Considerations:

1. Participation in WZO Bodies

At the time of the WZO Congress we decided to participate in the WZO Executive. This decision was based on the assumption that meaningful negotiations were continuing. As this is not so this policy decision should be reviewed. In my opinion, our ongoing participation in the WZO Executive has become meaningless and even counterproductive.

A. We have granted de facto legitimacy to an Executive which has been appointed by a process we characterized as undemocratic. In doing so we are humiliating ourselves and projecting an image of political naivete and impotency. What are we gaining?!

B. Our de facto participation in the Executive potentially neutralizes tactical initiatives which might further our strategic aims regarding the establishment of the new world Jewish Zionist body. Our credibility in promoting the above strategy vis-a-vis the activists outside of the WZO would be enhanced if we publicly distanced ourselves from the WZO establishment without leaving the Zionist movement. It also gives us additional leverage and credibility in furthering the democratization of the UIA/KH.

Our operative conclusion could be to announce (preferably as a faction) that as the result of the non-recognition of our terms, both in the area of democracy and in the area of portfolios, we are ceasing to participate in the WZO Inner Executive. We should not resign. Our continued participation in the outer executive is also an open question. At the same time we will continue to participate in the Zionist Federations of the Diaspora as well as the Vaad Hapoel and its subsidiary bodies. Clearly we will continue to participate in all the institutions of the Jewish Agency and the Joint Authority for Jewish Zionist education.

---

1. Absorption.
2. Settlements.

In practical terms we are not doing ourselves a disservice by absenting ourselves from the inner WZO Executive. Its ongoing work is insignificant and our influence within it is close to nil. On the other hand, the psychological pressure we can bring to bear by absenting ourselves — in particular on Simcha Dinitz and the Conservative movement will be significant. We may even find it easier to get material advantages in negotiations with individual Departments.

We have an additional option — second best but possible. We could leave the *Shinui Hanhala* member in place and take out the ARZENU representative. I do not recommend this option.

2. The Joint Authority for Jewish-Zionist Education

A. As a result of the disenfranchisement of the Jewish Agency Assembly, we should submit our education resolutions to the Commission in February. To do so we must submit them to the Authority *Hanhala* now. In addition to the type of resolution already referred to above (p. 56) we also submitted a resolution recommending a gradual increase in the size of the Joint Authority budget. The resolutions are appended for your ready reference.

Failure to follow through on resolutions we submit projects a lack of resolve and amateurism on our part. This is negative not only in our relations with others but also in terms of our own constituency and our faction partners.

B. There is an ongoing attempt to blur the amount of Joint Authority money being spent in or on behalf of various countries and regions. This is not in our best interests — nor is it in the interests of the various regional advisory councils. Admittedly, not all money spent can be accounted for regionally. Even so, we should push for budget presentation by region and population served. Not only is this in the general interest but also the current system is generally detrimental to our movement. Budget presentations by region will help us to focus on anachronistic features of the budget.

C. The question of *shlichim* is to be discussed at the February meeting of the Commission. In fact, the relevant focus is not allocation of *shlichim* but allocation of resources to the youth movements and organizations. It should be up to the latter how best to utilize these resources. Principles of utilization may vary from movement to movement and from region to region. We should submit our proposal on this subject to the Joint Authority Commission in February. If possible, we should attempt to coordinate such a presentation with Hanoar Hazioni.[1] Hopefully such a proposal will be circulated to you and the ARZENU executive in the next six weeks.

D. In the area of Research and Development we should take initiative in pushing for case studies of successful Jewish Zionist education to be determined by the Authority Executive on the basis of advice from the professional staff. Such case studies would then point the direction where the Joint Authority should go. We should then suggest at least one focus where Netzer is very strong (England, Australia) in order to ensure that future criteria for Jewish Zionist education take into account the potential success of a Zionist youth movement linked to a religious, non-orthodox ideology.

E. We should attempt to initiate an amendment to the Joint Authority charter at the 1993 Jewish Agency Assembly in order to re-enfranchise the Assembly to deal with matters of Jewish Zionist education. The aim should be to give the Assembly the same powers in relation to the Authority that it enjoys in relation to the Board of Governors. This is in our interest because our potential political strength gets less as we go up in the hierarchy and hence our ability to lever from the Assembly is most important.

General Remark:

We must consider the implications of our policy in the Joint Authority for the on-going financing that some projects of our Diaspora constituency receive from the Special Allocations program of the Jewish Agency. It is questionable that the current arrangement (money from both the Authority and the Special Allocations program) is viable in the long run.

Procedures For Tactical Operation

1. The ARZENU Executive should hold telephone/fax consultations, coordinated by the General Secretary of ARZENU in Israel, in order to reach conclusions on the directives with regard to the tactical suggestions in this memo and/or other tactical suggestions relating to the matters raised in this memo. It should be possible to do this by mid-January.

2. The ARZENU committee in Israel should:
   a. Continue to receive directives from the ARZENU executive with regard to negotiations (or non-negotiations) from an ARZENU viewpoint prior to discussing them with our faction partners.[2]
   b. Initiate in-depth discussions with our faction partners with regard to

---

1. Coalition partners of ARZENU in the WZO ("The New Faction").
2. Faction partners — Hanoar Hazioni, Shinui, Ratz.

ARZENU strategic interests (which may or may not conflict with some of theirs) and encourage them to present their parallel interests.

c. Act as a sounding board for ARZENU executive directives regarding operational policy stemming from this memo and/or other suggestions.

d. Convene monthly meetings prior to faction meetings. We should ensure that monthly faction meetings do indeed take place.

In conclusion, it is my belief that in order to build ARZENU as a movement and our faction as an effective political force, it is essential for us to have a movement strategy backstopped by tactical plans and organizational procedures for putting them into operation.

B'vracha
Michael Livni

Affirmative Action — Reform Zionist Aliyah[1]

11 Cheshvan 5755
October 16, 1994

Rabbi David Lilienthal
Chairperson, ARZENU
Liberaal Joodse Gemeente
1079 RM Amsterdam, Netherlands

Dear David,

<u>Subject: Affirmative Action — Reform Zionist Aliyah</u>

Enclosed please find my paper "A Rationale and Program for Reform Zionism"[2] which I have submitted to Rabbi Ami Hirsch for the Reform Zionist Journal. It might also be useful for discussion groups in ARZENU even though most of the paper is oriented to the North American scene. However, the subject of Reform Zionist *Aliyah* is relevant to the entire movement and hence I would like you to raise the subject of affirmative action for Reform Zionist *Aliyah* at an ARZENU executive meeting in the hope that the member movements will have discussed the subject in their home movements.

A practical program for promoting *Aliyah* must be a central aim of ARZENU. The creative tension generated by dealing with the question of *Aliyah* is one aspect of the differentiation between a Zionist movement as against a pro-Israel support group. Reform Zionist *Aliyah* would not only strengthen our movement in Israel — it would also have certainly have a positive effect on Israel-Diaspora relations for Reform Jews in the Diaspora.

The following steps could constitute affirmative action by ARZENU for Reform Zionist *Aliyah*:

1. A contacts office in Jerusalem which would receive information from congregations regarding congregants (especially young people) coming to Israel for extended visits. The contacts office would attempt to link people

---

1. Unpublished, 1994.
2. See Section 1:7.

to the Reform movement and its institutions in Israel. Too many people (especially young people) come to Israel without coming into any real contact with the Reform movement. This is especially true of those countries such as the United States and Canada that have no informal youth movement networking through their Netzer Olami affiliation.

2. A revolving loan fund for housing, index linked but interest free, should be established for adult Reform congregants making *Aliyah*. Their membership fees in one of our congregations of their choice should be paid for the first three years.

3. A retraining fund for our *Olim*[1] should be set up in order to supplement what is available from the Ministry of Absorption. Such retraining involves Hebrew language proficiency as well as vocational adaptation. Most of "our" *Olim* are university graduates. Functioning in Hebrew at a level comparable to their ability to function in their native language makes a great difference in their absorption process. It also empowers them to do Reform Zionist outreach more effectively in Israel. This type of assistance is of particular relevance to our Kibbutzim which, relative to their small size, absorb many *Olim*.

4. For young singles and/or students a number of apartments located in a particular area could be rented by the movement. This would enable joint socio-cultural and Reform Zionist movement activity. The apartments would be made available at subsidized rates on condition that those renting commit themselves to some area of part time Reform Zionist outreach (for example, among other foreign students at the universities, projects in coordination with the Israel Religious Action Center).

5. A debt forgiveness program should be established for graduates of our academic institutions (Hebrew Union College, Leo Baeck College) who choose to make *Aliyah*.

Practical Implementation

The augmentation of the ARZENU and Netzer Olami infrastructure would be the basis for implementation. Chances are that most candidates (but not all!) are young people and hence the involvement of Netzer Olami is cardinal. Our Kibbutzim might be approached to institute a "first home" (Beit Rishon B'Moledet) similar to the program for *Olim* from the former Soviet Union.

---

1. Olim — Immigrants.

A movement wide discussion on the subject will surely result in additional ideas as well as further practical suggestions for implementation.

B'vracha

Dr. Michael Livni

cc: ARZENU Executive (to be distributed by the Jerusalem Office) — Paula
    Mazkirut Netzer Olami — Leah, John
    ARZA — Rabbi Ami Hirsch — for distribution to the ARZA Board

A Rationale and Program for Reform Zionism[1]

A Rationale as Prerequisite to Reform Zionist Outreach

North American Reform Zionism must project a coherent rationale to two groups of relatively committed and searching Jews. The first group comprises those Reform Jews who are not yet Reform Zionists. The second group is made up of those who identify as Zionists but have not yet contended with a rationale for Reform Zionism.

Currently, most Reform Zionist energy has been expended on Reform Jews. However this energy has gone into mobilizing the Reform Jewish polity for specific projects such as democratic elections to the Zionist Congress and support for the Israel Religious Action Center. As yet, Reform Zionism has not adequately developed an overarching rationale and action program within the Reform constituency defining positions not yet within its general consensus.

In addition, Reform Zionism has neglected outreach to those Zionists (both in Israel and in the Diaspora) searching for alternative ideas and ideals on which to base their Zionist outlook within the Jewish world reality of today. Such outreach requires a credible rationale. Without it Reform Zionism will remain a parochial phenomenon of a particular (Reform) constituency.

An adequate Reform Zionist rationale must accomplish a double task. Firstly, it must relate to the existential problems of Reform Judaism (and in effect of the larger Jewish community). These problems focus around the rapid dissipation of Jewish commitment (not just identity) in the Diaspora with its concomitant demographic attrition as illustrated by the 1990 National Jewish Population Survey of the Council of Jewish Federations.[2]

Secondly, Reform Zionism must define an approach to Jewish peoplehood including Jewish purpose which relates to current political and social reality in the Jewish world including Israel. In order to do so it must explain itself in relation to the historical categories of Zionist thought — Political Zionism and Cultural Zionism.

---

1. Published in slightly abridged form in: *Reform Zionist Journal* (ARZA) No. 2: March 1995.
2. Council of Jewish Federations, Highlights of the CJF 1990 National Jewish Population Survey, New York, 1991.

Political Zionism Has Become Pro-Israelism

Historically the aim of Political Zionism's founder Theodor Herzl, was embodied in the platform of the First Zionist Congress (1897) promulgated in Basle: "...the establishment of a home for the Jewish people secured under public law in Palestine."[1] Herzl's program was focused on solving the problem of the Jews and the inability and/or lack of desire of many modern Nation States to fully accept the Jews in their midst. The climactic events which engulfed the Jewish people in the second quarter of this Century bore out in nightmare fashion the somber prognosis of political Zionism and created a significant Jewish consensus for the Basle program.

The internationally sanctioned establishment of Israel in 1948 did not signify the end of the political (and military) struggle by and for the State. However, since 1948 the instrument for furthering that political struggle has become the sovereign State of Israel. The seminal political events taking place in our day are the ultimate demonstration that the sovereign State of Israel is responsible for ensuring Israel's viable political continuity and not the World Zionist Organization, the instrumentality originally created by Theodor Herzl to further the establishment of the Jewish State. The peace process has dramatically exposed the irrelevance of Political Zionism.

Political Zionism has become redundant. Its aim has been achieved. In the Diaspora, the consensus that formed around the establishment of the State has become the pro-Israel consensus. In our generation, this consensus is normative to the organized Jewish community outside of Israel and includes the Reform movement. This consensus expresses itself by means of philanthropic, economic and political support. This support is surely desirable and constitutes an essential part of our world of Jewish values, but its auxiliary nature precludes it from constituting a movement program.

Cultural Zionism — the Forgotten Program

Cultural Zionism preceded Political Zionism. Its primary exponent was Achad Ha'am (the pen name of Asher Ginzburg — 1856-1927). The central ideas of Achad Ha'am have particular value in Reform Zionist outreach which seeks to clarify Reform Zionism's position to those who already identify as Zionists.

Achad Ha'am believed that the continued creative survival of Judaism was threatened by the impact of modernity. On the one hand the Enlightenment had exposed the bankruptcy of traditional Judaism. On the other hand, Reform

---

1. Quoted from Ben Halpern, The Idea of the Jewish State, Harvard University Press, 1961, p. 28.

Judaism in the West was negating Jewish peoplehood and reducing Judaism to a religious denomination. Achad Ha'am posited that Jewish creativity depended on the on-going interaction with ever-changing reality, an active national existence with its accompanying national feeling in the real life of love and work.

For Achad Ha'am the creative element within Judaism, the Hebrew national spirit, was defined by Prophecy and its uncompromising striving for Tikun Olam. The prophets embodied the idea of mission (*shlichut*), which gave Judaism its sense of purpose. Achad Ha'am first developed this thesis in his essay, "Priest and Prophet,"[1] published in 1894 (three years before the First Zionist Congress).

Achad Ha'am recognized that Prophetic striving for Tikun Olam would have to be modified by political reality as represented by the "Priest." It was the dynamic interplay between them that would be the leaven of Jewish creativity. The restoration of this mythic-historic interplay between "Priest" and "Prophet" into a meaningful and creative force for modern Judaism was the core concern of Cultural Zionism. The restoration of a Jewish National Home was an indispensable prerequisite to this end.

Israel and the Diaspora: "Interdependent, Spiritually Inseparable...Strong and Creative"

For a post 1948 perspective on Herzl and Achad Ha'am it is particularly fitting to quote Rabbi Abba Hillel Silver, one of the minority within Reform who espoused Zionism. Silver became the outstanding American-Jewish spokesman for political Zionism during the Forties. Two years after the achievement of Zionism's central political aim to which he had dedicated so much he said:

> It was fortunate that the sound political vision and program of Theodor Herzl governed the course of the movement until the State was established. A premature overemphasis of the concept of a spiritual or cultural center would have found the Jewish people unprepared for the final political and military struggle without which the State could not have been established...

> But Herzl's political triumph now paves the way for the vision which was Achad Ha'am's — that of the radiating center in a reconstituted Jewish State which would also serve as a unifying influence for world Jewry...

---

1. In Leon Simon, Selected Essays by Achad Ha'am, Meridian Books, Jewish Publication Society, Philadelphia, 1962, p. 125.

> The Jewish communities of the Diaspora will look eagerly for all
> stimulating influences which might emanate from Israel But
> Diaspora Jewry need not remain a mere passive recipient of
> outside cultural influences. It can become, as indeed so often in
> the past it did become, creative in its own right, wherever the
> religion, language and literature of the Jewish people were
> fostered... (my underlining — M.L.)
>
> This is a good program for Jewish survival from here on. Israel and
> the Diaspora should remain interdependent, spiritually insepa-
> rable though politically separate and apart. Both should be helped
> to become strong and creative.[1]

Can Reform Zionism formulate a rationale and carry through an action program
which would further Abba Hillel Silver's vision of a relationship within which
Israel and the Diaspora are both strong and creative, interdependent and spiritually inseparable? Can Reform Zionism formulate practical programs, both in
Israel and the Diaspora, which will constitute *shlichut* in the prophetic spirit?
How will Reform Zionism relate to the challenge of Jewish-Zionist literacy within
its constituency?

In my opinion, it is the task of ARZA to build on the pro-Israel consensus and
to define issues which are not yet within the general consensus today but are
essential for realizing a Reform Zionist action program. Today, these issues relate
to Jewish culture — political, national and religious.

A Political Basis for Interdependence

In part, the Reform Zionist movement (with ARZA in the lead) has recognized
that, in the light of the general pro-Israel consensus, the existing institutional
world of Jewry (its political culture) needs a far-reaching overhaul.

As Rabbi Richard Hirsch has pointed out, official Zionist ideology as
formulated in the Jerusalem Platform of 1968 and the so-called "non-Zionist"
pro-Israel outlook of the "fund raisers" as expressed in the Jewish Agency
Mission statement of 1990 are in essence identical.[2] It is the recognition of this
fact that has lead ARZENU (the international umbrella organization of which

---

1. Abba Hillel Silver, "Problems and Prospects of American Judaism" (Founder's Day Address, Hebrew
   Union College, March 12, 1950), in Herbert Weiner, ed.,Therefore Choose Life: Selected Sermons,
   Addresses and Writings of Abba Hillel Silver, World Publications, New York, 1967, pp. 409-10. Also in
   Reform Zionist Perspective, UAHC Youth Division, 1977, p. 255.
2. Richard G. Hirsch, The Israel Diaspora Connection: Reorganizing World Jewry to Meet the Needs of
   the 21st Century, ARZENU — World Union for Progressive Judaism, Jerusalem, 1993, p. 10.

ARZA is the U.S.A. constituent) to espouse a new world-wide democratic reorganization of the Jewish people in an all-encompassing Jewish-Zionist body which would reflect that existing consensus.

It would be ideal to convene the first convention of such a new world Jewish-Zionist body in August 1997 on the 100th anniversary of the founding Zionist Congress.

However an adequate rationale for the changes necessary in order to achieve world-wide democratic reorganization has not been proposed. In the absence of such a rationale we are in constant danger of compromising the essence of our ideas. For example, if Reform Zionists really propose a new world Jewish-Zionist body the energy invested in attempting to reform the existing World Zionist Organization from within may be superfluous and possibly self-defeating.

The Problematics of Democracy in the Diaspora

Democracy is not normative to Judaism nor is it a part of traditional Jewish communal political culture in the Diaspora.

The pre-modern, authoritarian Jewish community was governed by a power elite of *parnasim* and *chachamim* — the wealthy and the learned. Today we would call them the big giver and the professional Jew. By and large both in the past and today this was and is an elite of responsible, caring and often dedicated individuals. However, it was and is patronizing. It was not and is not democratic. The traditional system is maladapted to dealing with current problems facing the Jewish people in the Diaspora, particularly in the United States, because it confirms the indifference and/or alienation of an ever widening margin of passively identifying Jews.

The current system of Jewish communal organization disempowers the average Jew of modest means and undercuts motivation among many to become involved in community affairs. The days of reflex ethnic commitment which tolerated the traditional power structure are no more. Jewish community activism (not to be confused with interest in Judaism) is increasingly the game of the rich and the Jewish professional.

The Jewish professionals in turn have become increasingly beholden to a select group, appointed by a buddy-system of their wealthy peers and essentially not accountable to a wider public. They have introduced the culture of the corporation board into Jewish community affairs. There is little policy input from the general public nor is it sought. As one leading American Jewish professional with the United Israel Appeal put it: "We go by the Golden Rule — he who has the Gold rules."

Tikun Am — mending the institutions of the Jewish people should be a "natural" for Reform. The principles of democracy and Israel-Diaspora interdependence should guide Reform Zionist policy.

Universal Jewish Suffrage

It is my thesis that a precondition to interdependence between the Diaspora and Israel is a common, democratic institutional framework for all of world Jewry with universal suffrage in elections for that framework. The unique idea of Jewish peoplehood, "We are One," expresses not just mutual responsibility but also necessitates a world-wide institutionalized democratic forum for the ongoing development of that mutuality. Democratic elections for a world-wide Jewish-Zionist forum would surely mobilize interest and commitment to Jewish peoplehood in both Israel and the Diaspora.

In reality, the Reform movement as such and its leadership as individuals are integrally a part of the traditional power elite scenario. It would be naive to assume that the Reform establishment can take an initiative in demanding universal Jewish suffrage with its implications for the General Assembly of the Council of Jewish Federations, the General Assembly of the Jewish Agency and its Board of Governors. But ARZA could raise this issue in tandem with the demand for a new world Jewish-Zionist body. This demands determined and knowledgeable lay leadership. Reform Zionism must beware of becoming over-professionalized. By means of a nationally coordinated effort, ARZA activists could raise this issue at the grass roots level in Federations across the country.

Is ARZA prepared to conceptualize a world Jewish-Zionist body based on universal Jewish suffrage as defined by a minimal contribution to the United Israel Appeal/Keren Hayesod in the Diaspora or Israeli citizenship? In effect, this would be a renewal of the idea behind the Zionist "shekel" of pre-State days. It also means separate elections in Israel for the new body. To compromise on Diaspora elections only is to catalyze Israel-Diaspora polarity and to undercut the institutional basis for interdependence.

Israel and a World Jewish-Zionist Body

In Israel, the Shekel to the Zionist Congress was replaced by the Israeli parliamentary system. This left a vacuum insofar as a participatory relationship between Israeli Jewry and Diaspora Jewry is concerned. Israeli delegates to the

Zionist Congress of today are nominated by their parties on the basis of elections to the Knesset. They purport to represent voters who sent them to the Knesset but this is a fiction. To the Israeli voter, issues of concern to the Jewish people are marginal at best. Israelis have no way of expressing their approach to problems affecting the Jewish people nor is there a venue for Diaspora Jewry to dialogue with the Israeli Jewish-Zionist community.

The result is doubly negative. Firstly and most damaging of all, the Israeli public is not exposed in a comprehensive way at given intervals to issues concerning the Jewish people as a whole (e.g., Israel-Diaspora relationships, the Jewish nature of the Jewish state, *Aliyah* absorption from the West). Elections to a world Jewish Zionist body would raise awareness regarding the nature of Israeli and Jewish identity. The issues involved would find their way into public debates and would legitimize (and possibly authorize) discussions in the Israeli classroom. Obviously this would be a tremendous opportunity for Reform Zionism.

Secondly, the Zionist institutions have become a dumping ground for Israeli political party functionaries who are no longer relevant on the Israeli political scene. While some of these people are capable and dedicated practically speaking they are not really accountable to anyone once appointed. The Simcha Dinitz affair has highlighted what can happen when an arrogant personality insulated from any real accountability is appointed by an indifferent party machine to a position of cardinal importance in the Jewish world. The real agenda then becomes personal political power and survival.

The Components of "Spiritual Inseparability"

Abba Hillel Silver's vision of "spiritual inseparability" necessitates a further development of Jewish norms — both in Israel and in the Diaspora.

There can be no "spiritual inseparability" in today's world of pluralist approaches to Judaism if the State grants legitimacy to only one interpretation of Jewish religious culture. Quite aside from the negative impact on Israeli spirituality, this situation limits the degree to which significant sectors of Diaspora Jewry can identify with Israel spiritually. Cultural Zionism assumes that the Jewish State will be a laboratory for creative Judaism and that all trends within Judaism will be able to utilize it as such. The attempt by the Orthodox (and to a large extent non-Zionist) establishment to de-legitimize Jewish pluralism is an attempt to straight jacket Cultural Zionism.[1]

---

1. Michael Langer (Livni), "Democracy, Religion and the Zionist Future of Israel," *Judaism*, Vol. 36, No. 4, Fall 1987, pp. 400-415. See Section 3:3.

The pioneering work of the Israel Religious Action Center in furthering the legitimacy of Jewish pluralism is beginning to bear fruit and I believe that it will prove to be a catalyst of historic importance in shaping the relationship between religion and state in the Israel of tomorrow. It is an accomplishment in which ARZA can take great pride but there is still a long way to go.

In leading the battle for Reform rights in Israel, Reform Zionism represents activist Reform Judaism as a whole. However, it would be a mistake for Reform Zionism to make this issue the rationale for its existence.

If Reform Zionism is to be an instrumental factor in creating spiritual inseparability it can do so only by creating a far more significant bridgehead within Israeli society. This is a function of the nature of Reform outreach in Israel, an increase in committed Reform *Aliyah* and the implementation of Reform Zionist education in the Diaspora.

The Nature of Reform in Israel

Will Reform in Israel be cloned from the Diaspora format or will it develop a different methodology? I have raised the issue of "Reform Judaism and Reform Zionism in Israel" elsewhere[1] and it will suffice to point out here that given limited resources (money and people) there is a conflict between developing congregations as against outreach by means of an educational system. It is my opinion that we should do everything in our power to ensure equal rights for our congregations. But the long term impact on Israeli attitudes to Jewish culture will be only marginally affected by an increase in the number attending Reform services. On the other hand a viable educational system is the more realistic path, ideologically and economically, for Reform Zionism to influence the future spiritual nature of Israeli society. In the present political circumstances a window of political opportunity for Reform education in Israel has arisen.

Affirmative Action for Reform Zionist Aliyah

The miniscule size of our movement in Israel makes it imperative that Reform Zionism develop an affirmative action program for *Aliyah*. The aim should be a few hundred Reform Zionistically committed *Olim* per year from the world constituency of one and a half million Reform Jews. Currently the Reform Zionist bridgehead is not large enough for the outreach necessary in order to impact on

---

1. Michael Livni, "Reform Judaism and Reform Zionism in Israel," *Journal of Reform Judaism*, Spring 1991, p. 49. For another view see also: Mordecai Rotem, "Israeli Reform Judaism: An Alternative View," *Journal of Reform Judaism*, Spring 1992, p. 61. See Section 2:5.

Israeli society. In any case, an *Aliyah* program is an ideological imperative for the credibility of any movement calling itself "Zionist."

For Reform Jews spiritual inseparability is also a function of personal bonds and identification. This does not mean that *Aliyah* is a defining criterion of who is a Zionist. It does mean that a practical program for promoting *Aliyah* must be a central aim of ARZENU in general and ARZA in particular. A more significant Reform Zionist presence in Israel would certainly also have a positive effect on Israel-Diaspora relations for Reform Jews in the Diaspora.[1]

Pro-Israel or Reform Zionist Education

Clearly, one implication of Reform Zionist education is that there will be more Reform Zionist *Aliyah*. However the real significance of Reform Zionist education is in the Zionizing impact this will have on the Reform movement as a whole in the Diaspora. By "Zionizing impact" I mean commitment to Jewish peoplehood in personal life-choices and commitment to community activism, both lay and professional.

Pro-Israel education for Diaspora youth is part of the pro-Israel consensus. However, there is no agreement within that consensus on the desirability of Jewish-Zionist education. How do we differentiate between them?

In addition to "learning about" Israel in various formal and informal frameworks, pro-Israel education opts for a relatively short Israel experience (usually in the summer) and/or experiences which by their educational design do not permit value clarification and confrontation so necessary in the process of making life choices and commitments. Most pro-Israel trips are really a kind of educational tourism whose purpose is to reinforce Jewish identity and in the short run they generally do so. However, the long term impact on Jewish community commitment is questionable.

Furthermore, the tourist ambience inherent in the pro-Israel approach may augment Jewish identity but it also strengthens the We-They polarity between Israel and the Diaspora rather than promoting spiritual interdependence.

In Jewish-Zionist education the educational process is conceived as an organic whole, embodying a strategy from early childhood through college and beyond, and encompassing both formal, and informal education. Jewish-Zionist education takes place in dynamic "fields" of community such as Day schools, camps and Israel experiences. Every educational framework is a field within

---

1. It is beyond the scope of this article to outline the specific initiatives which the institutions of Reform Zionism (ARZENU, ARZA) could take. They have been submitted in a memo to the ARZENU Executive. See Section 1:6.

which relevant role models (professional and lay) act as agents of acculturation to Jewish-Zionist norms. The Israel experience is part of this process.

At some stage (certainly after Secondary school) the control of this process must pass from professionals to youth and young adults working in a lay or semi-voluntary capacity. They must be empowered for otherwise they cannot be motivated to commitment. In North America, the current hegemony of the professional makes such a development problematic unless it is actively supported by a committed and understanding laity.

The end aim of Jewish-Zionist education is a Cultural Zionist commitment to personal participation, with like minded others, in some action program of Tikun Olam. The Cultural Zionist commitment may lead to *Aliyah* but in such a case *Aliyah* is only a stage in a particular path of Jewish-Zionist commitment. In the main the benefits accrue to the Diaspora community upon which graduates of the Zionist educational process have a vitalizing effect.

The Zionist Israel experience has distinguishing characteristics. Teaching about and seeing are not enough — that is the difference between short term pro-Israel educational tourism and a long term Zionist program. However, time is not the only factor. The program must not only be of sufficient length — it must also be planned so that a variety of Jewish-Zionist options are experienced and processed.

Optimally, program participants should come from a common background and interrelate with ease. On the other hand, there must be adequate opportunity for extended interaction with peers representing gradings of differing value options.

In terms of group dynamics the program must constitute an "educational field." Within this "field" the avenues of continuity after the Israel experience are made apparent and available to the participants. The participants must feel that inter-personal relationships and new norms developed during the year can continue to play a significant role in their lives upon their return to the Diaspora.

On the issue of Reform Zionist education, Reform Zionism finds itself in a paradoxical position. A number of its member movements, Britain and Australia in particular, have Zionist youth movements which are second to none. Since the establishment of Netzer Olami in the early Eighties, these Reform communities have begun to feel the cumulative vitalizing impact of a decade of Zionist education (an integral part of which is a year on a Reform Zionist program in Israel). Reform Zionist education has become a norm for a significant percentage of their youth.

Netzer Olami is slowly establishing itself in other countries of the Diaspora as well. Unfortunately this does not include North America, the main reservoir of Reform youth.

Is ARZA prepared to take the initiative within the UAHC to legitimize the idea of a Zionist Youth movement and to create Zionist programming in both formal and informal education? The fact that ARZA has formally recognized NFTY as an affiliate simply means that the mantle of Zionist legitimacy has been granted to a pro-Israel youth organization. A good starting point would be to recruit NFTY graduates to Israel programs where they can interact significantly with Reform Zionist and other youth from other countries. Some of those returning from such programs should then be empowered to create a semi-autonomous Reform Zionist youth movement. Because such a movement is likely to take stands outside the general consensus because of its Zionist nature, it will have to be associated with ARZA. At the same time, ARZA will have to ensure locally, regionally and nationally that a Reform Zionist youth movement has access to NFTY frameworks and UAHC Camps.

It is Reform Zionist education for all Reform youth that will be the decisive factor in making the concept of "We Are One" and "spiritual inseparability" viable for Reform Jews in the next generation. Reform Zionist education is potentially a centrifugal force countering the centripetal attrition faced by Reform Judaism, quantitatively and qualitatively. Hence, the issue of Reform Zionist education is central in the interfacing of Reform Zionism with Reform Judaism in the Diaspora.[1] The continued creative development of Reform Judaism in the Diaspora is dependent on inculcating that sense of Jewish purpose, that sense *of shlichut* which only Reform Zionism can provide.

11 Cheshvan 5755
October 6, 1994

---

1. For a further discussion on Jewish-Zionist education see: Michael Livni, The Meaning of Zionist Education in our Generation, Dept. of Jewish Education and Culture in the Diaspora, Joint Authority for Jewish Zionist Education, Jerusalem, 1992. See Section 4:6.

Reform Judaism and Reform Zionism in Israel

* IMPJ = The Israel Movement for Progressive Judaism (also — "Telem")

Synopsis of the Section

This section deals with the implications of the interface between Reform Judaism and Zionism to the particular situation of Reform Judaism in Israel. In particular, the strategy and tactics of the Israel Movement for Progressive Judaism (IMPJ) are discussed. The central question arises: Should the IMPJ take the form of a federation of professionally run congregations on the Diaspora model or should it be an educational movement democratically led by lay leadership?

The articles in this section reflect three stages in my relationship to the question of Reform Judaism and Reform Zionism in Israel.

In 1977, after my return to Israel from my *shlichut* to the UAHC (see Preface), I was full of the ambition of a new "convert" to adapt the ideas of Reform Judaism to kibbutz life. I hoped that at least some kibbutzim (in addition to the expressly Reform kibbutzim) could be an effective venue for Reform Zionism in Israel as a further outgrowth of a culturally oriented Labor Zionism (See also, Section 7:2).

TIKKUN IN JUDAISM (1978) was a position paper aimed at the Kibbutz movement within the framework of a symposium held on the newly founded Kibbutz Yahel, co-sponsored by the World Union for Progressive Judaism and the Ichud Hakvutzot Vehakibbutzim movement (today a part of the "Takam" — the United Kibbutz Movement). I helped organize this symposium. However, against the backdrop of increasing ideological and then economic disarray within the Kibbutz movement, such issues did not arouse real interest. The Kibbutz movement limited itself to practical assistance that the UKM extended to the Reform Kibbutzim and the youth movement, Tzofei Telem.

The second stage in my relationship was a direct result of my being recruited to be youth movement coordinator (again: see Preface). It quickly became apparent (to me) that internal changes in the Israel Movement for Progressive Judaism (IMPJ) would be necessary in order for Reform Judaism to strike root in Israel. PROGRESSIVE JUDAISM AND THE JEWISH STATE (1979) was my first foray into this field.

By 1982, as a result of my intensive involvement with the youth movement, MORE THAN WORSHIP IS NEEDED was written. This article was published within the framework of a symposium in the Quarterly, JUDAISM. The symposium focused on the doctoral dissertation of Ephraim Tavory of Bar-Ilan University on the (marginal) state of Conservative and Reform Judaism in Israel. Not being part of the "establishment" within the IMPJ, I was not invited to participate in the symposium. By chance I heard that such a symposium was contemplated and "invited" myself to participate. My contribution was accepted by the then editor, Dr. Robert Gordis.

The question of the role of the Rabbi in the IMPJ became (and still is) a central issue within the IMPJ and is reflected in AMERICAN RABBIS IN THE ISRAELI SETTING (see also: Section 6: Articles 1 and 10).

By the mid-Eighties I was prepared to advocate wide ranging changes in the aims and methods of IMPJ activity. In a memo to the Ninth IMPJ convention (1988) I raised two central tenets.

Firstly, the IMPJ had to find a way to play a role within formal education. One option might be the TALI[1] educational stream. It would not be possible to create a significant potential for a Reform Zionist movement (beginning with youth movement) without a base in a part of the formal educational system. This was the lesson to be gleaned from the pre-State Labor Zionist educational system and youth movements. More recently, the post-Six Day War development of ultra-nationalist Yeshivot has constituted the soil within which a new Bnei Akiva has emerged.

Secondly, the IMPJ reliance on "Jewish professionals" and their increasing empowerment seemed to undercut the potential for a committed movement of lay people. Indeed, this over-empowerment threatens the democratic nature of the movement. On a practical level, in the light of financial constraints (uncertainty of consistently increasing Diaspora financial support) the IMPJ would find itself at a dead end.

These developments led me to the formulation of the core conflict facing the IMPJ — is the IMPJ primarily an organization of Diaspora style Reform congregations in Israel or is its point of departure a movement for Reform Zionist *tikkun* and impact in Israel. 1988 marks the third stage of my involvement. The English version of my memo to the 1988 IMPJ convention appeared in 1991 (REFORM JUDAISM AND REFORM ZIONISM IN ISRAEL).

In 1989 I was asked by the principal of the Leo Baeck School in Haifa, Rabbi Reuven Samuels, to join the purely advisory IMPJ Education Committee. (MEMOS TO THE EDUCATION COMMITTEE OF THE IMPJ). At the Twelfth IMPJ Convention (1994), I was elected to a two year term on the IMPJ Executive on the strength of my strong pro-education position. However, financial constraints as well as the traditional approach of giving priority to subsidies of congregational (mainly Rabbinic) staff eroded the tentative IMPJ Executive support for education and exacerbated the tension between congregational needs and educational programs. This controversy extended to the Association of Reform Zionists in America (ARZA).

---

1. TALI — acronym for *"Tigbur Limudei Yahadut"* (reinforced Jewish learning). Established in the early Nineteen Eighties by interested groups of parents backed by the Israel Movement for Traditional Judaism (Conservative).

HAS THE IMPJ GONE FORTH OUT OF EGYPT?, FIRST, LET'S MEND THE MOVEMENT, RESPONSE TO THE ARZA EDUCATION COMMITTEE and, finally, A SUGGESTED PROGRESSIVE ZIONIST PLATFORM AND ACTION PROGRAM reflect my alternative points of view on the future movement nature of the IMPJ. The elections held in the IMPJ in April 1998 where I was a candidate for Chairperson of the movement, demonstrated that my position is a minority position among the 2000 odd members of the IMPJ. The majority preference is for a professionally (in the main Rabbinically) led congregational organization heavily subsidized by the Reform movement outside of Israel. It is an open question whether such a congregational organization has any significant Zionist future. Nevertheless, there is some hope that a determined minority (as always in Zionist history) will ultimately succeed in making the transition to a Progressive Jewish Zionist movement in Israel.

Tikkun in Judaism:
What Do We Mend and What Tools Do We Need?[1]

In my opening comments, I would like to review what elements of Judaism offer the potential for Tikkun, as I see them, and what tools are required to this end. I shall do so without claiming to offer any guidelines as to what the actual content of Tikkun should be. That is a question that those actually involved in this work — and I consider all those here today to be so involved — will have to decide for themselves over the course of time. Accordingly I shall relate only to the fields in which Tikkun should be reflected, as well as offering some criteria for examining the tools I feel will be needed for Tikkun in Judaism.

As I see it, Judaism is a cultural and religious totality which, as a practical guide for life, cannot really be divided into separate theoretical components. Accordingly we should see the analysis of such components as an artificial process, albeit one that is essential for the purpose of our discussion here.

With this in mind, we may define three spheres of Judaism in which Tikkun — and, according to my perception, ongoing Tikkun — is required:

1. Faith.
2. Halacha.
3. Society.

Faith

I am not a philosopher, a rabbi or a theologian, but to my mind "faith" implies that I have faith and values that shape my world outlook and define objectives toward which we may strive continually without their being achieved during the life of an individual. Thus, faith and values will be at least partially absolute or axiomatic, and not given to proof or rational explanation. This has two aspects:

a) The practical aspect: Our sages already pointed out that "It is not for you to finish the task, but neither are you free to desist from it." Kibbutz

---

1. Colloquium: Tikkun in the Judaism of Our Generation: What Do We Mend? Pesach 5738 (1978), Kibbutz Yahel (translated from the Hebrew).

members in particular should arm themselves with this belief in order to resist internal and external criticism of the gulf between theory and practice.

b) Abstract faith, such as Maimonides' Principles of the Faith.

Both the objectives and abstract faith have been the subject of ceaseless Tikkun over the generations. We should recognize that partnership in life demands some type of common denominator regarding objectives, though the same does not apply in the case of abstract faith.

Regarding such questions as the coming of the Messiah or the properties of God, an entire range of views is possible. Having just mentioned Maimonides, it is worth recalling that his "Principles" were not universally accepted by his contemporaries.

Halacha

To me, Halacha means the way of life that results from togetherness in a communal framework whose members accept its authority, whether formal or informal. In other words, a prior condition for the existence of any Halacha is a community.

By "way of life," I refer to three spheres:

1) Relationships between individuals;
2) Relationships between individuals and the community.
3) The reflection of the foundations of Jewish tradition in the public life of the community.

Please note that I did not say "observing the commandments between individuals, or between individuals and God." I do not want to get into that argument, although those who do wish to adopt such an interpretation may certainly do so within the above-mentioned framework. On the other hand, I do want to say that Halacha in its real sense goes beyond the traditional meaning of Rabbinical Halacha, which would seem no longer to provide an effective tool for Tikkun in the modern era. I will reiterate that I do not believe that there can be any Halacha or any Tikkun of Halacha without a base of community. There can, therefore, be no discussion of Tikkun in the absence of that social Tikkun that leads to Jewish community.

Society

In this respect, there can be no doubt that Zionism, and particularly the cultural Zionism of the Labor Zionist movement, has already said and achieved much in ideological terms in recent generations.

As a member of the kibbutz movement, I still believe that a life of cooperation in a rural community in Israel, organized in a network of such communities on the regional and national levels, constitutes a foundation for a process of Tikkun in Judaism.

However, I would not argue that in principle social Tikkun could not also be realized in other frameworks, perhaps even in the Diaspora, though this would seem to be a much more difficult task.

In any case the process of Tikkun must take place **in all three spheres: faith, Halacha**, and **society**. Accordingly, the channels for Tikkun in modern Jewish faith and Halacha must develop social frameworks that can provide a concrete infrastructure for Tikkun over a period of generations.

Equally, though, the existing communities, and particularly the cooperative communities based on social Tikkun, cannot ignore the need to tackle openly questions of faith and Halacha in order to constitute a more complete force in the process of Tikkun of Jewish tradition.

The kibbutz could develop norms and Halacha in a variety of fields. In particular, the kibbutz as a community has the potential to give new meaning to the dimension of time, and as a public entity it has the potential to revitalize the concepts of sacred and profane, in terms of the individual lifecycle, Shabbat and the annual calendar. This is a long-term endeavor, however — even in terms of several generations — and we should caution ourselves that there is no point in the members of Kibbutz Yahel engaging in daily soul-searching on this matter.

The tools required — a youth movement

What are the tools, particularly the educational tools, that I believe are required in order to forge cooperative communities (or communities of any kind) characterized by an approach to Tikkun in Jewish tradition, faith, Halacha and society?

We must not ignore the experience accumulated to date by the kibbutz movement. I believe that this experience might be summarized by stating that without the pioneering and educating youth movements, firstly abroad and then in Israel, we would not have succeeded in forging the kibbutz movement as we now know it. Even today (perhaps particularly today), when the movement has a younger generation, the youth movements still play a vital role in the continued existence of this movement. Accordingly, the current crisis in the youth movements (which can no longer be divorced from the problematic ideological and educational situation within the kibbutz movement) overshadows all our successes in the organizational and economic spheres.

A movement for Tikkun in Jewish tradition that seeks to establish social units for ideological realization must therefore be based on a youth movement. I shall briefly itemize the criteria that I see as defining a pioneering youth movement. While we are here discussing a pioneering youth movement with its own unique identity, this is not significant in terms of these criteria.

1. **An ideology of Tikkun:** The vision of Tikkun must be both universal and particularistic/Jewish. This point has already been elaborated. In other words, the movement is a political body (not necessarily in the sense of party-political), insofar as it seeks to change the shape of society.

2. **Ideological realization:** This is where a youth movement differs from adult organizations and movements. This realization must be in the following spheres:
   a. Personal self-realization on the part of members of the movement;
   b. A movement plan of action for realizing its ideas for Tikkun;
   c. Mended inter-personal relations within the movement and an ongoing willingness on the part of the movement itself to engage in Tikkun of the movement.

3. **A policy on Aliyah and realization:** It is not enough for a movement abroad to preach Aliyah, or for an Israeli movement to preach self-realization. The movement must have a policy regarding an Aliyah and self-realization framework in order to maximize its impact. This usually implies the creation of *Garinim*[1] and specific objectives designed to reinforce and consolidate the ideology of the movement, and to point the direction to those who do not achieve realization through the movement's *Garinim* and projects. At the same time, these frameworks must give the individual member maximum possibilities for self-fulfillment.[2]

   Once again, I must emphasize that in principle this does not relate solely to kibbutzim.

4. **Educational character:** Gradual education toward a revolutionary objective: The revolutionary objective is to be achieved through the gradual development and education of the individual. In terms of societal norms, self-

---

1. *Garinim*: settlement groups.
2. A detailed discussion of the terms self-realization and self-fulfillment will be found in *Self-Fulfillment and Self-Realization: Two Terms, Two Outlooks*, Section 4:2.

realization through pioneering movements was always a revolutionary step, but the path to this step was the product of an educational process that lasted for years.

5. **Combination of organizational and movement activities:** Organizational activities, which might also be termed "bureaucratic," are designed to ensure the proper continued existence of the organization. It will be possible to sketch an organizational diagram of departments, authority, etc. The organization will seek to fill all functions in order to ensure proper functioning and continued existence.

   Movement activities must be related to the organization, yet separate and independent thereof. The nature of activities are determined by two main variables:
   a. Current problems.
   b. The nature of the leadership available at that point in time.

In other words, activities are developed around the existing situation and people, rather than being dictated by an abstract and pre-determined organizational plan.

Note my emphasis on the need to integrate organizational and movement activities.

6. **Faith and commitment:** We have already discussed this point in a slightly different context. It need only be stressed here that this is the cement that must bind together the other principles of the movement.

Where will we find theories and tools for Tikkun?

"For the Law shall go out of Zion, and the word of the Lord from Jerusalem." But is it really that simple? The process would seem to be rather more complicated.

In discussing the theories of Tikkun that will be used to built the "Third Temple," we should recall that insofar as it is possible to talk of historical precedents, the Judaism fashioned during the centuries following the Return to Zion was initially influenced mainly by Babylonian Jewry.

The first Aliyah to the Land of Israel during the period of Zerubabel would have become assimilated were it not for the ideological, organizational and social support it received from Ezra and Nechemiah.

In modern times, the ideological basis of the kibbutz movement and the tools used for the movement's development (the youth movements) have not exactly been labeled Made in Israel. It is true that Israel has served, and continues to serve, as a melting pot, and that the Diaspora foundations have been used to create new patterns which may then even return to influence the Diaspora. But here, too, we are speaking of a process that will require many generations.

The theories of Tikkun that have emerged in Judaism over the past century and a half may exert a strong influence on the patterns of Tikkun that will emerge in the Jewish State, both in terms of what it is we are trying to mend and in terms of the social tools needed for this task. These theories should not be seen as inherently alien to Israel, although these movements will have to be open to considerable change.

This, it seems to me, is the challenge facing a Zionist pioneering movement established as part of those streams that advocate Tikkun in Jewish tradition.

Progressive Judaism and the Jewish State:
A Plan of Action[1]

A discussion of the nature of the State of the Jews is a discussion about Zionism, and we need to decide for ourselves what kind of Zionism we mean. It is clear that we are still (or once again) talking about the old distinction between political and cultural Zionism.

Political Zionism was established as the people's reaction to anti-Semitism or, to put it another way, as the reaction to the failure to fulfill the promise of the liberal emancipation. The essence of political Zionism was simple: in modern times, with the rise of nation states, the Jewish people also requires a state of its own, like all other peoples, in order to solve the distress faced by the Jews, who had become the victims and scapegoats in the whirlwind of violence sweeping through the peoples in whose midst the Jews lived. Political Zionism generally painted a bleak picture of the future of Jews in the Diaspora. Accordingly, for Herzl and Nordau a State for the Jews (*Judenstaat*) was the issue of the moment and a burning need.

Naturally, different approaches emerged among the advocates of pure political Zionism concerning questions relating to the political tactics to be adopted by the Zionist movement, and concerning the general political and social character of the future state. In terms of tactics, the division was between moderate nationalism (Weizmann) and militant nationalism (Jabotinsky). In terms of general issues, the division was between a private economy (the General Zionists) within a liberal state according to the European model, and a public economy and a society free of sharp class distinctions (the Labor Zionist movement). These issues were not unique to the Jewish national movement — in one way or another, almost all the national movements of the late nineteenth century addressed such questions, and positions were based on the ideologies that had emerged in the Western word as a whole. It should therefore be noted that the various streams of political Zionism were not obliged to address **specifically Jewish** questions. Indeed, those with a grounding in the history of the Zionist Organization will recognize that such discussions would have been seen

---

1. Shalhevet, IMPJ, Autumn 1978 (translated from the Hebrew).

as a recipe for division, in place of the national unity that was required in order to establish a State for the Jews.

By contrast, **cultural Zionism** was established as a reaction to the collapse of traditional Jewish communal life, reflecting a feeling that in modern times, only through an autonomous Jewish center in the people's historic homeland could the Jews ensure their continued creative existence as a people. In other words, Achad Ha'am saw the goal as a Jewish State, rather than as a state for the Jews.

Cultural Zionism thus believed that the continued existence of Judaism in the Diaspora was dependent on the presence of a Jewish center in the Land of Israel. The establishment of a state was seen as a long-term objective. The more immediate need was to establish a center with a distinctly Jewish character. Before the First World War, it was still possible to argue that if anti-Semitism were really the core of the problem, the Jews could emigrate to America.

Thus we can see that the question of the "Jewish way of life in the revived Jewish State" (as distinct from the "State of the Jews") assumes the adoption of the viewpoint of cultural Zionism. Within the Progressive Jewish movement, we would really do better to talk of the "Jewish State." Cultural Zionism was not a defensive reaction to the violence of which we have been and continue to be the victims. Rather, it is a movement for the Tikkun of the Jewish people and Jewish tradition.

Political Zionism was certainly correct in its diagnosis of the urgent nature of the problem. Circumstances have prevented us from engaging in a gradual development of a cultural enterprise. Cultural Zionism and its advocates (such as Yehuda Magnes and Martin Buber) found themselves marginalized between the World Wars and up to the establishment of Israel. For almost three generations, we have been obliged to relate primarily to political Zionism. This historical imperative has caused us to forget the principle of cultural Zionism, namely that the state is a means, not an end.

Only one movement insisted on the importance of the unique character of the future state. The "Mizrachi" movement was the only one that, by its very nature, related to specifically Jewish content within the context of the Zionist Organization. This movement even imposed on the Zionist Organization — and later on the state — its own perception and exclusive authority as the interpreter of the Jewish character of the state. The Mizrachi had a more or less clear position on the question of cultural Zionism, i.e., to the three spheres of Judaism: faith, Halacha and community (including the "community of communities," the entire Jewish people). In historical terms, Mizrachi won this monopoly due to the fact that non-Orthodox religious forces refrained from activity in the Zionist organization. Now the pendulum is swinging back again. The level of interest in the Jewish nature of the state is increasing, and for the first time a variety of approaches to cultural Zionism are being heard, and one may begin to speak of different streams within cultural Zionism. These streams must now develop ideological theories and a plan of action designed to lead to alternatives for a Jewish way of life in the Jewish State. We hope that from among these alternatives significant Jewish recipes for life will emerge for modern Jewry in the coming generation.

The two Tikkun movements that arose within the Jewish people in recent generations were Reform and the Zionist pioneering movement. These movement exerted a tremendous influence on the Jewish people, yet both of these movements were flawed. On the one hand, Reform advocated Tikkun as an ongoing principle in faith and Halacha, but negated — in principle — the community based sphere of affiliation to the people as a whole. On the other hand, the principle of the Zionist pioneering movement was to call for Tikkun of the nature of Jewish community and the national basis of the Jewish people, while negating the religious basis of faith and Halacha. Reform negated the community element in the hope that this could be replaced by the principle of a universal mission to all the nations, but in so doing it negated the social basis for the maintenance of any type of Halacha and faith. The pioneering movement negated faith and Halacha, which it sought to replace with universal philosophies drawn from the Socialist streams. Yet in so doing, it led to a crisis in the Jewish State over the question of Jewish identity and the meaning of the term "Jewish State."[1]

In conceptual terms, what is required in current-day Israel in order to forge a renewed Jewish way of life is a combination of these two approaches to Tikkun in which one complements the other, creating a movement for Tikkun including community, Halachic and faith-related elements. Only a "complete" cultural Zionist movement along these lines will be able to serve as an effective cultural bridge for Diaspora Jews, most of whom do not belong to the Orthodox stream.

At present, both Reform Judaism and the Zionist pioneering stream are in a transitional phase. Within the established kibbutz movement, for example, a tendency may be discerned to seek the development of Jewish content, at least in terms of festivals. There is also a degree of interest in the study of Jewish thought and texts. These trends have been reflected in the establishment of committees to

---

1. For further discussion of this point, see Michael Langer, *Pioneering Zionism and Reform Judaism — New Ideological Horizons* (Hebrew), Shdemot, Vol. 62, Winter 5737. See Section 7:2.

organize festival programs, in the development of classes in Judaism and Jewish thought at Oranim,[1] and in a willingness to cooperate with the Reform movement.

At present, however, these developments are indicative only of the general mood. A conscious effort to grapple with questions of faith and Halacha is still at a very early stage.[2]

In the Progressive movement, meanwhile, there are efforts to seek an appropriate formula for Tikkun in the community capable of constituting the framework for a Progressive Jewish way of life. While no one would challenge the important role of the congregation, this institution is not in itself a sufficiently broad communal foundation for the creation of living tradition. The congregation does not usually offer an adequate manifestation of life partnership in practical fields. In other words, the congregational community does not embrace the life of the individual and/or of the nuclear family at most points in time. The only exception to this is, of course, the community of Kibbutz Yahel.

Kibbutz Yahel and other similar groups due to be established in the future are potential (though not yet actual) symbols of the possibility of a synthesis between communal, social and religious Tikkun in a comprehensive and broad-based context. Yahel represents an attempt at integration, and — to quote M. Buber — this is "an attempt that has not yet succeeded, but surely also an attempt that has not failed."[3]

The Reform movement is examining its approach to community, and without community there can be no Jewish way of life. Before rushing to whip out a scalpel and begin to dissect what is happening in Yahel, we should thoroughly consider the lessons to be learned from the Labor Zionist movement.

The Labor Zionist movement left its mark on the pre-State community and on Israel during its early years, and secured important achievements in the field of social Tikkun from which we would do well to learn. I am not referring here to the present movement, but to that which existed before the establishment of the State — and not exclusively to the kibbutzim. However, there is a common

---

1. Kibbutz teacher's seminary.
2. Rabbi Shalom Lilker, a member of Kvutzat Kfar Hamaccabi, wrote a doctoral thesis on this subject: *Kibbutz Judaism: A New Tradition in the Making*, HUC-JIR, New York, 1974. Published as *Kibbutz Judaism*, Herzl Press, New York, 1982. See also Moshe Kerem, *A Movement of Jewish Renewal in the Kibbutz Movement* (Hebrew), Petachim, Vol. 3 (39), Sivan 5737, p. 17.
3. Martin Buber, *Paths in Utopia* (1949), Beacon Press, Boston, 1958, p. 139. *Reform Zionist Perspective*. See also: Michael Langer, *Reform Kibbutz and Religious Pioneering*, in *Reform Zionist Perspective*, p. 371 (see Section 7:1). Adi Asabi, *Yahel — A Reform Jewish Kibbutz* (Hebrew), Petachim, Vol. 2 (39), Sivan 5737, p. 51. Matthew Sperber, *Some Preliminary Thoughts on the Approach to Halacha for the Reform Kibbutz*, in *A Reform Zionist Perspective: Judaism and Community in thd Modern Age*, UAHC Youth Division, New York, 1977, p. 360.

misconception regarding the purpose of the kibbutzim. We often hear that the creative zenith of the Labor movement, the kibbutz, is no longer relevant to Israel in the 1970s, and that its importance as an economic and social force and its importance for security is a thing of the past. It is impossible, we are told, that the IMPJ will base itself on kibbutzim. What we see here is total confusion between the kibbutz as an agent of political Zionism and the kibbutz as a manifestation of cultural Zionism.

The lesson to be learned does not relate to the kibbutz *per se*, but rather to the **kibbutz infrastructure**. After all, the kibbutz never accounted for more than 7.5% of the Jewish population in the Land of Israel (this was the figure in 1947; today it is 3.2%). Despite this, its influence in terms of shaping values and ways of life was decisive, for better or for worse (as far as religious matters are concerned, perhaps for worse). Why was this so? Because the Labor Zionist movement succeeded in establishing the instruments and channels required to magnify the influence of the pioneering movement, providing the impetus needed to inculcate pioneering values among the majority of the Zionist community in the Land of Israel. What were these instruments?

1. An independent education system — the "Labor Stream" and, of course, the education system in the cooperative settlements. These schools legitimized the world view of the Labor movement, not only in terms of the material studied, but also through the educators who personified the Labor Zionist movement.
2. An informal education system in the form of the youth movements, which served to enable an entire generation in Israel and abroad to undergo a socio-cultural educational process in the context of Jewish Tikkun, albeit with the emphasis on social rather than religious themes. It must be recalled that relatively few people realized pioneering values on a permanent basis, yet this process carried with it most of the young people and, indirectly, their parents. It was this process that inculcated the pioneering and kibbutz experience among wide sections of the public.

    This is not the place to enter into a discussion of the complex historical problems that led to the abandonment of this framework in the context of historical circumstances. Political Zionism triumphed over cultural Zionism within the Labor Zionist movement. That section of the public that **refused** to dismantle its educational system in spite of the demand for a "general State of Israel[1] approach," and which continued to maintain the religious schools

---

1. *Mamlachtiut.*

and Yeshivot, eventually formed the nucleus of religious power through such expressions as Gush Emunim.

3. Political organization within the world Zionist movement in order to ensure the resources required to operate the education systems. This point refers to organized political power in terms of cultural Zionism (e.g., support for youth movements in Israel and in the Diaspora).

What lessons should we draw?

1. The value of the Progressive Jewish kibbutz movement lies not only in the fact that it will enable several hundred young people from the world movement to enjoy a framework for maximizing self-realization, but also in the fact that it will provide a symbol around which a youth movement and Nachal *Garinim*[1] may be developed, offering a chance to experience communal life in its maximum manifestation for Progressive Jews. It may certainly be possible, in the context of such a movement, to experiment with *Garinim* to targets other than the kibbutzim, such as the Netzer *Garin* currently being organized in America, with the aim of settling in the development town Shderot.

2. Maintaining the educational infrastructure required by the frameworks detailed above means that the Progressive Jewish movement must maintain its own education system, i.e., a Progressive Jewish stream. This is an enormous task and here, too, I believe that only graduates of the movement — those who have completed the unifying movement process inculcating a comprehensive world view — will be capable of persevering in such a tremendous task.

3. There can be no doubt that goals such as these require political organization in the context of Jewish and Zionist institutions. The recent Zionist Congress saw the first signs of such organization. In the present generation, and given the small number of members in Israel, the IMPJ will be obliged to concentrate on such political work abroad, although not exclusively so. **All these points are inter-related**: Kibbutz Yahel provided the impetus for the establishment of ARZA (the Association of Reform Zionists in America), and ARZA as a Zionist political party was the impetus for the victory at the Zionist Congress — the recognition of the rights of non-Orthodox Jewish streams in the Zionist Organization.

I believe that we must continue to struggle to achieve changes in the World Zionist Organization — changes which may in the long term be of

---

1. Settlement groups based on joint army service.

assistance to the Progressive Jewish movement. For example, the Zionist organization should be separated from the political organization in Israel — in other words, elections to the Zionist Organization in Israel should be separate from the elections to the Knesset. This is the only way that we can strengthen the cultural Zionist streams as distinct from the political streams.

In terms of the plan of action, we could naturally discuss possible Halachic directions and the possibility of finding a common denominator on questions of faith with sections of the so-called "secular" public. However, it seems to me that this would be putting the cart before the horse. I believe that **in the absence of any educational or political infrastructure, there can be no real achievements**. Such an infrastructure cannot be based on congregations alone. Community action, Reform pioneering self-realization, the development of an educational infrastructure and cautious but determined political activities are all required. If these develop, the content-related aspects will emerge in the course of action. The fact is that it is practice rather than theory that will determine the future, just as in the past it was the acts of the pioneers, rather than their abstract ideology, that determined and forged pioneering "Halacha."

These, it seems to me, are the guidelines that should shape our plan of action in seeking to develop a Jewish way of life, and in seeking to fashion a Jewish State open to innovations in Judaism.

More Than Worship Is Needed[1]

Ephraim Tabory's description of congregational Reform and Conservative Judaism in Israel today is largely correct. In part, however, his analysis misses the central question — *can the congregation based on religious worship, à la the Diaspora, be the focus and/or source of cultural-spiritual commitment in Israel?*

The student of Israeli and Zionist history must conclude that the basic Israeli-Zionist ethos of commitment projected by the founding fathers of the Zionist Labour Movement over a period of two generations succeeded in making its seminal impact because the cultural-spiritual commitment of its elite was expressed by *action orientation and total life style and involvement* (e.g., the kibbutzim). In recent years, this phenomenon of linkage between total life involvement, action orientation and cultural-spiritual commitment has been an identifying feature of the Gush Emunim movement's elite.

Such total life involvement and commitment is not characteristic of the religious congregation in the Diaspora. The Diaspora congregation is not the traditional *Kehillah Kedoshah* unquestioningly committed to the Sanctification of the Name in everyday life, its earthly existence predicated on the proposition that the community exists for the observance of mitzvot. Neither does the religious congregation conceivably constitute a group focus of cultural spiritual commitment reflecting a particular vision of Jewish community and purpose (e.g., classic secular kibbutz community). *The religious congregation in the Diaspora, since the Emancipation, has confined itself to being a community of ritual and "cult"* (kultusgemeinde), *and has ceased to be a community of life and/or life-purpose.* Maintaining the ritual is one of the expressions of Jewish identity in the Diaspora. But with the possible exception of some of the "professional" Jews (an inherently un-Jewish concept) it is *not* an integral expression (almost a natural by-product) of total shared life-purpose and community.

It is very difficult within the context of modern society to achieve such total *religious community* outside of Israel. On the other hand, it has been one of the signal failures of the secular Zionist movement that, in its attempts to create

---

1. Published in *Judaism*, Fall 1982, Vol. 31:4.

community and community of purpose in order fundamentally to reform Jewish society, it failed to integrate an innovative approach to Jewish tradition.

There is a place for alternative visions of Judaism in the Jewish State. Indeed, the current polarization in Israel between Orthodox Judaism and Orthodox secularism is fraught with problematic consequences for Israeli society and the Jewish people as a whole. It is questionable whether a Jewish State "like all the nations" without a particular and special spiritual-cultural élan and commitment is viable. Unfortunately, Jewish history would seem to suggest that whenever we became "like all the nations" our autonomous existence in Eretz Israel became non-viable. However, as Tabory implies, the introduction of alternative forms of Judaism within the framework of communities of ritual (*Kultusgemeinde*) would seem to be a dead end.

In the last five years we have witnessed new attempts to create total communities of alternative Judaism. These more recent developments have not been adequately dealt with by Tabory, whose field work was done three to four years ago. The ideological basis for these very tentative beginnings has been Reform Zionism, a point of view which is a synthesis of two classically opposed but fundamentally complementary ideas:

1. Classic Reform Judaism — affirmed Judaism as a religion but demanded ongoing reform within it. But Reform negated the principle of Jewish corporate community — nationality as a continuing determinant of Jewish existence. Judaism was to be a brotherhood of the spirit alone.

2. Classic Labor Zionism — affirmed the principle of Jewish nationality and community but demanded far-reaching reforms in the socio-economic structure of Jewish community and its transfer, at least in large part, to Eretz Yisrael. Labor-Zionism negated the relevance and authority of the Jewish heritage faith and Law (halakhah) and observance for the vision of the new Jewish Society of the Jewish State. For the latter, it substituted various Schools of Socialism.

The essence of the Reform Zionist synthesis is the acceptance of a holistic view of Judaism and a rejection of the "negations." Such a view affirms both religion and community, both in Israel and in the Diaspora, but is predicated on the principle of continuous development (reform). This ideological synthesis has led to close cooperation between the United Kibbutz Movement and the World Union of Progressive Judaism and the Union of American Hebrew Congregations — particularly its Youth Division. The result has been the establishment of the first Reform kibbutz and recruitment is already under way for a second one. This development also reflects the increasing concern of kibbutz educators with questions of Jewish identity and roots. The first kibbutz, Yahel, was founded five years ago by Americans and Israelis. However, it soon became apparent that the Israeli congregations of the Movement for Progressive Judaism (Reform) were a totally inadequate base for recruiting youth.

Currently, there is an ongoing attempt (again with the active help of the kibbutz movement) to create an Israel-Reform youth movement. Most of the several hundred members of the youth movement and most Israeli members of Yahel do not come from "Progressive" homes. The Youth movement attempts to constitute an independent youth community whose path in Judaism and Reform Judaism is determined by its members. Similarly, decisions regarding "religious" questions in Yahel are decided on the same democratic basis as all other decisions — i.e., the weekly kibbutz general assembly is the ultimate authority. There is no kibbutz "Rabbi."

During the past year some leaders of the Conservative Movement have begun to put out feelers to the Kibbutz Movement in order to recruit its assistance in establishing the first Conservative kibbutz.

An additional development which may well be indicative of a possible future trend has been the initiative of Conservative families in Jerusalem. They have established a primary school oriented towards providing a Jewish traditional atmosphere. This school was established within the framework of a Ministry of Education ruling that if a majority of parents are in agreement, some 25% of school time is apportioned according to their demand.

Another example: The World Union for Progressive Judaism is, formally speaking, the patron of the Leo Baeck Secondary School in Haifa. The Principal is a Reform Rabbi. The School has become a center for the new Progressive (Reform) Youth Movement and has built a synagogue as an integral part of the school. It has also established a popular community-center type of program. Again, the students and participants in the programs are not associated with Reform Congregations. However, a community is beginning to emerge as defined by common interests and involvements, especially via the children.

The kibbutzim, the Youth Movement, and the Schools are indications of some of the paths open to Reform and Conservative Judaism in Israel. They are all predicated upon an involvement much beyond the community of ritual, the *Kultusgemeinde* of Diaspora origins. Unfortunately, the congregation orientation and mentality of the Movements is not changing quickly enough. Even the handful of young Israelis who are recruited into the Rabbinate seem to be Congregation oriented. The developments mentioned above, kibbutzim and schools, have been the result less of institutional policy than of individual initiative.

A central problem of both the Conservative and Reform movements in Israel has been their lack of action-oriented aggressive leadership. They have been far too diffident in not raising "embarrassing issues" for the sake of *Shalom Bayit*. But, then, up until the very last year or so they have represented constituents for whom congregational involvement is a marginal part of their lives. Three developments may change the passivity of the movements in the near future.

1. The more aggressive orientation of those whose commitment is more all-encompassing (educators, youth movement leaders, kibbutz members).
2. The establishment of Reform and Conservative Zionist parties within the framework of the World Zionist Organization.
3. The development of an Aliyah movement (of even a few hundred per year) with an ongoing commitment to alternative Judaism.

Much ado is made of the government's attitude to the Conservative and Reform movements. While the struggle for equal rights for all trends within Judaism is justified, in and of itself, it is not a primary requisite for the stimulation of a "grass roots" Conservative and Reform Judaism. Religious freedom does exist. Nobody (not even the Reform movement) can tell members of Kibbutz Yahel how to interpret their Reform Judaism. But the Ministry of Religion will not cover the religious expenses of Yahel nor can marriages there be legally conducted by Reform Rabbis. On the other hand, government recognition of Conservative and Reform Judaism will not necessarily change their marginal nature, especially if they continue to limit themselves to congregations of worship.

My conviction is that alternative trends in Judaism will take root in Israel but only if the forms (as distinct from content) are indigenous and relate primarily to real needs of community and not merely to religious worship as such.

American Rabbis in the Israeli Setting[1]

20 April 1982

Oren Sela
UAHC — Pacific Southwest Council
13107 Ventura Boulevard
North Hollywood, CA 91604, U.S.A.

Shalom Oren,

My response to your letter of March 5 has been delayed because of Machanot[2] Pesach and the absence of a secretary to type this letter. In fact, your address should be Yair Palmoni who is now Chairperson of the Vaadat Higui.[3] Within the context of my work in Telem Noar I'm not capable of being involved on an operative level in the project of the type you envision.

However, I do want to relate to your suggestion in more than a cursory way on the basis of my general involvement, interest and perspective. I'm convinced that your idea should be developed.

The Need for Reform Educators

There is a critical need for Reform Rabbis willing to be educators here in Israel. When I say "critical" I mean from the point of view of introducing the idea of Progressive Judaism into the fabric of Israeli society and creating a real Progressive Jewish Movement in Israel over a period of a generation. Hence "critical" means critical for those of us who have a certain relationship to Judaism and to the Jewish people.

The problem is that the Reform Movement (the World Union, the Israel Movement for Progressive Judaism and the Hebrew Union College) have not developed a practical policy geared to Israeli reality and the logistical-financial limitations of the movement itself. Such a policy would also have to be minimally

---

1. Unpublished letter to Oren Sela (emissary), to the UAHC Youth Division in the Los Angeles area.
2. Camps.
3. Joint Kibbutz — Reform steering committee (advisory).

reflected in the educational approach of the Hebrew Union College. What does all the above mean?

Rabbis in Israel do indeed have to be educators: this means a year of additional study for most to achieve an adequate level of Hebrew. The reason is two-fold:

1) They have to get a salary from somewhere. The Reform Movement does not have the money.

2) The educational infrastructure for Reform has to be created in the schools — within these schools a youth movement can be created to realize the ideals of Reform Judaism as a way of life. There is an absolutely realistic possibility of pinpointing a number of schools open to being "taken over." In fact, even the Leo Baeck School could absorb half a dozen educators from the Reform Movement if it could find them. It's a wide open situation if we could only move in the right way.

I have seen that a major stumbling block is the expectations of the HUC students themselves and their educational program here in Israel.

The self-image of congregational rabbis and leaders with all the ego rewards and career rewards implicit is simply not a realistic scenario for Israel. The role has to be teacher (in the sense of educator, Mechanech and/or Madrich). The tradition has to be the Zionist one of personal example. Only in this way can Reform Judaism become part of the spiritual tradition and precedents that formed the ethos of Israeli society up to the establishment of the state. The fact that this whole tradition is in desperate need of ideas to rejuvenate itself is Reform Judaism's opportunity. So far, the Reform Movement has simply not grasped that its ideas (creative, developmental and democratic Judaism) have tremendous potential but cannot strike root in Israel by means of congregations in the American fashion. It is a source of continual amazement to me that this simple basic fact has been ignored in Reform thinking in Israel. Academically, it's a lack of understanding in Comparative Sociology and Israeli Cultural Anthropology. It also reflects a dearth of exposure to the spiritual ideas and ideals of the Zionist pioneering movement.

The Role of HUC

Up to now there has been no real possibility of presenting this option to HUC students during their year here. At an operative level, the Hebrew Union College is not yet prepared to allocate two weeks of time for us to present the spiritual tradition of the Zionist renaissance as an option for their self-realization as Reform Jews.

The Hebrew Union College has not yet grasped that such a two-week program is of the essence even to enable American Rabbis to correctly interpret Israel to American Jews. The students are almost totally isolated from Israeli reality while they are here. It's quite a paradox that Reform Judaism, which once saw itself as the banner bearer of the idea of Judaism's "universal mission," should shy away from exposing its students to the idea of "mission" in the Jewish State. As long as the policy is dictated by fear of "Jewish Brain-Drain" from America to Israel we have a problem. As long as the Hebrew Union College evades its historical responsibility in this matter and limits itself to the assumption that its responsibility is to American Reform Judaism because that is who gives the money — we have a problem.

I have gone into this detail because of a key sentence in your letter quoting Richard Levy — "preferably as soon as possible after ordination."[1] That means serious commitment of HUC to the program, preparedness (which I think exists) to write off debts of students who go on Aliyah — or put in a minimum of five years on "shlichut." The principle of worker-Rabbi sounds fine — I'm not sure it isn't just as necessary in urban and development town settings, always providing that it is integrated into a general strategy for promoting Reform Judaism.

For example, if we are talking about kibbutzim, then in my opinion a small group of Rabbis has to go to such an area on the basis of openness of the kibbutzim in the area to the idea. Perhaps they would have to do a year in Oranim (financed by the Absorption Ministry within the framework of olim re-training) in order to prepare themselves.

The major hitch in your proposal is its inherent limitation if we are talking about a one-year program. Such a program would seem to me to be superficial and not relevant to the central aim of Reform Jewish Aliyah — impact on Israeli society in terms of strengthening the movement which is trying to develop a path for a positive alternative to the secular-orthodox polarity which is currently stifling Jewish creativity in the Jewish State.

Oren, I have taken the liberty of sending a copy of your letter and my answer to a number of additional people and I'm suggesting that the subject be raised at the Vaadat Higui to which representatives of HUC should be invited.

B'virkat Chaverim,
Michael Langer

---

1. Reference to a plan of "a year of service in Israel" for Reform Rabbis after ordination.

Reform Judaism and Reform Zionism in Israel[1]

The Movement for Progressive Judaism in Israel (Reform[2]) numbers only a few thousand members, but that number does not reflect its potential importance as a means of Jewish identification and as an alternative path for Jewish education for many who cannot accept an increasingly militant Orthodoxy as the only alternative to sterile secularism. Moreover, the fate of the movement constitutes an important concern for many Diaspora Jews (especially in North America) when thinking about Israel. Thus it is important to understand some of the developments and tensions within the movement whose future development in Israel could well be significant for Israel as a whole.

Two Origins of Progressive Judaism in Israel

There have been two paths to Progressive Judaism in Israel. The first was the direct "import" of Reform congregational patterns from abroad. During the past ten years another path, rooted in the Zionist enterprise in Israel, has developed. Mutual interaction and a degree of friction have resulted.

The clear separation between belonging to a religious congregation on the one hand, and Zionist activity on the other, characterized Progressive Judaism in Israel from the end of the 1950s to the end of the 1970s. (This was so in the Diaspora as well.) Neither did the *de facto* recognition by the World Union for Progressive Judaism of the centrality of the State of Israel — as expressed by moving its head office to Jerusalem in 1971 — change the self-image of the movement in Israel during this period as an organization of Reform religious congregations. The congregational model suited German and British as well as American immigrants. It has even drawn a small number of native Israelis who were attracted by a Judaism unfettered by Halacha and which reflected the religious equality of men and women.

As individuals, Reform Jews in Israel undoubtedly identified strongly with Zionism. Many came to Israel from the affluent West because of their Zionist

---

1. Published in *Journal of Reform Judaism*, Spring 1991. Shorter version, Hebrew leaflet, 1988.
2. Throughout this paper, Progressive Judaism refers to Reform. The Israel Movement for Progressive Judaism (Tenu'a Leyahadut Mitkademet — acronym Telem) is the Israeli affiliate of the World Union for Progressive Judaism.

identification. Among Israelis who joined Reform congregations, many considered Reform Judaism as a way to better the cultural climate in Israel. However, unlike classical Zionism, neither the personal adherence of Reform Jews to a liberal form of congregational membership and worship nor Progressive Judaism as a movement developed an overall program for molding Israeli society.• The main political focus for Progressive Judaism in Israel has been the struggle for Jewish religious pluralism in general, and the rights of Reform Judaism in particular.

Even in cases where commendable projects have been undertaken at the initiative of Reform movement bodies — such as the Leo Baeck School's pioneer community outreach program and special projects for integrating immigrant children, and the Ramat Aviv Progressive congregation's Jewish-Arab summer camp and its work with children in distress — these initiatives have not projected themselves as organically linked to Progressive Judaism; nor are the people involved in these projects necessarily identified with the Movement for Progressive Judaism.

The other root of Progressive Judaism in Israel was the Zionist enterprise itself. In the second half of the 1970s, its particular focus was Ichud haKevutzot vehaKibbutzim — the most pluralistic of the three major kibbutz movements, historically associated with the Mapai element and currently a part of the United Kibbutz Movement.

From its very beginnings the kibbutz movement perceived itself as a "way of life." The Ichud was historically the least doctrinaire of the kibbutz movements. A small number of activists in the Ichud kibbutz movement became concerned by the Jewish-cultural vacuum in their way of life. A confluence of interests developed with those educators in the American Reform movement who identified as Zionists and perceived Israel as a means of strengthening the Jewish identity and commitment of American Jewish youth. These activists also hoped to set up projects in Israel where American and Israeli youth could creatively grapple with alternative expressions of Judaism. A number of Ichud kibbutz members of North American origin with ties to leaders of the Reform movement in America served as matchmakers in initiating a joint program between the two movements. As a result, two kibbutzim, Yahel and Lotan, were established in the Arava and the rural settlement, Har Chalutz, was established in the Galilee.

It must be noted that the initiative of melding Reform with Zionism, coming as it did from the kibbutz movement and from abroad (the UAHC Youth Division in particular), was not an organic development stemming from Israel's Progressive Jewish congregations. It became clear in the late 1970s that Israeli youth could not adapt to the concept of Liberal Judaism *ex nihilo*. A youth movement educating to an alternative approach (alternative both to Orthodoxy and to secularism) would have to be established. The Ichud was asked by representatives of the World Union for Reform Judaism and youth educators in the UAHC to help in establishing such a youth movement.

For a small number of youth in the Progressive movement congregations, joining a Progressive Zionist youth movement was a revolt against what was perceived as a sterile, ritualistically-oriented establishment that had uncritically sought to import a Diaspora format for Liberal Judaism as the way in which Liberal Judaism would be expressed. They became the leadership of Tzofei-Telem ("Telem Scouts").

The attempt to establish an educational movement process in Israel via the Telem scouts, in cooperation with the kibbutz movement, resulted in controversy over the meaning of Progressive Judaism in Israel.

As is true of the scouts in general, Tzofei-Telem are educated toward serving in Nachal.[1] In Nachal, after a pre-army service period, the men and women soldiers are attached to a kibbutz identified with their particular youth movement for a portion of their army service. But like the scouting movement's other Nachal nuclei (groups organized to serve together in a kibbutz) the kibbutz is not the only option. A year of movement service or an urban collective are other options. Netzer Olami (Noar Zioni Reformi — Zionist Reform Youth) abroad (in particular, England, Australia, and South Africa) is also influenced by this spirit.

Tzofei-Telem and Netzer perceive themselves as links in the chain of cultural Zionism.

The new Progressive Zionism draws from the traditions of cultural Zionist fulfillment. Its outlook is rooted in the social ideas of Martin Buber,[2] and to a lesser extent A.D. Gordon.[3] The philosophy is combined with the activist movement spirit of Berl Katznelson[4] into a modern interpretation of prophetic values. Historically, the egalitarian lifestyle of the kibbutz and its orientation to Zionist *shlichut* embodied this tradition.

In the area of culture and ritual, Reform Zionism espouses communal initiative and authority as against *de facto* rabbinic authority and largely passive congregational participation. This rejection of rabbinic primacy is a reaction against both the idea of the charismatic Chasidic Rebbe as well as the "pastor and

---

1. Noar Chalutzi Lochem, Pioneer Fighting Youth — a branch of the Israel Defense Forces that combines military service with work and life on the kibbutz, particularly in border areas (e.g., Yahel and Lotan).
2. See in particular his "The Experiment That Did Not Fail" (1949), in *Paths to Utopia* (Beacon, 1958).
3. Labor Zionist philosopher and pioneer who believed that a regeneration of Jewish culture could take place only if the Jewish people returned to Israel and worked the land without exploiting others.
4. Labor Zionist ideologue and educator — 1887-1944.

his/her flock" pattern so much in evidence in contemporary congregational life. In spirit, the Reform Zionist approach is close to those circles in the kibbutz movement that see themselves as an alternative trend in Judaism. Innovation and creativity in prayer and ritual as a modern *derash* of ancient symbols are characteristically nurtured by Reform *chalutziut*.

In terms of social ideology, Reform Zionists are groping (most are still relatively young) with fashioning a way of life that combines cooperative living with a mission. The source of their inspiration is the entire heritage of Israel, including the ideology and activism of the Zionist movement. There is an attempt at formulating guidelines for a communal way of life in both the social and the cultural-ritual realms. The individual and his/her community constitute a framework for the fulfillment of the existential needs "of the hour" with some observance of a ritual within the Reform Jewish framework. But there is more — individuals and their community are involved in "world mending" (*Tikun Olam*), beginning with themselves as individuals and including their community, the Jewish people, and the world. In the words of A.D. Gordon, this constitutes *hagshama atzmit* (self-realization), which connects the individual to "eternal life." Here the concept of *kehila kedosha* (holy — read dedicated — community) is infused with new meaning. Progressive Zionism is a way of life that blends well with the concept of Judaism as a "developing civilization" in the spirit of Mordecai Kaplan. Consonant with Kaplan's theory, there is no obligation toward any specific theological belief. Indeed, with its strong orientation to community, Progressive Zionism is *de facto* a form of Reconstructionism.

The return to Zion has a great influence on the ideology of a movement that "makes *Aliyah*." In the past, Eretz Yisrael was the crucible in which a unique blend of socialism and Zionism emerged three generations ago. Reform Zionism today also seems to be on the way toward fashioning a Reform Judaism that is different in expression from the mother movement abroad.

Thus the life of the Movement for Progressive Judaism in Israel today is marked by a natural division between those for whom Progressive Judaism constitutes religious organizational (Reform) affiliation in the familiar Diaspora sense (i.e., a rather circumscribed commitment for a small area of their lives) and those for whom it constitutes a total expression of personal commitment and an indication of the direction in which Progressive Judaism would like to move society. Naturally, just as there was sympathy in pre-state Israel for the Labor Zionist pioneers, there are members of urban congregations who sympathize with the aims of Reform Zionism, even though they themselves will not attempt to realize it. Nor do the more radical Reform Zionists question the legitimacy of

Reform congregations for those who so choose. However, the efficacy of such congregations in terms of long-term impact is currently a matter of disagreement.

The Issues in Dispute

The Nature of the Reform Rabbinate

Is the rabbi primarily a teacher and/or someone well-versed in the Jewish heritage who serves the congregation as a resource person, or is the rabbi also a religious adjudicator in certain areas? In particular, what is the status of the Israel Movement for Progressive Judaism's Council of Progressive Rabbis (MaRaM)?[1] Certain council members seek the movement's legitimization for adjudicating in matters of personal status, and even to represent the movement in discussions with other trends in Judaism. It is as if these rabbis seek a Reform parallel to the Orthodox rabbinical judicial system.

Another question is: What should be the guidelines for training rabbis who wish to serve in Israel? Currently the Israeli program of the Hebrew Union College has not projected a clear policy in this regard and would appear to be in need of input from the Israeli movement on this subject. The issue is in dispute in the movement and even among the rabbis themselves.

Most of those who identify with Progressive Zionism negate the principle of rabbinic authority. Authority is perceived as a congregational function, even in matters of Halacha and custom, including the laws of personal status. Moreover, many believe that Liberal Judaism means applying principles of democracy to the area of ritual and to what is allowed or forbidden. For example: there has been dissatisfaction with the position of many rabbis that there be four witnesses — two men and two women — to a marriage. To the minds of many, this seems to be giving in to the Orthodox position which invalidates women as witnesses. On the other hand, many members are prepared to compromise for the sake of Kelal Yisrael, but even among them are those who deny the right of the rabbis to adjudicate the issue.

Social Action

Currently there appear to be three different points of view. There are those in the movement who contend that Progressive Judaism is solely an organization dealing with religious (ritual) matters. A religious congregation may engage in

---

1. Mo'etzet Rabbanim Mitkademim — the umbrella organization of all Reform rabbis living in Israel. About 15-25, mainly congregational rabbis, attend monthly meetings.

charitable work, but no more, they say. A somewhat larger group advocates social action, as practiced by the Reform movement in America on the basis of a broad movement consensus. Finally, there are those who believe in political activism as a prerequisite for *Tikun Olam*. This last group is identified in the main with graduates of the Reform Zionist youth movements.

Progressive Zionism advocates political action (not necessarily in terms of a political party) as a principle for repairing the world. Political action is one of the ways of fulfilling a mission. The young people in the Progressive Zionist camp are not, however, mature enough to present a total political program. A broad consensus, but not an absolute majority, approve the principle of social action, especially in the spheres of religious pluralism, equality of the sexes, and changing the electoral system in Israel. The position of the movement regarding Israel-Arab relations is a "gray area," even though it is an open secret that most members of the movement in Israel tend to a dovish view.

In actuality, during the past decade the movement has come a long way on the question of social activism. The latent difference between the desire for an *ad hoc* expression in actual matters and the desire to formulate a comprehensive ideology has not yet crystallized.

Priorities in Movement Activities

What area of Telem's activity should be prioritized? Congregational outreach? Legitimization of Jewish pluralism? Formal education? Informal education?

On the fact of it, there seems to be general agreement to act in all areas. On the other hand, there are deep divisions concerning priorities, especially against the background of growing budgetary constraints. In actuality, the priority in recent years has been congregational outreach and public relations.

Many (and all of those in the Progressive Zionist camp) believe that emphasis should be placed on the development of a formal educational system — perhaps in conjunction with the Tali (*Tigbur Limudei Yahadut* — reinforced Jewish studies) school programs of the Israel Ministry of Education, initiated some ten years ago primarily by activists in the Conservative movement.

However, an agreed-upon Progressive Zionist educational philosophy within the framework of formal education does not exist. Nor has Tali succeeded in formulating a clear educational rationale. Since many of the initiators of Tali come from Conservative backgrounds, the Schechter day schools in America have served as a guide. There is some pressure for Tali to become "Conservadox" in practice. The Reform movement faces the question of whether to integrate within

Tali and cooperate in shaping it or whether to opt for a separate Reform Jewish school stream.

At present options are open for Progressive Jewish education in Israel, and the movement has indeed initiated a number of kindergarten and primary grade frameworks. It is beginning to cut its teeth in the educational field. For staffing, teacher retraining workshops must be held, first for kindergarten teachers and then gradually for grade school staff, to train staff for a Progressive Zionist educational system. In my opinion, the movement cannot by itself establish a college for nursery and grade school teachers. It could cooperate with an existing teachers' college on the basis of similarity in educational philosophy. This, too, would force the movement to clarify its educational direction.

As for informal education, the innovative thinking in Tzofei-Telem in and of itself is a reason to continue nurturing an independent movement process of informal education.

In order to deal with the complexities of education, the Education Committee, currently a non-elected subcommittee of the Telem executive (*Hanhala*) dealing with formal education, will have to become a central priority within the movement. Given current economic constraints, the hiring of professional staff will have to reflect the priority of education over or within community outreach.

There are many in Progressive Judaism who believe that without an educational system from kindergarten onward, the movement will not succeed in striking deep roots. This is the lesson derived from the Orthodox educational systems (Zionist and non-Zionist), which have given rise to the Orthodox streams, whether Gush Emunim or Shas.[1] There is also another difficulty and challenge: How does one educate with the same measure of intensity and identification as does the Orthodox educational system without endangering basic values such as pluralism, equality, and democracy in all areas of activity — including religion?

Progressive Zionism has reservations with regard to the current policy of community outreach geared chiefly to expanding the congregations. Professionalization by community workers and rabbis will at best create a public of passive consumers of subsidized social, cultural, and religious services. This subsidy will have to be paid by contributions from abroad. There is no foreseeable way in which congregations can be weaned from dependence on subsidies in the near future. Moreover, it is doubtful whether these "consumer congregations"

---

1. Sephardic Orthodox non-Zionist party.

will ever constitute a political factor motivated toward active Progressive Zionism.

In the Israeli context, a more rational way to budget would be to subsidize the activities of volunteers and by so doing develop initiative, mutual responsibility, and an identification of the members with the movement. In fact, the Tzofei-Telem program has had this effect, and today it is becoming increasingly clear that much of the movement's lay leadership (and even some of the professional leadership) will come from Tzofei-Telem graduates. However, it is an unfortunate fact that some among the current professional leadership are threatened by this development.

An Area of Consensus — with a Catch

There is no doubt that the Movement for Progressive Judaism's struggle for equal rights for all religious streams has almost unanimous support from everyone in the movement. For well-known political reasons, Progressive Judaism's rights in Israel are negated. Progressive Judaism, of course, negates this negation. The catch is that negating a negation does not necessarily constitute a positive program of action. At the moment when the movement will win its rights, the question of its identity and what it wants to do with those rights will emerge far more sharply. Will the movement be a sterile clone of American Reform, or will it develop a unique Zionist way of life in Israel?

Memo to the Education Committee — Israel Movement for Progressive Judaism[1]

The Ideological Basis of Progressive Jewish-Zionist Education

This proposal relates to Jewish-Zionist education for the Jewish people as a whole, both in conceptual and experiential terms.

Our educational objective is to inculcate a sense of commitment to Jewish-Zionist culture without attributing binding authority to the Torah or to its traditional interpretation.

Basic values

a. Progressive Jewish-Zionist education means education in the spirit of humanism. In other words, the sovereign individual stands at the center of the educational process and its purpose.

b. Human equality is a basic value from which other values are derived, including tolerance, pluralism and democracy. This is where we stand with regard to interpersonal relations in general and Judaism in particular. The realization of this value necessitates the replacement of rabbinical authority with sovereign Judaism on both the individual and community levels.

c. Progressive Jewish-Zionist education is based on the belief that the Jewish people, the Torah and the Land of Israel form a union symbolized by the Rock of Israel (Tzur Israel).

d. In the spirit of the vision of the Jewish prophets, Progressive Jewish-Zionist education seeks to inculcate a commitment to peace, friendship and solidarity among peoples, and a sense of mission to mend the individual, the Jewish people and the world.[2] In order to achieve this objective, the ability to think critically and independently must be nurtured, as must a willingness to act altruistically.

---

1. 1989-1992 (translated from Hebrew).
2. *Tikkun Ha-adam, Ha'am ve Ha-olam.*

e. "The world stands on three things: On Torah, on labor and on good works."

Torah: The study of Jewish and other sources from all periods, and the clarification of values reflected in these sources.

Labor: The fruits of the individual's labor to maintain his/her physical and spiritual existence as a Jewish-Zionist human.

Good works: Mutual responsibility according to the precept "Love your neighbor as yourself."

Realizing values

In order to creatively implement the value-based education outlined above, the following frameworks and tools are required:

1. An educational center that is not just a place of learning but also provides a social fabric. Accordingly, the unique aspects of our educational centers will include:
    a. The educational and educating community of children/ youth.
    b. An egalitarian approach to pupils of both sexes.
    c. Educating students in how to communicate.
    d. Good works toward others in the school.
    e. Good works that relate to the surrounding community.
2. The children's farm will function as an academic and experiential tool promoting education for labor and Land of Israel studies and inculcating a relationship to the workings of nature.
3. In addition to cognitive study of Jewish sources and heritage, the Progressive Jewish-Zionist education center will also be characterized by:
    a. A short, creative daily service (Ma'amad) at the start of the day reflecting different aspects of traditional and innovative Jewish culture.
    b. Weekly study of that week's Torah portion and discussion of the values that can be drawn from the portion for our times.
    c. Joint celebration of the Jewish festivals and holidays.

DRAFT FOR DISCUSSION AT THE IMPJ EDUCATION COMMITTEE[1]

The IMPJ education system espouses the declared goals of the National Education Act: "To base education in the State on the foundation of Jewish cultural values and scientific achievements, on love of the homeland and loyalty to the State of Israel and the Jewish people, on a conscious memory of the Holocaust martyrs and heroes, on belief in agricultural and manual labor, on pioneer training and on the desire to create a society based on liberty, equality, tolerance, mutual assistance and human fellowship."

We see our educational institutions as frameworks characterized by an open[2] Jewish-Zionist identity. Their objective is to develop a comprehensive educational-experiential system that will forge learning, creating and **contributing** communities in which students, educators and parents are all partners.

Our educational centers place special emphasis on Jewish heritage as manifested in each generation, including in modern thought and practice. Our approach to the **inculcation** of this heritage is pluralistic, egalitarian and **non-coercive**. We believe that Israel's central objective as a Jewish state is to constitute a means for our people to renew its Hebrew-Jewish culture in its homeland in a spirit of "many paths lead to the holy."[3]

We believe that in modern times the values of our heritage should be interpreted and implemented in accordance with the democratic humanistic tradition that has developed in the Western world over the past few centuries.

With this in mind, we will interpret such values as:

1. The essential value of each human, since **"He created them in God's image; male and female He created them."**
2. The community as a framework enabling each individual to realize his/her unique identity, and **to take part together with others in realizing Zionism in our generation.**
3. A mission that gives purpose both to the life of the individual and the community.

    We hope to shape individuals with the ability and desire to realize these values through a ceaseless commitment to mending oneself, the Jewish people and the world.

We see the Jewish heritage and the humanistic tradition, when taken together, as the guiding ideological foundations shaping our approach to those we educate.

---

1. May 21, 1992 (translated from Hebrew).
2. Non-coercive, non-dogmatic.
3. *Harbei Petachim Lamakom.*

They are the focus of educational and academic activity; accordingly, we aim to achieve excellence in **all** fields. This implies a desire to enable each student to realize his/her skills in the emotional and academic spheres. In realizing this objective, we will respect the unique character of each individual, while expecting those we educate to take on responsibilities toward others, toward the community and toward society in general.

Has the Israel Movement for Progressive Judaism Gone Forth out of Egypt?[1]

For the People of Israel, exile in Egypt was both physical and spiritual. The spiritual enslavement was no less severe than the physical. Forty years' wandering in the desert were needed in order to evolve a generation freed of the mentality of dependence on others who dictate the conditions of the people's existence.

In modern times, the Zionist movement was established for two reasons. According to the First Zionist Congress in Basle, political Zionism of the Herzlian school sought "to establish a homeland for the Jewish people in the Land of Israel guaranteed by international law." Herzl was concerned by the threat to the continued physical existence of the Jewish people in exile. By contrast, Achad Ha'am was afraid that the Emancipation would threaten the unique spiritual character of the Jewish people. Anticipating the danger of assimilation in exile, Achad Ha'am rejected the formula of political Zionism — the "normalization" of the Jewish people — and saw the future state as a means for reviving Jewish culture in the spirit of the prophets, thus ensuring its continued creative existence both in its homeland and in the Diaspora.

Herzl's political Zionism emphasized liberation from physical enslavement, while Achad Ha'am stressed the problem of spiritual enslavement. Due to the historical circumstances in which the Jewish people found itself during this century, political Zionism had no choice but to develop a practical plan of action. Cultural Zionism found itself marginalized.

Reform Zionism constitutes an interpretation of Cultural Zionism. It rejects assimilation within Western culture, on the one hand ("Hebrew-speaking Gentiles"), and spiritual enslavement to Halachic Judaism, on the other. It is widely agreed that Israel has today reached a point where it is possible to advance activities in the spirit of Reform Zionism. However, the question facing us is whether we are capable of developing and proposing a program as a Reform Zionist movement in current real time.

---

1. Leaflet: March 12, 1995 (translated from Hebrew).

Is the IMPJ a Zionist movement?

One might argue that, as people who choose of our own free will to live in Israel
as the national state of the Jewish people, to identify as Jews, to receive the rights
and to accept the duties commensurate with our status as Israeli citizens, we may
therefore define ourselves, individually, as Zionists. It is however important to
note a contrary view which postulates that an Israeli Jew is only a Zionist insofar
as he or she is personally involved with others in an attempt to realize some
vision reflecting a commitment to the concept of cultural Zionism. It is doubtful
whether we could claim today that by coming together as an association of
Reform Jewish congregations we thereby constitute a **Reform Zionist
movement** in Israel. There are two inter-related reasons why this is so:

1. The IMPJ is not a **movement**, since it lacks any agreed plan of action for
    changing Israeli society. Our advocacy of pluralism and democracy in
    Judaism does not detail what we intended to do as a Progressive Jewish
    movement when were have the chance to act (a situation which effectively
    exists already).
2. The IMPJ is not essentially Zionist, since it is **enslaved spiritually and
    materially to Reform Judaism in the Diaspora**. In its dependence,
    Progressive Judaism is reminiscent of the "Halukka" system in the old,
    pre-Zionist Jewish community. Emissaries (*Meshulachim*) from the old
    Yishuv traveled throughout the Jewish exile in order to collect donations
    for the "Holy Labor" (i.e., worship) in the Holy Land. Halukka Jewry lived
    a life of exile in the Land of Israel, and I fear that the same applies to the
    IMPJ. **We have not yet "gone forth out of Egypt."**

IMPJ: A plan of action for a free movement in its own land

1. On the basis of an updated platform of values we must propose a plan of
    action in such fields as education, culture and society, which will reflect an
    attempt to implement a Reform Zionist world view in practical terms.
2. In both material and spiritual terms, the IMPJ must prepare a plan to become
    self-sufficient within a few years. The Diaspora patterns of the "professional
    Jew" (rabbi or other workers) as the leader of a passive congregation is inap-
    propriate for a Zionist movement. By what right do we demand that Reform
    Jews in the Diaspora should finance personnel in our congregations? This
    enslaving dependence prevents our supporters in the Diaspora from
    allocating funds to the development of the buildings and institutions we

urgently need to house our congregations and to promote the Reform Zionist path within the environment in which we work. Many of the professional Jews should be replaced by voluntary activity, supported by the allocation of small amounts to cover expenses incurred by the volunteers, in order to ensure that activism in the movement is not a luxury reserved for the well-off (once again, the pattern of moneyed members leading the communities is a Diaspora import).

3. The training of those planning to be active (rabbis and others) should be guided by considerations relating to the needs of Israeli reality, rather than by the standards of the Diaspora. At this time movement workers should be making their living mainly from the education system in Israel rather than from movement budgets. Their training must prepare them for this. Otherwise we shall be chained as a movement to the salaries of unsuitable workers (in objective and/or subjective terms). We will be unable to adapt to rapid and far-reaching changes now occurring in the reality in which we exist and work. These changes represent an opportunity and a challenge for a Zionist movement in the spirit of Progressive Judaism, if we will be prepared with the necessary spiritual and material resources.[1]

---

1. These comments were submitted twice to the editors of "Kolot," the IMPJ newsletter. The editors did not see fit to print these remarks. They were disseminated to activists in the Director's Circular of the Summer of 1995.

First Let's Mend the Movement[1]

- Tikkun Olam entails all the circles of Tikkun — Tikkun Adam (mending the individual), Tikkun Am (mending the people) and Tikkun Olam (mending the world).
- Translating Tikkun Olam into concrete steps requires the existence of a movement as a tool for implementation. Without a plan of action supported by the human and financial resources necessary for its implementation, there can be no movement. **Adopting declarative positions has no real value in terms of Tikkun.**
- The Israel Movement for Progressive Judaism is currently incapable of taking on the task of changing society, since it is not a movement. At present, the IMPJ is an umbrella organization of Jewish congregations in Israel which hold Reform-style religious activities. There is an organization of Reform Jewish congregations in Israel, but there is no movement seeking to promote a Reform Zionist vision in Israel.
- The IMPJ is an organization devoted to recruiting the necessary means for its own existence, particularly personnel costs ("professional Jews"). One of the characteristics of professional personnel employed on what are virtually tenure conditions is a lack of flexibility and an inability to divert personnel to different tasks as circumstances change.
- In recent years, there has been a welcome expansion in the fields of activity of most of the congregations, including such areas as establishing pre-schools, encouraging immigrant absorption (including conversion), and campaigns focusing on good works. We must certainly not disparage these activities. However, they have exerted only a marginal impact on Israeli Jewish society. These activities — unlike the Religious Pluralism Center — do not constitute consistent and long-term work to promote political aims.
- Things have recently reached the stage of fierce conflict in the movement institutions between movement tasks and the desire to ensure the existence of

---

1. An open letter on the occasion of the movement study day on the subject "Tikkun Olam: From Theory to Practice" (translated from Hebrew), May 5, 1996. Distributed together with *Has the Israel Movement for Progressive Judaism Gone Forth Out of Egypt?*

congregation-based systems of a non-Zionist character (as explained in detail in my article "Has the IMPJ Gone Forth Out of Egypt?")

The main avenue for influencing the future is education. We must reach out to a secular public looking for values and meaning to life in Israel. We must influence teacher training seminars and schools (through Tali[1] and in other frameworks). This requires a new order of priorities in the allocation of resources and personnel. New immigrants also form a key target for our messages. We must also work to enhance contacts with Reform youth from abroad who spend time in Israel in various projects.

The IMPJ Convention approved education as a key priority, but in practice the Executive has failed to accept the programs prepared by the Education Committee, which have not yet been discussed by the National Committee. The approved budget for 1996 is clearly marked by a commitment to the existing patterns of personnel functions.

In order to mend the movement, we need

1. A periodical committed to ensuring freedom of expression, and appearing sufficiently often to enable real-time discussions and updates on the movement.
2. Within two years, half the professional personnel of the IMPJ should be integrated into educational work **funded by external bodies** (the Ministry of Education, seminaries). The goal should be that the congregational rabbi will work in the broader community on a regular basis and achieve long-term influence. This program will be accompanied by assistance in partial professional retraining, and by the provision of compensation payments where necessary.
3. The dependence on professional personnel (rabbis and community workers) must be reduced. Professional activity will be replaced by volunteers from the communities, who will be reimbursed solely for direct expenses as necessary.
4. A special plan of action will be developed for working with new immigrants, as well as a plan to encourage Reform Zionist Aliyah from the Western countries, with the assistance of ARZENU.

The process of thinking engenders the accomplished deed *"Sof ma'ase bemachshava t'chila"*

---

1. Some 15 schools offering "Jewish reinforced" learning (non-Orthodox).

Response to the ARZA Education Committee

MEMORANDUM

Date: May 5, 1997

To: Rabbis and Educators
From: Ruth Frankfurt, Chair, Education Committee (ARZA)

Philip Meltzer, President of ARZA, asked me to chair a committee to explore the viability of ARZA giving major support towards a center for Liberal Jewish Education in Israel. The committee in America consists of:

Ruth Frankfurt
Rabbi Karyn Kedar
Rabbi Arnold Gluck
Seymour Lipton
Rabbi Eric Gurvis
Norman Schwartz

To begin this exploration, we decided that each committee member would write his/her vision, expressing his/her dreams of how to effectively bring the message of Reform Judaism to Israelis and how to help secure religious pluralism in Israel, through Education.

To this end, we invite you to participate with us, by writing your vision of an Institute for Progressive Jewish Education. Please include how this vision interfaces with other needs of the movement. Please send me a mission statement and your goals for a Resource Institute for Liberal Jewish Education in Israel. Our plan is to circulate the mission statements and goals, without their authors, for the benefit of enlightened discussion and dialogue.

Our committee will be in Israel during the last two weeks in June, and we hope to follow up our discussions with meetings and interviews. June 20th and June 22nd seem like two good days for group meetings. We will also arrange for some individual interviews between June 17th and June 27th.

We are looking forward to your "mission statements" and "goals" for our discussion as soon as possible. Please fax to Ruth Frankfurt: (212) 689-9220...
Thank you for your immediate attention.

B'Shalom
Ruth Frankfurt

AUTHOR'S RESPONSE:[1]

How To Bring The Message Of Reform Judaism To Israelis And How To Help Secure Religious Pluralism In Israel Through Education

*I wish to demur from the way in which the Association of Reform **Zionists** of America has framed the question.*

*The question should be framed: "How to bring the message of Reform **Zionism** etc...." We should be seen as a **Zionist** alternative to the varieties of Orthodox Zionism and secular Zionism. In Israel, our Reform Judaism should be seen as a source of the principles and practices whose aim it is to shape the religio-cultural character of the Jewish State. Reform Judaism plays a role in the individual life of every Reform Zionist — what that role is will ultimately be an individual matter (in Israel or anywhere else). But in Israel, Reform Zionism should be an ideological approach with an action program to further an alternative vision of society in the Jewish State. Reform Zionism is our means for achieving Tikkun of our People, a mended society in our National Home.*

A few words on what that vision should be are necessary. What is the message of Reform Zionism in Israel? Currently we have failed to project any message at all. Our fight for pluralism and our rights is fully justified and (thanks to IRAC[2]) gets good publicity but this is the cry of our pain — it is not a message. My vision as an Israeli (ex North American) Reform Zionist can only illustrate what our message could be.

Our vision of the Jewish society in Israel should be that of a society committed both to democracy and the Jewish heritage. The Reform Zionist commitment to democracy leads to our affirmation of the rights of minorities in general and to the legitimacy of pluralism in matters pertaining to our Jewish heritage.

However, within that pluralistic framework we have a particular outlook which it is our task, our shlichut, to promote. In our Zionist view, it is the purpose of the Jewish state to ensure the creative continuity and unity of the Jewish people both in the Diaspora and in Israel. We believe that this requires the freedom of each generation to

---

1. Unpublished memo.
2. Israel Religious Action Center — established with the help of ARZA.

encounter the Jewish heritage within the context of its contemporary situation. Indeed, such encounter is both the right and the obligation of the committed Jew and his/her community.

Authority within the decision making process generated by encounter lies with the (hopefully Jewishly literate) individual and his/her community. Our belief as Reform Jews is that all the Jewish (and some universal) sources, both classical and modern, serve to inform us. However, no single authority (e.g., the Halacha) has exclusive authority and no group can claim to have a particular prerogative in authoritatively interpreting the tradition. This belief in the non-authority of specific sources differentiates between us as Reform Jews and other streams of Judaism. The message of Reform Zionism is that the status quo by which secular authority legalizes Halachic authority not only undermines the unity of the Jewish people — it cripples the Zionist potential for cultural creativity.

As Reform Zionists in Israel the challenge before us is to educate a generation which will be committed to observing Judaism in family and in community without being shackled (sometimes self-shackled) to non-democratic authority. But observance is not enough. In Israel, shlichut must be the defining characteristic of the Reform Zionism and set him/her and his/her community apart from simply being a Reform Jew in Israel who attends services in a Reform congregation. The Reform Zionist view of the Jewish State is that it serves as a crucible for the development of new paths in Judaism compatible with modern thought as understood by the humanist tradition of the western world. It is our belief that the unique venture in human history which began some four thousand years ago with the call to Abraham to go forth unto the Land, will be heard again if we can succeed in establishing an educational system capable of motivating at least a part of the future generation to pioneer new paths for the Judaism of the 21st Century.

This Is the Mission

A system of Reform Zionist education, formal and informal, cognitive and experiential, from kindergarten through to the end of high school and beyond (Institute for Progressive Jewish Education) should be the backbone of a Reform Zionist movement in Israel. An educational system is a necessity not only to "bring the message of Reform Zionism" but also to **develop the message** and to **prepare the messengers**.

Preparing the messengers is not only a question of imparting knowledge — it means inculcating commitment to personally living and creatively projecting the Reform Zionist alternative within religious, cultural, social and educational contexts in Israel. At one level examples of such creative projection are creative prayers and alternative methods of marking life cycle events (e.g., weddings). In other contexts we need a laity that can contend with confrontation at the neighborhood level. The Reform education system, the formal interacting with the informal, must generate the critical mass of graduates (hundreds) for evolving and establishing committed Reform Zionist communities capable of backing both the message and the messengers.

"An Institute for Progressive Jewish Education: A Resource Institute for Liberal Jewish Education in Israel"

I am assuming that we are ultimately talking about one institution serving a multiplicity of aims.

A number of years may be necessary to create such an institution. Hence a plan to provide long term financial is essential. **A critical first step would be to do joint in-service training programs with existing teacher colleges.** *This is a necessity because the Hebrew Union College is not yet adequately rooted in Israel to initiate such ventures on its own. By means of their regular and continuing in service training, the Teachers Colleges (the better ones are currently affiliated with University Schools of Education) provide access to the present and future public of educators. In addition to the general value of outreach, making "converts" within the existing public of educators will provide educators for the future Reform Zionist educational system. Here is a key to Reform Zionist outreach in general. The lesson of history is that in the pre-State period the Labor orientation of a major part of the formal and informal educational system had a significant influence on the initial pioneering egalitarian ethos of the State of Israel. From the late Fifties, the system of Orthodox Zionist education, formal and informal, constituted the soil which nurtured Gush Emunim. Today, the central activity of the non-Zionist, ultra-Orthodox is the development of their educational system. It should be noted that the religious congregations in Israel have an ancillary role. The "action" is in the Yeshivot and the settlements.*

These are the Goals of the Institute and Resource Center

The Institute and Resource Center for Progressive Judaism (the name should include the word Zionist) would serve the following needs:

1. The training of professional personnel for both formal and informal education for schools/communities seeking a Reform Zionist approach.
2. The training of lay leadership for a variety of roles as the needs evolve.
3. Seminars for in-service training.
4. Adult education seminars.

5.   The general public seeking resource material from our viewpoint.

A central task of this institution would be to create and propagate Reform Zionist curriculum alternatives for the **existing** "secular" school curricula — particularly from the Junior High School age up. This involves in-service training workshops (in cooperation with existing Schools of Education) in integrating Reform values and approaches to existing approved Ministry of Education syllabi. Ultimately, our curriculum alternatives would involve both our interpretation of content as well as a methodological approach. Without going into details in this memo, this means applying a multi-disciplinary, confluent approach to both the cognitive and the experiential aspects of the school year. This approach would not be limited to "Jewish Studies." All the humanities as well as some of the sciences would be involved.

The establishment of the Center in stages, in cooperation with existing Schools of Education is both a logistical necessity as well as serving the goal of recruiting educators.

"Interfacing With Other Needs of the Movement"

We have no "movement" in Israel. "The emperor has no clothes." As stated above, the educational system has to be the backbone of the movement that currently is not. The IMPJ is an organization, an umbrella framework of the Reform congregations in Israel. Its primary function is to regulate the allocation of funds (mainly from the Diaspora) to the congregations — in particular to ensure the funding of the professional (mainly rabbinical) staff. This does not a movement make....

The question should be: "How do the congregations interface with the need to create an educational system?"

ARZA would do well to learn from its success in initiating and developing the Israel Religious Action Center. Although it has a long way to go, it is the Israel Religious Action Center that has had a major impact on furthering religious pluralism. (It has not brought the actual message of Reform Judaism/Zionism to Israel because that was never its task.) It has opened doors and created possibilities for a Reform Zionist movement. No such movement exists to take advantage of the possibilities that have emerged.

*In addition to its outstanding leadership, one of the reasons for IRAC's success has been **its minimal "interfacing" with the IMPJ**. The lesson that ARZA will have to internalize is that the proposed Institute will have to be independent of the IMPJ and independently financed. It is legitimate (as in the case of IRAC) for the IMPJ to be represented on the Israel steering committee (responsible to ARZA) of the planned institution. Those who claim that, in contrast to IRAC, there is no "leadership" for an* *educational policy independent of the IMPJ, are engaged in a self-fulfilling prophecy. No educational leadership can emerge within the IMPJ where existential priorities of congregations are paramount.* **The Education Committee of the IMPJ ceased to function when it became impossible to generate policy initiatives (which can take a number of years to mature) within the context of the day-to-day constraints of the existential priorities of the IMPJ.** *Hence, "The viability of ARZA giving major support to a center for Liberal Jewish Education in Israel" is contingent on following the administrative precedents set in establishing and furthering IRAC.*

An Educational Center could serve the needs of the IMPJ in the following ways. (Please note: the opinions re IMPJ needs are those of this writer and the examples are illustrative and not exhaustive.)

1. Train lay leadership in order to reduce dependence on professional leadership and in order to make Reform Judaism in Israel something that "everybody can." This makes sense both in order to expand the movement as well as in order to do it in an economically viable way.
2. Train professional leadership (in cooperation with Schools of Education and/or Social Work) so that they can function as accredited teachers and/or social workers. This is both a springboard to community outreach and a way of financing our professions.
3. Serve as Resource Center for congregational adult education including Reform conversion programs.

Congregations could serve the needs of the Education Center in the following ways:

1. Demonstration centers for Reform ritual and community.
2. Practical experience for students in early childhood education.
3. Professional staff seconded to the Educational Center for satellite activity in their locality.

Good Luck!

A Suggested Progressive Zionist Platform and Action Program[1]

February 15, 1998

Our aim in the **Progressive Jewish Zionist Movement** is to **make an imprint** on Israeli society. Our movement has a **mission to further our unique Zionist vision**.

Our Path To The Vision

"When there is no vision, disorder reigns among the people"
Proverbs 29:18

1) We see the Jewish heritage as a **unifying** factor within Jewish Zionist society in Israel, and between the Jewish people in Israel and in the Diaspora. The **togetherness** of the tradition intensifies the **sense of partnership** in the fate and destiny of the Jewish people. We recognize the pluralistic nature in which the Jewish people addresses its heritage. In a society of patience and tolerance, each person will live according to his/her own beliefs — "there are many paths to the divine."

   We take upon ourselves the task of Tikkun Olam — mending ourselves, our people, our land, and our world. Our path in Tikkun is a blend of Jewish heritage and Western humanism. We are guided by three basic principles. The independent life of the people in its own land enables full participation in all spheres of particularistic and universalistic Tikkun. People and their environment constitute the focus for remedial social action here and now. Our joint Jewish Zionist heritage constitutes a means of recruiting those who will mend society and the environment, despite the pluralism in belief inspiring the action.

   a) **The equal value of human life as dictated by our common descent as those created in God's image.**

      Our Progressive Zionist position is that the equal value of all humans

---

1. Prepared for the IMPJ Elections, April 1998, (translated from Hebrew).

demands a democratic and pluralistic state. All the citizens of Israel are equal before the law and have equal civic rights and obligations toward the framework of the state.

b) **The Jewish state is the national home of the entire Jewish people.**
The goal of the Zionist state is to ensure the continued creative existence of the Jewish people as such. As well as serving as a national home, the state provides a framework for renewing the heritage of the Jewish people in Israel and elsewhere. As long as a century ago, cultural Zionism predicted that in order to meet the challenge of modernity in our age Judaism would require a spiritual center in our own land providing meaning and creating Jewish commitment. In this context, the status quo that grants exclusive rights to one stream of Judaism (and a stream most of whose adherents in Israel do not define themselves as Zionist) negates and restricts the renewal of Jewish heritage in our own land.

c) **We adopt the principle "do not destroy" in our attitude toward the land.**
We are charged with maintaining the existence and quality of creation. We are enjoined "to tend and to maintain it" for the coming generations. This commandment raises a particular challenge in the State of Israel. From Beersheva north, Israel is one of the most densely-populated areas in the world. On the other hand, in the Negev and the Arava there are particularly vulnerable ecosystems that we must take care to protect.

2) **Our approach to the commandments, symbols, and festivals is based on identification and love.**
Faithful to the Zionist goal of renewing the Jewish people in its homeland, we see our heritage as a foundation for renewal. The Bible is the infrastructure for this entire heritage — a heritage that also includes the Oral Law, the literature and achievements of two thousands years of exile, and Jewish and Zionist thought and action in the modern era. Progressive Zionism does not attribute exclusive authority to any component of our heritage. Over the coming generations, history will make clear the ways in which the Jewish people can exist as a constructive force among the nations of the world. Our spiritual development depends not only on accepting our heritage but also on our ability to create and renew through identification and love.

3) **We advocate the integration of democracy in the process of Jewish renewal.**
Only through a commitment to democracy (majority rule with due respect for individual rights) can we facilitate the free and pluralistic development of

Jewish heritage. In order to promote this process the separation of religion and state is necessary.

The Tools For Realizing Our Vision

1) **A community of communities reflected in the institutions of the national movement.**
   Each community must see itself as responsible for maintaining and partici-pating in national institutions such as the National Board and the Committees advising the Executive, such as the committees for Education, Community Development, Media, Aliyah and Absorption, and other committees according to the needs of the hour.

2) **A formal and informal education system functioning as a creative workshop for Progressive Zionism.**
   In experiential terms, those we educate will learn in the "Progressive Tali"[1] framework, whose values will reflect our path to our vision. This system requires the investment of resources in order to develop a rationale for education and study from the kindergarten through the 12th grade.

   a) There is an urgent need to develop ways to integrate Progressive "Tali" education in the junior-high and high schools. The challenge is to inculcate values in youth based on the foundation acquired in the elementary classes.

   b) The Progressive Tali framework requires an immediate program and long-term plan of action to recruit and train educators. To this end we should cooperate with existing teacher training colleges. Involvement in the existing colleges is required not only to recruit personnel for the Progressive Tali framework, but also to expand the horizons of the next generation of educators in Israel.

   c) As a parallel process, the Hebrew Union College should adapt itself to train educators. The IMPJ institutions must be involved in shaping the educational directions at a future college of Progressive Jewish-Zionist education.

In Zionist history, those who educated reaped the rewards

3) **Different models for communal activities and Havurot based on leadership development among rank-and-file members.**
   This requires training seminars for activists and mentoring for communities.

---

1. "Tali" — Reinforced Jewish Studies.

The IMPJ should also be involved in developing training tracks for professional personnel (rabbinical and other) to serve the movement.

4) **A periodical allowing free expression of Progressive Zionist and emerging Progressive Zionist identity.**
The movement must publish a journal committed to allowing free expression and appearing sufficiently frequently to enable updates to be disseminated and discussion promoted in real-time. A program is required to ensure that the movement's books and periodicals (in Hebrew, English and Russian) are available at public libraries and during Book Week.

5) **Special action plan to encourage Reform Zionist Aliyah and promote absorption in the movement.**
   a) Intensifying and expanding activities among Olim from the former Soviet Union.
   b) Implementing the ARZENU proposal to establish an Aliyah Desk to promote Progressive Zionist Aliyah from the West.

In the Israeli public arena

1) Raising the unique ideological profile of the Progressive Zionist movement in Israel by means of all the tools discussed above. We must develop an identity that is clearly demarcated from that of secular Zionist circles, on the one hand, and from that of Zionist circles that accept Halachic authority, on the other. We must develop alternative paths for a life based on a "post-Halachic" commitment to Jewish heritage.

2) A continuation and intensification of the struggle for equal rights for all streams in as many areas as possible, including a strategic direction of striving to secure the separation of religion and state.

3) In cooperation with ARZENU, a struggle to introduce separate elections (separate from the Knesset elections) to a world Jewish-Zionist body. In these elections, the IMPJ will stand as the Reform Zionist movement of ARZENU in Israel.

In order to act, the IMPJ Convention must elect a Chairperson and Executive committed to an action plan to promote a **national movement** program. There is currently a window of opportunity to engage in movement action. Creating facts on the ground is a Zionist tradition.

A Reform Zionist Approach to Zionist Politics

Synopsis of the Section

These articles deal with political issues within World Jewry — i.e., that great majority of World Jewry which relates to Israel positively. How can Israel Diaspora relations be institutionalized in a democratic fashion? Can the formally Zionist Jewish polity (including the State of Israel) exercise principles of democracy in relating to Jewish identity? The author advocates political Reform Zionist initiatives regarding democratization of world Zionist-Jewish bodies as well as separation of religion and State in Israel.

SECTION 3 • INTRODUCTION

The main reason for the establishment of ARZENU, the World Union of Reform Zionist parties was to give Reform Zionism a voice in the affairs of the Jewish people. In particular, the Association of Reform Zionists of America (ARZA) has seen political action as its *raison d'etre*. ARZA was instrumental in establishing the Israel Religious Action Center (IRAC) in 1986. Its main purpose has been to fight for equal rights in Israel for all streams of Judaism. The establishment of a government committee in 1997 (chaired by the then Minister for Finance, Yaakov Neeman) to deal with the right of non-Orthodox Rabbis to perform conversions in Israel, in which Reform and Conservative representatives participated, may be seen as a major victory after a decade of Reform Zionist political activity. This is so even if the operative results of the Committee's deliberations prove to be negligible. However, the question may be asked: Should the fight for legitimacy and equal rights be the sum total of Reform Zionist political strategy?

The fight for legitimacy is surely a just fight but it is not enough. Nor is the rationale of "democracy" as the exclusive rationale for these rights sufficient from my Reform Zionist point of view to justify the on-going struggle (see in particular: 1:7 and 2:5). As I pointed out in DEMOCRACY, RELIGION AND THE ZIONIST FUTURE (1985-1987), the legitimacy of Reform (and Conservative) Zionism in Israel is essential for Israel to fulfill its cultural Zionist task of being a creative center for meaningful Judaism in the future. This article evolved from a study seminar (*"Kallah"*) on State and Religion organized by Tzofei Telem in 1985. The context at that time was the emergence of Rabbi Meir Kahana's "Kach" party. However, the entire gamut of religious issues was also involved.[1]

The American approach to creating movements which relate to specific issues (e.g., equal rights for all streams of Judaism in Israel) is not an adequate strategy, in my opinion, from a Reform Zionist point of view. The reason for this is that Zionist movements have historically embodied a total world outlook. It is of course true that in contemporary Israel the "secular" political parties have become ideologically empty. However, the Religious Zionists (Mafdal) and the

---

1. Zalman Abramov, Perpetual Dilemma, World Union for Progressive Judaism, New York and Jerusalem, 1976 is an early, still readable review of the questions involved. See also in this book, 7:3.

non-Zionist ultra-Orthodox have become aggressively ideological. I would hope that Reform Zionism will never adopt the style and tone of the orthodox religious parties. Nevertheless, Reform Zionism, as a religious movement will have to develop a comprehensive approach and outlook if it wishes to project a Jewish-Zionist alternative to the existing religious parties and to the drifting, nominally secular Israeli public. As outlined in Section 2, the development of an educational system is a prerequisite. An educational rationale ultimately necessitates an ideological and political rationale.

Democracy in Jewish Public Life

Over the years I have consistently argued that the democratization of Jewish public life is a central need of our times. This concern was certainly shared to some extent by ARZENU in general and ARZA in particular. For the realization of the unique nature of Jewish peoplehood we need a democratic framework to process question relating to Jewish peoplehood and Israel-Diaspora relations. *Participation in such a framework would also be an essential element in ongoing adult Jewish-Zionist education.*

Since my article ISRAEL DIASPORA RELATIONS: CHANGING THE WORLD ZIONIST ORGANIZATION (1978) some change has come about in democratizing the World Zionist Organization. The democratic elections held in the United States to the 33rd Zionist Congress were a direct result of ARZA leadership on this issue. The elections resulted in a sweeping victory for ARZA and Merkaz (Conservative Zionists). However, there has been no real confrontation of the lack of democracy in the Jewish Agency for Israel and the related structure of Jewish Federations in the Diaspora. In addition, no progress has been made on the question of separate democratic elections in Israel to the WZO. The current situation is that the Israeli delegation to the WZO is a function of its strength in the Knesset. There is no real political accountability on behalf of the Israeli delegation to any public forum. Lack of WZO elections in Israel is one factor in preventing real involvement of the Israeli Jewish Zionist public with issues of Jewish peoplehood.

In the past I believed that the World Zionist Organization could be reformed. The short articles, ZIONIST PARTIES: A LETTER TO TRUDE WEISS-ROSMARIN (1981) as well as WORLD ZIONIST ORGANIZATION: PARTISAN — YET DIVERSE. argued for reform from within. In the early Nineties, as a result of my actual contact (as Director-General of the Department of Jewish Education and Culture in the Diaspora) with the realities of the WZO and the Jewish Agency for Israel (JAFI), I came to the conclusion that a new democratic worldwide Jewish Zionist body had to be created. (See Section 1:5)

A DEMOCRATIC POLITICAL BODY FOR WORLD JEWRY (1993) fleshed out the rationale and a partial blueprint for such a body. (See also Section 1:7)

Israel-Diaspora Relations[1]

Changing the World Zionist Organization

The question of a representative forum of the Jewish people encompassing both Israel and the Diaspora has not yet found a satisfactory solution. The possibility of creating *de novo* a new world-wide Jewish body which might evolve into such a forum does not appear to be real. The mythic force of the Zionist idea has achieved almost absolute primacy in the context of modern Jewish history. Jewish reaction to the "Zionism is racism" resolution at the UN, both in Israel and in the free Diaspora, has confirmed this vividly. The Jewish people will continue to exist in the shadow of the seminal events of the past 50 years during the rest of this century, and probably well beyond. Hence, with all its faults (some of which we will discuss in detail) the World Zionist Organization is the most logical forum for the development of Israel-Diaspora relationships. However, the World Zionist Organization as presently constituted is in need of radical transformation in order to play such a role, and such a transformation would raise both ideological and political questions.

Zionist Ideology and the Israel-Diaspora Relationship

There is no point in trying to find a Zionist consensus acceptable to every individual Jew. On the other hand, it does seem to me that we can begin to formulate an ideological view of Zionism that might represent a consensus among the majority of those Jews who identify Jewishly through national organizations and movements, whether secular or religious. Hence, although the following emendation of Zionism will be unacceptable to some — both in Israel and the Diaspora — it is in my opinion one of the many possible interpretations of the Jerusalem Programme[2] of the World Zionist Organization.

The aim of Zionism is to ensure the continued creative survival of the Jewish people as one people — both in the Diaspora and in Israel. The function of the Jewish state is central in this regard for three reasons. Firstly, we have the triple

---

1. **TO THE 29TH ZIONIST CONGRESS**, Published in *Midstream*, February 1978.
2. *The Jerusalem Programme*, An Analysis of the New Zionist Platform, World Zionist Organization, Jerusalem, 1970, pp. 3-5.

bond (for secularists) or triple covenant (for the religious) which constitutes the core of Judaism — the link between the Jewish people, the Torah (cultural heritage for secularists) and the Land of Israel. Secondly, at least one Jewish center where it is politically possible to develop autonomous social and political institutions up to and including statehood is necessary to enable the Jewish people to contend creatively as a community with the impact of the modern age. Thirdly, only within such a Jewish center can the national language of the Jewish people, Hebrew, be a living medium within which Jewish culture can continue to evolve.

Such a definition of Zionism purposely leaves more questions with regard to Israel-Diaspora relations unanswered than it answers, and so it should! After all, the spectrum of views on the problematics of Jewish existence both in Israel and in the Diaspora would itself presumably be the focus of deliberation within Zionism. Therefore, there is no need for full agreement on the practical implications of the centrality of Israel. The Zionist movement would presumably develop a much greater cultural emphasis — i.e., programs based on the unity of the Jewish people that give expression to and heighten Jewish-Zionist commitment. Such commitment would be valid whether expressed in Israel or the Diaspora. While one cannot rule out groups within Zionism that will continue to demand *Aliyah* as a *sine qua non*, the normative approach would eventually be that *Aliyah* is an individual decision and valued act which Zionism has a special responsibility to encourage and support. It would become a primary task of Jewish-Zionist education to afford the individual with the possibility of realistically weighing the options of Jewish commitment and self-realization at an appropriate age.

Are Israel and the Diaspora Equal?

Would this make the Diaspora "equal" to Israel? The answer would be a qualified "yes." Within a Zionist framework predicated upon this very broad ideology, the "political right" of committed Zionists whether in Israel or the Diaspora, insofar as world Jewish affairs are concerned, would be equal in a formal sense. I say qualified "yes" because the political questions raised by even a qualified "yes" have no precedent in contemporary affairs. The Jewish people is unique and, hence, so is the problem. For example, actions (or the lack of them) by the political state Israel can be perceived as affecting the possibility of continued creative Jewish survival. But what is to be the *modus operandi* of Diaspora Zionist input into the affairs of the Jewish state? Similarly, no less significant (even though much less publicized) is the concern of Israeli Zionists (in the sense defined above) with regard to voicing their views effectively with regard to internal Diaspora Jewish affairs and not just the Diaspora's attitude to Israel.

On the other hand, as distinct from possible formal political equality, Zionism does and always will imply a *potential* of cultural inequality between the Diaspora and Israel. Arthur Hertzberg has noted that:

> In no version of Zionist thought is it possible to assert the notion of the co-equality of Israel and the Diaspora, *not even of a Diaspora on which Israel may be overdependent* (my italics — ML). To assert the paradigm of "Jerusalem and Babylonia" is to maintain that there is no difference between living in one's own language and existing, even in power and freedom, in a culture such as the American, which may be unique in not being alien to Jews, but which certainly is not totally one's own.[1]

After all, every Jewish child in Israel does attend Hebrew Day School for a minimum of nine years with Bible, Jewish history and literature as mandatory subjects. The fact that sometimes these subjects are taught in an Israelocentric way that can be problematic for Israel-Diaspora relations hardly detracts from this basic point.

An equally significant point (generally unappreciated in the Diaspora) is the imprinting of the *Eretz Yisrael* landscape — historical, biological and geological on the psyche of the young Israelis. This leads to a *potential* for total Jewish identity totally outside the scope of Diaspora Jewish emotional experience. There has also been in the past the potential to excise the Jewish component deliberately from such identity with the land. But here we speak of Israeli Zionism and not Canaanism. As Eli Schweid has pointed out, many sensitive young Israelis attempt (unconsciously) to subsume all their Jewish identity in love for the land.[2]

The bond with the land is partly a result of the fact that only in Israel does a real Jewish *rural* ecology exist. But it is also catalyzed by the deliberate policy of formal and informal education which systematically integrates field trips and excursions through the entire country into the educational experience. The mass phenomenon of *Yediat Haaretz* (knowledge of the land) gives expression to the infatuation with physical contact with the landscape of *Eretz Yisrael*, its geography, its flora and fauna, and its archeological remains, including their links to Jewish history and tradition. If you will — there is the possibility of a cosmic

---

1. Arthur Hertzberg, "Reflections on Zionism Today," *Forum*, 1976 (2) 25, World Zionist Organization, Jerusalem, p. 34.
2. Eli Schweid, "Ahavat Nof Vezikat Moledet," *Shdemot* 43, Summer 1971 (Hebrew).

unity to one's Jewish identity in Israel, which has absolutely no counterpart in Diaspora Jewish life.

Hence, ideologically, a Zionist perspective would have to conclude that there is a latent and perhaps at present actual cultural inequality between Israel and the Diaspora, when the two are juxtaposed. But all of this is *relative* and not absolute. There are clearly many individuals in the Diaspora whose Zionist Jewish identity and commitment will be greater than that of many Israelis. Nor does this formulation rule out or negate the possibility for Jewish creativity in the Diaspora, which can indeed inform and enrich Israel. Actually, most of the ideals that shaped Israel's society inevitably trace their origins to the Diaspora. But Israel can also have the potential for transmuting Diaspora creativity, in a way that can enhance and invigorate Diaspora Judaism even further. This is the kind of dynamic reciprocity which should underlie Israel-Diaspora relations — a mutually fructifying relationship which should enrich both communities (some early signs of this are already present).

The Anachronistic Politics of Zionism

However, even if the Zionist idea can be interpreted broadly enough to provide a conceptual consensus within which Israel-Diaspora relations can be expressed and developed, this does not mean that the World Zionist Organization as presently constituted can be a meaningful framework for discourse on Jewish public policy as presumed in my definition of Zionism.

To begin with — the entire system of elections to the World Zionist Congress which ultimately determines World Zionist Organization policy, is undemocratic. The World Zionist Organization constitution determines that 38 percent of the delegates shall be from Israel, 29 percent from the United States and 34 percent from other countries in the Diaspora.[1] But this is not all — the Israeli "delegation" is not elected at all! The WZO constitution states that there will be no elections to the World Zionist Congress in Israel, and that the Israeli delegation is to be appointed "in accordance with the relative strength of Zionist parties in the last Knesset prior to the holding of the Congress."[2]

There are two implications here:

1) The Israeli delegation is simply a "carbon copy" of existing Israeli parties.
2) No formal forum exists within Israeli Zionism for Zionist deliberation.

---

1. Article 17, Section 3: *The Constitution of the World Zionist Organization and Regulation For Its Implementation*, WZO Executive, Jerusalem, 1967, amended February, 1974.
2. *Ibid.* Article 21, Section 1.

There is an assumption that Knesset debates represent Israeli Zionism but in fact substantive questions bearing on world Jewish questions have very low priority in terms of the Knesset's business. Israeli Zionists have absolutely no way of expressing a vote on "Zionist issues" as distinct from any other issue. Are the ideological premises of Zionism as presented earlier acceptable to every Israeli (including Israeli Arabs who also vote in Knesset elections)? Does every Israeli by virtue of living in Israel automatically merit a Zionist vote? On the basis of recent surveys, a majority of Jewish Israelis do definitely consider themselves Zionists, but there is also a significant minority that does not.[1] Yet, their votes are "co-opted" for Zionism by virtue of their voting in the Israeli Knesset elections.

What is even more irritating is that committed Israeli Zionists cannot differentiate in their voting between the best interests of the political State of Israel as they perceive them and their perception of world Jewish affairs. (For example, those participating in a large protest vote against an Israeli Labor Government might nevertheless not want that protest to be reflected in a vote against the World Labor Zionist Movement at the level of the World Zionist Organization.)

In addition to the basically non-democratic way in which representation to the Congress is determined — in particular with regard to the predetermined ratios of delegates and the inherent farce of an Israeli Zionist delegation, we have a further built-in anachronism in terms of the party structure of the World Zionist Organization and its implication for the World Zionist Organization power structure.

The party structure originated during the development of the World Zionist Organization as the political means by which the aim of securing, in the words of the Basle Congress, a "publicly recognized legally secured homeland in Palestine" was to be realized. Political philosophies of European nations and nationalist movements extant in the early 20th century had a formative influence on various interpretations of political Zionism. The paths by which the homeland was to be secured and its society shaped, were informed by the ideas of liberal democracy (progressive and general Zionism), various schools of socialism (Labor Zionism), and by different approaches to national self-determination (Revisionism). Each party within political Zionism developed a network of affiliates in the Diaspora. Hence, we have the World Confederation of General Zionists (in America — ZOA); the World Labour Zionist Movement (in America — Labor Zionist Alliance); World Union of Tnuat Herut-Hatzohar (United Zionists Revisionists

---

1. Simon N. Herman, "Zionism and Pro-Israelism: A Social and Psychological Analysis," *Forum*, W.Z.O. 1976 (2) 25, p. 27.

in America). The tendency has been for the Palestinian (later Israeli) affiliate of each individual political Zionist movement to become predominant in determining the stand of its particular world movement. The end result is that today not only does the Israeli delegation to Congress have 38 percent of the seats, but also it is instrumental — through the *primus inter pares* status that Israeli affiliates have in each particular world Zionist Party — in determining the stand of much of the Diaspora delegation. (The major partial exception to this rule being Hadassah.) In summary, the political composition of the WZO is still determined by the various stances within the political Zionism of pre-State days. These stances may or may not have relevance to the State of Israel today, but they surely do not relate to any possible spectrum of choice in terms of the Jewish nature of the Jewish state.

The definition of Zionism that I have posited presumes that with the establishment of the State, Zionism has evolved to where it must concern itself with questions inherent in the Jewish state being a means to ensure a vital collectivity of which both Israel and the Diaspora are an integral part. This is not to deny that there may be political implications in such questions. But the point of departure must increasingly become "Jewish" ideology and not adaptations of Western political philosophies. Western political philosophy was useful to political Zionism as scaffolding for establishing the State and very definitely has a significant role to play in shaping Israel's emerging political institutions. But *Zionist* ideology and deliberation must increasingly concern itself with cultural Zionist questions.

Cultural Zionism as Jewish Ideology

During the first decade of its existence, the WZO was ambivalent with regard to including cultural (including religio-cultural) content within Zionist activity as distinct from political activity and practical work of settlement. The Jewish nature of the Jewish state in embryo was a potentially divisive issue. Any cultural Zionist activity might detract from the Zionist presentation of a united political front. Nevertheless, in 1911, at the 10th Zionist Congress, the importance of cultural work to nurture Jewish national consciousness (the Achad-Ha'amist view) was affirmed. As a result, the Mizrachi (Religious Zionist Orthodox) party crystallized, committed to "The Land of Israel for the People of Israel according to the Torah of Israel." (Those Orthodox Jews who objected strongly to Zionism's cultural involvement as an encroachment on religious prerogatives joined Agudat Israel.) The Mizrachi remained for the next 60 years the only party within the framework of the WZO which was defined by "Jewish ideology" rather than political philosophy adapted from the Western world.

It is true that a certain "Jewish ideology" was also latent among culturally oriented Labor Zionists, such as A.D. Gordon and Berl Katzenelson. As I have pointed out elsewhere, this ideology related specifically to the nature of the Jewish community to be created in *Eretz Yisrael*.[1] As Maurice Samuel noted, the fact that various Socialisms figured prominently in shaping the formulation of this ideology served to partially conceal it as an authentic product of specifically Jewish tradition.[2]

Katzenelson, the ideological "guru" of Palestinian Labor Zionism, from the early 20s to his death in 1944, was extremely sensitive to what he perceived as the indiscriminate secular-socialist onslaught on Jewish tradition within the Yishuv. However, he believed that this problem could be contended with only after the establishment of the State. As early as 1934, Katzenelson gave what amounted to an ideological promissory note on the question of cultural content:

> We are now in a period wherein we are engaged only in constructing the frame of the building. Our thoughts have not yet turned to furnishing the house, to its interior decoration. We are expending the greatest efforts to make the frame strong and spacious so that it will be able to accommodate all those who want to come in. We ourselves do not yet know how to enjoy living in the building. We have not known such an edifice since the days of the Babylonian captivity. We do not as yet have the leisure for profound spiritual life... but the day will come. Some day there will be many Jews in the country and they will give us no rest. What is made light of today — due to hard labor or to dulled spirits — will become a cause of great spiritual distress for those who come after us. And as we now struggle with questions of Hebrew labor... in time to come they will struggle with questions of our cultural fate.[3]

The current ideological malaise of the Israeli Labor Movement, whose ethos was so instrumental in shaping the social and political fabric of Israel, is both a cause and effect of not redeeming this "promissory note." It is also a major contributory cause to its political decline.

---

1. Michael Langer, "Zionism and Reform Judaism," *Midstream*, April, 1977, p. 30. See Section 1:1.
2. Maurice Samuel, "The Chalutzim," *Level Sunlight*, Knopf, 1953.
3. Quoted from Ephraim Katzir, *The Humanist Values and Objectives of the Israel Labor Movement*, Attitudes Series, World Labor Zionist Movement, Tel Aviv, 1974, p. 16.

It is to be emphasized again that cultural Zionist emphasis means a *Jewish ideology* — a Jewish world view whose point of departure is the Jewish tradition and history. This is not to deny that contemporary schools of political philosophy may supplement such an ideology secondarily in Achad Ha'am's spirit of "competitive imitation."[1] Of course, in a very general sense, Zionism could always be (and was) interpreted as a Jewish ideology. But the only formally Jewish ideology that existed in Zionism until recent years was Mizrachi Religious Orthodox Zionism and this fact was reflected by and confirmed in the status given to the Orthodox Religious Zionist establishment in the State of Israel. As the only organized political contender with a specific point of view on the political implications of cultural Zionism, Mizrachi has had a "field day" for more than a generation in extracting concessions from Israeli parties for whom cultural Zionism was a secondary rather than a primary focus.

The Emerging Politics of Cultural Zionism

But what are the possible variables within Jewish Zionist ideology — options whose origins lie outside the Western tradition and stem from traditional Jewish discourse? These variables are Jewish theology and *halachah* (Jewish law). The political implications of differing approaches to these variables are still inchoate stirrings not truly reflected in the institutional and political structure of the World Zionist Establishment (or the State of Israel).

The "theological variable" which has of late drawn the most attention, relates to the interpretation of Messianism in Jewish history. Mizrachi always viewed the Zionist enterprise as the beginning of redemption in which secular ideologies too (in spite of themselves) were an instrument of divine will. (The ultra-Orthodox denied this religious Zionist interpretation which they saw as *dechikat haketz* — an unseemly and sinful "pushing" of God in order to bring about the Messianic Age.) But today the events of the last 10 years have brought forth a particularly aggressive and militant Messianism which no longer sees fit to work in tandem with the secular appreciation of politics, insofar as politics is a secular art of the possible in human affairs. Hence, the theology of Gush Emunim (and in a sense, its Neanderthal expression in America, the Jewish Defense League) is to "push God" fanatically in the direction of Messianic realization of Jewish political hegemony over all of *Eretz Yisrael* conquered by the force of Jewish arms. This is in consonance with Gush Emunim's particular interpretation of traditional texts

---

1. Achad Ha-Am, "Imitation and Assimilation," in Leon Simon, ed., *Selected Essays of Achad Ha'am*, Meridian Books, 1962, pp. 107-124.

and Jewish history. Even more significant, in their Messianic theology (Jewish ideology):

> ...They have opted for a one dimensional integralist mode of understanding and regard *Western cultural influence as a threat to be warded off completely.* (my italics — M.L.)[1]

Gush Emunim is a growing minority within religious Zionism. There can also be little doubt that this disturbing phenomenon is a vital expression of a new Jewish Zionist ideology which is transforming Mizrachi and wielding some influence among elements of the "secular" public.

But perhaps of greater ultimate ideological significance is the second variable which lends itself to differing interpretations and this is the approach to *halachah* (Jewish law) and the creation of alternative non-Orthodox communal norms. Clearly, here is an area of discourse with implications for reciprocal influence for both Diaspora and Israel. Early signs of such a development are already discernible both in the Diaspora and in Israel. The affiliation of both the World Union of Progressive Judaism (Reform) and the World Council of Synagogues (Conservative) with the World Zionist Organization, are milestones in this regard. But while such affiliate status is a symbolic step for these major Diaspora constituencies, they do not as yet represent any real political influence within the World Zionist Organization. Real influence and power are wielded by the constituent political organizations whose roots are in the traditional party structure as explained above. The Reform Movement is now actively undertaking to achieve constituent status within the World Zionist Organization in order to further its particular point of view regarding the continued creative survival of the Jewish people. This would be a step for which there had been no real precedent in Zionist political annals for 60 years.

Within Israel itself the question of a new *halachah* has been gingerly raised in — of all places — the Kibbutz Movement. After all, basic to *halachah* is communal consensus. But how can one develop such a consensus without real community? Can the communal consensus reached within kibbutzim be seen as a possible basis for a new approach to *halacha* and Judaism? Rabbi Shalom Lilker, member of Kibbutz Kfar Hamaccabi, answers in the affirmative.[2]

The logical synthesis of these gropings for other than established Orthodox alternatives within the Jewish state is between Progressive Judaism and Labor

---

1. Janet O'Dea, "Gush Emunim: Roots and Ambiguities," *Forum*, W.Z.O. 1976 (2) 25, p. 46.
2. Shalom Lilker, *Kibbutz Judaism: A New Tradition in the Making*, D.H.L. Dissertation, Hebrew Union College-Jewish Institute of Religion, New York, 1974. Published in book form, Herzl Press, New York, 1982.

Zionism. The current attempt to establish a Progressive Jewish kibbutz is a para-digmatic expression of such a combination.[1] But such a fusion, if successful, would also be a healthy precedent for a reciprocal and dynamic Israel-Diaspora relationship. Reform and Conservative Judaism (and more recently, *Chavura* Judaism) have been Diaspora phenomena. Doubtless, as "ideologies" they will be altered in Israel to something different from what they are in the Diaspora. This was also true for the secular ideologies which were introduced from Diaspora settings. On the other hand, there is every reason to suppose that alternative forms of Judaism developing in Israel stimulated by the Diaspora will have in their altered form a further vitalizing impact on the Diaspora.

In conclusion, Zionism, both in the Diaspora and in Israel, will have to express itself in ways which speak from within a Jewish *Weltanschauung*. New expressions of religio-cultural Zionism are still stifled in the strait-jacket of a long obsolete political framework. There must be political equality for a Zionistically identifying Diaspora community within the world Zionist forum. This will encourage major Jewish organizations in the Diaspora to become increasingly involved in Zionist affairs. The ensuing interaction will surely have a salutary effect on Israel-Diaspora relations. The initiative for constitutional changes in the World Zionist Organization must come from the Diaspora. The prospects for such an initiative are good given the recent political changes in Israel which have weakened the existing WZO party structure. Major American-Jewish organiza-tions (in particular the synagogue movements) are maturing ideologically and are prepared to integrate Zionist commitment as an organic part of their policies and programs.

For the future, a renaissance of Zionism based on Jewish ideology both in Israel and the Diaspora holds the greatest promise for the rejuvenation of the World Zionist Organization. Only thus can the WZO become the unique and relevant political expression of contemporary Jewish corporate existence that we need today.

---

1. Michael Langer, "Zionism and Reform Judaism" *Midstream*, April 1977, pp. 34-35. See also Section 1:1
   — p. 30.

"Zionist Parties":
A Letter to Trude Weiss-Rosmarin[1]

While agreeing with the spirit of your editorial "Party Zionism Is Obsolete" (Winter 1980), it seems to me that you have oversimplified the issue.

Jews are a unique people and the Diaspora's relationship to the Jewish State is *not* analogous to that of the Irish in America to Ireland. If the Jewish State is to constitute a center or the center for *all* Jews, then there *are* aspects of that state's policy which do affect Jews outside of Israel as *Jews*. With regard to those aspects, Jews outside of Israel are entitled to a voice. The World Zionist Organization, with all its imperfections (many of which await grass roots initiative to be corrected) is the most suitable and *potentially* representative forum for Israel-Diaspora dialogue on practical policy. No other body has this potential.

Let me give a few examples which are illustrative, although not exhaustive.

a) The disenfranchisement of Reform and Conservative Judaism in Israel must be of direct concern to all those who believe that equal rights for all trends within Judaism should exist in the Jewish State.

b) The settlement policy of the Government of Israel is aided by funds mobilized by World Jewry. Surely the representative World Zionist body has the right to some say in that settlement policy. Ninety percent of the housing units allocated to new settlements last year (1980-81) were allocated to the West Bank.

c) Insofar as Israeli foreign policy can have an effect on Jewish communities, both in the "free" world as well as in lands of persecution, it is a legitimate subject for discourse between Israel and the Diaspora.

d) Immigrant absorption is a fourth area of mutual concern. If Aliyah is a central aim of Zionism, then the organization that is called upon to bear the responsibility must also have greater authority in exercising that responsibility. This was in effect one of the conclusions of the shelved Horev Report. The report recommended the abolition of the Govern-

---

1. Published in *The Jewish Spectator*, Summer 1981.

ment's Ministry of Absorption, and the re-establishment of a central Aliya and Absorption authority under the aegis of the WZO — Jewish Agency.

Each of the above policy areas exemplifies the implications of a mutually interdependent relationship between Israel and the Diaspora. We have not yet perfected the World Zionist Organization as a *democratic* instrument expressing differing approaches — tactical and strategic — in the battle for *creative* survival. One of our conceptual difficulties is the continued exclusive identification of Zionism with *political* Zionism.

If the purpose of Zionism was and is the normalization of the Jewish people — to make us "like all the nations" — then Trude Weiss-Rosmarin is correct. After the establishment of the State of Israel, a political party structure within the World Zionist Organization is not an anomaly. However, if the State of Israel is a means to an end (and not an end in itself), and if we believe in the unique interdependence between the Jewish people the world over and the Jewish State, then Weiss-Rosmarin's analysis misses the point.

If we accept the point of view of *Cultural Zionism* as distinct from *Political Zionism* then the purpose of the Jewish State is to ensure the creative revival of the Jewish people. Given this assumption — I know there are political Zionists especially in Israel who reject it — then it is unavoidable that there will be areas of mutual concern which will require institutional frameworks to express them. It is also highly likely that there will be different philosophies regarding the strategy for creative Jewish survival and hence different *parties*. This does *not* mean that such parties will necessarily reflect the Israeli political party scene.

Most of the Zionist parties are based on the assumption of Political Zionism. There are socialists, capitalists, moderate nationalists, activist (Revisionist) nationalists, etc. Religious parties can be said to have had a particular vision of *cultural* as distinct from *political* Zionism. The significant development of the last five years has been the rise of alternative cultural Zionist groups — Reform and Conservative.

Diaspora Jewry cannot infringe on the *sovereignty* of the State of Israel. But does this mean foregoing a *voice* — even an active voice? And what if certain aspects of Israeli policy are seen as *detrimental* to the unity and survival of the Jewish people, such as secularism currently leading to a crisis of *Jewish* identity and a large emigration?

Dr. Weiss-Rosmarin is correct in castigating Party Zionism. We must democratize the World Zionist Organization. In order to break up the party fiefdoms and to bring democracy into the WZO, we must have elections to do away with self-perpetuating oligarchies. We must also call for an end to the anachronistic way in which Israelis "elect" their delegations to the WZO Israeli elections to the Knesset determine Israeli representation in the WZO I am sure that the majority of Israelis today are totally unaware of their participation in the WZO.

Finally, for democracy to work, we need an informed and committed *electorate*. Ideally, such an electorate will support those groups that project a program for creative Jewish survival. It is within the pluralistic tradition of Judaism as well as within the democratic tradition that differing visions of our people's future will have legitimate expression in political groups.

A committed Zionist electorate within a pluralistic framework implies political groupings of some type to reflect differing outlooks within that Zionist commitment. This is the contribution that Reform and Conservative Zionist groups can make to the democratization of the World Zionist Organization.

Democracy, Religion, and the Zionist Future[1]

It is the thesis of this article that religious (halakhic) authority in Israel is not only undermining democracy, but, also, threatening the Zionist nature of the Jewish state. We will first examine the interface between the ideological assumptions of democracy as against those of halakhah and then comment on the implications of the current evolving relationship between religion and state for future Zionist cultural development.

I

"Government of the people, by the people, for the people" has become the accepted political norm to which the free world subscribes. The purpose of democracy has been defined as "a form of government in which the rulers are fully responsible to the ruled in order to realize self-respect for everybody."[2] This concept of self-respect is inseparable from the idea of self-fulfillment and we find a classic statement of it in the Declaration of Independence of the United States:

> We hold these truths to be self-evident, that all men are created equal, that they are endowed by their Creator with certain unalienable Rights, that among these are Life, Liberty and the pursuit of Happiness. That to secure these rights, Governments are instituted among Men, deriving their just powers from the consent of the governed....

Democracy as it is understood today is based on a number of assumptions, among which are:[3]

---

1. 1985, *Tzofei-Telem* (Hebrew). Published in English: *Judaism* 36:4, Fall 1987.
2. William H. Riker, *Democracy in the United States* (New York: Macmillan, 1953), p. 34.
3. I have adapted in part the summary of Zechariah Goren, *"Al Hahiloniut Ve-al Maskanot Pedagogiot Ahadot Hanovot Mimena,"* (Some Pedagogical Conclusions Stemming from Secularism), *Oranim: Sugiot Hinukh VeHora-a* (Oranim Teachers Seminary, 1982), pp. 177-185.

1. A Guarantee of Individual Liberties

In his essay, "On Liberty," John Stuart Mill identifies three areas in which individual liberty constitutes a prerequisite for a free society.

- liberty of conscience, thought and feeling; absolute freedom of opinion and sentiment on all subjects, ...the liberty of expressing and publishing opinions....
- liberty of tastes and pursuits; of framing the plan of our life to suit our own character....
- liberty of combination among individuals; freedom to unite for any purpose not involving harm to others.

No society in which these liberties are not, on the whole, respected, is free, whatever may be its form of government; and none is completely free in which they do not exist absolute and unqualified.[1]

2. Truth As Relative

There is no one absolute truth. Hence, there is no justification for any kind of coercion. The principle of tolerance and pluralism in no way negates the right of individuals to believe and act and preach according to their understanding of "truth," on condition that they in no way detract from the rights of others to believe in, and propagate, contrary views.

3. Rational Thinking

Rationality is the guiding principle of human action. This does not imply that humans are, by nature, entirely creatures of reason. Reason and intellect are to be mobilized in order to regulate emotions and in order to promote both the welfare of the individual and the public as a whole.

4. The Negation of Supra-Human Authority

There is no Supra-Human authority which grants special rights to some form of government (e.g., the divine right of Kings) or system of law (e.g., Divine Revelation). Hence, it is necessary to separate political authority from religious authority. Government is secular, i.e., of this world, and its legitimacy derives from human and not supra-human frames of reference.

---

1. John Stuart Mill, "On Liberty" (1859), in Max Lerner, ed., *The Essential Works of John Stuart Mill* (New York: Bantam Books, 1961), pp. 265-266.

This does not negate the possibility (or even desirability) of ideological and moral values stemming from religious belief (the "Judeo-Christian" ethic). However, no idea, dogma or doctrine, in and of itself, constitutes authority.

The American motto, "In God We Trust," has not been interpreted as granting divine authority to any individual or political institution where public affairs are concerned. Similarly, the closing paragraph of Israel's Declaration of Independence reads: ..."Placing our trust in the Almighty (*Zur Israel*) we affix our signatures to this Proclamation." In addition to being a formulation acceptable to all the signatories, the reference to *Zur Israel* (referred to as the Almighty in the official English translation) satisfied a similar need for a consensus value expression.

While religion may be perceived as contributing to the value consensus of society and state, it is the function of the democratic political process (and not of any authority purporting to represent divine revealed truth) to determine *public norms*. Furthermore, it is incumbent upon the political process to determine such norms without infringing on individual liberties.

Prophetically, John Stuart Mill wrote:

> The great writers to whom the world owes what religious liberty it possesses, have mostly asserted freedom of conscience as an indefeasible right, and denied absolutely that a human being is accountable to others for his religious belief. Yet so natural to mankind is intolerance in whatever they really care about, that religious freedom has hardly anywhere been practically realized, except where religious indifference, which dislikes to have its peace disturbed by theological quarrels, has added its weight to the scale...[1]

Democracy, Liberty and Judaism

Modern democracy is the outcome of social and political processes which characterize the modern age. It has no basis in Judaism. Judaism was never democratic, just as no other traditional society had democratic government in the modern sense of universal suffrage and guaranteed civil liberties. In ancient Israel, authority was (divinely) vested in the King, the Priesthood and the "true" prophet. After the destruction of the Temple, the Rabbis emerged as an aristocracy (at times hereditary, at times of merit) which collectively determined *halakhah* and what became normative Judaism up to the Emancipation.

---

1. Ibid., p. 261.

This is not to deny that the religio-cultural legacy of Israel was particularly rich in ideas and ideals which could constitute an ideological value-infrastructure for the development of democracy. For example, the separate delegation of divine authority to prophets, priests and Kings is reminiscent of (without necessarily paralleling) the separation of powers in the modern democratic state. During the period of the Second Temple we also have a certain degree of pluralism (not necessarily accompanied by mutual tolerance): Pharisees and Sadducees, the House of Hillel and the House of Shammai.

Rabbinic tradition interpreted the ambiguous biblical passage in Exodus 23:2 as an injunction to take one's lead from majority opinion. The Ethics of the Fathers (*Avot* 1:1) specifically states that it is man's task to set limits to (i.e., interpret) the Torah. The Rabbis even tell the tale of God Himself descending from on high to help decide a dispute regarding the ritual purity of an oven. A majority of the Rabbis disagree with the Divine decision even though God makes miracles happen to prove His point. In the end, God recognizes that His rule is in heaven and that He must leave the interpretation of His will to the Rabbis (note: the Rabbis — not the people).[1] The modern Jew can surely find much that is positive in this aspect of the rabbinic tradition. But it is not democracy.

The Inherent Equality of all Human Beings

Values such as the equal, intrinsic worth of all human beings can be derived from the Book of Genesis: "And God created man in His image, in the image of God He created him; male and female He created them" (*Gen.* 1:27).

In Judaism we find evidence that at least some of the Rabbis felt the tensions inherent in the Tradition regarding intrinsic human worth. The rejoicing of Israel as the waters of the Red Sea engulf Pharaoh's host evokes God's response in the Talmud: "The work of My hands is drowning in the sea, and you desire to sing songs!" (*Sanhedrin* 39b). In the same context, we have the custom of pouring out a drop of wine for each of the ten plagues that were visited upon Egypt. Surely this human sensitivity to the suffering of one's foes represents a value-orientation of universal and not just Jewish significance. There is much in the social ambience of Jewish tradition which is compatible with democracy and the spirit of democracy. However, we must refrain from confusing our proclivity to the democratic spirit, our tradition of messianic longing for a just world, with the norms of modern political democracy.

---

1. *Baba Mezia Nun-Tet* (59): Ch. N. Bialik and Y. Ch. Revnitzky, *Sefer HaAggada* (Tel Aviv: Dvir, 1951), p. 171 — No. 98.

The Concept of Freedom

The idea of freedom is a seminal contribution of Judaism to human society. The right to self-determination of all peoples, of freedom from subjugation to another people, are ideas that draw their inspiration from Moses' demand: "Let my People go!"

But Freedom as a symbol is shared by two rather different concepts. The modern one is based on the secular, humanistic, anthropocentric view of humankind — man inherently free and as the measure of all things. The traditional Jewish concept is conditional on the acceptance of theocentric obligations within the framework of a covenant whose purpose is "world-mending" (*tikkun olam*). Individual self-fulfillment has no meaning in isolation from a life of fulfilling the *mitzvot*. Are these two concepts of freedom, in fact, antithetical? As we will see, this is an open question in terms of modern Jewish thought and in terms of Israeli political practice. Certainly some creative *drash* (interpretation) is needed. In any case, it is hardly tenable to claim simplistically that as pioneers of the freedom-idea the People of Israel laid the groundwork for the future emergence of democracy.

Democracy and Halakhah

For some 1700 years, from the destruction of the Second Temple and until the Emancipation, normative Jewish behavior in all matters, sacred and profane, individual and communal, was determined by the halakhah. A line of authoritative interpretation generally accepted by Jews everywhere extends from Beit Hillel to our own day. The essential truth of this generalization overshadows the relatively insignificant nuances between Sephardic and Ashkenazic Jewry. Above all, the Rabbis arrogated to themselves the authority of kings, priests and prophets. "On the day that the Temple was destroyed, prophecy was taken from the prophets and given to the Rabbis" (*Baba Batra* 2).

Shneur Kopelevitch, a militant activist in the cause of Israeli secularism, has emphasized the anti-democratic nature of halakhah, stemming as it does from rabbinic interpretations of divinely ordained immutable and absolute truth.[1] Its features are:

1. The hierarchic nature of halakhah. Different status and laws govern Priests (*Kohanim*), Levites and Israelites.

---

1. Kopelevitch grew up in an Orthodox home and, after the Six Day War, joined a secular kibbutz. He is an instructor of Judaica at Oranim, the Teachers Seminary of the kibbutz movement, as well as a frequent lecturer on subjects cognate to this article.

2. The rights and obligations of Jews and non-Jews are not the same. There is also a basis for relating differently to different peoples.
3. The different status of men and women.

Hence, halakhah is not compatible with the modern idea of equality before the law. Neither are halakhic decisions made in democratically constituted forums.

We must not confuse the basic incompatibility of the halakhah with the *exacerbations* of the problem caused by the increasing rigidity of the halakhic process itself — especially within Israel's obscurantist religious establishment. Had the halakhah retained its original flexibility, the conflict between it and democracy would perhaps have remained latent for a longer period. But the evolution of the halakhic process itself has gone in the direction of increasing codification (*Shulhan Arukh*). As a result of the Emancipation we have the birth of modern ultra-Orthodoxy (Hatam Sofer: "*Hadash assur min HaTorah*"), which has effectively prevented adequate creative exegesis in our time.

Halakhah and the Modern State

The controversy regarding the possibility of governing a modern state according to the precepts of halakhah exists within the camp of observant Jews as well as between the religious parties and the actively secular. A most comprehensive and aggressive statement from the secular point of view has been made by Gershon Weiler, whose thesis is that halakhah has always presupposed limited Jewish autonomy and, hence, is not a viable framework for the functioning of a modern Jewish state. Weiler takes great pains to differentiate between an autonomous Jewish *society* and an independent Jewish *state*.[1] The Orthodox iconoclast, Professor Yeshayahu Leibowitz, argues in favor of the separation between religion and the state because it is demeaning for the halakhah to be juxtaposed with the secular legal system of the state.[2]

II

The Secular Roots of the State of Israel

The modern Nation-States emerged from traditional feudal society. An important corollary of the elimination or, at least, the transfer of authority to the Nation

---

1. Gershon Weiler, *Jewish Theocracy* (Hebrew) (Tel Aviv: Am Oved, 1976), (English — Brill, Leyden & New York, 1988).
2. Yeshayahu Leibowitz, *Judaism, The Jewish People, and the State of Israel* (Hebrew) (Jerusalem: Schocken, 1976), pp. 155-191.

State was the demand that the Jews divest themselves of their traditional society. This "emancipation" of the Jews from the authority of the halakhah in their daily lives exposed them to those same influences which had engendered secular humanism and the Enlightenment from the end of the 15th century onwards.

The modern Zionist movement, ideologically, was conceived in the womb of the Jewish enlightenment of the 19th century and became possible only when a critical mass of the Jewish people rejected the authority of halakhah and its rabbinical interpreters. The political Zionist vision as embodied in the Basle Platform of the first Zionist Congress (1897) was the establishment of a western, liberal secular state. Achad Ha'am railed against the concept of a state for the Jews "like all the nations" but in no way did he suggest that the Jewish values which he hoped to nurture should be expressed by authoritative halakhic norms. Within Orthodox Judaism, religious Zionism emerged and joined the Zionist movement. But the final aim that it envisioned — the Torah State — was incompatible with the vision of secular Zionism.[1] Even so, religious Zionism remained a small minority within Orthodox Judaism before the Holocaust.

The Labor Zionist movement, in particular, rejected the passive nature of the traditional Jewish community in the light of the crisis which began to engulf the Jewish people towards the end of the 19th century. It also rejected the oligarchy of the *shtetl*, based as it was on the oligarchy of *parnasim* and *hakhamim*. The founding generation of the future Jewish State consciously opted for a new Jewish society based on the equal worth of all as a central value and democracy as a concomitant principle. Above all, the Labor Zionist *halutzim* saw themselves as being "called" — in the prophetic sense — to realize the vision of social justice in the Jewish National Home. The renewal of prophecy by Man, not God, expressed the total rejection of halakhic authority.

Religion and the Limits of Democracy in Israel

The Declaration of Independence of the State of Israel says:

> The State of Israel will... foster the development of the country for the benefit of all inhabitants; it will be based on freedom, justice and peace as envisaged by the prophets of Israel; it will ensure complete equality of social and political rights to all its inhabitants

---

1. See, for example: Yosef Tirosh, ed., *Religious Zionism: An Anthology* (Jerusalem: World Zionist Organization, 1975), pp. 11-34, and, also, *"LeOfia shel Medinat HaTorah"* (The Nature of the Torah State) in *HaZionut Hadatit Ve-Hamedinah* (Religious Zionism and the State) (Jerusalem: World Zionist Organization, 1978). The writer, Yehuda Leib Cohen-Maimon, was Chief Ashkenazic Rabbi.

irrespective of religion, race or sex; it will guarantee freedom of religion, conscience, language, education and culture...

The State of Israel was intended to be governed by law, democratically enacted. It was not intended to be a "Torah State." However, the spirit of the Declaration of Independence has been realized only partially by Israel's legislative process. In a large measure that spirit has been stymied by the religious parties which hold the balance of power or are perceived as potentially holding the balance of power by the major political parties. There has been creeping expansion of the "status quo" (exclusive rabbinical jurisdiction in matters of personal status, extensive curbs on public and private amenities available on Shabbat) as inherited from the British Mandatory government which, in turn, had adapted the Ottoman Empire's policy of internal religious autonomy. The political situation in Israel has resulted in granting a new lease of life to an authoritarian vestige from pre-modern times. Laws limiting archeological and pathological research have been enacted. Regulations forbidding abortion have been tightened. The net result has been the curbing of individual liberties to the extent of religious coercion. No civil, Reform or Conservative marriages, divorces or conversions are recognized. No public transportation is allowed on the Shabbat (except in the Haifa area where it existed before 1948).

A number of additional reasons have given momentum to the creeping expansion of religious legislation. The passing of the founding generation after the Six Day War was complemented by the emergence of a generation outside of the tradition of pioneering Labor Zionism. While outwardly secular in behavior, this generation (to a large extent the offspring of parents of Asian-African background) is prepared to accept passively the legitimacy of some of the religious legislation. The dismantling of Labor Zionist schools in the early Fifties in favor of a system of "general" education within the framework of Ben-Gurion's "Statism" policy resulted in a general loss of Labor Zionist élan. On the other hand, a new generation of Religious Zionists arose from the Religious public schools and the Yeshivot which became the backbone of the *Gush Emunim* movement. They see certain questions of public policy (the borders of Eretz Israel) as "beyond" the democratic process.

The end result of these social and political changes has been *the emergence of a partial consensus on a national level that certain areas are legitimately exempt from the democratic process.* Moreover, civil liberties in the Western tradition are not always understood as being an integral part of the democratic process. All Israelis are deprived of certain liberties by law (e.g., civil marriage for reasons of conscience).

Certain groups face more discrimination in varying degrees — e.g., Arabs, Reform and Conservative Jews, various Christian groups.

III

Can Democratic Norms and Non-Democratic Norms Coexist?

Contradictory norms can generally coexist if they are not on the same political plane. There is rarely a conflict for an American Jew who takes upon himself the life of an observant Jew — subject to halakhic authority — and is at the same time an American citizen who demands and enjoys all democratic prerogatives inherent in such status. At the political level of the state such a dichotomy is more problematic.

The ambiguous message which the young Israeli gets is something like this: There are certain areas which are outside of the law as understood in democratic process. The definition of such "extra-territorial" status is ultimately a matter of political clout at the critical moment. The authority within the area outside of democracy is that of *poskei halakhah* and their authority is absolute even if differing rabbinical bodies differ radically in their attitude to the State. And, so, halakhic authority can be the basis for the Greater Israel movement and the Jewish "underground" on one hand, while, on the other extreme, halakhic authority negates the very existence of the Jewish State (Neturei Karta). This analysis provides an understanding of the ideological roots of "Kahanism." Rabbi Meir Kahane's basic contention is that, within the Jewish State, the basic rights of the Arabs are not equivalent to those of the Jews.

In effect, in Israel everyone has the democratic right to organize for the purpose of substituting halakhic authority in place of the democratic process and/or curtailing civil liberties in the name of the halakhah. The Knesset can attempt to pass legislation limiting the right of those who would formally propagate racism to participate in the democratic process. But if the purpose of what can be interpreted by some as racism is the fulfillment of a particular halakhic interpretation regarding Eretz Israel, or the status of Ethiopian Jews, then is it racism or is it halakhic interpretation of God's will? In the long run, the central question facing Israeli society is can two diametrically opposed norms — western democracy and halakhic authoritarianism — coexist in the same body politic?

Unfortunately, in the short history of democracy, all of the precedents where such coexistence was attempted, have been failures. Furthermore, the attempt to

maintain different criteria in terms of basic rights for different groups of inhabitants of the same body politic, or even the attempt to maintain equal but separate
status, has inevitably proved nonviable. The frictions generated by the coexistence of incompatible political norms inexorably leads to violence. The classic
case is the American Civil War. At Gettysburg, Abraham Lincoln had no doubt
regarding the fundamental question at issue:

> Fourscore and seven years ago, our fathers brought forth upon this
> continent a new nation, conceived in liberty and dedicated to the
> proposition that all men are created equal. Now we are engaged in
> a great civil war, testing whether that nation — or any nation, so
> conceived and so dedicated — can long endure...

A society and economy based on slavery could not exist within a political
framework which espoused the value of individual freedom. Lincoln's belief in
democracy was vindicated, but at a terrible price. Moreover, it has taken more
than an additional century for American Blacks to begin reaping the benefits of
what was theoretically promised in the Declaration of Independence in 1776. The
formulators of the Declaration (Jefferson) were not necessarily talking about the
rights of their slaves (or of their wives and daughters). But, surely, of all people,
we Jews, on the basis of our historical experience of several millennia, know how
words (even those of the Torah) can change their operative meaning with the
passing of time.

If we examine Lincoln's proposition within the general context of this century
we have no cause for optimism. Although a doctrine of apartheid can be viewed as
an anachronism, the fact remains that most people do not live under democratic
regimes. Nor is democracy perceived as the wave of the future. In many instances
the attempts to substitute democracy for traditional authoritarian regimes
(Russia, China) have failed and non-traditional, but no less authoritarian,
regimes have emerged. The failure of democracy in Germany after the First World
War resulted in the monstrosity of the Third Reich. Most of Africa and Latin
America are governed by non-democratic regimes. Of the major third world
powers, only Japan and India can be said to be in the democratic camp. Certainly,
in the Middle East, only Israel (in spite of the flaws which constitute the subject
of this article) deviates from the authoritarian norms of the region. However, are
we justified in assuming that Israel, the Jewish State, is different? "We Jews have
always been different" and so we will succeed in grafting elements of divine
authority onto a democratic polity, even if it has not worked elsewhere.

Our political capabilities have not been tested for more than 1800 years (since the revolt of Bar Kochba). Our "track record," politically, during the 250 years spanning the latter part of the Hasmonean Dynasty and culminating in Bar Kochba's revolt is hardly encouraging. The Sages commented that social strife and moral depravity were central causes for the destruction of both the First and Second Temples. Worst of all was the blind hatred engendered by the civil war that paralleled the revolt against the Romans.

> Why was the First Temple destroyed? Because of three things — idolatry (materialism), adultery and bloodshed. But the Second Temple — in which Torah was studied and mitzvot observed and charity dispensed — why was it destroyed? Because of blind hatred. Thus, we learn that blind hatred is equal to the three transgressions of idolatry, adultery and bloodshed taken together.[1]

Unfortunately, a considerable part of our political tradition was shaped by fanatic devotion to an absolute truth without any tolerance for deviation from divinely ordained norms. This is the political tradition which legitimates the total legal disenfranchisement of Conservative and Reform Judaism in Israel — better no norms than avowedly deviant norms regarding the interpretation of Judaism. Nor can we ignore the political implications of the biblical concepts of *Herem* (the total elimination of people and their culture as described in the Book of Joshua) and the mitzvah of annihilating Amalek. The direct or indirect appeal to such elements in the Jewish tradition comprises part of the "ideology" of nationalist religious extremism and widespread intolerance in Israel today regarding our relationship with the Arabs.

Political Options for the Jewish State

Modern Israel is politically rooted in the tradition of western democracy but, as a Jewish state, it confronts the relationship between State and religion. Nevertheless, fifteen percent of its citizens are non-Jewish. Furthermore, a small but vocal Jewish religious minority either rejects the state outright (Neturei Karta) or rejects the Zionist rationale for the state's legitimacy as a Jewish state (Agudat Israel).

What, then, is the commitment of the state to Judaism? What is Jewish tradition and who decides on the paths of its further evolution? (The Orthodox would deny evolution and substitute the term elucidation or interpretation.) A significant number of Israeli Jews affirm the responsibility of the state somehow

---

1. *Yoma Tet* (9), *Sefer HaAggadah*, p. 145 — No. 4 (my translation — M.L.). *"Sinat Hinam"* has been translated as "blind hatred."

to further Jewish values while they reject, on a personal and/or public level, the authority of the halakhic process to determine personal and/or public behavioral norms stemming from Jewish values. In 1958, David Ben-Gurion was queried by youth movement members on the place of religion in the State of Israel. The question was asked within the context of the "Who is a Jew" controversy. The reply was:

> If you wish to know what is the legal status of religion in the state then I advise you to refer the question to a lawyer. I will summarize what the relationship should be:
> 1) The possibility for every religious Jew to live according to his belief and to educate his children in that spirit.
> 2) Freedom of conscience for every individual to act as he wishes in his private life.
> 3) The bequeathing of the Hebrew cultural legacy, especially Bible and Legends (Aggadah) to the younger generation.
> 4) The celebration (*hagigat shabatot*) of the Sabbath[1] and the festivals of Israel (*moadei Israel*).[2]

We might say that this constitutes a minimum answer. A generation has now passed and it would be difficult to claim that this basic minimum has been realized. More to the point, this minimum can no longer be considered adequate.

The Separation of Religion from the State — An Option?

The ideological roots of separation between religion and the state in modern democracy are the secularism and humanism discussed at the outset of this essay. Any political process which imposes a religious position on its individual citizens violates freedom of conscience, a basic civil right. On the other hand, the state is the guarantor of another civil right — freedom of association for those who would voluntarily unite for any purpose which does not constitute an infraction of the law and which cannot be construed as violating the public order. In Israel, the religious establishment has not hesitated to use its political leverage to impose laws which, in effect, impinge on the individual citizen's freedom of conscience. Moreover, the religious establishment has done all in its power to limit freedom

---

1. Ben-Gurion's use of the term, *hagigah* (celebration), instead of the term, *shmirah* (observance), in referring to Shabbat and the Festivals can hardly be accidental.
2. This statement appears in a symposium on the place of Judaism in the State. David Ben-Gurion, "The Place of Religion in our State," *Petahim* (January 1985): 33 (translation — M.L.).

of association insofar as other trends of Judaism are concerned (political pressure
to forbid building permits, hate propaganda in the press, total exclusion from the
budget of the Ministry of Religion).

Social Process versus Religious Legislation

Martin Buber believed that the Jewish nature of the Jewish state would be
determined by the nature of *voluntary community* within the state — not by the
degree of ritual observance or by state legislation. His vision of "a renewal of
society through a renewal of its cell-tissue"[1] led him to focus on the potential of
collective villages (the kibbutzim) for spearheading a social process which would
create a Hebrew humanist society.[2]

The theme of social-educational process as distinct from political process has
appeared at many junctures in Zionist history: Achad Ha'am versus Herzl, A.D.
Gordon versus Ber Borochov, Chaim Weizman versus Vladimir Jabotinsky. But in
the past history of the Zionist movement the issues were not argued within a
politically independent state. In addition, historical priorities within Zionism
were such that the question of the Jewish nature of the Jewish state was left to an
indefinite future date. But in the last twenty years the question has become a
major focus of conflict within Israeli society. What concerns us here is not the
growing religious fundamentalism in alliance with nationalism. Rather, our
subject is a less well known and as yet amorphous trend actively to seek alternative paths to revivify Jewish commitment. This grass-roots phenomenon has led
to a new-old perception of the relevance of the ideas of Buber, Achad Ha'am and
A.D. Gordon as cultural, rather than political, Zionists.

*In order for nascent trends in cultural Zionism to bear fruit, the separation of
religion from the state may not only be an option in order to ensure Israel's democratic
character — it may be a necessity if Israel is to serve the Zionist aim of enabling Judaism
to express itself creatively within the context of modernity.*

IV

Israel as a Zionist State: Renewal or Halakhic Continuity

We have already pointed out that there are differences of opinion regarding the
ability of the halakhah to provide a legal framework and legislative guidelines for a

---

1. Martin Buber, *Paths in Utopia* (Boston: Beacon Press, 1958), Foreword.
2. Ibid., Epilogue, p. 139 and Martin Buber, "Hebrew Humanism" (1942), *Israel and the World* (New York: Schocken, 1963), p. 240.

modern democratic state. But it would seem that the more central question *from a Zionist point of view* is: What right does the religious Establishment have to determine Jewish norms in the National Home of *all* the Jewish people according to theocentric absolutist and, hence, non-democratic principles? Only 15% of the electorate casts its ballots for the religious parties even though twice that number may be observant. But all of the major parties have been willing to trade off the basic civil rights and liberties of at least part of the citizens in order not to alienate those who might give them the balance of power.

Moreover, *if Zionism means a commitment to ensure the continued creativity of the Jewish people in the modern age, and if Israel's Zionist purpose is to constitute a means to that end, then legally straitjacketing the Jewish National Home into the halakhic mold is, in effect, a betrayal of that Zionism.* Unfortunately, the major Israeli political parties of today function, ideologically, on the basis of political Zionism alone — i.e., ensuring the physical existence of the State "like all the Nations." Religious Zionism (or even non- or anti-Zionist religion) remains the legitimate arbiter of Israel's cultural fate as determined by secular law of the Jewish state.

Ideological Sources for Cultural Zionism

Are there ideological sources for cultural Zionism outside of Orthodoxy — foci of commitment to the renewal of the Jewish heritage without *a priori* halakhic limitations.

We tend to forget that over a period of a century and a half the Jewish people has developed alternatives to halakhah as the basis of legitimate authority in Judaism. During this time two movements arose which rejected the priestly-rabbinic monopoly and declared that emancipation implied the renewal of prophecy and an age of *Tikkun Olam* (world-mending) mediated by the free will of humankind. Both of these movements are a part of the post-emancipatory Jewish heritage which assimilated democratic values and norms of civil and political behavior.

From the first half of the 19th century, the Reform movement claimed that, in order to stem mass assimilation and in order to adapt to changed socio-political circumstances, rabbinic Judaism would have to be re-formed both in substance and in process. Three generations later, at the beginning of the 20th century there arose the pioneering Labor Zionist movement which rejected traditional Jewish society as a whole and opted for self-realization by building a society based on the prophetic vision of social justice in Eretz Israel.

The ideological roots of these two movements differ. The Reform movement drew on liberalism and humanism in its approach to Judaism and rejected the Jewish particularism which led to Zionism. The Labor Zionist movement rejected religion, as such, and utilized various socialist rationales, in part utopian, in part Marxist, as guidelines for its version of building the Jewish National Home. Reform Judaism and Labor Zionism were both movements of *Tikkun* and, in a sense, mirror images of each other: Reform affirmed religion while demanding fundamental changes within it but rejected community and peoplehood; Labor Zionism affirmed Jewish peoplehood and community but demanded fundamental changes in its ecology while rejecting religion. Complex historical circumstances beyond the scope of this essay prevented these two movements from becoming alternatives to rabbinic Judaism in Israel.[1] But today we are witnessing an as yet inchoate groping of elements from both of these movements in the direction of a synthesis.[2] Within non-establishment Labor Zionism voices are being raised demanding cultural initiatives and denying the inherited *status quo* of exclusive Rabbinic legitimacy.[3]

In short, for the first time we are witnessing a potential challenge to Rabbinic Judaism in Israel on the ideological basis of a cultural Zionism, which has an avowed commitment to Judaism and its symbols and which intends to interpret that tradition and its symbols outside of the halakhic process. This new cultural Zionism perceives modern Jewish and Zionist thought and literature to be the latest accretion of source material for Judaism. No source — from the Bible to the contemporary (and very definitely including all of the Rabbinic) literature — is

---

1. Michael Langer, "Reform Judaism and Zionism as Responses to the Modern Age," in M. L., ed., *A Reform Zionist Perspective: Judaism and Community in the Modern Age* (New York: UAHC, Youth Division, 1977), pp. 3-17. An abridged version appeared in *Midstream* (23, No. 4, April 1977). See Section 1:1.

2. The establishment of two Reform kibbutzim, Yahel and Lotan, as well as a Conservative kibbutz, Hanaton, with the active assistance of the United Kibbutz Movement, is one example of this synthesis. The integration of a small Reform Zionist Youth movement within the Israeli Scout Movement (Zofei-Telem) is also indicative.
   On the urban scene, the proliferation of Judaism modules in the secular school system (generally with a Conservative orientation) is another phenomenon with a potential for long term impact. North American *olim*, many from Conservative, Reform and/or Labor Zionist backgrounds, have been prominent in initiating this trend.
   Two periodicals, *Shdemot*, the intellectual journal of the Kibbutz movement, and, in particular, *Petahim*, Quarterly of Jewish Thought, are in part devoted to discussing the issues dealt with in this article. *Shdemot*, with a different but related content, also appears in English.

3. Yariv Ben Aharon, *"Al Shloshah Shlabim B'Darko Shel Am Israel: Me-Samkhut Rabanit LeRibonut Leumi"* (Three Stages in Jewish History: From Rabbinic Authority to National Sovereignty), *Shdemot* (Sept. 1980, No. 76) and, also, *Shorshei Yenikah* (The Roots of Sustenance) (Tel Aviv: Efal Leadership Training Institute, United Kibbutz Movement, 1984). Ari Elon, *"Higiyu Shamayim Ad Nefesh"* (The Heavens Are Drowning My Soul), *Shdemot* (June 1980, No. 75): 11. Michael Langer, "Our Ideological Approach to Socialism and Judaism," *Shdemot* (English) (1978, No. 10): 59. Beeri Zimmerman, *"Oz L'Midrash B'Et Poranut"* (The Courage to Interpret in a Time of Trouble), *Shdemot* (No. 92, Winter 1984/1985): 16.

foreign to the modern Israeli Jew. But authority stems from individual conscience and contemporary community. This approach has been developed by a group of second- and third-generation Israelis centered in the Oranim Teachers seminary of the Kibbutz movement. However, in affirming their commitment to Jewish symbols, this new cultural Zionism has as yet not come to grips with the question of God — whether as being or as symbol. Nor has it really confronted the difference between *inculcating knowledge and an attachment* to Judaism and its symbols as distinct from *educating to commitment*. What is needed is: *a committed alternative cultural Zionism, identifying with all of the major symbols of Judaism, freely drawing on all of the sources — classical and modern — and compatible with norms of democracy. The task of such an alternative cultural Zionism (a committed alternative to Orthodox Zionism) is to evolve Jewish norms during the coming generation which can be meaningful to significant numbers of Jewish Israelis.* Hopefully, we have that much time.

If the Zionist purpose of the State of Israel is to constitute the framework within which Jewish tradition is to be renewed, then equal encouragement, or at least full freedom must be given by the State to all trends of Zionistically oriented Judaism. It is within this context that the delegitimization of Reform, Reconstructionist and Conservative Judaism is not only a blemish on Israel's democracy but is retrogressive in relation to the Declaration of Independence. *It is, in essence, an anti-Zionist act which attempts to throttle the potential creativity of alternative cultural Zionisms.*

Clearly, halakhic Judaism remains a legitimate and important trend within Judaism. Orthodox Zionism as a way of life has demonstrated its vitality — which is not meant to imply endorsement of its policies by this writer. It is the democratic right of those who are observant, in the traditional sense, to live in communities or neighborhoods where the law will protect them from those who would violate the Shabbat norms which they have chosen for themselves. It is *not* their democratic right to arrogate to themselves the position of exclusive arbiters of Judaism in the Jewish state — a state whose Zionist purpose it is to be a National Home for *all* of the Jewish people.

Zeev Falk, who is an observant Jew and a Professor of Law at the Hebrew University, has felt that the *legal* problem regarding the status of alternative trends in Judaism is secondary.

> The fundamental problem is spiritual... We need pluralism by
> virtue of our recognition that we are in the midst of a crisis so deep
> that only by mobilizing all our resources, everyone in his own way

competing to overcome that crisis... only by utilizing all our strengths do we have any chance of overcoming that crisis.[1]

If the state as a Zionist state has a commitment to encourage the unhampered and even freely competing alternative trends in Judaism then, surely, the normative educational curriculum, formal and/or informal, has the responsibility to expose the younger generation to all of the options, present and potential. Unfortunately, the fuzziness of most of the teachers' Jewish identity, as well as the fear of political repercussions, has neutralized the general (non-religious) educational system in Israel. In spite of a few promising steps it is questionable whether Israel's educational system, in and of itself, can grapple with the problem of Jewish Zionist identity and democracy in an integrated way. Perhaps the Kibbutz Movement, if it will at least in part overcome the problem of its own Jewish identity, might provide a lead.[2]

The Religious educational system constitutes a particular problem. Insofar as it is committed to inculcating halakhah as an absolute value, we have a situation where a substantial minority of students are being educated to a value system which differs from that of the majority. *Gush Emunim* has been one of the results of this process. The burgeoning independent educational system of Agudat Israel (propelled by a birth rate almost three times higher than the Jewish average) is a time-bomb whose consequences it is difficult to predict. In short, the educational system (reflecting socio-political realities) is creating a situation where two societies, increasingly militant, will coexist within the same body politic with the potential results alluded to above. If alternative forms of cultural Zionism do not strike root in Israel within the next half-generation it may be too late and the effect on Israeli society and Israel as a Jewish state may be irreversible.

In Summary

The western democratic tradition of civil rights and liberties that guarantees freedom of religion and conscience has not been realized in Israel in spite of Israel's Declaration of Independence which is, however, declarative only and not legally binding. The separation of religion from the state would further Jewish pluralism in Israel. It would make halakhic authority an option for those individuals and groups who wish it. Such separation of religion from the state is necessary if Israel is to realize its Zionist destiny as a crucible for the development

---

1. Zeev Falk, Remarks in "Symposium on Religious Pluralism in the State of Israel," *Petahim* (Sept. 1981): 20. The entire symposium is relevant to this article.
2. See footnote 3, p. 160, Beeri Zimmerman above, and, also, Shalom Lilker, *Kibbutz Judaism, A New Tradition in the Making* (New York: Herzl Press, 1982).

of new ways in Judaism compatible with modern thought as understood by the humanist tradition of the western world. We cannot afford to have Rabbinic Judaism (and a particularly recalcitrant variety at that) neutralizing the Jewish state as an instrument for Judaism to confront modernity.

Ultimately, the realization of the idea of the Jewish state, the development of meaningful Jewish content for this and future generations, is not something that can be legislated. Rather, as Buber and the Labor Zionist pioneers recognized seventy years ago, this is the task of committed social process, of community and perhaps of a community of communities based on free will and conscious of their Zionist *Shlihut* (mission).

The sooner that religion and state are separated the better for the renewal of cultural Zionism. The sooner we renew a pluralistic cultural Zionism the greater the prospect that the unique venture in human history, which began some four thousand years ago with the call to Abraham to go forth unto the Land, will generate a call that can be heard by this generation as well.

World Zionist Organization: Partisan — yet Diverse[1]

I AM A FREQUENT reader of Charles Hoffman's well-informed and discerning articles on Jewish affairs. I don't know what happened to him this time, but "WZO barons fighting over the spoils" (*The Jerusalem Post*, June 8) comes close to just plain demagoguery.

There are indeed abuses, and there is indeed corruption in the World Zionist Organization. Clearly, its functioning — particularly in the field of education — must be reformed. It is, nevertheless, the only democratic worldwide Jewish organization focused on the centrality of Israel that we have. I know of no democracy (Israel included) where abuses have not crept in. That is hardly a reason for abrogating democracy.

Hoffman in fact suggests returning authority in Jewish affairs to pre-modern times. The power-elite in the traditional Jewish community was composed of an alliance between the wealthy and the rabbis. That elite sometimes ruled efficiently, honestly, devotedly and in the best interests of the Jewish Community of its time. Nevertheless, it was hardly democratic, and hardly free of abuses.

In principle, Hoffman is suggesting that Jewish affairs be turned over to a new but similar alliance, one made up of the philanthropists and our new secular rabbis, the Jewish professionals. The latter, as in the case of the traditional Jewish community, are funded by the former. He suggests that "waste, duplication and lack of effectiveness" is a prerogative of the WZO departments.

I suggest that he study the Jewish Agency's Comptroller's Report on the work of the Jewish Agency Education Committee (as distinct from the WZO) issued two years ago. It clearly pointed out the danger of funding certain professional Jewish establishments which, in effect, police and evaluate themselves. Such establishments (under the guise of "professional expertise") are notoriously impervious to public input. Education is too important to be left to the educators, insulated from public review by funding from wealthy philanthropists and foundations.

The article completely ignores questions of ideology. It is symptomatic of the

---

1. Published in *The Jerusalem Post*, June 15, 1989.

times. If we don't have ideology, then we won't have Zionism. We will have an ever more sterile pro-Israelism which, in turn, will also wane as it distances itself from Zionist commitment.

Hoffman constantly refers to *Jewish education* without in any way differentiating it from *Jewish-Zionist* education. Zionist education is always Jewish education, but not all Jewish education is Zionist education.

In the free world, where Zionism is not a function of an immediate external threat to the physical or cultural existence of the Jewish people, Zionist education presupposes an ongoing long-term process of becoming socialized within groups where Zionist commitment is a norm.

The process of Zionist value clarification and value confrontation will always be inherently partisan (unless we mean some kind of blind reflex ethnic loyalty to the State of Israel) and it is such partisanship that generates commitment. We need such commitment among the Jewish laity of the next generation in order to ensure the continued creative survival of a Zionist-oriented Judaism.

Without such commitment (usually partisan), there can be no meaningful Aliyah, nor will there be a committed laity of money givers and money raisers in the Diaspora.

It is the function of the Zionist movement and Zionist education to ensure unity within partisan diversity. That has been the strength of the Zionist movement and, of course, a potential weakness as well.

THE FOCUS of Jewish education in the Diaspora is Jewish identity and knowledge. The additional focus of Zionist education means personal commitment and action to changing the status quo of the Jewish people.

There has been no *public* discussion of the educational rationale to be implemented by the proposed joint educational body (WZO and Jewish Agency). Jewish Agency officials have treated it as a purely organizational problem. Hoffman too does not differentiate between Jewish (including pro-Israel) education and Zionist education.

Personally, I hope that the WZO and the Jewish Agency will be able to agree that a rationale for Jewish education in the Diaspora today must be a democratic Zionist rationale.

There is no doubt in my mind that an overall coordinating body for *Zionist* education in the Diaspora should be established. There is no doubt that research and evaluation are necessary. But the structure and function of such a body cannot be dictated by the corporate mentality of a number of philanthropists and their professional advisers.

In a pluralistic and democratic society there are differing views of what the nature of Zionist commitment should be. The Zionist movement has served as the *relatively democratic* umbrella under which differing interpretations of Zionism have functioned. In recognition of this reality, one of the major developments in recent years has been the emergence of Zionist movements affiliated with Reform and Conservative Judaism.

These movements are certainly partisan, but their nascent political traditions are relatively untainted by the Zionist party politics of yesteryear. They are also much more attuned to the current realities of Diaspora Jewry.

My (admittedly partisan) belief is that they hold the key to formulating the new modus operandi which must emerge on the Zionist education issue between the Jewish Agency and the WZO.

There are many who feel that the ideological partisanship has no place in education. Perhaps this is true in the case of educational systems whose function is to ensure the continuity of an existing society.

But a *movement* education system is a priori committed to change in accordance with its ideas and ideals. This means competition for the hearts and minds of young people for differing visions of the Zionist ideal. It means an open and pluralistic Jewish-Zionist educational system in tandem with autonomous Zionist youth movements which provide an ongoing social and intellectual environment leading to Zionist commitment.

It is irrelevant for a coterie of Jewish professionals (highly paid at the Jewish people's expense) to point out that such a scenario is totally at odds with the reality of today's Diaspora Judaism. Of course it is. *It is the function of movement to change "reality."* Classically, this has been the function of the Zionist youth movements.

THE TRAGEDY of Zionist education in the Western Diaspora over the past generation has been that leadership at the youth movement level has been stifled by *shlichim* (envoys) representing Israeli party political interests. Hence a spectrum of ideas and ideals, indigenous to the new Diaspora generation and reflecting their Zionist aspirations could not develop — to the detriment of the present WZO. Funding for indigenous leadership with a good part of the money allocated to *shlichim* should have been instituted years ago. Nevertheless, the current policy of doing away with funding the Zionist youth movements (in the guise of not funding *shlichim*) is an example of some of the real issues involved, which Hoffman simply ignores. The substitution of professionally run value-neutral programs (even in the format of an Israel experience) in fact means inculcating pro-Israel attitudes and Jewish identity, but it does not necessarily lead to Zionist commitment.

Yes, there are serious flaws in the WZO educational effort. The competing Jewish Agency structure is no less problematic, and has in fact aggravated those flaws. The corporate-professional solution envisioned by Charles Hoffman went out when Herzl replaced Baron Rothschild.

Let us renew and revitalize the Zionist educational effort, by all means. But there is no point in throwing out the baby with the bathwater.

A Democratic Political Body for World Jewry: A Rationale and a Proposal[1]

Foreword

In his paper of June 1993, *The Israel Diaspora Connection: Reorganizing World Jewry to Meet the Needs of the Twenty-First Century*, Rabbi Richard Hirsch proposes creating "a new democratic representative world body to advance and enhance the interdependence of Israel and the Diaspora," which would "create a unified institutional framework which most Jews already believe exists." This paper concurs with Rabbi Hirsch's analysis and initial conclusions. However, the additional rationale and further development of Rabbi Hirsch's thesis in terms of operative proposals are the responsibility of the undersigned.

Why Do We Need Democratic Institutions for the Jewish People?

The current situation is inconsistent with the world of values to which most Western Jews subscribe, whether in Israel or in the Diaspora. The main exceptions are certain elements of the ultra-orthodox. In Israel we all participate in a political process which focuses on public issues such as the peace process and the economy for which those elected are ultimately accountable. In the Diaspora, we are mostly citizens within political frameworks with similar democratic processes. Paradoxically, the Jewish people whether in the Diaspora or Israel, deviates from the norm of democracy on questions of concern to the Jewish polity as a world wide entity. Both in Israel and in the Diaspora democratization of Jewish Zionist public affairs is an organizational prerequisite for *Tikun Am*. However, the question of democratization impacts on both communities in different ways.

The Relevance of the Issue in Israel

In Israel, since the establishment of the State, the Jewish community has been *de*

---

1. Position Paper for Seminar on "Reorganizing the Jewish World," Beit Shmuel, Jerusalem, Oct. 15, 1993.

facto disenfranchised from participating in the world-wide Jewish political process. The representatives of Israeli Jewry to the Zionist Congress, the (so-called) democratic body of the Jewish people, are appointed by the political parties according to the percentage of votes garnered in the elections to the Knesset. There is no general awareness among the Jewish public in Israel when voting in Knesset elections that they are voting for a Congress slate nor is there any political process of accountability to the Israeli Jewish public for decisions taken in the WZO/JAFI[1] framework by their "representatives."

The indifference and even ignorance among Israeli Jews regarding the reality of Jewish existence in the Diaspora is in part a result of their being cut off institutionally from issues within the Jewish world. It is doubtful if we can overcome the growing chasm between "we" and "they" that characterizes Israel-Diaspora relations if we cannot be joint participants in processes dealing with some of the focal questions that confront Jews today. Examples of such questions are: how should the institutions of the Jewish people relate to the differing interpretations of what and who is a Jew, what is the role (or should there be a role) of the Jewish state in the lives of Jews outside its borders, by what criteria should the Diaspora community undertake responsibilities, philanthropic and other in Israel. In Israel, political channels by which such questions of concern to the Jewish people as a whole can be confronted do not exist. Involving Israeli Jews in such a process would also make a salutary contribution to the Jewish identity of the Israelis, especially those in the younger generation. In effect, the direct participation of Israeli Jews in such a process would constitute adult education in Israel with regard to the meaning of Jewish peoplehood in the 21st century.

Democratizing Traditional Jewish Politics in the Diaspora

In the Diaspora, Jewish political process has remained traditional (pre-modern). The power elite of the traditional community consisted of the alliance of *parnasim*[2] and *chachamim*.[3] In our day the big givers and the professionals have taken over the parallel roles. Mostly they have acted sincerely and in good faith but it has not been democracy. However, we have reached the point in the Diaspora where it has become counter-productive to moot the "practicalities of fund raising" as the reason for organizing community federations and national organizations in their current format. It has become counter-productive because

---

1. WZO — World Zionist Organization; JAFI — Jewish Agency for Israel.
2. Parnasim — providers of funds.
3. Chachamim — "wise ones" (the Rabbis).

the real problem is no longer raising money but rather ensuring the continued creative survival of the Jewish community in the Diaspora.

The findings of the 1990 National Jewish Population Study conducted by the Council of Jewish Federations clearly point to a process of accelerating disintegration within the largest Diaspora community — that of the United States. The well publicized phenomenon of 50% plus intermarriage among those coming of age today should not be seen as the cause of this disintegration. Intermarriage is only one of a number of *symptoms* of a situation where almost total lack of external constraints to assimilation combine with an absence of internal motivation to invest resources (time, money, energy) in order to ensure meaningful Jewish continuity in the next generation. Judaism and the Jewish people are not a priority.

The problem is not money; it is motivation. No matter that Jewish professionals (the *chachamim*) are among the highest paid public service professionals in the world. No matter that we have marginal success in ensuring Jewish identity among a small number by means of Israel experiences, summer camps and Jewish Day Schools. *We have failed to ensure commitment and involvement as distinct from passive identity among the majority of Diaspora Jewry.* For a growing number of those identifying passively as Jews, Judaism simply has no significant priority in their day to day lives. The well of Jewish voluntarism needed to maintain Jewish family and Jewish commitment as viable entities in the contemporary reality of Western society is drying up. The demographic situation is that a declining number of young Jews who care less and less are to be saddled with the task of maintaining a viable community with a rapidly aging population.

Unfortunately the internal structure of the Jewish community has become a significant factor in exacerbating the problem. Transposing the culture of the corporate board room into the realm of community affairs has further alienated the widening margin of the weakly affiliated. "Baal Hameah Hu Baal Hadeah"[1] may have been a functionally adequate way to run community affairs in the previous generation whose motivation for remaining committed Jews was a given. Currently, this system has led to an incestuous relationship between the moneyed and the Jewish professionals dependent upon them while what remains of "Amcha," the ordinary, somewhat marginal and not necessarily affluent Jew, has no real access to community institutions except as an occasional consumer of services on an *ad hoc* basis. Jewish community structure has become counter productive to the development of an involved caring Jewish laity.

But worse is yet to come. The possible phenomenon of continued leveling off

---

1. Baal Hameah Hu Baal Hadeah — "he who pays the piper calls the tune."

of economic achievement in the upper middle class of Western society means that the present and future recruiting ground for *parnasim* (the wealthy donors) to maintain and finance the traditional politics of the Jewish community and its *chachamim* (the professionals) is drying up economically as well as sociologically and psychologically.

We have not evolved a culture of responsible Jewish citizenship in symmetry with what the surrounding civil culture inculcates in relation to the general polity. The lack of democracy in the Jewish Diaspora together with the growing lack of relevance of Judaism already noted above for those coming of age (many in mixed marriage homes) two generations after the Holocaust and after the establishment of the State of Israel have created a growing alienation from Jewish institutional life. Who needs it? What does it have to do with me?

The necessity for an involved and responsible Jewish citizenry as a prerequisite for the survival of a world-wide Jewish polity and as an important factor in giving meaning to Jewish commitment requires that we find a new mechanism to replace that unique contribution of the WZO to Jewish democracy — the Zionist shekel. Although the State of Israel inherited the democratic system inherent in the shekel — the politics of the world Jewish community reverted to its pre-modern form. It may be argued that in the past the current form of political organization within the Jewish community served a significant role in mobilizing community wide support for the economic support of Israel. Today this support in relation to Israel's Gross National Product is marginal. However, it would seem that at present the strategic interests of Israel itself would dictate policies more in line with enabling the American and other Diaspora communities to survive as viable and vital entities in the next few generations.

THE PROPOSALS

Democracy in the Diaspora

The basic principle of one wo/man one vote must be reinstituted in Diaspora Jewish life. As Rabbi Hirsch has shown in his paper, ideologically the JAFI Mission Statement of 1990 has essentially become identical with the WZO Jerusalem Platform of 1968. It represents a consensus position of the vast majority of Diaspora Jewry (excluding ultra-orthodox enclaves). Hence some minimum contribution to the UIA[1] or KH[2] ($25 ?) should entitle one to vote at

1. UIA — United Israel Appeal.
2. KH — Keren Hayesod, fund raising apparatus for Israel outside the U.S.A.

the community level for representation to a new World Jewish Zionist-Jewish Assembly. The groupings in such an assembly, nationally and/or internationally, would evolve. The groupings might be ideological or community independent. Such elections should be held in the year preceding the quadrennial meeting of the General Body (see below).

Elections in Israel

For educational reasons it would be preferable to have elections in Israel to the new body on a particular date. A second choice would be to hold elections in Israel at the same time as national elections — there would be separate polling boxes in the booths for elections to the Zionist-Jewish World Assembly. All Israeli citizens of Jewish nationality as well as those with immigrant certificates would be entitled to vote. The problem of temporary residents would have to be solved.

Institutions of the New Body

A new constitution would be drawn up for the new body. While WZO/JAFI rules and regulations might be instructive they would not constitute binding precedents on those formulating the new constitution.

The general body (500 members) would meet quadrennially. The division of seats would be on the basis of the absolute number of votes cast. For the first twenty years the Diaspora would be guaranteed a minimum of 50% of the seats.

A meeting of the international council (125 members) would be held annually.

The full executive (45 members) would meet three times a year.

The inner executive of 15 would meet every two weeks. The 15 members of this "government" would draw full salaries equivalent to the salary paid to members of the Israeli Knesset. They would be politically responsible for the function of various departments and committees.

A Proposed Timetable

It would be fitting to schedule the founding Congress of the new World Zionist-Jewish body for August 29, 1997 — the 100th anniversary of the first Zionist Congress convened by Herzl in Basle.

Aspects of Zionist Jewish Education

* JAZE: Joint Authority (World Zionist Organization and Jewish Agency for Israel) for Jewish Zionist Education.

Synopsis of the Section

The articles in Section 4 deal with the subject of Zionist education. All Zionist education is also Jewish education but not all Jewish education is Zionist education — even if its orientation is pro-Israel. The articles relate to the issue of defining and educating to Zionist values which are not normative in the Jewish community. The questions are discussed from an ideological and professional (educational) point of view. The target audience is sometimes the young Zionist leadership and sometimes the institutional world of Jewish education.

From the early Nineteen-Fifties as a *Madrich* (youth leader) in Vancouver Habonim, I have been involved in Zionist Jewish education. Indeed, my doctoral thesis for the M.D. degree at the University of British Columbia, "An Adolescent Subculture," sponsored by the Dept. of Psychiatry, dealt with the social psychology of Habonim Labor Zionist Youth in Vancouver.

It was the late Professor Simon Herman of the Hebrew University, himself a student of Kurt Lewin, the founder of Group Dynamics, whose writings shaped my approach to the field of Zionist Jewish education. His unpublished doctoral dissertation (1948), "The Social Psychology of *Chalutziut* in North America" (MIT), has unfortunately been bypassed by two generations of Zionist educators. I am in debt to Professor Herman for the entire concept Zionist education as a dynamic process of acculturation to a non-normative subculture. Similarly, Herman's differentiation between Zionism and Pro-Israelism is fundamental to articles 3 to 6 in this section.[1]

In the mid-Eighties I was active for a period of time on the education committee of the United Kibbutz Movement (UKM). The absence of an educational and ideological rationale in the Israeli youth movements (symptomatic of the severe ideological anemia in the kibbutz movement) was leaving its mark.

MOVEMENT, YOUTH MOVEMENT, ZIONIST YOUTH MOVEMENT: A CLARIFICATION (1987) deals with educational parameters of youth movement from both an organizational as well as a philosophical point of view. SELF-FULFILLMENT & SELF-REALIZATION: TWO TERMS — TWO OUTLOOKS seeks to clarify what I believe to be a root conflict between Judaism in its cultural Zionist expression and the extant norms of Western liberal capitalist philosophy.

These were two of many articles I wrote during this period on kibbutz education.[2] However, the above articles stemmed directly from my involvement

---

1. Simon Herman, "Zionism and Pro-Israelism: A Distinction with a Difference" in Jewish Identity: A Social Psychological Perspective, Sage Publications, London 1978 — pp. 117-135, 140; also "Yesodot Hachinuch Hayehudi Zioni," Kivunim, 2, (New Series) December 1990, W.Z.O. Jerusalem.

2. See: "Lelamed Hashkafah Rayonit" (Teaching an Ideological Outlook), *Iggeret L'chinuch* 79-80, July 1987. "Tigbur Limudei Hayahdut B'beit Sefer Kibbutzi" (Reinforcing Jewish Studies in the Kibbutz School), *Iggeret L'chinuch* 81, January 1988, "Hachinuch L'Kibbutz" (Educating to the Kibbutz) *Shdemot*, June & October 1988. "Hanchalat Arachim b'Chativat Habeinaim" (Value Education in Junior High School), *Iggeret L'chinuch* 83, October 1988.

over the previous decade in Reform Zionist education. They were written in order to provide background for programs of Zionist value clarification and confrontation in general. But in fact, the intention was to create discussion material for Reform Zionist youth work in particular.

The Department of Jewish Education and Culture in the Diaspora

As a result of the elections to the 31st Zionist Congress, the World Reform Zionist confederation, "ARZENU" received the chairpersonship of the Department of Jewish Education and Culture in the Diaspora. Rabbi Henry F. "Hank" Skirball was asked by ARZENU to chair the Department. In 1989 I was asked by Rabbi Skirball to serve first as adviser and then as his Director General. I served for over three years, until after the 32nd Zionist Congress when ARZENU left the coalition with the World Labor Zionist movement — see Section 3. All the Departments of Education were soon to be integrated into the Joint Authority (World Zionist Organization and the Jewish Agency for Israel) for Jewish Zionist Education (JAJZE). What would be the distinct ideological and educational input of Reform Zionist thinking to this process?

This was the context within which I wrote the memoranda and essays — EDUCATING TO ZIONISM, MODEL COMMUNITY FOR JEWISH ZIONIST EDUCATION, POLICY GUIDELINES FOR THE JOINT AUTHORITY FOR JEWISH ZIONIST EDUCATION and THE MEANING OF ZIONIST EDUCATION IN OUR GENERATION. An abridged version of EDUCATING TO ZIONISM was published in Hebrew ("Lechinuch Yehudi Zioni," Kivunim, 2, New Series, December 1990, WZO, Jerusalem).

MODEL COMMUNITY FOR JEWISH ZIONIST EDUCATION was specifically formulated to include a geographic model (Metrowest, New Jersey experimented with it) as well as the regional religious community model. My hope was that UAHC Regions would define themselves as communities. The Center for Jewish Education (Reform) in London, under the leadership of Dr. Michael Shire, did in fact meet with most of the criteria and in 1992 was awarded the Shazar prize for Jewish Zionist education by the Department of Jewish Education and Culture.

Movement, Youth Movement, Zionist Youth Movement — A Clarification[1]

What is a movement?

The word "movement" comes from the word "move." The basic concept is to cause movement from a given social situation to a different social situation. In order for this to be achieved, people must be motivated and the system set in motion in order for this desired "movement" to occur.

Movement and politics

Aristotle defined politics as the science of human affairs. It therefore follows that a movement — which by definition seeks to influence events, and to shape society, or part of society, according to its attitudes and/or visions — will always be political. A political party is a formal political organization that proposes a platform of proposals agreed by its members concerning the desirable character of society and the means to be employed in order to move society and the state toward the realization of these proposals.

Movement and organization

The usual frameworks used to address and promote social issues of all types are **organizational**. They are based on the assumption that what exists is more or less desirable. Each type of framework — school, community center, municipality, army, state, trade union or commercial company — seeks to ensure its own existence and advancement through integration with other existing frameworks. Each body of this kind develops appropriate organizational mechanisms to ensure its correct functioning (bureaucracy). Bureaucracy ensures that the system is staffed by people who will run it according to the needs of each organizational slot.

    A **movement** emerges only when people experience a **sense** of spiritual, psychological and/or material deprivation within existing organizational

1. From: *Shdemot*, Issue 100, January 1987 (Kislev 5747), (translated from the Hebrew).

frameworks and within a given reality. Only if groups of people within this given reality manage to adopt a vision of a different reality, and to develop a **plan of action** to which they are personally committed, does a movement develop.

A movement does not force its activists into organizational slots. It attempts to utilize those who seek to become involved according to their abilities and personality in order to promote the movement's objectives.

However, any movement that operates over an extended period of time will also encounter the need for a measure of institutionalization, in order to create the organizational system necessary to ensure the proper functioning of the movement. Accordingly, the characteristic of a movement is not the **absence** of an organizational system, but **tension between the organizational aspect and the movement aspect**. In a purely organizational system, such tension is not legitimate.

Faith and ideology

A person who belongs to a movement is one who believes. For our purposes, it does not matter whether this faith is the product of a prolonged educational process or the result of a sudden personal revelation. Neither does it matter whether this faith reflects a rational and intellectual process or religious inspiration. The faith must lead to a world outlook that goes beyond the normative world view of the immediate environment. In order to create a movement, this world view must lead to an ideology.

Individual feelings of deprivation due to the absence of appropriate conditions to live according to a particular faith must be developed into a common position with others. The cry of the lone individual will remain just that (a voice crying in the wilderness) unless a group of people is motivated to take up the "cause."

Ideology is a plan of action designed to realize a faith and a world outlook in the present and in the future.

There can be no movement without faith, an outlook and ideology that lead to an action program.

Finite faith and infinite faith

The Christian theologian Paul Tillich distinguished between true or infinite faith and false or finite faith.[1] Any faith based on an objective that may be realized in the historical present (national or individual) in a final and concrete manner is of

---

1. Paul Tillich, *The Dynamics of Faith*, New York, Harper, 1957.

necessity a false faith. The vision of the Nazi Reich, which was supposed to last one thousand years, is an example of a false faith that produced a disastrous national movement. A true and infinite faith always exists as part of a vision of the end of days. It is true that a movement based on such a vision may undergo a process of institutionalization. The institution rather than the vision may subsequently become the reason for its existence. However, if the institutions exists in accordance with open democratic principles, it will always be possible to rekindle the vision. Even in cases when the institution suppresses the movement foundations, these may still have a chance to break through.

Types of movements

A movement may be confined to addressing a topical issue (e.g., Parents Against Silence[1]), or it may concentrate on a particular sector (e.g., the women's rights movement). Equally, a movement may be of a general nature, with a **general** world view relating to the entire social structure of a people and/or of the world. Thus, for example, the goal of the Zionist movement is to change the face of the Jewish people. The Socialist movement aims to change the shape of human society as a whole.

Socialist Zionism was a combination of the national type movement and the universal type of movement.

A Zionist youth movement

The Zionist movement emerged among the Jewish people as a reaction to the deprivation — material and spiritual or psychological — faced by many Jews due to the enormous changes resulting from the impact of modernity. In particular, against the backdrop of the disintegration of traditional society among all peoples, including the Jews, the Zionist movement called for far-reaching change in the "ecology" of the people. Both the physical location and the spiritual and psychological character of the people were to be transformed.

In the context of the history of the Zionist movement, the youth movement has been a voluntary educational and movement framework. The means (or, more precisely, the **path**) for realizing this vision is **self-realization**.[2]

The classic Zionist youth movement developed during and after the First World War, and was a general movement in terms of its national and universal-

---

1. An Israeli movement of soldiers' parents protesting the children's involvement in the military occupation of the occupied territories.
2. For a detailed analysis of the term "self-realization" (*Hagshama Atzmit*) see *Self-Fulfillment and Self-Realization — Two Terms, Two Outlooks*, Section 4:2.

istic content and goals. The movement's values and plan of action were drawn from its **socialist Zionist interpretation** of the travails facing contemporary Jewish society. The way to realize these values, self-realization, meant educating youth toward the vision of the movement in social frameworks that would continue to exist as an adult society. Thus as the generations passed and the Jews moved to the Land of Israel, a new adult society would emerge characterized by these corrected and alternative values. The social framework of the "former" youth movement would continue to maintain the new way of life as an adult society, thus creating *ipso facto* a new society. In other words, the way to educate toward a different society and vision is to educate through social frameworks which have a natural continuation in adult society. When the youth become adults, they then actually embody and become the reformed and corrected adult society in concrete terms.

The alternative path in education: Knowledge, experience and identification

Every society maintains a system of formal and informal education that transmits its basic values, norms and world views to the next generation. This process begins in the family, and continues at kindergarten, elementary and high school. In Israel, the army also forms an important link in this chain, the last link of which is higher education. At all stages, this process is subject to influence from the environment and from the mass media. All these elements promote socialization and culturalization to existing society; in other words, they help shape an individual capable of functioning properly within existing society.

It is obvious that this process is about much more than just imparting knowledge. The meaning and purpose of knowledge are absorbed by young people on the basis the **experience** through which knowledge is acquired, and according to the extent of their identification with the individual person responsible for providing education.

This is complex. It would be absurd to argue that is impossible to learn mathematics except by means of a positive experience including identification with the teacher. Equally, however, it is very rare in education for the elements (knowledge — experience — identification) to be completely divorced from each other.

Youth movements engage primarily in the establishment of alternative experiential paths. These paths provide an opportunity for young people to identify with their leaders, who embody (by means of self-realization) a world outlook that differs from the status quo. The following diagram illustrates this point, and relates specifically to the existing **organizational** state of the Israeli youth movements. It illustrates the alternative path branching out from existing society into a movement educational path leading to a different society.

Element/Institution	Figure (Role Model)
Family	Parents
Kindergarten	Kindergarten teachers
Elementary school	Teachers

Toward existing society		Toward an alternative society	
Institution/Element	Figure (Role Model)	Movement/Stage	Figure (Role Model)
Children's and youth organizations	Counselors	Youth movement: Junior sections (5th-8th grades)	High School age junior leaders
High school	Educators, teachers	Youth movement: Senior sections (High School)	Young adults from the "other society" Leaders post high school (pre-army)
Army	NCOs/officers	Nachal[1] settlement group (*Garin*)	NCOs and officers in Nachal, adult members of the alternative society
Higher education	The academic world Professionals	The alternative society	Internal leadership

Self-realization begins in the adolescent age groups

In many respects the junior (children's) age groups resemble the traditional process of socialization and culturalization into existing society. In symbolic terms, the transition from a "children's organization" into a movement takes place at the end of the eight grade (at the oath-taking ceremony) and the ninth grade (junior leaders' movement activists' course). This point represents the beginning of self-realization.

---

1. *Nachal*: An army framework which enables youth to maintain partial links during their military service with a view to encouraging their continued (joint) projects (e.g., settlement) after their service.

At this stage, the youth begin to be led by older youth leaders. Most importantly, they themselves begin to engage in self-realization — i.e., the new junior leaders take on responsibility for society by counseling the junior (children's) sections and by taking on responsibility for the organizational framework (scout troop, movement branch), thus enabling the alternative educational process to take place. It is not necessary for all members of the youth movement to complete the entire process. It is desirable for a nucleus of members who have been through the junior sections to absorb new members during the highschool period.

As mentioned above, a movement is born out of material and/or spiritual want. There can be no doubt that in modern-day Israel this distress is largely of a spiritual nature. With the exception of certain Orthodox Zionist circles, young Israelis lack examples of society that could serve as examples for those on the path to self-realization.

This situation increases the importance of providing role models **along the path to self-realization**. Such role models (e.g., post-army young adults) ensure the existence of the movement, while also engaging in reflection on questions relating to the path the movement should take.

Interaction between the movement and existing society: Dangers

The interrelationship between the movement and existing society can be seen as a dynamic field fraught with dangers in two directions. If the movement ideology is insufficiently distinctive and cannot be embodied in the personality of its leaders, the movement will be drawn toward existing society. While it will continue to maintain the name and the trappings of a **movement**, it will actually have become an organization. This situation is typically accompanied by a struggle for organizational existence, but an absence of inner ideological tension.

However, the other direction also entails dangers, namely that the level of tension with the norms of existing society will be so great as to prevent any possibility of communication. If communication is cut off, the movement becomes a cult. A cult no longer seeks to exert an active influence on changing existing society, but rather strives to **"save"** individual members of that society, cut them off from it and draw them into its ranks.

Brainwashing is a cult tactic, and is possible only in a framework that is cut off from existing society (regardless of whether this isolation is taken on voluntarily by the individual or imposed on him/her).

In times of socio-economic crisis, existing society may move toward the plan of action proposed by a movement that seems to offer a response to the profound distress faced by society as a whole. This was the case with the Jewish people and the Zionist movement in the wake of the events before and after the Holocaust. The partial realization of political Zionism led to the consolidation of the Zionist movement in the form of the political establishment of the State of Israel. The dream became reality! The question which then arises is, where will the forces be found to renew the movement tension? The answer to this question would seem to me to lie in the special nature of the Jewish people.

Judaism and Movement

The very beginning of the Jewish heritage was rooted in the injunction to "Go forth" from an existing society to a different society. In responding to God's call to leave his land of birth, Abraham was the first person to take on himself a mission in the name and for the sake of something infinite.

As the national leader, Moses caused the People of Israel to leave Egypt on the basis of their physical hardships, but he educated the people to become aware of the spiritual distress that had accompanied enslavement. Through its perception of unity, monotheism posed a challenge of peace and perfection as a vision for the Jewish people and for all humanity. This ensured that the course of Jewish history would be accompanied by an unceasing tension between reality and vision — i.e., between existing society and an alternative, more perfect society. The mission of the Jewish prophets was an example and an inspiration to those who challenge any reality that falls short of the absolute dominion of justice.

The belief that by living a way of life according to the Divine constitution as transmitted to Moses the Jews promote world-mending (*Tikkun Olam*) under God was the key factor explaining the spiritual strength of the Jews throughout the generations.

The social tension that strives and struggles to achieve change in the name of something better and more just is one of the great contributions the Jewish people have made to humanity. No other traditional society had legitimized foci of social tension. Socrates drank the cup of poison due to his belief that he had no right to oppose the existing regime.

In his essay **Priest and Prophet**,[1] Achad Ha'am analyzed the tension between the priest, as the representative of the organizational establishment of existing society, and the prophet, who strives to achieve an alternative society founded on

---

1. Achad Ha'am, *Priest and Prophet* (1893), in Leon Simon (ed.), *Selected Essays of Achad Ha'am*, Jewish Publication Society of America, 1962, Reprint, p. 125.

absolute justice. According to Achad Ha'am, the destiny of the Jewish people as a nation is to strive to realize the prophetic vision, and to this end the people require a national home. In our terms, Achad Ha'am saw the Jewish people as a "movement" entity within the global reality of existing society. The unending mission to mend the world in the direction of absolute justice as reflecting the Jewish desire for monotheistic perfection is one of the main foundations of Zionism in general, and cultural Zionism in particular.

The axes of movement tension may be summarized as follows:

Existing society	←——————→	Alternative society
The family of nations	←——————→	Israel
Priesthood	←——————→	Prophecy
Organization/Establishment	←——————→	Movement

It would seem that the Zionist movement is currently largely synonymous with the establishment of the State of Israel.

There is also a danger that the state may come to be seen as the goal in its own right, rather than as a means for realizing the ongoing mission of *Tikkun Olam*. Does the partial realization of political Zionism imply that there is no longer any need for a Zionist movement or for Zionist youth movements? Has the feeling of need which generates a movement passed?

There is clearly spiritual need and ideological confusion among those who do not identify with a Messianic Orthodox Zionist approach and/or with Jewish nationalism as a total message. The socialist movement as the sole, or even the main, element in a philosophy of the pan-human mend has proved a disappointment.

For the founders of Israeli society, who had a solid grounding in Jewish culture, Socialist Zionism provided a universalist path for national regeneration. The following generation was totally preoccupied with the physical struggle for existence. The reality of the Holocaust and the struggle for Statehood left no room for soul-searching. However, some of those in the third generation of Israeli society seek to understand who they really are. Many repress and reject the confrontation with their distress and confusion. They escape into the immediate present by limiting themselves to concern for their family and the pursuit of economic security and material wealth. Many Israelis leave the country in order to seek fulfillment free of Zionist commitment.

We are not only seeking to address that minority that is willing to struggle with the feeling of spiritual need. We also attempt, by means of education in a democratic and voluntary youth movement, **to develop an awareness of the spiritual vacuum by means of interpreting knowledge through the prism of alternative experience and identification. This then constitutes an alternative path to that of existing Israeli society.**

For Those That Seek: Self-Fulfillment and Self-Realization (Two Terms — Two Outlooks)[1]

Self-Fulfillment (Mimush Atzmi): Here and Now

Self-fulfillment is the right to a full life in the here and now. Man and woman are in and of themselves the end aim of human endeavor. This is so because of the intrinsic inner value of the human being. From this follows the right to life, to freedom, and to self-fulfillment. Self-fulfillment means the right to fully develop physical, intellectual, and spiritual abilities in the here and now on condition that achieving this fulfillment does not undermine that same right for someone else.

The fulfillment of happiness will find expression both in the realm of work and in the realm of love. Work is to be differentiated from making a living. Work answers the psychological need of the individual for self-expression and satisfaction through shaping, controlling, manipulating, and processing the physical, social, and spiritual environment. In general, society (or a part of it) will ensure that self-fulfillment at work expresses itself in a way useful to that society. (The ways in which society may do so will differ.)

In the realm of love, man/woman expresses his/her need to combine his existence with that of another or others. The prototype is the full relationship between a man and a woman. But, in fact, we are referring to the full spectrum of human experience that awakens emotional openness to be "with" or "part of" nature, the arts, an intimate group. Work is doing. Love is experiencing.

The individual's intrinsic right to self-fulfillment as a result of being the end aim and ultimate value of existence constitutes the humanistic inheritance of the fifteenth and sixteenth centuries. *Humanism established the individual human being as an end and not just as a means to fulfill God's will.*

Since then, many controversies in social and political thinking centered around the question: How can society be ordered so as to enable the individual to achieve maximum self-fulfillment?

---

1. Published in English in *Kibbutz Trends* 9 (Spring) 1993. Originally published in Hebrew in 1988.

How Do We Realize Humanism?

Liberalism favored free competition and maximum freedom for the individual in his/her quest for self-fulfillment. The responsibility for using his/her strength and abilities to fulfill himself/herself is placed upon the individual.

The opponents of liberalism point out that there is no practical possibility of guaranteeing equal opportunities for self-fulfillment. Hence liberalism perforce undermines (directly or indirectly) the right of someone else to self-fulfillment.

Private Versus Public Responsibility

The *rationale of socialism* in attempting to relate to the inadequacies of liberalism is *that the responsibility for ensuring maximum self-fulfillment is a public matter,* that is, the general responsibility of society and government.

Critics of socialism claim that this approach necessarily leads to a limitation of the individual's freedom and is therefore unacceptable.

Where is the Focus of Public Authority?

Centralist socialism believes that public responsibility should be expressed through the central authority. (This is a common denominator for both democratic socialism and totalitarian socialism.)

Decentralist (anarchistic) socialism claims that the collective responsibility has to be expressed through a voluntary and egalitarian community of mutual responsibility. The state should constitute the minimal national framework necessary for supporting such an arrangement of voluntary community associations. Otherwise a state bureaucracy (a "New Class") will inevitably arise and become oppressive.

Centralist socialism rails against such a "Utopian" solution, which, in its view, is impossible to bring about in our modern complex world.

The centralist (anarchistic) socialist response is that the community of true partnership is the necessary crucible for creating the prototypes of human relationships that ultimately ensure both freedom of the individual and collective responsibility for self-fulfillment. Only in a community framework reflecting the idea of mutuality in human relationships will it be possible to combine the realm of work with the realm of love.

At the national level, the humanistic ideal of self-fulfillment led to the idea of a people's right to self-determination. Within this context, many national movements have arisen in the last 200 years, including the national political movement of the Jewish people — the Zionist Movement.

Self-Realization (Hagshama Atzmit): The Link With the Eternal

The essence of the human (created in the Divine image) can be realized only by melding one's life with the purpose of human existence — that is, on-going "mending" of the world (*tikun olam*). This is the meaning of what A.D. Gordon called *chayei olam* (life eternal).

According to Jewish tradition, the aim is for the sovereignty of heaven to become indistinguishable from sovereignty on earth. This hope for *tikun olam b'malchut Shaddai* is part of the daily *Aleinu* prayer.

Just as the human's intrinsic value confers upon him/her the right to self-fulfillment, so does it impose the obligation to live a life of purpose. Without a link to the eternal (or perhaps — without being a link in an eternal process), momentary self-fulfillment is meaningless in truly human terms (as distinct from the animal-existential). For this reason, self-realization calls for a dimension of work and love beyond the dimension of the here and now (*chayei sha-ah*). Without denying the validity of the finite, self-realization relates to the infinite and eternal — *chayei olam*.

Only through social existence of full togetherness, "shared land, shared work, a shared way of life, shared faith" (Buber), can we realize fleeting expressions of those relationships between people that herald the realization of the Eternal in the here and now.

It is the mission of humankind and the human community to live lives of self-fulfillment that are also self-realization. This is the significance of "world mending" — *tikun olam*. The contemporary Jew, no longer sure whether he/she was/is chosen for this vocation, must confront the issue of his/her personal choice. The question is not "Are we a chosen people?" Rather, the question is: "What do I and my community choose?" Do we freely and willingly become part of the eternal challenge?

Alternatives to Self-Realization

The joining of one's personal life to the life of one's people as "people-person" (A.D. Gordon: *am-adam*) by working in and on the land (*am-adam-adama*) was the Zionist pioneering interpretation of how the prophetic ideal (*tikun olam*) was to be furthered in practical terms in their own lives (*hagshama atzmit*[1]). Moreover,

---

1. Self-realization.

the social framework for the practical realization of this vision was to be based on a radical interpretation of the equal value of all humans and their human endeavor (work). This was the essence of the *kvutza* idea for many of the Second *Aliyah* founders of the kibbutz idea.

But today the issue before us is not merely the confrontation between the right to personal self-fulfillment and the obligation (self-imposed) for self-realization as it appeared to the protagonists of a previous generation. Today, alongside a renewed concern with personal self-fulfillment (catalyzed by an ever greater feeling of powerlessness to shape events in mass society), we also have alternative paths for realizing the eternal.

The philosophies of the Far East tempt us to seek the eternal not through social action in community but rather by an inward journey to coalesce with our personal essence.

Christianity also offers an alternative. Christianity (and Protestantism in particular) justified personal self-fulfillment in the here and now because self-realization could be achieved only in Kingdom Come.

Jewish Self-Realization: Then and Now

Past generations saw themselves as commanded from on high to fulfill divine injunctions (*mitzvot*) for the sake of self-mending and world mending. From the belief in a Creator who commands stems compliance with commandments. Those constitute norms of behavior not necessarily compatible with the contemporary ideas of freedom and sovereignty. Thus we have the clash between humanism based on the ultimate intrinsic value of the individual and between traditional *Halachic* Judaism where ultimate intrinsic value is assigned to the divine commandments.

The Zionist pioneering movement (*chalutziut*) innovated and legitimized the concept of self-realization as a willed act on the part of an individual where he/she joins together with others for the purpose of self-mending, people mending, and world mending. This was the path to both self-fulfillment and self-realization. This requires taking on obligations that will express themselves both in the life of the individual and in the life of the community.

A community of self-realization will be one unit in a federation of communities. The quality of the relationship amongst the communal units reflects the quality of interpersonal relationships within the individual communities. The federation will be a community of communities that constitutes a base for a movement active politically and educationally in the propagation of and agitating for true community in the surrounding society. (This conceptual description is derived from Martin Buber's *Paths to Utopia*.)

The Zionist pioneering ideal of self-realization is a synthesis of Western humanism, with its focus on individual *rights*, and traditional Judaism, which focuses on the *obligations* of the individual *and* the community and where the rights of the individual stem from his/her obligations to fulfill *mitzvot* (commandments).

An example of this synthesis is our relationship to the value of freedom as illustrated by our redemption from slavery in Egypt. We were not redeemed because of our democratic-liberal "right" to self-determination, but rather our freedom was necessary to fulfill the commandments of God, the traditional norm for self-realization. The creative tension between rights and obligations in the call of Moses, "Let my people go that they may worship me" (Exodus 7:26), was inherited by the Zionist pioneering movement.

The Dilemmas of Self-Realization in Our Time

The Zionist pioneering movement internalized the synthesis between Western humanism, self-fulfillment, and democracy in its path of self-realization, though it would be a gross misrepresentation to suggest that this was accomplished without tremendous tensions. *Hagshama atzmit*, as a modern way of interpreting the purpose of Jewish existence, that is, *tikun olam*, was the unique spiritual and practical contribution of the *chalutzim* — and it became an integral component of the ethos of the embryonic Jewish state.

But in our time, the idea of self-realization has run aground for a number of reasons. First, because of our inundation by Western culture, we have become unable, at the conceptual level, to differentiate between self-fulfillment and self-realization. What was crystal clear to the pioneering generation has become blurred since the establishment of the state. Is the state an *end in itself* (national self-fulfillment), or is it a *means to national self-realization*? A basic tension has always existed within Zionism between national self-fulfillment (our right to self-determination "like all the nations") and national self-realization (the necessity of having our own political framework in order to fulfill our special obligation — whether imposed from without or within — to strive for *tikun olam*). A *state of Jews* does not need *tikun olam* more or less than any other state. A *Jewish state* cannot do without it.

The establishment of the state immediately "legitimized" the appellation "self-realization" for all those who chose the state as a career. Certainly, the personal motives of many of those who did so (and still do so) are praiseworthy. But that is not the issue. Nor can we avoid the ideological implication that for many, state-careerism was linked to the idea of the state as an aim rather than the state as a means for *tikun olam*.

Second, and perhaps the more essential reason in understanding our estrangement from *hagshama atzmit* lies in its being an extension of *shlichut* — mission.

Hagshama Atzmit: The Zionist Drash[1] on Shlichut

The idea of *shlichut* for the sake of *tikun olam* began when God commanded Abraham to "Go forth." For the *chalutzim, chalutziut* was their conscious affirmation of "going forth" to an alternative form of Judaism and Jewish identity. The *chalutzim* came from a totally Jewish environment. Their Jewish identity was not in question, but the abandonment of Jewish tradition by the original *chalutzim* left their children bereft of Jewish identity. *Chalutziut* became a symbol of the New Jewish State for many, but of a new Judaism for only a few.

A nontraditional point of view could maintain that every generation has the right and the obligation to relate to the symbols of Judaism in a way relevant to the felt needs of that generation. This includes the idea of God itself — which might possibly be seen as the word symbol for that state of ultimate completedness and harmony which is the end aim of *tikun olam*.

The secular Zionist movement of self-realization (*hagshama atzmit*) did not find or create an educational alternative to the *symbols* of traditional Judaism for inculcating the ideas of *shlichut* and *tikun olam*. In traditional Judaism, the idea of mission and purpose is immanent in the annual cycle of holy days, the weekly cycle of creative work and creative rest, and the individual's rites of passage. The intellectual rationale for a universal ideology (socialism) without these symbols has remained an intellectual rationale — as sterile as the sterility in many cases of Jewish ritual in the Diaspora that it sought to replace.

A community dedicated to self-realization is characterized by its allocation of resources both to working for a decent existence in the here and now as well as to sustaining the spiritual tension necessary in order to nurture a constant awareness and practical expressions of *shlichut* to promote *tikun*.

The function of traditional symbols in the Jewish community is their potential power to maintain that awareness, which then expresses itself in action. No less important is the educational function of the symbols referred to above.

---

1. Interpretation

Abandoning these symbols exposes the individual and then the community to the danger of a crisis of identity and purpose leading to that sense of drift and ideological malaise characteristic of the kibbutz movement in its third and fourth generation.

The resultant vacuum is quickly filled in by the values of normative Western society with its liberal worship of the right to self-fulfillment. Can an autonomous Jewish polity maintain itself in its historic homeland without active commitment to self-realization as expressed in the value quality of its social fabric?

It is the same question that the prophets asked and our sages pointed out.

It is not for you to finish the task — nor are you free to desist from it.

Education to Zionism (excerpts)[1]

Introduction

All Zionist education is, perforce, Jewish education. However, Jewish education as such is only potentially Zionist education — even if it includes Hebrew language study, Israel study and even an Israel experience. The substantive content of Jewish education and Zionist education may at many stages of the educational process be similar, but the rationale of Jewish/Zionist education — from preschool through college age — is distinctive.

A prominent Zionist educator has summed up the interdependence of Jewish and Zionist education: "Judaism without Zionism has no root; Zionism without Judaism will bear no fruit." This paper subscribes in a large part to the differentiation between Zionist education and Jewish (including pro-Israel) education made by Professor Simon Herman of the Hebrew University. The most relevant chapter from his book, *Jewish Identity: A Social Psychological Perspective*, Sage Publications, Beverly Hills, 1977, is "Zionism and Pro-Israelism: A Distinction with a Difference."

The development of a comprehensive model of Jewish/Zionist education is the natural responsibility of the Zionist movement. Ultimate public responsibility to this end is vested in the Zionist Actions Committee (Vaad HaPoel) and the Zionist Congress.

For some time now there have been ongoing discussions regarding reform in structure and function of WZO/JAFI in the field of education. An overall body for education has been posited and in the meantime, a coordinating committee of just the WZO educational departments has been established...

...Unfortunately, much of the thinking evidenced on the subject of any posited overall body has been the attempt to formulate structural reform without relating to essential function. This stems naturally from the absence of an agreed theoretical model of what Zionist education is and how it should function. This absence of agreement does not mean that there is disagreement; it simply means that no comprehensive model has been posited in the position papers presented...

---

1. Booklet published by Department of Jewish Education and Culture in the Diaspora (World Zionist Organization), April 1989.

...A RATIONALE FOR JEWISH/ZIONIST EDUCATION

A viable rationale for Jewish/Zionist education must relate to the following considerations:

1. The multi-disciplinary nature of the Jewish/Zionist educational rationale

a. Social Psychology — Field Theory

Zionist education takes place in a dynamic field in which all factors in the field relate to and influence each other. This is the basis of our rejection of the over-departmentalization of Zionist education.

Kurt Lewin, the founder of field theory, is often quoted as having pointed out that "there is nothing as practical as a good theory." Simon Herman, a student of Kurt Lewin, has applied concepts of field theory to Zionist education (see "The Social Psychology of Zionist Education," *Forum*, WZO, January 1962).

Jewish/Zionist education takes place in five major "fields" represented by the diaspora communities of North America, continental Europe, Britain and the former Dominion countries, Latin America and the communities behind the now radically changing Iron Curtain. Since these communities differ greatly in character, resources and needs, it is beyond the scope of this paper to detail the application of the proposed educational rationale in each of them.

b. Cultural Anthropology of Judaism

"Judaism stands or falls with the concept of the 'Holy Community'" (Jacob J. Petuchowski, "Toward a Modern Brotherhood," *The Reconstructionist*, Vol. 26, No. 16, 1961).

Jewish culture has always developed in structures of intentional community. Martin Buber (*Paths in Utopia and Other Essays*, Am Oved, 1982, ed. A. Shapira) and Uriel Tal[1] have informed this viewpoint regarding the centrality of intentional community to the Zionist endeavor. The recently emphasized relevance of purposive community to questions of Jewish demography (see proceedings of 31st Zionist Congress) have given added weight to this viewpoint.

---

1. Uriel Tal, from "Structures of Fellowship and Community in Judaism," *Conservative Judaism*, Vol. 28, No. 2, Winter 1974, pp. 3-12; also in Langer, Michael, ed., *Reform Zionist Perspective*, UAHC Youth Division, New York, 1977, p. 304.

c. Jewish History from a Zionist Viewpoint

Zionism is a part of Jewish history. In particular, it is the major response of the Jewish people to the impact of modernity. By their structuring, many curricula (including those of Israel's Ministry of Education) imply that modern Jewish history and the Zionist idea can be studied as discrete topics. On the one hand, the position of this paper is that there can be no separation between Jewish history and Zionist history. On the other hand, Jewish history, and modern Jewish history in particular, can be taught from a Zionist point of view. For example, Achad Ha'am's paradigm of "Priest and Prophet" (1893)[1] as archetypes and the ongoing tension between them relates to the essence of the Zionist interpretation of Jewish history. It is a model for an historical/educational interpretation of the element of "movement" in Zionism.

d. Educational Philosophy and Theory

Who can be educated to what? How and when do we educate to Jewish symbols? How and when do we introduce the context of Jewish/Zionist values? How do we reflect a Zionist outlook, cognitively and effectively to the child, adolescent, young adult, and adult? While these questions must be related to, a detailed discussion is beyond the scope of this paper.

Dr. Michael Rosenak has raised fundamental questions regarding Jewish education in his *Commandments and Concerns* (Jewish Publication Society, Phila., 1987). Although his focus is the question of religious education in secular society, the problematics mooted apply equally to Zionist education. For example: To what degree should Zionist education be explicit or implicit at given stages in Jewish/Zionist education? Is Zionism to be presented as a normative idea or is it to be a subject on which educator and pupil "deliberate" together? There will be variables in educational approach stemming from differing Zionist ideologies as well as those stemming from differing socio-cultural environments. Furthermore, the way in which youth movements relate to such issues may well differ from the way in which a formal educational network relates. In general, youth movement education in any given environment will be relatively explicit in educating to specific Zionist norms.

This paper does take a clear stand on the philosophical roots of our educational approach — humanistic, pluralistic, democratic. It also reflects a bias in

---

1. Leon Simon, ed., *Selected Essays of Achad Ha'am (1912)*, Jewish Publication Society, Phila., 1962, pp. 125-138.

favor of explicit education to Zionist norms at some stage in the Jewish/Zionist educational process.

2. An Outline of the Rationale

The basic model of the ideal progression of Zionist education takes place in a "field" of community. Formal education constitutes an educational learning community (beit chinuch) and not just an organizational framework for learning (beit sefer).

Informal education — camps and, classically, the youth movements — are perceived as frameworks of community within which socialization is accompanied by acculturation to Zionist norms.

Critical to the inculcation of Zionist norms is the process of identification with relevant Zionist role models. This paper identifies the absence of young adult Zionist role models indigenous to the Diaspora communities as a "missing link" in the continuum of role models from preschool teacher, school teacher at various levels, junior leader, young adult leader to adult graduate necessary for the emergence of adult Zionist commitment. (We do not rule out the possibility of Zionist commitment via personal search, but not all of us are made of the stuff of Herzl!)

Experiential education within community is to be complemented by cognitive education regarding the centrality of community to Jewish continuity.

The relationship between formal education, informal education and a necessary tension between them is seen as a sine qua non for Zionist "movement" as distinct from mere "organization." This tension is the heart of the dynamics of Judaism, lying at the core of Jewish existence and purpose. The systole of the prophetic drive for *Tikun Olam* alternates with the diastole of priestly continuity. Zionist education is committed to their mutually fructifying interdependent coexistence and seeks to replicate this tension in the personal lives of all young Jews. It constitutes the matrix within which Zionist value clarification and confrontation take place while on the educational path of acquiring Zionist norms.

a. The Tension Between Movement and Organization

Jewish/Zionist education posits itself as being in constructive tension with the Jewish community as a whole. Nevertheless, Zionist-oriented schools are perforce institutions for Jewish education and continuity. As such, they are charged with the formal transmission of the Jewish people's heritage. However, the Jewish/Zionist schools are expected to be open to Zionist movement process — in particular by cooperation with Zionist youth movements and by integrating properly structured long-term Israel programs as part of the curriculum.

The tension between formal education and informal (movement) education in the Zionist context should not be resolvable. To be more precise, it is resolvable only by the elimination of movement. This can take place in one of two ways.

The movement becomes unable to withstand the tension between itself and the adult Zionist organizational establishment and becomes youth *organization* rather than youth *movement*. The dynamics involve the replacement (for whatever reason) of indigenous semi-voluntary movement leadership by educators and/or quasi-educators from Israel (*shlichim*) or "professionals" from the Diaspora. In both cases they are not responsible to *movement* and are responsible to *organization*. (It is quite irrelevant if organizational headquarters are in New York or in Tel Aviv.) Thus organization co-opts movement. The re-introduction of indigenous semi-voluntary *movement* leadership is central to the rationale presented here. There cannot be responsible autonomous movement without this "missing link."

The other possibility by which movement can eliminate the tension between itself and organization (normative society) is by cutting itself off from society. It becomes a sect. It may attempt to "convert" vulnerable individuals but it no longer sees itself engaged in the outreach of an educational/political action program to change existing society.

The commitment to the rationale of necessary tension between organization and movement, between formal education and informal movement education must be shared by educators in both sectors. The development of indigenous leadership among Jewish/Zionist educators is likely to facilitate the process of a shared Jewish/Zionist rationale.

A particularly problematic focus of Zionist education, in particular Zionist *movement* education, is the role of the professional educator (*shlichim* or local educators). On the one hand, the professional may be capable of raising standards both in terms of affective and cognitive education. On the other hand, because of the absence of an organized body of knowledge regarding the educational methodology of *movement* education, the professional is likely to become an agent of *organization* rather than *movement*.

b. The Rationale for Pluralism in Informal Zionist Education

The question of pluralism in both formal and informal education has been dealt with by the Zionist Congress.

There are differing interpretations of Zionist realization. "Harbei Petachim Lamakom" (many paths to the Divine).

Formal Zionist education will take the differing interpretations of Zionism into consideration in the process of inculcating Jewish knowledge from a Zionist point of view. It is then obligated to give free access to different viewpoints in Zionism which seek to recruit young people into their processes of socialization.

Does this mean that formal Zionist education should tolerate "political indoctrination" of youth? Those who put the question in this fashion betray either a misunderstanding of the concept of movement or wish to co-opt it within the framework of organization.

Education is politics. Our sages knew it. Plato knew it. Tikun Olam means politics. (*Tikun Olam* is not to be confused with *Gemilut Chassadim*. *Gemilut Chassadim* commits one to social responsibility in the here and now. *Tikun Olam* commits one to changing the here and now.) After Bar/Bat Mitzva the teenager is intellectually and emotionally capable of confronting differences in values and norms in Judaism and Zionism. This is also a vital part of the youngsters' experiential education to democracy and pluralism in Judaism and Zionism.

In return for access to pupils, formal Zionist education must make one educational demand of the youth movements — mutual respect and tolerance. If the leadership in informal education has itself graduated from a democratic pluralistic educational approach in the Diaspora, this constructive interplay will doubtless be facilitated.

c. The Israel Experience

Ideally, the properly structured long-term Israel experience constitutes the centerpiece of the process of Zionist value clarification and confrontation. But as in the case of any other centerpiece, it has little meaning in terms of Zionist process unless there is a "before" and "after." In fact today the Israel experience often initiates the Zionist process.

Within the context of this rationale of Jewish/Zionist education, the elements of proper structure in the long-term Israel program, regardless of ideology, are:

1) Group organization and some group norms influenced by role models embodying a more evolved focus of Zionist commitment within the process of Jewish/Zionist education.
2) Cognitive and experiential consideration of additional Israel experiences and/or personal Aliyah options.

3) Imparting an acceptable (to the participant) intellectual rationale for his/her emotional affinity to Zionism.
4) Exposure to differing interpretations of *Tikun Olam*.
5) Projecting an expectation regarding the participants' continued involvement in Zionist educational process and providing skills and attitudes which can be utilized to this end upon the return to the Diaspora — i.e., some "leadership training" for all participants.

Model Community for Zionist Jewish Education[1]

What is Zionist-Jewish Education?

The purpose of this paper is to advance ideas for communities interested in developing an overall strategy for Zionist-Jewish education. The purpose of Zionist-Jewish education is to catalyze an ongoing process of commitment to the Jewish Community, the Jewish People and to its National Home — Israel. Commitment in a pluralistic society results from conscious confrontation and creative tension between alternative modes of identity and action. Zionist-Jewish education seeks to crystallize Jewish identity and commitment within the context of alternative modes of identity and action made possible by the Zionist endeavor.

Model Community — A Comprehensive Approach

The unique feature of the Model Community idea is a *comprehensive approach* to which a community will commit itself for a period of years.

This concept is proposed as a practical guideline for the Regional Advisory Councils of the Joint Authority for Zionist Jewish Education. The underlying assumption behind the adoption of an overall strategy for Zionist Jewish Education is that the cumulative impact of its implementation will be greater than the sum of the individual components.

The Principles of the Comprehensive Approach

The components of the strategy are a concurrent approach to three definable elements in the Community which can be related to as sub-communities:
1) The Young — Children, Youth, Students.
2) The Educators — formal and informal, professional and Volunteer.
3) The Parents — the parents of children reinforce the impact on the young, but they also constitute a starting point for Adult Zionist Jewish education in general.

---

1. Unpublished Mimeo Circular, Department of Jewish Education and Culture in the Diaspora, Joint Authority (World Zionist Organization and Jewish Agency for Israel) for Jewish Zionist Education — JAJZE, June 1991.

Each sub-community necessitates a particular strategy in order to achieve a state of creative tension inherent in the Zionist idea. However, the sub-communities would share a common ideational rationale at least in part. Hence, over a period of time each such sub-community also serves as a partial support system for the other sub-communities. For example, young parents involved in a school program where in the evening parents tell stories chosen on the basis of a peoplehood/Israel orientation may be stimulated to learn more (adult education) and will probably be relatively more supportive of their child going on an Israel program.

The major emphasis will be on the sub-community of children-youth-students. The entire period of maturation is seen as a time period within which a Zionist-Jewish approach is integrated both formally and informally in order to internalize Zionist-Jewish identity. A properly structured Israel experience is viewed as a desirable norm for all Jewish youth. A significant proportion of these should be long-term programs oriented to educating participants to be active in their communities upon their return.

The particular tactics suitable fur furthering a general strategy will vary among different countries.

What Communities

Communities may number from 10,000 to 250,000. They may be defined on a geographic basis. They may be defined on an affiliational basis. An example of such an affiliational basis would be a region of a synagogue movement. The community must have a representative body (committee) which speaks in its name.

THE SUGGESTED COMPONENTS OF THE COMPREHENSIVE APPROACH IN NORTH AMERICA

1. Promotion of the long-term America-Israel Secondary School Programs (Grades 10-11), 3-6 participants from the community. These programs will be modified where necessary in order to integrate leadership training and junior pedagogic modules in order to enable participants to return to their communities as youth leaders and supplementary school assistants in the movements / organizations / institutions of their choice.

   A particular focus on long-term programs at high-school age in North America is dictated by the following considerations:

a. The participants return to their home communities for a minimum of 1-2 years and hence become part of the process generating model community by being active role models for other youth.

b. The age of 15-16 is ideal for a combined experiential-cognitive program incorporating Zionist Jewish value clarification and confrontation leading to activist Zionist-Jewish identification.

c. A possibility exists of organizing parent-youth committees (program graduates and their parents) as lay Zionist-Jewish lobby groups for Zionist-Jewish education.

It is to be noted that within most other countries of the Diaspora age 18 (post-highschool) is a more practical option. In the case of affiliational communities even in North America the possibility of re-integrating into the same affiliational community in a different geographic location is a viable option.

2. Promotion of the integration of day-school programs and the Israel Experience.

a. For those communities with day-school education up to Grades 7-8, the final program module will consist of a properly structured short-term Israeli program of 4-6 weeks.

b. For those communities with day-school education at the high-school level, a minimum of one semester (Grade 10 or 11) should be programmed in Israel within the total class framework (including part of the educational staff). Day-school programs will be planned in cooperation with the appropriate Departments of the Authority.

3. Day-schools (receiving Federation funds) will retain one teacher-shaliach on the staff of their school. "Shaliach" in this context means a qualified teacher sent via the Joint Authorities' Departments. If the teaching staff of the school numbers over 20, it is suggested that the school will retain two teacher-shlichim. The purpose of shlichim is not only instruction of particular subjectmatter but also to project an alternative mode of Jewish identity within the school community of children, educators and parents.

4. Day-schools will give reasonable access (from Grade 5) to Zionist youth movements to recruit pupils.

5. The community will sponsor a 3-4 week educational seminar for local educators in Israel every two years. The seminar program will be planned jointly by the Joint Authority Departments and representative community institutions.

6. The Community together with the Authority will sponsor local/regional seminars once a year in the areas of:
   (a) Hebrew Language instruction
   (b) Modern Jewish history (including Zionist history)
   (c) Israel
7. Community Education (Parent-Child):
   A Jewish-Zionist program of community education involving kindergarten to Grade 4, integrating both parents and children will be established. Modules will include supplementary schools and day schools. In this way the school will also become a venue for adult education.
8. The Community will sponsor Hebrew Language ulpanim for adults.
9. The Community will promote Hebrew and Jewish ethnic studies in local Public School systems and colleges where feasible.
10. Follow-up: The community and the Joint Authority by means of the Steering Committee will be responsible for follow-up and evaluation according to the guidelines to be developed for all the model communities.

IMPLEMENTATION WITHIN THE COMMUNITY

1. An authorized body representing the components of the Authority in that particular Community and the community itself will sign a commitment to this program for a five-year period.
2. A local Steering Committee will be established representing:
   Federation (lay)
   Zionist Council
   Jewish Youth Council (lay)
   BJE and JCC (or equivalent professional body)
   Joint Authority representative
   Zionist Youth Council of the community (lay)
   This committee will have public responsibility vis-a-vis the Authority for conducting the Model Community project.
3. The question of partial incentive funding for an initial three-year period for the Israel components of the Model Communities will be brought to the Authority.
4. The Steering Committee will act to secure funding for the continuation of the project beyond the initial stage of outside funding participation.

Policy Guidelines for the Joint Authority[1] for Jewish Zionist Education[2]

Education for Zionism

Any Zionist education is by definition Jewish education. Only potentially, however, is Jewish education Zionist education — whether or not it engages in Hebrew language study, Israel studies, or even an Israel Experience. The contents of Jewish and Zionist education may be similar in many stages of the educational process, but the whole rationale of Jewish-Zionist education, from preschool to the post-secondary level, is unique. The policies of the Joint Authority for Jewish-Zionist Education should give expression to the uniqueness of Jewish-Zionist education.

The special attributes of Jewish-Zionist education are the following:

1. It regards the educational process as a single organic entity, embracing cognitive and emotional components, that begins with early childhood and continues to university studies and beyond.

   It entails cooperation among its constituents: formal and non-formal education in the Diaspora, and the Israel Experience. There must be a measure of dissonance — educational tension — among these components. This constructive tension is a prerequisite for Zionist educational "movement" as distinct from "organization" for pro-Israel Jewish education.

   This being the case, the Authority should formulate practical criteria leading to an overall strategy. The Authority's budget policies should provide incentives to communities and/or sectors that adopt such an overall strategy.

2. Jewish-Zionist education takes place in dynamic "fields" of community and intimate partnerships. Any educational setting is a "field" in which relevant role models promote processes of socialization and acculturation that inculcate Jewish-Zionist norms.

---

1. Formalized in 1991 as a partnership between the World Zionist Organization and the Jewish Agency.
2. Unpublished Mimeo Circular, Department of Jewish Education and Culture in the Diaspora, Joint Authority (World Zionist Organization and Jewish Agency for Israel) for Jewish Zionist Education — JAJZE, July 1992.

The Authority should promote processes conducive to the formation of foci of role models that project a Jewish-Zionist culture which offers an alternative to the norms of existing Jewish society. It is especially important to present these alternatives to persons in their teens and early twenties, for these are the age groups in which personal identity coalesces. Youth movements are examples of frameworks which have role models personifying Jewish-Zionist alternatives, and hence individuals in the movement may opt for a Jewish-Zionist identity as they advance toward adulthood and formulate a personal ideal.

The Authority should select a policy promoting the development of Jewish-Zionist movement among selected target populations of Jewish youth, both within the existing youth movements and those outside the classic youth movements. Special effort should be made to foster these processes among youngsters who already take part in general organizational settings affiliated with the World Zionist Organization, such as B'nai B'rith and various religious groupings.

Thus, in non-formal education the Authority should promote, qualitatively and quantitatively, the training of counselors for work in direct contact with the young. These would serve as role models for the acquisition of Jewish-Zionist norms. Thus numerous focal points of Jewish-Zionist education would be created, which, by virtue of the Zionist role models and attractive experiential settings, would attract others to the Zionist idea.

However, the frameworks that offer Jewish-Zionist education must adopt an explicit program of value clarification over and above the experiential dimension. This value clarification should help the young cope cognitively with the Zionist idea and the alternatives for its fulfillment in personal and public life.

3. We regard Jewish-Zionist schools as more than schools per se; they are educational centers and study communities which inculcate Jewish-Zionist culture and, above all, our national language, Hebrew. To accomplish this in day schools, there should be a policy of enough hours of Hebrew language study so that students will be able to study Jewish subjects (e.g., Bible, Jewish history, tradition, calendar) in Hebrew.

    Formal Jewish-Zionist education should strive for an integration between general-Jewish subjects so as to impart cognitive understanding of and emotional identification with the uniqueness of Hebrew civilization in the context of the surrounding culture. The Joint Authority should develop principles of integrative and value education of this kind. The Authority should train teachers and pedagogical counselors to become adept at formulating such Jewish-Zionist curricula in diverse cultural surroundings.

To promote formal education of this type, the Authority should also emphasize teacher training for skills in direct contact with students. A teaching staff imbued with Jewish-Zionist values and equipped with pedagogic skills for imparting them is a prerequisite for formal education in a Jewish-Zionist educational center.

The Joint Authority, collaborating with Diaspora organizations committed to Jewish-Zionist education, should encourage the writing of study units — Hebrew, Jewish and Zionist studies — suitable for supplementary schools. The Authority should also develop study units for non-formal education settings in which formal education takes place, such as summer camps.

4. The Israel Experience, when properly structured, is the centerpiece in the process of Zionist value clarification and confrontation. However, as with any centerpiece, the significance of the Israel Experience as a part of the process of Zionist education is gravely limited, unless there is both a period of preparation as well as follow-up after returning to the Diaspora.

    The Authority should give clear priority to long-term Israel Experiences. Such programs are far more likely to provide an educational basis for value changes in the direction of Jewish-Zionist norms. The long-term programs are the most likely to develop a potential for Aliyah as well as Diaspora Jewish-Zionist leadership. Therefore, long-term Israel Experience activities should be promoted in non-formal education and should be included as part of the curriculum in formal Jewish education.

    As for the short-term Israel Experience, its value in Jewish-Zionist education is chiefly when it is part of a process that has continuity. Ideally, such continuity leads into an educational process that puts youth in confrontation with the challenge of alternative paths leading to personal Jewish-Zionist fulfillment.

◆ ◆ ◆

The Education Authority should allocate its resources commensurately with the size of the potential and actual target population groups. The Authority should encourage research that sheds light on factors that may foster Jewish-Zionist educational processes, with special reference to the centers of Jewish population in the West that face the risk of demographic decline and cultural and physical assimilation. In order to focus such research properly, such research should be preceded by in-depth, case-study examination of existing examples of successful Jewish-Zionist education.

◆ ◆ ◆

Jewish-Zionist education aims to perfect the individual, the nation, and the world. The tension that this generates is the very heart of the Prophetic trend in Judaism — a trend that the Zionist movement has revived in modern times. Zionist education is committed to the tension between the priest (the *cohen*), who adheres to the existing path, and the prophet, who strives for perfection. Zionist education aims to instill this tension, by educational means, in the lives of both the individual and the people. This fructifying tension constitutes the matrix in which the process of Zionist value clarification and confrontation takes place.

The goal of Jewish-Zionist education is to shape a mature young adult living in Zionist tension and striving to join others (we hope he/she does this in Israel) I the ongoing effort to resolve this tension in their personal lives and in the Jewish community, both in Israel and in the Diaspora.

The Meaning of Zionist Education in Our Generation[1]

Resources for Jewish-Zionist Education

We have become accustomed to hearing that $2 billion is spent each year on Jewish education in the Diaspora. In 1992, only $34.7 million of this amount was budgeted via the Joint Authority for Jewish-*Zionist* Education. This sum undoubtedly leverages additional sums, which amount to at least $60 million (authenticated) if not $100 million.

But what, really, is Jewish-Zionist education? In the absence of a consensus as to the criteria of Jewish-Zionist education, who can guarantee that the Authority's expenditures are indeed channeled to Jewish-Zionist education? Conversely, agents other than the Authority may also be investing in Zionist education.

The truth is that much of Jewish education recognizes, directly or indirectly, the centrality of Israel as the national home of the Jewish people. One might say that a considerable portion of Jewish education is "pro-Israel." Does that mean it is also Zionist education? Moreover, is the money spent by the Authority disbursed on the basis of a rationale espousing pro-Israel Jewish education or Jewish-Zionist education?

Jewish-Zionist Education and Pro-Israel Jewish Education — What's the Difference?

To bring the criteria into focus, let us compare Jewish-Zionist education and pro-Israel Jewish education. I am aware that nothing in reality is black or white, that there are shades of gray. Thus I propose to sharpen the contrast, since our public norm is to blur them; a habit that does not further meaningful discussion.

---

1. Unpublished Mimeo Circular, Department of Jewish Education and Culture in the Diaspora, Joint Authority (World Zionist Organization and Jewish Agency for Israel) for Jewish Zionist Education — JAJZE, August 1992.

Comprehensive Long-term Planning

First and foremost, Jewish-Zionist education means formulating a long-term strategy starting in preschool and extending to university and beyond. To implement such a plan of action, an agreed-upon community strategy is required — with the community being either geographical (i.e., a locality) or affiliational, e.g., associated with a religious stream.

In this comprehensive strategy, Jewish-Zionist education integrates formal and non-formal education and embraces education for parents, educators, and youngsters. The Israel experience (and optimally, experiences) with its cognitive and emotional components, is a major link in the entire process of Jewish-Zionist education. The Israel experience, however, must be part of an ongoing process. Preparation precedes the experience, and the experience serves as a basis for future learning. Pro-Israel Jewish education, by contrast, rarely functions within the context of an overall strategy. There is no coordination between levels of education and the educational authorities and agencies. The Israel experience is an isolated event, rather than part of an ongoing process.

Education that Uncovers Contrasts in Values and Principles

Values are preferred positions based on overt or covert beliefs (vis-a-vis other possible positions) in any given situation in which one must take a stance. For example, one group of values is related historically to the Greece-Israel dichotomy. In ancient Greece, determinism prevailed; values were governed by the belief that the individual's fate was predetermined. The Jewish belief affirmed predestination but asserted the existence of free will (i.e., free will can prevail over fate). Another example: in Greece, the concept of beauty was an aesthetic value and a goal to be achieved, as symbolized by the Olympic Games and contests held in the nude. The Jews regard beauty as an internal, qualitative concept, one connected with justice and ethics.

A value such as *Tikun Olam* — mending the world — cannot be implemented without a belief in our ability to fashion our world. It also assumes a commitment to that which is just and ethical.

It is not enough to take a position that rests on values. This alone cannot guide us in behavioral norms, i.e., principles. For example, one may embrace the value of *Tikun Olam* on the basis of belief in free will. However, those who believe in the dictum "Justice, justice shall you pursue" would not necessarily agree on what particular personal commitment this entails. Likewise, on the socio-political plane, the question of how to implement values may elicit fundamental differences of opinion. For example, Gush Emunim and Ha-shomer ha-Tsa'ir share the vision of *Tikun Olam*, but, as we know, they disagree profoundly on the way to bring it about.

Jewish-Zionist education is based on exposing contrasting values and principles between Judaism and surrounding society, and within Judaism itself. There are also different methodological emphases between formal and non-formal education as to how to achieve this objective.

The objective of any formal program of Jewish-Zionist education is to make the student aware and create tension with regard to the value alternatives that arise when s/he seeks a way to Zionist *Tikun* for him/herself, the People Israel, and the world. Jewish-Zionist education does more than clarify cognitive values from a Jewish-Zionist point of view; it also provides an experiential continuum based on role models who represent a certain tension between the realization of the norms (principles) of an existing society and those of some other society.

Pro-Israel Jewish education, by contrast, strives to inculcate Jewish values (including identification with the People Israel and the State of Israel). The objective is active integration into an existing Jewish community and an emotional link with the Jewish people and the State of Israel. Pro-Israel Jewish education does not expose or pinpoint the basic contradictions inherent in the attempt to realize values. Similarly, pro-Israel Jewish education has no fundamental, conscious interest in exposing students to the tension between different ways of realizing given values.

Educational Staff: Permanence versus Transience

As a result of the nature of role models in Jewish-Zionist education, there may be a high turnover of educational staff. This will be true both for *shlichim* and for local youth counselors.

Role models in pro-Israel Jewish education, by contrast, identify with a particular cross-section of an existing community. For them, educational work is probably a career, which takes place within the community's norms. Thus one would expect less turnover in pro-Israel Jewish education than in Zionist education.

Senior Educators versus Direct-Contact Staff

For Jewish-Zionist education to succeed, a large number of counselors and educators must come into direct contact with the youngsters — in classes, in summer camps, and in youth groups. This is because Jewish-Zionist education conveys complex value messages not only through the curricula themselves but by means of direct, face-to-face contact — in class, in the youth group, in summer camp, or in the Israel experience.

Pro-Israel Jewish education places more emphasis on senior educators who can build and strengthen stable, permanent educational systems, formal and non-formal, in the Diaspora.

An example of the distinction is the controversy concerning the involvement of Jewish-Zionist education in financing and training senior educators. One could claim that since these senior educators are likely to assume leadership in pro-Israel Jewish education systems, it is unfair to finance them with the small reserves earmarked for Jewish-Zionist education. What remains to be asked, however, is how much Jewish-Zionist education should contribute to courses in Israel for senior educators, and who should be responsible for such contributions. As complex as this controversy is, one should not flinch from confronting it in a practical and civilized manner.

Naturally, there is a paradox here, one that attests to the close relationship between pro-Israel Jewish education and Jewish-Zionist education. For example, there may be a consensus that the best candidates for senior positions in pro-Israel Jewish education are precisely those who received a Jewish-Zionist education.

The Political Aspect

Jewish-Zionist education leads automatically to *political* education in the *Jewish* domain, i.e., personal involvement on behalf of some particular vision of a Diaspora community and a Jewish state in Eretz Israel. It is an education that posits the People Israel and the Land of Israel as values, with the addition of principles that point to a particular way of implementing these values. The student must cope with the alternative ways of realizing the values.

Pro-Israel Jewish education regards itself as neutral in the field of Jewish politics. It strives to find and make full use of the common ground and to blur that which is particular to a specific point of view. It teaches that the People and Land of Israel are values but avoids dealing with specific principles for realization that may overstep the general community consensus.

Democratic Processes in Education

As one component of political education, Jewish-Zionist education promotes democratic involvement in Jewish and Jewish-Zionist institutions. Zionist education that strives to achieve *Tikun Olam* almost always requires the principle of democracy in order to influence undemocratic, oligarchic community systems.

Pro-Israel Jewish education does not deal actively with democracy in Jewish and Jewish-Zionist community institutions, even if it ostensibly supports the concept. Neither are the educational institutions themselves always open to public, democratic criticism. At the present time, for example, the institutions of the Joint Authority for Jewish-Zionist Education have not solved the problem of accountability — either that of the representatives of the fundraising organizations or that of the representatives of the World Zionist Organization.

1. The Israeli political establishment is content with the undemocratic administration of Zionist institutions because this permits it to maintain control of these institutions and utilize them for partisan needs. Democracy (e.g., special elections for the Zionist movement in Israel) would be a threat to the current situation.

2. Abroad, an alliance between big donors and "professionals" is the present incarnation of the alliance that characterized the traditional community — between wealthy lay leaders (*parnassim*) and the rabbis (*talmidei chachamim*). The professionals, sometimes wearing the mantle of academe, act as "gatekeepers" for the big givers; from these positions of power, they can screen out anything incompatible with their conceptions and, *ipso facto*, anything that challenges their institutions' financial interest.

One may hope (although there is no guarantee) that, by means of democratic processes, we can ensure that at least the funds spent and/or influenced by the Joint Authority for Jewish-Zionist Education will be utilized according to criteria of Jewish-*Zionist* education. It may also become possible to arrange further funding for Jewish-Zionist education from community resources.

Ideological Processes in Jewish-Zionist Education

In the past 20 years we have witnessed the accelerated decline of ideological Zionism as represented by the World Zionist Organization, and the ascendancy of the fundraising "appeals" (UIA/Keren Hayesod) as expressed in the Jewish Agency for Israel. Furthermore, the influence of private foundations with no a priori commitment to public systems (e.g., the Jewish Agency) is on the rise. Accessibility to these private foundations is carefully guarded by professionals who have gained the confidence of their wealthy patrons.

The root cause of the ideological decline is the fact that the principal goal of political Zionism was achieved with the establishment of the State of Israel. This left people who supported the idea of a Jewish state with two options: make Aliyah to the Jewish state or accept the "demotion" of becoming a supporter of Israel. To support Israel, one need not be a declared Zionist.

My hypothesis is that today we are facing the educational implications of having embraced an obsolete and ossified political Zionism. In the free, developed Western countries (and in Israel, too, in my opinion, but that is not the issue here), *we face the necessity of basing the Zionist idea and Zionist education on an outlook of cultural, not political, Zionism.*

The Educational Significance of Political Zionism

Political Zionism is based on the model of a state for the Jews "like all the nations." This nation-state model comes in various shades of Western political philosophy.

Classically, the assumptions of this model are:

1. We have always been an *'am*, a people, and in today's terms we are also a *le'om*, a nation.
2. The national home of the Jewish people is the Land of Israel. Our national language is Hebrew.
3. In the modern age, our existence in exile as an *am/le'om* is untenable because of
   a. cultural and physical assimilation;
   b. antisemitism, which threatens our physical and economic existence.

Note: Political Zionism *does not need to have a unique Jewish message.* Such a message can exist, but it is not essential.

An education derived from this view accomplishes two things: (a) it inculcates a *national* (not just religious/ritual) identity, and (b) it promotes immigration to Israel, at times in tandem with the negation of the Diaspora. Sometimes one encounters an attempt to integrate a political ideology (usually that of an Israeli political party) into the realization of the national cause. In the final analysis, classical political Zionism generates polarization between Israel and the Diaspora. Today, however, political Zionism usually disregards the question of content and focuses only on support for the framework.

The rationale of the model of political Zionism — a state for the Jews — is easy to comprehend. The dramatic changes in the former Soviet Union have created the illusion of a comeback for political Zionism. In principle, however, the era of classical political Zionism as an ideological factor in the Western world has expired.

The West is not receptive to the classic message of political Zionism. Therefore, the current diluted (pro-Israel) version is characterized by the following emphases:

1. national identity (identification with the Jewish people);
2. a national home for the Jewish people (Israel) and a national language (Hebrew);
3. an undefined connection between Zionism and Judaism.

To summarize the position of this diluted political Zionism: We are Jews, one people, and as such we have a national home. We must support our national home politically and materially, in the spirit of the historical Jewish principle of shared responsibility (*Kol Israel arevim ze le-ze*). Furthermore, educationally, an experience in Israel as an educational norm for our children will ensure the survival of the Jewish identity. Hebrew, the national language, is of secondary importance.

Let us note that the Israel-Diaspora bipolarity that has always been an aspect of political Zionism still exists. However, supporters of Israel accept this situation as Jewishly "normal." Classic political Zionism, by contrast, rejected the Diaspora on principle. It never came to terms with the "Jerusalem-Babylonia" polarization that strives to legitimize the existence of the Diaspora.

The Educational Significance of Cultural Zionism

On the other hand, *Cultural Zionism* regards Israel as a national home — a spiritual and cultural center — for the Jewish people. The center exists so as to ensure the *particularity* of the Jewish people, wherever they may be, in the modern era. The Hebrew language is an essential component of this particularity. This also means that the state of the Jews is a *Jewish* state with unique Jewish tasks. Hence the Jewish state is not strictly comparable to other national-political frameworks that came into being to manifest other people's right to self-determination. Note: Cultural Zionism does not assume that Jews should live only in the Jewish state; it does not negate the Diaspora. However, the Jewish state is central by virtue of its giving the Jewish people a chance to express their particularity among the family of nations in the modern age.

The Problem of Models (Education)

What model, then, should give expression to the uniqueness of the Jewish state and constitute a basis for Cultural Zionism? The model cannot be based on Western ideologies; it must draw on the Jewish heritage itself.

In 1893, even before the First Zionist Congress, Achad Ha'am offered a rationale justifying the Zionist enterprise as relevant to the Jewish people in the modern age. In his essay *"Kohen ve-navi"* (Priest and prophet), he proposed a model for cultural Zionism based on the tension between the priest and the prophet in ancient times. According to Achad Ha'am, *this tension is unique to the Jewish people and is the source of our special contribution to the history of nations.* Unless this constructive tension is revived as an active force in the modern age, the culture of the Jewish people will ossify. To revive this tension, however, requires the establishment of a national home in the Land of Israel, even if a majority of Jews continue to live in the Diaspora.

The "priest and prophet" concept may be represented as two vectors pulling in opposite directions, with a field of tension between them. The "priest" vector is akin to existing Jewish society, which lives in a state of compromise between the prophetic ideals of *Tikun Olam* and current Western social realities. Synonyms for the priestly vector would be "organization" or "establishment."

The vector that aspires to be prophetic, to reform the individual, the people, and the world, represents a vision of another society. The prophetic vector is synonymous with "movement." A movement tries to move a society from point A to point B and formulates a plan of action to bring this about.

As we know, yesterday's movement is today's organization or establishment. One might say that this was the fate of political Zionism.

It is precisely this dynamic tension between priest and prophet (establishment and movement) that makes it necessary for them to relate to and influence each other. The dynamic relationship may be severed for one of two reasons. First, the movement may turn into an organization by achieving its goals or by surrendering to "reality." Alternatively, the potency of the tension between establishment and movement may cause the movement to break away and become a "cult." It will try to convert individuals, but it no longer interacts with or influences the existing society.

The priest and the prophet express their Jewish commitment and identity differently. For the priest (today, the establishment) the emphasis is on performing religious precepts relating to the individual — generally rituals, acts of kindness to others, and charity. The emotional thrust of activity will be in the direction of integration with the existing community norms.

For the prophet (today, the movement), the key word expressing the nature of the commitment is "mission." This term does not rule out organizational affiliation alone. When the movement agenda includes *Tikun Olam*, the emotional thrust of activity will be a plan of action intended to cause change. Every stream of Judaism with a vision (or a potential vision) of its own can develop a plan of action for the future of the Jewish people and the national home based on its interpretation of prophetic ideals.

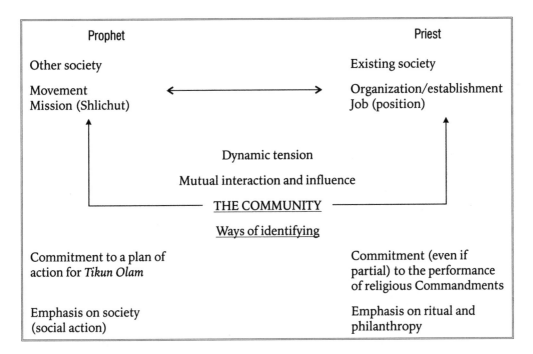

We shall explain the priest-prophet dichotomy further by examining the educational ramifications. Above we have described a field loaded with centers of influence that have competing norms. There is a possibility of children, teenagers, and adults being exposed to a diversity of norms by processes of socialization and acculturation.

The aim of Jewish-Zionist education is to impart the priest-prophet tension as an activating factor. To live with tension within surrounding society while striving for prophetic ideals requires more than a passive Jewish identity or performance of religious commandments on the individual level. What one needs is a *commitment to the Zionist idea of* Tikun Olam *and readiness to act for its fulfillment together with others.* It means being ready to undertake "mission" (*shlichut*) in the context of a movement.

In the light of the foregoing, we have highlighted the differences between pro-Israel Jewish education and Jewish-Zionist education. The former is based on political Zionism, which means, mainly, identification with the centrality of the State of Israel for the Jewish people and active support for it. The latter is based on cultural Zionism with everything this implies, including the imperative of active participation in and commitment to the realization of some Zionist vision, a vision that manifests itself both in the Diaspora and in the National Home.

Educational Ramifications of Cultural Zionist Education

With respect to *formal education*, the curriculum in pro-Israel Jewish education and Jewish-Zionist education may be virtually identical (language, Bible, literature, Jewish history). However, there will be an essential difference between the message communicated by teaching in the spirit of "culture like all the nations" and by teaching in the spirit of a unique culture whose purpose is mending the world (*Tikun Olam*). The integration of general subjects into Jewish education will also be different.

To illustrate both the potential and the problematics of this issue, we mention only that there are two systems of Zionist education in Israel. We are actually raising two peoples in Israel, and their values overlap only in part. In my opinion, one system is based on political Zionism (secular State schools) and the other on a *certain type* of cultural Zionism (State religious schools). Let us remember that there is also an "independent" education system in Israel that is not committed to the Zionist idea at all.

In *non-formal education* one may find numerous common denominators in routine summer-camp activities. The experience offered in Camp Ramah or Young Judea camps, however, differs from that provided by most camps run by Jewish community centers. Yes, some camps make sure to employ Israeli *shlichim* during the summer, but these people can only reinforce the polarization between "them" and "us." They cannot challenge the youngsters' set of values for the long term as can local Zionist graduates of Israel programs. The questions in non-formal education are always the same: who are the counselors, what are their values, and does the establishment give this value system the backing that it needs if it is to be presented to the youngsters as an alternative?

◆ ◆ ◆

I conclude my remarks with a few words on the common denominator, and the mutual interests, of Jewish-*cultural*-Zionist education and pro-Israel Jewish education.

As we recall, cultural Zionism assumes that Diaspora Jewry will continue to exist and that its vitality must be ensured. The Zionist educator will claim that its vitality will not just be a function of passive Jewish identity but will depend on the Jewish-Zionist tension within it. This tension stems directly from the commitment, the need to act, that such tension engenders. Perhaps this commitment will not always lead to Aliyah, but it must lead to personal involvement in raising a successor generation that is motivated to play an active role in the continued creative existence of the Jewish people. This commitment will affect the flow of resources for both the Diaspora communities and the national home.

Therefore, Jewish-Zionist education and pro-Israel Jewish education share an interest in the active component that we are interested in inculcating: *commitment*. The postulate presented here is that only a comprehensive educational strategy based on cultural Zionism can succeed. Incomplete, fragmented activity may augment Jewish identity, but this is not enough. Therefore, for the sake of its vitality, the Jewish community would do well to adopt a comprehensive educational strategy based on cultural Zionism, rooted in the criteria that we set forth in the beginning of this article.

This is the role, the challenge, and the vision for Zionist education in the Jewish community of our generation.

Educating for Reform Zionism

* Aliyah — "Going up" to settle in Israel
** ARZA — Association of Reform Zionists in America

Synopsis of the Section

The articles in this section synthesize between Reform Zionist ideology (Sections 1 & 2) and Jewish Zionist educational principles (Section 4) and seek to apply them to the youth frameworks of Reform Judaism, both in the Diaspora and in Israel. They represent active advocacy for Reform Zionist Education — in particular within the framework of informal (youth) education.

Logic would have dictated that the writings in this section would constitute the outcome of the theoretical bases established in Section 4. In fact, the confrontation with actual situations and challenges in many cases triggers the process for formulating more general statements.

It was a primary purpose of my *shlichut* to the UAHC in North America to lay the groundwork for a Reform Zionist Youth Movement. In forming the *"Garin Arava"* framework (see Introductory Preface) I felt that the infrastructure for such a movement was being laid. It was not to be. The lack of suitable *shlichim* and in particular the resignation of Rabbi Stephen Schafer, the Zionistically oriented head of the Youth Division, led to the substitution of Pro-Israel programming for the Reform Zionist orientation introduced by my *shlichut* and continued by Gidon Elad of Kibbutz Chatzerim until 1979.

A ZIONIST YOUTH MOVEMENT FOR REFORM JUDAISM (1977) was a call that was ignored in North America. However, the more Zionist orientation of the Reform communities in England, Australia and South Africa resulted in the formation of Netzer (Noar Zioni Reformi) as a Reform Zionist Youth Movement. Unfortunately, these small communities could not fill the gap left by the absence of North American participation in such an enterprise. My participation in the symposium REFORM ZIONIST COMMUNITIES AND VALUES (1984) and my 1987 letter to the then *Mazkira* of Netzer in England (WHAT IS THE MEANING OF YOUR ALIYAH FRAMEWORK?) were attempts to relate to the Netzer graduates' search for a meaningful role. The dearth of Netzer graduates' involvement (those who have, made *Aliyah*) with the IMPJ indicates that this problem, reflecting fundamental defects in the Netzer educational process, remains open.

My memo, ARZA AND REFORM ZIONIST YOUTH PROGRAMMING constituted a renewed attempt to raise the issue of Reform Zionist (as distinct from Reform Pro-Israel) youth education within the UAHC framework (see also Section 1:7). The great harm done to the IMPJ by the lack of Reform Zionist *Aliyah* was, in my opinion, a direct result of ARZA's unwillingness to advocate a Reform Zionist youth education program and to challenge the Youth Division's minimalist pro-Israel approach. However, into the mid-Nineties, ARZA remained primarily committed to political action on behalf of Reform Judaism in Israel. Nor was the approach of the Hebrew Union College to its Year in Israel program for American (and Israeli) Rabbinical students conducive to promoting Reform Zionism. A REFORM ZIONIST POLICY FOR THE HEBREW UNION COLLEGE was written in response to Rabbi Sheldon Zimmerman's request for input by Reform Jewish educators in Israel at a meeting held in July 1996.

A Zionist Youth Movement for Reform Judaism[1]

The time has come for the development of a Zionist youth movement within Reform Judaism. Such a development would relate to both the needs of Reform Judaism and of its youth constituency.

Reform Judaism today affirms the unity of the Jewish people and is vitally concerned with its continued creative survival wherever it may be. The tradition of social action developed within Reform Judaism during the Sixties is now seeking meaningful expression and engagement within the life of the Jewish people. As a result, a Zionist consensus has emerged within Reform over the past decade — a consensus which perceives the Jewish State as a central force in the life of the people and Reform Judaism's growing involvement with Israel as a reflection of the creative potential inherent within Liberal Judaism. Reform Judaism is transcending its immediate organizational concerns and its preoccupation with religious forms. It is emerging as a movement committed to a certain vision of Jewish life. It is seeking the leadership of those who will take upon themselves the vocation of realizing such a vision in their own lives.

The Need: Educating Towards Reform Jewish Community

But the continued creative survival of Judaism and the realization of visions of Jewish life are dependent on *communities* of committed individuals — Judaism ultimately is a way of life that must be expressed in community. It was Martin Buber who pursued the problematics of the breakdown of community, and in particular, Jewish community, as a result of the advent of the Modern Age. The ramifications are many — absence of community means absence of dialogue between individuals, and it means the alienation of the individual from the group. In Buber's eyes, only through organic community could the individual relate to God. This led Buber to the position that without authentic Jewish community, there can be no authentic Jewish experience.

How do we create an environment of Jewish community within which we can educate our children and youth? Let no one think that this is not a real problem

---

1. 1977, unpublished. Appeared (mimeo) in Newsletter to North American youth considering Aliyah ("going up" to settle in Israel).

even in Israel. But it is a much greater problem in the Diaspora. In the past, an effective relationship to and identification with Judaism were achieved through an organic Jewish community. The effective relationship ensured effective cognition, socialization and acculturation. Such an organic Jewish community is no more.

Reform Judaism, child of the Emancipation from that organic Jewish community and heir to the Western liberal philosophical tradition geared to individual achievement and orientation, rather than group and community consciousness, is not confronting this question. In our society, adolescence is the age where such community consciousness must be developed.

Adolescence and the Peer Community

Adolescence is that period of biological, social and psychological maturation between childhood and adulthood, when identity and life commitment crystallize. In the middle class of American society to which the vast majority of American Jews (including Reform Jews) belong, this period extends from the post-Bar/Bat Mitzvah age through the college years.

The transition period from the defined dependence of childhood to socially recognized and sanctioned independence of adulthood is a stormy one in our society (by comparison to adolescence in other societies at other times). Western society has not defined the adolescents' role clearly — high school and college-age young people are in partial isolation — in a kind of "limbo." Hence the peer group, one's age-mates, becomes a key factor in socialization and acculturation. The great need for peer-group community at the age of youth stems from the necessity of having a framework within which the gropings for identity can express themselves. The peer group becomes the medium through which values and orientation can be transmitted and reinforced.

The openness and the relative isolation of adolescents from adult society in their search for meaning and identity, makes a small number of them vulnerable to such phenomena as Moon and Jews for Jesus. But this same quest for meaning and identity in community can express itself through channels which are ultimately integrative with the contemporary need of Reform Judaism for community. It was a classical function of Zionist youth movements to channel the energies of youth into activities and commitments that served the Jewish people. The time is ripe for a Reform Zionist youth movement to serve a similar function for Reform Judaism.

Implementing a Reform Zionist Youth Movement

Implementing the concept of a Reform Zionist youth movement assumes a Jewish education during childhood and the motivation to continue one's Jewish education, both formal and informal, during adolescence. A Reform Jewish Day School education would be optimal. For the youth constituency itself, it means the structuring of a progression of experiences in Liberal Jewish community which relate innovatively to the reality of contemporary Jewish existence.

A critical element within such a progression of experiential education is the contact that the adolescent has with committed Jewishly and Hebraically literate role-models, professional and lay, representing in their own lives current options for Reform Jewish commitment both in America and in Israel. Identifying with role-models is an on-going process in adolescence. In the case of youth movement, it is the *context* within which such a relationship takes place (in this case, the context of Reform Zionist community and commitment) that leads not only to identifying with a more adult individual, but also generates commitment to the community and group concerns.

Reform Zionist Youth Movement as such would probably manifest itself primarily at the post-High School level, at a time when more concrete demands for Jewish Commitment can be made. Clearly, a purposive Aliyah would be a central (not necessarily *the* central) option for Jewish commitment.

A primary responsibility of the UAHC Youth Division in providing the organizational infrastructure for the possible growth of a Reform Zionist movement is the maintenance and further development of a progression of properly structured and programmed experiential situations in innovative Jewish community settings both in Israel and America, so that various options in Jewish commitment can be weighed by the young individual. This is both the minimum that the UAHC *organizational structure* must provide for the youth constituency and, in a sense, it is also the maximum that it should do. It is axiomatic that when one wishes to give *organizational support* to generate a *movement process* one cannot predict in advance how or what will be generated. Qualitatively, however, we have a right to hope that as in the Zionist youth movements of the past, the works of a Reform Zionist youth movement will reflect its members' personal commitment to contribute in their own lives both as individuals and in community to the continued creative survival of the Jewish people.

A Progression of Experiential Education

The main steps in a progression of experiential community which could constitute the matrix for a Reform Zionist Youth movement already exist:

1. The UAHC Camps in the pre-teen and early teenager period; they provide total community and are a series of introductory experiences and a major stimulus for NFTY youth group activity during the winter. At present to be even more effective, the camps must up-grade the level of Jewish commitment and literacy — in particular among the lay junior staff members.

2. The properly structured Israel experience with a Liberal Jewish orientation. In particular, long-term programs — six months and up — are critical in developing Hebraically and Judaically literate individuals. At present, the particular component of Liberal Judaism must be integrated more thoroughly into some of the Israel programs. The Israel experience is also decisive in imprinting Jewish identity and concretizing the concept of Jewish Peoplehood. Suitable graduates of long-term programs are natural role-models for younger age groups in the Temples and the UAHC Camps.

3. College-age Reform communities ("Batim") — these are a new development in those centers where there are numbers of committed Reform Jewish students. The basic requirements for participating in such a cooperative living arrangement are more than a mutually agreed level of personal observance. There must be a willingness on the part of the individuals and of the "Bayit" (house) *as a community* to take upon themselves the responsibility for Liberal Jewish "outreach" — whether on campus or within the rest of the community. Clearly, such college "chavurot" have implications for chavura structure in the congregations.

If a significant percentage of our youth will utilize such a progression of experiential education in Liberal Jewish community, then Reform Judaism will succeed in developing a committed fellowship, a "core community" and element of self-generating "movement" within Reform Judaism on a national and international level. Such a "core community" would constitute the future lay and professional leadership of a Reform Judaism capable of a relevant and meaningful response to the challenge of our times.

Reform Zionist Communities and Values[1]

A PANEL DISCUSSION HELD AT THE INTERNATIONAL CONFERENCE OF NETZER OLAMI

August 1984, Jerusalem

Panel Members: Michael Langer, Gidon Elad, Rabbi Tovia Ben Chorin

<u>Michael Langer</u>: I will try to take up where Mike left off and assume that my fifteen minutes will be a bit of an introduction on where I think that Reform Zionist community should be going.

You all hopefully remember this quick summary of Reform Zionism as a synthesis of classic Reform Judaism and classic *chalutziut* — Zionist pioneering.

Judaism	Classic Reform	Classic Chalutziut	Reform Zionism
"Religion" Belief Halacha	<u>Affirmation</u> with Reform	<u>Negation</u> (Substitute Universal Ideology-Socialisms)	Affirmative Synthesis
Peoplehood Community	<u>Negation</u> (Substitute Universal Mission)	<u>Affirmation</u> with Reform	Particular and Universal .... Reform Religion and Community

In the wake of the Emancipation and the resultant breakdown of the Jewish community, Classic Reform posited the continuity of Religion, whose injunctions and rituals would have to be reformed. Community was negated. Judaism was to be a brotherhood of the spirit, with a universal mission of being a "light unto the nations" by virtue of being dispersed among them.

On the other hand, three generations after Emancipation, the emergence of a non-viable situation for Jews (as a result of anti-semitism) and Jewish Culture (as

---

1. Unpublished minutes of a discussion in a Netzer Olami (Reform Zionist Youth Movement) conference.

a result of assimilation) spawned the Zionist movement. Within it, the *chalutzic* vanguard posited the continuity of Jewish peoplehood — radically reformed. *Chalutziut* negated particularistic religious culture and espoused universalistic ideology — various brands of Socialism.

The synthesis is Reform Zionism which believes in on-going reform and negates the artificial separation of Religion/Culture from Community/Peoplehood. But then we are left hanging, because the question becomes, what is the content, what is the texture, what is the nature of this Reform Zionism, this synthesis of classic Reform Judaism and *Chalutziut*. It is on this question that I want to share some thoughts with you.

1. Community Responsibility for all Aspects of Reform — From Its Inception

Community is responsible for all aspects of reform! If one of the questions is: should Reform Zionism community have communal responsibility for cultural, spiritual, ritual life, my answer is yes. If there is going to be a group of people living together in a Reform Zionist community, they must expend energy on spiritual, cultural, creative togetherness. They must say immediately: "This is why we are here. No, we will not wait until we have solved all our Klitah problems. And of course there should be democracy in spiritual-ritual matters as well as communal matters. Community responsibility for community spiritual life is a matter for immediate *hagshama* (self-realization) within the Reform Zionist community, and not deferred until we solve economic and social and personal problems.

But I also want to say a few words about what community means. There are many overused words, but community in the historical Jewish sense implies more than people living together in a particular geographic location. It implies more than people living together with some degree of mutual responsibility for each other within that particular geographic location — more than sharing certain life patterns on an existential level. All that is inadequate as a description of the historical concept of community in Judaism, as I understand it. *The concept of community is linked to purpose.* In other words we are talking about a community in which there is a *community of purpose*, a community of *shlichut*. A community of purpose in that sense (an English phrase) relates to the concept of community called "*Kehilat Kodesh.*" "Kadosh" means separated out for a purpose, separated out for the purpose of achieving the best possible world. This is the ideal of *tikun olam* (world mending) which became imprinted in the collective psyche of the

Jewish people. Perhaps in the *galut* (exile), *tikun olam* lost its meaning. People simply went and did all their 613 *mitzvot* (divinely ordained commandments), and these were an *end* in themselves. The idea that the purpose of existence is to bring about the best vision may have been back somewhere in some rear chamber of some people's minds, but it really went underground except for certain schools of Kabbalah. The central idea of Zionism, particularly cultural Zionism, is to recreate a contemporary political situation for that community of purpose — *kehilat kodesh* — to exist again.

That is the element of *shlichut*, of purpose, that must express itself in Reform Zionist community on a practical level. I have emphasized that purposiveness is something which expresses itself over and above meeting existential needs of mutual help and interaction, living together, praying together, playing together. So we are talking about the community, a true Reform Zionist community, immediately taking upon itself responsibilities of cultural creativity as a way of life. We are also talking about elements outside of that community. Now very clearly, Reform Zionist community of Netzer Olami is the *hagshama* of Netzer Olami. Hence, the first primary responsibility of Reform Zionist community of Netzer Olami graduates is continued involvement with Netzer Olami.

In Israel we have the precedent of institutionalization of this idea, even if the people have already forgotten where it comes from. In the kibbutz movement 5% of all people power is apportioned to this element of responsibility to the community of purpose as distinct from the community of day-to-day existence. My feeling is that, in Reform Zionist community, the 90-95% of the day-to-day efforts to maintain its own existence cannot become meaningful if it does not serve as the basis for the other 5 or 10%. At this time that investment must go into strengthening the Netzer Olami (including Tzofei Telem) movement process.

A community of purpose *from the beginning*, a community of *shlichut* — that is the central orientation that I see for Reform Zionist Community. At this stage the main beneficiary of such *shlichut* should be Netzer Olami.

2. Ideological Tension Within Reform Zionist Community

The concept of purposiveness and the concept of *"tikun olam B'Malchut Shaddai"* — perfecting the world in the divine image — implies an ongoing tension and this has been from earliest times. It is the tension between what is and what should be. It is the tension between the priest and the prophet, to use the name of the article by Achad Ha'am. The priests and the kings are the political establishment and without an establishment you can't really exist. But without the prophetic element pushing for this community of purpose, there may be community but not, in the long run, a truly Jewish community, not an activist Jewish community and, therefore, not a true Reform Zionist Community. By the way, I once heard a definition of Zionism as being activist Judaism. But in terms of ideological under-pinning Reform Zionist community must relate to the ideological tension inherent between taking care of established needs and going out on *shlichut* as a community of purpose, a holy community, a *kehillat kodesh*.

3. Cooperation, Mutuality — How Much?

It is very clear that community and mutual responsibility on a practical level must mean a certain amount of cooperative life within the community. At what exact level that is going to be determined, I don't want to say. I am a member of a kibbutz, and as such have my own specific ideas on that subject. However, you will not be able, in my opinion, to define Reform Zionist community as Mike has pointed out in his introduction, by negatives. To say: "We want a framework which isn't kibbutz, and doesn't have as much cooperation as kibbutz," is a negative definition. In other words you have to define what various frameworks of Reform are going to do in terms of positives.

Keep in mind, Reform Zionist Aliyah cannot be meaningful without being part of a Reform Zionist community. In other words, Reform Jews coming to Israel make for nice statistics for the Jewish Agency; however, it doesn't relate to Reform Zionist purpose. At this stage, I will say something, after my colleagues have spoken.

Mike: We will take two questions for each person, and then questions can be directed to whomever one wants.

Sylvia: You talk about the *kehilat kodesh* and the community of purpose. What ultimately is the purpose of *kehilat kodesh* as you see it?

Michael Langer: In traditional Judaism, the ultimate purpose is to live according to 613 *mitzvot*. A community which lives according to the 613 *mitzvot* will bring about *tikun* or the betterment of the community, and if all Jewish communities will do this, all the nations will eventually see the light in this way. The Torah will go forth from Zion to all peoples and then perhaps the Messiah will come. That's the traditional point of view.

I think that the Reform Jewish point of view on the question of the Messiah is that we try and strive for a better world which will, eventually, bring about a messianic age. *But our specific Reform Zionist contribution is that we must begin with our own community* and that means, first of all, establishing community perfection which is an infinite concept. If the question is asked in terms of today, then, in 1984, a Reform Zionist community which is not just a classic Reform *"kultusgemeinde"* (a community of ritual) is required to take stock of the situation and define goals for itself.

It must do this *not* as an isolated community dealing with its existential concerns. It should be in a federative relationship with other Reform Zionist communities and with the movement, Netzer Olami, in which future communities are gestating. The federative relationship should be the organizational reflection of *movement process*. This movement-federation must plan year by year: socially, politically and in terms of spiritual cultural life.

Sylvia's question regarding the "purpose" of the community is ultimately the question of the purpose of Jewish existence which I related to in my opening remarks. You yourselves must outline the specific goals year by year. I can only start talking to you about the social vision of the prophets and say to you now, it's your responsibility to take that prophetic vision, bring it down to the level of 1984, and decide on a program for your community that can bring between 1984 and 1985 that vision one step closer. *Lo Aleicha HaM'lacha Ligmor...* (it is not for you to finish the task, nor are you free to desist from it) fits here exactly.

The lecture today is what socially, politically, culturally, Netzer Olami communities should do this coming year. First of all, you have to decide if you accept, if you are committed, to the concept. Do you see it as being legitimate? That's what you have to do this year — decide on your self image — Reform Jews in Israel or Reform Zionists. What I fear is so-called Reform Zionist groups landing here and really worrying a lot about themselves, and about their partners and where they are going to live and what kind of job they are going to have and worrying about themselves existentially and forgetting that they are here for a purpose, otherwise there is no Reform Zionist significance for their being here. There is a danger of Netzer Olami focusing on frameworks to help Reform Jews make Aliya without any of the purposive commitment to *shlichut* I have emphasized.

Russell: It was mentioned that a Reform *kehila* in Israel will have to take into account the experience of those preceding it. Lotan considered Yahel and now the *mitzpe*[1] (Har Chalutz) should take into account the experience of Yahel and Lotan. My question is: Do you feel that a *mitzpe* 1) can be called a Reform Zionist community? 2) will they approach the questions which Yahel and Lotan have

---

1. *Mitzpe* — lookout, generally in a strategic location, its economic format is individual.

approached, with regard to religious practice, economic cooperation and all sorts of things from the same standpoint — in other words, the same attitude as developed on Yahel or Lotan? Would you say that the *mitzpe* is going towards a Reform Zionist *kehillah* (community, congregation), as you've spoken? Or Michael, will this be a community of purpose like Yahel and Lotan?

<u>Michael Langer</u>: It's my opinion that any group that organizes here that cannot assign some of its members to movement work, without, in any way, that having a negative economic effect on the individual so assigned, is not effective in meeting the needs of Reform Zionist Community, under the particular circumstances in which Israel finds itself today. So I cannot see any way around that point in terms of Israel 1984 and Reform Zionism organizing itself to have an impact.

The proof of my point is the current impotent state of the Israel Movement for Reform Judaism. The Reform Judaism here is based on congregations. They are called *Kehillot* (communities) but they are not in reality communities of the type I discussed. They are an import into Israel of the classical Reform concept of Ritual Community — *kultusgemeinde*. It is true some Israeli rabbis, perhaps Tovia among them, are trying to change that. I think they are shooting water pistols into an inferno. I don't think "professional Jews" (another problematic import from Diaspora conditions) can do it. And I admire the effort but don't believe that it can be effective. Leadership must be from within community. The professional Rabbi is a shepherd to his flock but sheep are no basis for Reform Zionist community.

At present only the kibbutz community can mobilize for movement work according to my criteria. If Reform Zionism wants to include other types of communities as well, then I don't believe — and I'll be happy to be proved wrong — that the present tactics and approach can succeed. In other words, I don't believe that out of nothing, a new framework which meets Reform Zionist community criteria can establish itself in Israel under the present circumstances. Rather I see a necessity for the next half of a generation, of strengthening the existing Reform Zionist communities that meet the criteria.

Currently what it boils down to is that Netzer Olami and Telem Noar are 90% dependent on that community structure for even putting on the line what exists at the moment. I'll be very practical. There is not and there will be no *adequate* funding. There will be no "sugar daddy" to fund Reform Zionism. It will have to be done by the people who are committed to doing it and who can organize to do it one way or another. Right now our bottleneck in Reform Zionist is that we have no activists. The Israel Reform movement does not have the organizational wherewithal to have any impact on the Israeli polity. We are incapable of making any kind of show versus the orthodox onslaught. Reform in Israel at this stage of the game is a failure. Read Tavory's analysis in the Fall '82 *Judaism*.[1] The community concept that is needed is an entirely new one. In the end, in terms of process, it will doubtless be heterogeneous in terms of its age framework. But I think the initial stage of creating community means that a group of people must take upon themselves the realization of different community concept. So at this historical juncture, there will not be age/heterogeneous community. An age-heterogeneous community would be subject to these economic limitations which prevent Reform Judaism right now in Israel from doing anything. That is my rather pessimistic analysis of the situation. So without anyway discouraging Reform Zionist Community concepts outside the established ones, I think that right now we are totally dependent on the established ones for people-power and help of all kinds from a kindred communal movement, called the kibbutz movement. I agree in principle that additional communal forms are necessary but they must *evolve from what we have*. They will not come about by spontaneous generation. The process may take ten to fifteen years.

---

1. Tavory et al., "Reform and Conservative Judaism in Israel Today and Tomorrow," *Judaism*, Fall 1982, Vol. 31:4.

What Is the Meaning of Your Aliyah Framework?[1]

Dear Caroline,

As per your suggestion, I am reviewing some of the questions we discussed in our short conversation during your stay in Lotan.

The central question which those of you who are seriously considering Aliyah must confront is whether Aliyah is a technical act or whether it is part of an ongoing Reform Zionist commitment. The reflex answer that you might want to give — "Obviously, both!" — is invalid in the absence of a concrete program of self-definition within the Misgeret[2] which reflects both purposes.

I want to clarify that I do not in any way deprecate the importance of an Aliyah framework which gives you mutual support and technical assistance in your preparation for what is under the best of circumstances a complex logistical operation for each and every one of you. Nor am I unaware of the many advantages that such a framework has in buffering the shock of your initial Klita[3] both in terms of the initial supportive environment and also in terms of dealing with the carnivorous bureaucracy.

Aliyah Within the Context of Reform Zionist Commitment

The sincerity of your individual Reform Zionist commitment is not in question. Undoubtedly you are also concerned with the question of how that commitment will express itself in Israel. But the message I hear is that you are saying: "Let us get to Israel first and let us get settled in our personal lives and livelihoods and then we will see about Reform Zionism!" You believe (wrongly, in my opinion) that your major immediate focus has to be Aliyah and Klita — and the rest will (hopefully) develop. Without any doubt there are many who would concur with this emphasis — in particular those whose primary concern is the annual "head-count." I don't negate the relevance of that consideration either but it is

---

1. Open letter to Caroline Walsh, Secretary, Netzer-England (Reform Zionist Youth Movement), 26/9/1987.
2. Misgeret — Framework.
3. Klita — Absorption.

not priority number one. *But in fact, your continuous and ongoing involvement with Reform Zionism, as individuals* **and more particularly as a group**, *will be a major factor in your successful klita.*

It seems to me that the basic point of departure of RSY Netzer has to be: "At this juncture of Reform, Zionist, and Jewish history what type of Reform Zionist commitment will have the maximum impact — on Israel, on Reform Judaism. Aliyah is just a technical step — albeit one of cardinal importance — in realizing Reform Zionist commitment. *Aliyah, in and of itself, is not an aim.*

There can be (and unfortunately is) Aliyah of Reform Zionist individuals which has little or no significance in terms of Reform Zionist impact. Please don't misunderstand. Of course such Aliyah is important — for the individual and for the State of Israel. Of course we want to encourage the Aliyah of any Jew who is willing to make his/her life a part of the Jewish National Home. But that is not what we are talking about here.

Only as a group/groups can you put your distinctive stamp on any part of the Israeli polity in which you lay down anchor. This is so even if part of your Misgeret makes Aliyah to a Kibbutz. However, as it is reasonable to assume that a significant part of the Misgeret Aliyah would eventually want to integrate within an urban framework, your prior commitment to some kind of group framework would seem to be an even more necessary prerequisite both for impact and for a more successful Klita.

Such a commitment to a group framework means not only an Aliyah commitment — it means making an initial commitment to an outlook of values and principles which in microcosm already reflect the Reform Zionist outlook by which you will try to live and the direction of the impact that you want to have. If you think that this is putting the cart before the horse, then in terms of "conventional wisdom" you are correct. The problem is that "conventional wisdom" has not gotten Reform Zionism in Israel very far at this point. Contemporary "conventional wisdom" on this point is also at variance with the historical record — most of the Aliyah organized by the pioneering youth movements from Chutz L'Aretz[1] (or from the Yishuv[2] itself) was organized through Garinim[3] and Hachsharot[4] in which commitment, values and principles were crystallized. The resultant impact determined the orientation and values of Israeli society up until the Nineteen-Fifties.

---

1. Chutz L'Aretz — Outside of Israel.
2. Yishuv — the pre-State Jewish community of Israel.
3. Garinim — Settlement groups.
4. Hachsharot — Training frameworks.

Reform Zionist commitment must become an ongoing *movement* process dedicated to furthering central theses of Reform Zionism in the personal lives of its members and within Israeli society in general. It means being involved in shlichut, and in a framework that support shlichut. Over the years such shlichut has to express itself from the base of a Reform Zionist community life situation here (ideally with like-minded Israelis) and its impact has to be felt both in Israel as well as in the Diaspora. This scenario is not compatible with the idea of individual Aliyah of individual Reform Zionists. The Aliyah framework/s of RSY Netzer have to project themselves forwards over a period of five years and this clearly means ideological education and commitment of a different order than the norm existing today. This includes confronting a number of questions which apparently are passed over in your present process.

What Seem To Be The Undiscussed Issues?

1. Is the Misgeret Aliyah interested in a total-life, purposive community? What is the ultimate rationale for such comprehensive community?

Keep in mind that at the level of religious commitment Reform Zionism must ultimately present a purposive total-life alternative to the various types of Orthodox total-life commitments (Zionist and non-Zionist) that exist in Israel. The Diaspora style of synagogue-centered or even community center Judaism *may* succeed in attracting a certain amount of organizational *affiliation and attendance* but that is not the type of *determined and even militant movement commitment* which is needed for Reform Zionist impact given current and foreseeable pressures within Israel's society and body politic.

And keep in mind another point. Building Reform Zionism on the basis of attendance and affiliation of individuals means in fact building the movement on the basis of professional organizers who will perforce become the professional Reform Zionist party machinery of tomorrow. Do we want to replicate the phenomenon of a professional bureaucracy within the Reform Zionism of the coming generation (your generation) that has become such a millstone around the necks of the classical Zionist parties? Only the total-community can send shlichim instead of what must become a group of Reform Zionist technocrats (be they rabbis, social workers or whatever) and only an actively concerned and involved total-community will be able to give them the political backing that they need. Please apply a little salt and pepper of sophistication to the above statements. Some professionalism will be unavoidable. But we can't have a *movement* of professionals.

Has your Misgeret really discussed Israel's political-social state, its prognosis and what the implications are for your having any impact here at all? Here is the "lay of the land" as I see it.

The forces of moderation in Israel are in disarray. They have been devitalized. Broadly speaking, this means the weakening of those forces whose major criterion for political action is furthering the good of the individual within a Zionist context — Buber once referred to it as Hebrew Humanism. The aim of political and social action is not the divinely ordained Mitzva (religious or national) nor is it the State. The aim of social and political action is a society in which every individual attains maximum self-fulfillment; and as Zionists we believe that maximum self-fulfillment is possible only within the context of Zionist self-realization.

The lack of new ideas in both the Labor party (including Mapam) and the moderate right (the Liberals) has resulted in the elements of grass-roots movement being eliminated. Much of the sense of purpose in the community elements of the Labor movement (the Kibbutzim) has been eroded and replaced by concerns of day-to-day existence. The moderate elements of the National Religious Party have been similarly affected. Instead there is a continual jockeying for personal position and endless political in-fighting. A new generation, largely Levantine has arisen. Its attachment to ideas and ideals is relatively superficial when compared to the pre-State norm. People are mainly concerned with and committed to the immediate welfare of their family-clan (that old Mediterranean phenomenon — the Mafia syndrome). In contrast to the society of the pre-state Yishuv, negative elements of an Israeli mass society without any real ideological or philosophical roots have emerged. Hence much of the younger generation is susceptible to slogans, demagogues and appeal to tribal loyalties on a primitive level. This basic Zionist rootlessness is also the cause of the Yerida[1] phenomenon. The actual percentage of Yerida is only the tip of the iceberg.

Only the extreme religious groups, Zionist (Gush Emunim and Kahana) and non or anti-Zionist (from Aguda and, more particularly, Shas all the way through to Neturei Karta) really know what they want. They are backed by significant numbers of purposive communities who are on call for shlichut at all times.

They have maneuvered the Government into financing their communities — the Gush Emunim settlements and more especially the Yeshivot. They have established a marriage of convenience with the economically opportunistic and populist, demagogic and nationalist right wing of Herut. The liberal nationalism

---

1. Yerida — "descending." Emigration from Israel.

of Jabotinsky is bereft of heirs. The ultra-nationalists of T'chiya are calling the shots for Herut nationalism. The Peace Now movement and Ratz[1] are rallying points of a small but basically isolated minority.

So here you are, a Reform Zionist Misgeret idealistically planning to put your lives and the lives of your future families on the line within this happy scenario. I am not being cynical. I know that your decision is motivated by ideals. But I'm nonplussed by your naivete. A Misgeret Aliyah under current circumstances that sends its chaverim on Aliyah into the Israeli pressure cooker as individuals will have most of their Reform Zionism cooked out of them in short order in their struggle for survival — unless they are directly maintained in their Reform Zionism by becoming Reform Zionist professionals and receiving continuous transfusions of Reform Zionist money from the Diaspora.

For the future of Reform Zionism the comprehensive community framework is the best chance for surviving and creating. It is the symmetric answer to the level of commitment and shlichut being put on the line by the ultra-orthodox and the ultra-nationalist. I would like to be unambiguous. *The life frameworks that Reform Zionism must create in Israel must be Jewish value alternatives to those of the ultra-orthodox and ultra-nationalist expressed at their level of commitment or shlichut.*

By the way, this opinion is not shared by the existing tiny Reform movement. There are those who feel that it is all a matter of more and better professionals. Any short-run political battles that Reform may win (and we all hope that they will win and we are all in favor of maximum political activism in this area) have no meaning without long-term lay commitments of tens (that is where we are at and that is why you are critically important and why it is critically important that your Aliyah be significant for Reform Zionism) and later hundreds — who are prepared to put their lives and personal futures on the line within frameworks of commitment. Can the varieties of Jewish Humanism generate the same level of communal commitment that Jewish "Humeini-ism" is capable of mobilizing? Once upon a time the secular Kibbutzim could and did. They have lost their "religion." Can Reform Zionist community be a relevant replacement — a rallying point for those who believe in democratic, humanistic, Zionistically committed Judaism?

Disagree with me if you must — but come with *your* version of a political-social map and how you think RSY Netzer (and all Netzer Olami for that matter) should negotiate the problematic terrain.

---

1. Ratz — Citizens Rights movement currently merged as part of "Meretz."

2.   What is Total-Life Community? Is it for me/us?

Now we have to get into the bugaboo of total-community and the individual. No doubt, this question reflects what is so far a non-success story in Netzer Olami.

There are all kinds of total-communities — including those where "total" really means totalitarian. That is so in many of the ultra-orthodox Kollelim and Yeshivot. We are obviously talking about democratic frameworks in the context of this letter.

About Comprehensive Community — and Your Experience

Theoretically you have all had experience with one type of total-community — the Kibbutz. Some of you have had personal experience with more than one Kibbutz. Re-im, Yahel, Lotan are all total-communities and yet they are different from one another as are three different people who can all be typed, biologically, as Homo Sapiens! And if a third Reform Kibbutz is established by the generation that will make Aliyah sometime in the early Nineties then doubtless it too will have a different personality. On the other hand, very few of you (if any) have had personal experience with total-community in an urban setting which is the major challenge that Reform Zionism must confront — I would guess by the mid-Nineties. I don't see the educational process in Netzer Olami (or Tzofei Telem) which will create adequate numbers before then. My guess is that the Kibbutzim will have to be strong enough to support such an endeavor which ideologically would be quite close to them.

Unfortunately, within the context of the experiences you had it would seem that the rationale of total-community for Zionist living (the possibility of mobilizing people and community for shlichut is just one example) was not discussed adequately. On the contrary, many of you even absorbed some fallacies — and you can hardly be blamed for this for even some Kibbutz members subscribe to them.

THE FALSE CONTRADICTION BETWEEN INDIVIDUAL SELF-FULFILLMENT AND ZIONIST SELF-REALIZATION[1]

Perhaps the major fallacy is the idea that there is an inherent contradiction between individual self-fulfillment and Zionist self-realization within a comprehensive community. In actual fact, the belief in the equal worth of all people in

---

1. See Section 4:2.

tandem with the belief that the aim of a humanist community is the maximal fulfillment of the individual provides the firmest ideological base possible for individual self-fulfillment. The base is firm because it exists *regardless* of one's personal ability (or the ability of one's children) to compete in an inhuman culturally sanctioned (by Western Society) race for individual achievement. Why inhuman? Because the purpose of the race (whether in London or in Tel Aviv) is the accumulation of status, power, money — in some combination and *not* the nurture of the human in the human being created in the divine image. The basic rule of the game is that most of the good things in life come only via the route of personal achievement in the competitive framework that constitutes the "natural reality" of life.

A life in community (let alone Jewish community committed to the ongoing attempt to maximize the realization of the divine image within it) is predicated to the basic value-proposition that as humans and as Jews *we create social reality*. And of course as Zionists with a certain outlook we feel that we did not come/are not coming to Israel to create a State and society "like all the Nations." Hopefully, Reform Zionist communities will be the building blocks to illustrate that point — in our own lives, for ourselves and, perhaps as an example to others.

Ultimately, the compatibility — indeed the advantage — of comprehensive community for the development of the individual is based on the belief that as humans we determine our cultural values and way of life congruent with those values. We must eat, drink, sleep and (in terms of the species) reproduce. We must protect ourselves from the vagaries of nature (clothing and shelter). Our innate drives of sex and aggression need outlets to ensure normative human psychological functioning but those outlets are not biologically predetermined. They find their human expression in an infinite variety of ways in which we can love and work. As human beings (distinct from animals) we reject the idea of a "natural reality," in the spirit of a modified Social Darwinism, to which we must adapt in the spirit of survival of the fittest.

Another aspect of the misunderstanding of the relationship between individual self-fulfillment and Zionist self-realization stems from the false assumption that Zionist self-fulfillment is possible without frameworks of self-realization. If we are talking about movement, and if the function of movement is always to move (change) society in some way then we must do so with others. But if the aim of the movement is to change a way of life (and not just a single issue before society at a given moment — e.g., Reform rights in Israel) then that way of life has to be lived by those who wish to change it. If Reform Zionism wishes to change the nature of Jewish society (not just the format of Jewish ritual in Israeli synagogues) then that way of life has to be lived and preached. To do so one must live in a community committed to that kind of shlichut. Ultimately, if the struggle of Reform Zionism is not your personal struggle, alongside any other work that you may want to do, then you are not a candidate for a community of Reform Zionist self-realization. But if the problem of Reform Zionism is your *personal* problem then you cannot really achieve individual self-fulfillment except in a community of Reform Zionist self-realization — i.e., a community of Reform Zionist shlichut.

Please note that I'm being very careful not to say "kibbutz" as code-word for community of shlichut. There are Kibbutzim where this element is weak or absent. There is nothing wrong in wanting to live on Kibbutz for a host of valid reasons — many of which I personally identify with fully. But this is not the subject of our discussion.

THE FALSE CONTRADICTION BETWEEN DEMOCRATIC ZIONIST COMMUNITY AND INDIVIDUAL FREEDOM

But what about freedom, you ask? What will happen to my basic freedom in comprehensive community even if I accept the necessity of Community for Shlichut?

What *is* freedom and what is its purpose? Here too we are confused as Jews, as Reform Jews and as Reform Zionists. We have all grown up in the cultures of the West. These cultures have taken the symbolic concept of Freedom as embodied in "Let My People Go" and applied it to the modern liberal concept of the individual freedom of individuals and nations. This idea of individual rights was the outcome of the Enlightenment and its human-centered secular as opposed to God-centered theocratic world outlook.

The original idea of freedom was purposive — freedom was a means and not an end in itself. The passage reads: "Shlach et Ami VeYaavduni" — i.e., Let my People Go and They Will Worship Me. In other words, the purpose of freedom for the People of Israel was to enable them to live according to God's commandments so as to being about "Tikun Olam B'Malchut Shadai."

Reform Judaism, at its outset adopted the Western concept of Freedom as a part of its adaptation to Emancipation. Zionism was of two minds — on the one hand, the Political Zionism modeled on other European national movements saw freedom in and of itself as an inherent right. On the other hand, most schools of thought in Cultural Zionism, while not negating the Political Zionist approach to freedom, related to freedom as purposive in terms of the continued role of the

Jewish People as an educative force in the history of nations. Reform Zionism as a whole has scarcely begun to confront such fundamental questions. But Reform Zionist community cannot evade the question. It exists as an affirmation of the proposition that a synthesis of the two concepts of freedom — freedom as a right and freedom as a means to fulfill our Jewish responsibility — is not only possible but also the only possibility for a contemporary Jewish society that can make a difference.

Simply put, the Western and Jewish concepts of Freedom must be melded — democratically, in voluntary frameworks. How, to what degree, under what circumstances, etc. — all these are part of the discussion that will have to take place (already is taking place) where Reform Zionist community exists.

The proposition that I would like to focus on is that a Reform Zionist Misgeret that merely constitutes a technical framework for furthering Aliyah and Klita of RSY Netzer graduates is not a Reform Zionist Misgeret in the true sense at all. It is a technical aid to young British Reform Jews making Aliyah period. And if your practical rejoinder is "But what about all those who have already reached a personal stage of development and commitment where they can non longer undertake a re-evaluation of their whole basic life outlook? — then I only have two possible answers (I am writing this during the Yamim Noraim).

Answer number one — insofar as we are human we always have the power within us for a change of heart and mind. We always have the power to wrestle again with question of our ultimate nature and identity and to discover in ourselves that mysterious quality within us that drives us to search for the eternal. It is easier to do it together with others on whom one can draw for support.

Answer number two was given to the generation that went out of Egypt. Individual, non-community Reform Zionist Aliyah is a contradiction in terms. Even those who "make it" materially in Israel will, in a sense, be condemned to returning to Egypt in spirit and wandering in the desert of non-purposive freedom that they have set up for themselves as an ideal.

Differentiating Between G'milut Chassadim and Shlichut

The third seminal question that you have not dealt with is the question of shlichut as a value and clearly distinguishing between Shlichut (mission) and G'milut Chassadim (good works, charity). Reform Judaism has a particular problem with this terminology because of its past history.

The Mitzva of G'milut Chassadim is essentially an act of grace, an act of love toward one's fellow for which no recompense is expected. The idea of the Reform Zionist community must surely include G'milut Chassadim as a central facet of interpersonal relationships between members. Moreover the community must also see itself as relating in this spirit to the outside world in ways commensurate with its ability. But this is not in and of itself Shlichut.

Shlichut means an action program of one kind or another (e.g., political, educational) in order to change the world. It is true that the political vision may be informed by a spirit of love. But that does not make it G'milut Chassadim.

We must keep in mind that much of the necessity of G'milut Chassadim in the pre-modern Jewish community stemmed from basic social inequality which existed as a norm within the community. Certainly, everyone including the wealthy have social responsibility. But the prophetic spirit of social justice calls out for an ultimate harmony in which some aspects of G'milut Chassadim will be superfluous. Of course this comment does not relate to such aspects of G'milut Chassadim as, for example, visiting the sick. But many if not most aspects of G'milut Chassadim ultimately relate to social problems. For Reform Judaism the active pursuit of social reform in order to abrogate the need for G'milut Chassadim can be problematic. This is without gainsaying that Reform Judaism (in America in particular) has been actively involved in social reform — but note, for purposes mainly outside the framework of the Jewish community.

Here in Israel the word "outreach" has been currently used as a term almost synonymous with shlichut. Again, outreach is a positive aim. (The current attempt to place it almost totally in the hands of "professionals" is a less positive manifestation.) However, "outreach" in and of itself is meaningless if its aim is simply to increase the "head count" of people affiliating with Reform. Outreach is only relevant if Reform Zionism has an action program to which those who affiliate will eventually commit themselves. There is not necessarily any relationship between the number of Jews affiliating with Reform and its political impact.

◆ ◆ ◆

All of the above constitute questions that the Misgeret Aliyah — and indeed all of RSY Netzer must work through. And if the Misgeret is not prepared to do so as a Misgeret then those who want to relate to these questions in their personal lives must form Garinim. The immediate tactical question of what such Garinim should relate to, organizationally in Israel, is for future discussions. But first — on with the work of self-definition as stated at the outset of this missive. This letter has been an attempt to describe some of the questions that you must deal with in the Misgeret's attempt to define itself. I have not claimed that these are the only questions.

One last sobering thought. The history of "Anglo-Saxon" Aliyah and its impact on Israeli society has not been a success story. Reform Zionism must inevitably base itself on significant Aliyah — qualitatively and then quantitatively. Much of the impotency of "Anglo-Saxon" Aliyah has been its inability to translate ideas into ideological action programs — and from there to long-term commitment of shlichut to further those action programs. It has to do with our cultural propensities, our inability to link our individual lives of self-fulfillment (even on the Kibbutz!) with *our* long-term program of Zionist self-realization.

My best wishes.
LeHitraot B'Aretz.[1]

---

1. See you again in Israel.

A Letter to ARZA[1]

May 6, 1992

Mr. Norman Schwartz
President, ARZA
1402 Fairoak Drive
Silver Spring MD 20902

Dear Norman,

Enclosed please find a position paper on ARZA and Reform Zionist Youth Programming in the UAHC Youth Division.[2] The purpose of this paper is to raise policy questions which deal with the *raison d'etre* of ARZA.

It may seem strange that with the Congress upon us I should choose this time to raise questions which some may feel are not within the purview of ARZA at all. Furthermore, within the context of the daily crises in my ongoing work as Executive Director of the Department of Jewish Education and Culture ("our" Department under the stewardship of Rabbi Hank Skirball), it never seems to be a suitable time to deal with other than immediate burning issues. Indeed, this letter has been put off time and time again since my visit to America in January because of constraints related to this situation.

I accept that one important purpose of ARZA and ARZENU[3] is to serve as a lobby for Reform interests (however defined) in the WZO and the Jewish Agency. But if this is the central purpose of the organized Reform Zionist movement then this paper will miss the mark. On the other hand, if ARZA and ARZENU seek to define essential interests and policy stemming from a Reform Zionist perspective, then hopefully this statement will contribute to the process of defining those interests and translating them into policy — including effective lobbying for our organizational interests.

It is precisely against the backdrop of the upcoming Congress (with the possible denouement between ARZENU and the established institutions of the WZO) that we should also be considering in terms of "deep background" seminal

---

1. ARZA — Association of Reform Zionists of America.
2. Unpublished memo to the ARZA National Board, 1992.
3. World Confederation of Reform Zionist Movements.

questions facing Reform Zionism not only at present but also after the Congress. This letter is not the place to review again the possible operational implications that I submitted to Rabbi Skirball and that I know he passed on to ARZA a number of months ago.

I do attach great importance to the current political initiatives of ARZENU to democratize the murky world of the World Zionist Organization and the Jewish Agency. Nevertheless, in my opinion ARZENU (and within it ARZA as the largest body by far within ARZENU) must deal with questions of Reform Zionist substance within the Reform movement in the Diaspora. Otherwise, the emphasis on "tikun" in the political and organizational instrumentalities outside the Reform movement becomes an exercise bereft of much of its potential significance and moral basis.

In the same spirit, the ARZA initiatives in Israel are to be commended — whether in the area of sponsoring the center for Democracy and Pluralism or whether in the area of funding the nascent system of education of the Israel Movement for Progressive Judaism (I also happen to be a member of the Israeli movements' education committee). Even though I feel these areas of activity are deserving of the support of all Reform Jews I do not suggest that ARZA lessen its efforts supporting projects of the Reform movement in Israel. However these activities fall into the category of Reform Jewish pro-Israel activity rather than Reform Zionist commitment. They do not deal with questions of Reform Zionist substance in the Diaspora with which the enclosed position paper and its appendices seek to contend.

Looking forward to seeing you at the Congress,

B'vracha, Michael Livni

cc: ARZA Board
ARZENU Executive
UAHC — Rabbi Alexander Schindler, Rabbi Daniel Syme, Rabbi Howard Bogot
Youth Division Staff — Rabbi Allan Smith, Rabbi David Frank, Rabbi David Forman, Paul Reichenbach
Shlichim — Meir Yaffe, Micha Balf
Netzer Olami — Lea Ronen, Mike Nitzan
Rabbi Stanley Davids
Rabbi Henry F. Skirball
Rabbi Richard Hirsch
Gidon Elad

POSITION PAPER

ARZA AND REFORM ZIONIST YOUTH PROGRAMMING
IN THE UAHC YOUTH DIVISION

The purpose of this paper is to raise policy questions which deal with the raison d'etre of ARZA.

It is my thesis that if ARZA seeks to have a substantive long-range impact it must become a serious advocate for a Reform Zionist educational policy within the Reform movement nationally, regionally, and locally. Of course adult education should be an integral part of the ARZA program for its own chapters as well as a means for outreach into the congregation and the region. But my concern here is with advocacy for Reform Zionism in the educational institutions of the Reform movement such as the Divisions of the UAHC dealing with education and the Hebrew Union College. However, this paper deals with the Youth Division of the UAHC in particular.

The Youth Division of the UAHC has been the focus of Israel activity in the past and has had *shlichim* assigned to it for this purpose. Hence it constitutes the logical venue for the implementation of a Reform Zionist educational policy. ARZA should find constructive ways to participate in policy formation of the UAHC Youth Division.

Background

Fifteen years ago as the first *shaliach* to the UAHC Youth Division I was involved in the initiative which resulted in the creation of ARZA. After the Yom Kippur war and the "Zionism is racism" resolution in the United Nations the temper of the times became ripe for the Reform movement to become more involved in the Zionist movement. The trigger to become a regular political party within the WZO (as distinct from the associate membership of the World Union) was the unacceptable system for allocating WZO resources for those not part of the system — in our case the Youth Division of the UAHC. The initiative of *Garin Arava*[1] of that time to submit a formal request for WZO membership was happily "preempted" by the movement as a whole. ARZA was founded and created a tremendous feeling of accomplishment and expectation with regard to the future of Reform Zionism in America among those who had initiated the process.

At that time it was my hope (and I know that this hope was shared by others) that ARZA would be that activist element in American Reform Judaism working

---

1. *Garin Arava* — settlement group composed of American Reform college-age youth.

within the institutions and the congregations of the movement in order to make Zionist commitment an accepted norm.

In particular we were hoping to create a degree of personal engagement with the Zionist enterprise on the part of American Reform Jewish youth as a norm for ensuring the ongoing creative continuity of the Reform movement within contemporary Judaism. We saw the task of Reform Zionism as imparting both the framework and content of what was to be an innovative phenomenon in modern Jewish spirituality. We felt that the synthesis of Reform and Zionism, the two major responses of the Jewish people to the modern age, had the potential for this kind of fructifying impact on Reform Judaism and the Jewish polity of the Diaspora and Israel in general.

The last decade has seen the partial realization of such a vision in a number of smaller Reform communities — particularly in Great Britain and in Australia. Reform Zionist youth movements (which founded Netzer Olami) have evolved there as a result of educational policy supported by the movement leadership in those countries. I don't want to paint an overly idyllic picture. The process in these countries was (and is) sometimes accompanied by friction and misunderstandings. However, the net addition to just plain Reform Jewish commitment (i.e., young people prepared to do for themselves and others and not just prepared to have others do for them) is proving itself. In these countries the Netzer Reform Zionist program has become the normative path for informal Reform Jewish education.

There is a difference between active commitment and passive identity. Netzer Olami has shown that there is an energizing potential to the synthesis between Reform Judaism and Zionism. That energy is beginning to express itself both in the home community and in a small but significant *Aliyah* movement. This is not just an *Aliyah* of individuals who feel that Israel is the answer to living a life of Jewish identity for them and their children — even though in and of itself this continues to be an excellent reason for an *Aliyah* decision. The significance of the *Aliyah* movement stems from the fact that it has a sense of Reform Zionist purpose vis-a-vis the Jewish National Home. This is precisely the type of Reform Zionist *Aliyah* that we so desperately need to catalyze the growth of Reform in Israel. For those who do not opt for *Aliyah* it is also the type of commitment needed for activist Zionistically oriented Judaism in the Diaspora.

The scenario we hoped for in North America fifteen years ago was an ARZA which would provide the political "backstopping" both within the Reform movement and within the World Zionist Organization for this kind of development. After all the bulk of Reform Jewry is in the United States. Of course there is no point in extrapolating numerically from the experience of Britain and Australia — they are very different kinds of communities.

Nevertheless, it is also true that THE YOUTH DIVISION HAS PURSUED EDUCATIONAL POLICIES WHICH COULD NOT (AND DID NOT) LEAD TO THE RESULTS THAT WE WERE ABLE TO ACHIEVE IN OTHER COUNTRIES. This is NOT 20/20 hindsight. In the late Nineteen Seventies, prior to the establishment of Netzer Olami,[1] the same policies in principle were suggested for the United States but rejected by the Youth Division which feared that they would be too disjunctive. Trite but true — there can be no movement without some friction.

The article, "Zionist Youth Movement for Reform Judaism" which I submitted to the Youth Division at the end of my *shlichut* to the UAHC in the summer of 1977 and published in the *Garin Arava Iggeret*[2] in October of that year is appended to this position paper.

I know there has been criticism of the *shlichim* assigned to the Youth Division during the past ten years and perhaps some of the *shlichim* could have been more adequate to their task. However the fact of the matter is that during the past ten years the *shlichim* did not have the support for an overall strategy of Reform Zionist programming that was given to the *shlichim* during the Nineteen Seventies. Nor would I say that the *shlichim* sent to other countries were inherently superior to the *shlichim* sent to America although they did of course work in a more favorable environment.

The ten years we have lost in terms of building Reform Zionism have seriously impeded our growth and vitality in Israel. My estimate is that we lost 50-100 committed young Reform Zionist *Olim*. This has had a negative effect on the growth of our kibbutzim as well as the emergence of alternative urban congregations. More specifically, this type of committed and knowledgeable *Aliyah* would have significantly augmented the future leadership — in particular the lay leadership — of the Israeli movement in both the urban and rural sectors. The lack of adequate lay leadership and the resulting over-dependence on professional (paid) leadership is proving to be the bane of the Israeli movement.

I do believe that it is the responsibility of ARZA to relate to policies within the UAHC Division which have a deleterious effect on the future of Reform Zionism in Israel as well as the Diaspora. Therefore I am suggesting that this become a central item on the ARZA agenda.

---

1. Netzer Olami — *Noar Zioni Reformi* — Reform Zionist Youth Movement outside of North America.
2. Garin Arava Iggeret — newsletter (the article appears in Section 5:1).

Current Youth Division Policy: Pro-Israel But Non-Zionist

In January of this year when I visited New York a meeting took place on my initiative between the staff of ARZA and the Youth Division of the UAHC with the participation of Gidon Elad (Noar and Hechalutz) and Etti Serok (Dept. of Jewish Education and Culture).

In my opinion, there were important substantive results. It was agreed that the Youth Division would highlight a NFTY[1] High School in Israel program for Grade 11. My understanding is also that ARZA will co-sponsor this program. I believe that the involvement of ARZA in an educational program must surely be seen as a truly positive precedent.

In Israel we are negotiating to make the planned new NFTY High School semester and the preparatory program leading up to it a joint project of both the Dept. of Jewish Education and Culture and the Dept. of Youth and Hechalutz. In cooperation with the Youth Division and the Division of Religious Education of the UAHC we hope to evolve a series of activities projecting options of Reform-Jewish identity for the Junior High School years (between Bar Mitzva and Confirmation). The program would be adaptable to both religious schools as well as to the UAHC camps. It would impart legitimacy to the idea that a significant learning experience in Israel should become a norm for every young Reform Jew. Hence the program would also constitute preparation for the NFTY semester in Israel. Such a project is also a legitimate recipient of financial and other support from our Department and will be submitted as such to the Joint Authority for Jewish Zionist Education.

On the other hand, the Youth Division remains adamant in its refusal to subscribe to an overall strategy of Reform Zionist education — in particular insofar as High school graduates and college students are concerned. The pro-Israel proclivities of the Youth Division remain unquestioned and its investment in the area of Israel programming over the years has been considerable. However, this investment has NOT been expended within the framework of an overall strategy of Reform Zionist education and hence it has had little or no Reform Zionist impact during the past ten years. Without the establishment of post High School programs with a Reform Zionist Orientation the NFTY Semester will not be a part of a potential educational continuum. Hence its Reform Zionist potential will not be adequately realized.

I pointed out at our January meeting that in the absence of a Reform Zionist rationale a *shaliach/shlicha* is reduced to being an Israel resource person servicing

---

1. National Federation of Temple Youth (of the Union of American Hebrew Congregations).

a pro-Israel youth program. It is questionable whether maintaining a *shaliach/shlicha* (or *shlichim*) for this purpose justifies the outlay of $90,000 per year of the Jewish people's money.

The purpose of pro-Israel education is to utilize Israel in order to strengthen Jewish identity as it relates to the existing community (of which support for Israel is an integral part). Pro-Israel education is a basis for Zionist education — but it is not Zionist education as such. Attached is a precis of my paper, "Educating to Zionism" which expands on this differentiation.[1]

Zionist education means cognitive and experiential exposure to alternative modes of Jewish Zionist self-realization. Classically, it is the task of the *shaliach* to counterpoint the normative path of Jewish identification (including pro-Israel Jewish identification) with an alternative path. The *shaliach/shlicha* has to be able to work with youth leaders who in turn will be role models for others as they contend in their personal lives with alternative value paths. The creative tension in the dynamic field between these alternative paths is the energizing factor in Jewish Zionist education. This creative tension is largely absent from pro-Israel education. It is this creative tension which creates Zionist commitment.

Clearly, if this concept is not acceptable to the Youth Division (as it once was) then having a *shaliach* becomes a symbolic act without real meaning. A meaningful *shlichut* program means a conscious decision to live with two partially contradictory educational philosophies within NFTY, the UAHC Camps, the College Age Department and of course the International Education Department.

As *Achad Ha'am* pointed out in his essay "Priest and Prophet" such an ambience is a quintessential part of the Biblical tradition. The task of Zionism and a Jewish State as *Achad Ha'am* understood it was to revivify the contradiction and tension that we find in the Bible between priests and prophets in a contemporary context. Only thus could Judaism remain meaningful and creative in the modern age. If the Youth Division seeks a "tame" Zionist program then this is a contradiction in terms.

The Desirable Educational Policies

What are the educational policies necessary in addition to the current pro-Israel policies of the Youth Division? To be more precise — what should be added to the building blocks already in place in the Youth Division in order to transform an educational policy geared to inculcating a pro-Israel Reform Jewish identity into a policy which has some prospect of leading to Reform Zionist commitment whether it expresses itself in the Diaspora or Israel.

---

1. See Section 4:3 for the ideas summarized in the precis.

1. There must be a semi-autonomous program, adequately funded and with a *shaliach*-advisor for graduates of Israel programs. This would be an American version of Netzer. As we are talking about a post-NFTY age group such a program should be the joint responsibility of the Youth Division and ARZA. The *shaliach/shlicha* assigned to work with this program should therefore be assigned jointly to the Youth Division and ARZA. (Such a *shaliach/shlicha* would also be available for adult educational work in ARZA.)

2. The following are operational examples of how the various departments of the Youth Division could up-grade their current pro-Israel orientation so that the implementation of an overall strategy of Reform Zionist education would be enhanced.

   A. The planned participation of NFTY graduates who are members of American Netzer at regional NFTY Conclaves.

   B. The staffing of every UAHC Camp with some qualified members of American Netzer. The integration of cognitive and experiential programming projecting Reform Zionist approaches to questions of Jewish identity. (Some of the UAHC Camps already try to do this).

      ARZA members serving on the various Camp boards which determine policy for particular camps could further this component of Reform Zionist education.

   C. The International Education Department of the Youth Division should be taking affirmative action to encourage attending long-term Reform Zionist Israel programs — see points 3 and 4 following.

   D. In a number of regions the College Age Department should seek to establish "Batim" (cooperative apartments or housing) for committed American Netzer activists which would not only serve as support groups for those already committed but also as centers for outreach to the larger campus community.

   In the Nineteen Seventies the *shlichim* (including myself) began to organize such a framework but there was no continuity to this effort in the Eighties. The Youth Division at the College Age level must be prepared to work in tandem with an American Netzer but in today's circumstances this should be the youth movement of ARZA. As distinct from other Netzer movements (which begin at ages 9-10), American Netzer should be a college age movement. However, the question of Netzer in Canada on the British model should be the subject of a separate discussion.

3. A NFTY Contingent of 10-20 per year, recruited from NFTY Leadership in the senior year of High School, must become a part of the existing Reform Zionist

contingent to the Youth and Hechalutz Departments' Leadership Training Course for Youth Leaders from abroad. This will catalyze the process of American Reform Zionist identity formation in a group of young leaders by virtue of being in ongoing contact not only with members of other Reform movements but with young people from differing Zionist backgrounds as such. A more general framework of a NFTY year in Israel (similar in its framework to the Young Judaea Year Course) should be established later.

4. A significant period of time (three to six months) in any Israel program of the Youth Division for the 18-20 age group must be spent in a Reform Zionist environment in Israel. Otherwise there is inadequate contact with older Reform Zionist role models and hence no basis for confronting the question of Reform Zionist *Aliyah* within the Israel experience.

By isolating its programs (particularly its long term programs) in Israel from the other Reform Zionist youth movements the Youth Division is severely hampering the emergence of a world Reform Zionist movdment.

The British and Australian experience have shown that four or five consecutive years of ten to twenty youth going through this kind of a program was necessary for building the critical mass which was able to bring about a sea change in the home communities. The South African movement which could not pursue such a policy because of governmental constraints has remained relatively small.

It is not the adoption of one or another of the above points which will lead to Reform Zionist impact. Only the deliberate implementation in an integrated way of ALL of these parameters during the coming decade can lead to the critical mass of young people (perhaps 200-300 by the end of the decade who are truly committed and perhaps half of these will make *Aliyah*). Of course they will be the visible minority of a much larger number that will have been influenced by going through the process of confrontation with Reform Zionist identity.

The Youth Division: Administrative Implications For ARZA-ARZENU

Given the current situation in the World Zionist Organization, the Jewish Agency and especially the Joint Authority for Jewish Zionist Education, it seems more than likely that ARZENU (in effect ARZA) will become involved in questions affecting the Youth Division that arise in these forums.

1. The Youth Division and Netzer Olami have partially parallel and overlapping administrative structures in Israel. In fact, if there were no ideological differ-

ences between Netzer and the Youth Division there would be no good administrative rationale for the coexistence of two such administrative infrastructures. Given existing financial constraints this question could become a public issue in the near future.

Both Netzer Olami and the Youth Division service the needs of their home communities for an Israel experience under Reform auspices. However, the Netzer Olami approach is an integral part of an overall Zionist educational program in the Diaspora geared to inculcating creative tension with a Reform Zionist ambience.

2. The ideological difference which does exist is exploited by those outside the Reform movement in order to discount the Zionist nature of the Youth Division and the legitimacy of investing shlichim and shlichim type resources in the Reform movement (especially in North America) at the expense of the "classical" youth movements.

Both Netzer Olami and the Youth Division will have to grapple with the implications inherent in the establishment of the Joint Authority for Jewish Zionist Education. The ability of ARZENU representatives to perform as advocates for the UAHC Youth Division while the latter maintains a Pro-Israel but non-Zionist structure which in essence competes with Youth and Hechalutz will become more and more problematic within the framework of the Joint Authority.

3. Because of the establishment of the Authority there is and will be continuing pressure to cease funding Diaspora clients (as distinct from Israeli clients and institutions) by special allocations from the Jewish Agency. This will have a relatively marginal effect on the UAHC Youth Division but will be most problematic for Netzer Olami.

◆ ◆ ◆

The veteran staff of the UAHC Youth Division have been my good friends and associates for some 15 years. I hope we will maintain that relationship. In a sense, this is a family argument and ARZA is part of that family. I have tried to follow the injunction: *"Hocheach Tochiach et Amitecha"* (Reprove your friend). I do not think I would be furthering the integrity of our relationship — or my personal commitment to Reform Zionism — if I did not, after ten years, raise these issues as central to the existence of ARZA.

Michael Livni
May 1992, Iyar 5752

A Reform Zionist Policy
for the Hebrew Union College[1]

August 18, 1996

Rabbi Sheldon Zimmerman, President
Hebrew Union College
3101 Clifton Avenue
Cincinnati, OH 45220

Dear Sheli,

As a participant in the meeting of July 7 held in Jerusalem I want to thank you again for your openness and patience in hearing the variety of views expressed. In addition, it was a pleasure to meet you again after so many years.

I'm going to accept your offer to all those present to submit their views in writing. I am writing you in a personal capacity, within the context of over 20 years of involvement in Reform Zionist education. In order to put my general views into perspective I am enclosing three articles published in recent years.

1. Democracy, Religion and the Zionist Future of Israel — for a general perspective on where Reform Zionism should fit in here in Israel.[2]
2. Reform Judaism and Reform Zionism in Israel — presenting the basic problems of the interface Reform Judaism/ Reform Zionism in Israel.[3]
3. A Rationale and Program for Reform Zionism — my perspective of what Reform Zionism in the Diaspora should be about.[4]

My comments will relate to:

1) The HUC program for American students
2) The HUC program for Israeli students.
3) HUC in Israel

1. Unpublished letter to Rabbi Sheldon Zimmerman, 1996.
2. See Section 3:3.
3. See Section 2:5.
4. See Section 1:7.

1) The HUC Program for American Students

I know that you have heard many people say that the HUC Jerusalem program is in fact a year inside a "Cincinnati bubble" located in Jerusalem. I agree but I assume you are interested not only in metaphors but also in practical suggestions. Mine is predicated on an assumption which I am not certain has been shared by the HUC in the past. That assumption is that a central consideration in having the students spend a year here is spiritual encounter with relevant foci in the Jewish National Home. The experiential is more important than the cognitive. If that assumption is incorrect then what follows is not very relevant. The student experience will certainly continue to contribute to a certain superficial familiarity with Israel but it will in fact reinforce the Israel-Diaspora dichotomy instead of promoting a sense of interdependence.

I do agree that the wisdom of spending the first year (instead of the third year) in Israel is questionable. I am well aware of the personal (family) constraints that may preclude this option as well as the implementation of some of my suggestions below.

Spiritual encounter means value clarification and confrontation. For myself, as an engaged Reform Zionist in Israel (a category which exists in limited numbers) the indirect proof of the lack of spiritual encounter in the HUC program is the rarity of an HUC student who makes the decision to fulfill himself/herself Reform Zionistically in Israel. Nor do I find myself being called upon to engage in such encounter.

Spiritual encounter is best done in smaller groups than the current HUC classes. In my opinion the class should be split up with sub-groups spending three or four months in the framework of willing Israeli teachers colleges such as Oranim, Seminar Hakibbutzim, or David Yellin. The key is that some of the subjects would be taught partly by their staff and that there would be a structured program of ongoing interaction between students at the teacher colleges and HUC students. I know that there are major logistical questions and educational questions (e.g.,. The preponderance of women students at some of these institutions). On the other hand, most of these colleges are capable of fielding intensive *Ulpan* programs and utilizing their students as tutors to HUC students thus facilitating even more interaction. One idea would be to divide the class into two groups — half the class would spend the first semester in Jerusalem and half would start in the teacher colleges. They might have to be divided according to level of Hebrew knowledge.

As for the cognitive program, I can vouch for Seminar Hakibbutzim and especially Oranim that they have people who can deal with central Jewish value questions such as the value and meaning of Wo/man, *Kehilla*, *Shlichut*, Torah, *Avoda* and *G'milut Chassadim* and *Eretz* Israel. (The Oranim dialogues of the early Seventies paved the way for the establishment of the Reform kibbutzim.) These institutions would utilize sources classical and modern from a "secular" point of view — but that is part of the encounter.

This idea of spending significant time in Israeli teacher seminaries also connects with topic 3 below. Such a semester would be rounded out by two additional two week modules. The group would again sub-divide for a month (one quarter of the entire class)

A. A two week module with the cooperation of the Religious Zionist movement. I refer to the liberal "Meimad" (Rabbi Aharon Lichtenstein) wing of the Religious Zionists and their institutions in Gush Etzion. I can't guarantee that they will agree to have HUC but in the interests of *Clal Israel* they might. I think that such an encounter would be of tremendous importance for both sides. Religious Zionism is not monolithic.

B. A half month (two *shabbatot*) within the framework of the Reform kibbutzim. This should combine learning (Reform Zionism from the kibbutz point of view), work and encounter. Ideally the group would be divided into half between the kibbutzim and "A" above. Even more ideally, in order to foster integration, the groups should be small, split between Yahel and Lotan.

In fact, currently the HUC groups get a three day Negev tourist tour led by Yahel and a three hour look-see stay on Lotan. I think this is a travesty. After all, the kibbutzim represent authentic value encounter from a Reform point of view.

The semester in Jerusalem should include much more structured contact with the Israeli Youth movement, Netzer Olami and Telem. I know that "it takes two to tango." Nevertheless, the ball should be put into the court of the Israeli movement. The Jerusalem stay should also be used to learn about the institutions of the Jewish people, the World Union and ARZENU.

2) The HUC Program for Israeli Students

I approach this question from my perspective within the Israeli movement. My perspective is not shared by most of my fellow members on the *Hanhala*[1] of

---

1. Hanhala — Executive Board.

Telem. On the other hand, at your meeting with us in July you heard the unsolic-ited comments of dismay regarding Telem voiced by of a number of those involved in education. The matter is also dealt with in my enclosed articles.

Simply put, the idea of training Israeli Rabbis for congregational posts in Israel is a total misconception and has no future within Israeli reality. If pursued further in its present form the Israeli Rabbinic program will die. The very notion that congregational Judaism (of any stream) can be cloned from the Diaspora and can be the focal point of Jewish identity in Israel (for which an Israeli will pay congregational dues) is simply a non-starter. Only the ultra-Orthodox who live in the "Israel as Diaspora" mode can make it work. I don't suggest that we emulate them.

The Israel Rabbinic program has to be a program which centers on education. It must grant a teaching certificate (recognized by the Ministry of Education) in Jewish subjects and humanities. The rabbinic element should be a part of such a program and should be recognized as equivalent to an MA so that teachers can get salaries at the MA level. Israelis have to be prepared to teach as their economic mainstay and in order to outreach for Reform Judaism. Part of their training has to be integrating Jewish values into the general curriculum. They have to be familiar with the syllabi of the humanities and Jewish studies as they exist. They have to do lots of exercises planning modules in various subjects that fit in with the curriculum. They have to teach in specific schools open to our integrative liberal approach to Judaism. They have to staff Reform Tali[1] schools such as we have started in Jerusalem. Right now we don't even have enough Reform teachers for Leo Baeck in Haifa let alone for the general educational system which is wide open for us to place qualified teachers.

I don't think all this is possible in the absence of at least an initial stage of cooperation with university affiliated Israeli teacher seminaries.

3) HUC in Israel

A number of people have told you that HUC (and the very name of the HUC) projects a Diaspora image. I know that HUC cannot suddenly become the type of educational institution that we need here in Israel. The Conservative movement with their Beit Midrash is way ahead of us. And yet, paradoxically, with the ideo-logical mandate of Reform Judaism, we have potentially more to offer. The way to begin is by cooperating with existing teaching colleges which already have recog-nition. That would work in with points 1 and 2 above.

---

1. Tali — Tigbur Limudei Yahadut — reinforced Jewish learning.

One way to begin is to offer joint In-Service training with the seminaries in areas of Jewish Studies. Such a policy has the additional advantage of outreaching to the staffs and students (Israel's future teachers) instead of locking ourselves up in the HUC Campus. HUC could offer the Jerusalem Campus as home for Jerusalem modules of those seminaries with whom HUC cooperates. They could be introduced to the Reform movement from that vantage point.

Keep in mind — the Reform movement in Israel is small and isolated. The Israel Religious Action Center has given the word "Reform" word recognition in the media but vanishingly few, (even in the miniscule "movement" that we have), can talk about Reform Judaism as a Zionist alternative which could play a vital role in the emerging culture of the Jewish State. HUC could play a major role if it chooses — in doing so it would strengthen Reform Israel-Diaspora ties and make the concept of Jewish peoplehood more meaningful for the entire movement.

These are my thoughts — but they are not only abstract ideas. Given a suitable framework, I will be happy to assist in the implementation of the above proposals.

B'vracha

Dr. Michael Livni

cc: Rabbi Shaul Feinberg — HUC Jerusalem
    Rabbi Joel Oseran — WUPJ, Jerusalem

SECTION

Reform Zionist Youth Movement in Israel

6

Introduction

1. **Authority in Telem Noar***

2. **Shabbat in Telem Noar**

3. **Telem Noar as a Movement and as a Community**

4. **The Circle of Friendship**

5. **From 5741 to 5742 in Telem Noar/Tzofei Telem****

6. **The Sixth Convention of the IMPJ**

7. **It's Not Every Day That a New Youth Movement Arises**

8. **Telem Noar and the Future of Positive, Creative and Relevant Judaism in Israel**

9. **A Year of Service as a Norm on the Path of Self-Realization**

10. **Clarification of the Term: Rabbinical Adviser**

11. **A Station on the Road to Ideological Clarification in Tzofei Telem**

12. **To Garin Kave on your Day of Celebration**

13. **Excerpts from "A Letter to Garin Arava"*****

14. **The Idea Behind the Ma'amad (Creative Prayer)**

* Telem Noar — Israel Movement for Progressive Judaism (IMPJ) Youth
** Tzofei Telem: Telem (IMPJ) Scouts. When Telem Noar affiliated with the Israeli Scouts in 1982 it changed its name.
*** Settlement group framework for American Reform Youth until 1987

Synopsis of the Section

This section reflects the author's personal involvement and struggle to establish an Israeli Reform Zionist youth movement as a synthesis between principles of

Reform Judaism and Zionist Jewish education within the framework of a youth community of dialogue.

During the years 1980-1996 informal education for youth in the IMPJ was conducted within the framework of an autonomous youth movement (as opposed to a federation of congregational youth groups). During much of this time the youth movement was a joint venture of the United Kibbutz Movement, the IMPJ, and was loosely affiliated with the Israeli Scouts.

Most of these articles were written in the period when the author served as Coordinator of the Reform Zionist youth movement in Israel. (Telem-Noar and later Tzofei Telem). They are position papers on internal issues — educational and political — that arose. The articles fall into several categories and some fall into more than one.

Articles 1, 6, and 10 deal specifically with internal questions in the youth movement that interfaced with the adult Israel Movement for Progressive Judaism (IMPJ).

Articles 2, 4, 14 confront questions of (religious) observance arising as a result of the movement's activities (particularly on Shabbat).

Articles 1, 5, 9, 11, document stations on the path of internal self-definition and development of the youth movement.

Some of the articles (3, 7, 8, 13) explain the youth movement to outside audiences linked with the work of the youth movement. In doing so, they document the author's personal understanding and perspective of the youth movement's significance at that time.

During the years 1979-1983 I served as the coordinator of Telem Noar/Tzofei Telem (see preface). I remained active in an advisory capacity for a number of years thereafter. Most of the articles in this section were written during the years 1980-1985. The articles were all written in response to "needs of the hour" and fall into several categories.

1. Articles dealing with the self-definition of the Reform Zionist Youth movement in terms of its internal educational needs — both in matters of Jewish norms and in matters of organization.
2. Articles responding to the necessity of interfacing with adult movements (in particular the IMPJ).[1]
3. Articles describing Tzofei-Telem to outside publics.

Authority in Telem Noar

AUTHORITY IN TELEM NOAR (1) had a seminal function in the process of Telem Noar's self-definition as an autonomous youth movement. The first educational council (in fact, a convention), held in Kibbutz Yahel, decided to adopt the platform of the IMPJ while resolving that it would seek to determine norms of movement behavior at movement activities by means of learning, movement discussion and finally movement decision. Every ten members of the age of 14 and up, and all members of the leadership staff including Rabbinical advisors, were allotted a vote in the Educational Conventions. This general format theoretically reflected the norm in the classical pioneering youth movements even though I was well aware that by the early Eighties the classical youth movements were no longer truly autonomous from their political party affiliation or Kibbutz movement bureaucracy.

There were two major points at issue in defining authority in Telem Noar. The first point was the *de facto* negation of Rabbinic authority and the relegation of rabbis to an advisory and teaching role as distinct from being Rabbinic directors with ultimate authority. In term of the *de jure* internal development of the

---

1. IMPJ — Israel Movement for Progressive Judaism.

movement, this matter was finally defined in 1984 — see CLARIFICATION OF
THE TERM: RABBINICAL ADVISER (10). The second point at issue was the
relation of Telem Noar to the existing congregations in the IMPJ. The youth
movement in essence defined itself as an independent congregation within the
IMPJ — see TELEM NOAR AS A MOVEMENT AND AS A COMMUNITY (3).

Contending With Educational Dilemmas of Jewish Observance

As a youth movement in Israel with its six day school week, Telem Noar (later
Tzofei Telem) had to function mainly on *Shabbat*. As a Reform religiously
committed movement, it immediately faced the question of how *Shabbat* should
interface with the type of activities to be conducted. Telemm Noar was called
upon to study, discuss and decide on norms — in effect to democratically
determine its own *"Halacha."* SHABBAT IN TELEM NOAR (2) seeks to contend
with this dilemma.

A similar process ensued regarding the nature of prayer. My experience in the
UAHC Camps and National Federation of Temple Youth (NFTY) during my years
of *shlichut* convinced me that creative prayer could be a powerful tool for
motivating young people to invest in personal and group spiritual processes.
Those leaders who had participated in the Exchange program with the UAHC in
America were open to the innovation. There was some opposition on the part of
Israel Reform Rabbis to introducing this "foreign American" feature of Reform
Judaism into the IMPJ. THE IDEA BEHIND THE MA'AMAD[1] (14) was written in
two stages to provide a rationale for this innovation. An entire *Kallah* (learning
seminar) of ten days was devoted to this subject in the summer of 1982.

Organizational and Educational Problems in Integrating With the Scouts

The decision to integrate Telem Noar into the Israel Scouts was accompanied by a
number of educational and ideological dilemmas. These are reflected in FROM
5741 TO 5742 IN TELEM NOAR/TZOFEI TELEM (5). It was strongly felt that a
number of the symbols of the Israeli Scouts (Tzofim) were not acceptable for
Tzofei Telem. The hierarchical nature of the Scouts symbolized by differing
kerchiefs for different age groups was rejected in favor of a uniform kerchief
(symbolizing equality of status for all) chosen after a year of discussion in the
movement. The military style drill with which scouting activities generally began

---

1. MA'AMAD — Creative Prayer.

was replaced by THE FRIENDSHIP CIRCLE (4). In addition, the practice in the Israeli Scouts of separate activities for boys and girls was not accepted.

The Interface with the IMPJ

The necessity arose of contending with the dilemma of youth movement self-definition within the IMPJ. A number of leaders in Tzofei Telem stemmed from the IMPJ congregations and were alienated from what they perceived as an organization of sterile congregations limited to ritual worship. Indeed, their agreement to be active in Telem Noar was conditional on maximum separation from the adult body. It necessitated intensive educational work on my part to convince these leaders that they must participate as a congregation (with votes) at the IMPJ conventions. THE SIXTH CONVENTION OFTHE IMPJ (6) has to be read in the light of this conflict.

Contending With Future Directions

A STATION ON THE ROAD TO IDEOLOGICAL CLARIFICATION (11) describes the process of internal ideological clarification in the youth movement. The educational conventions, the *Kallot* and the landmark *Efal*[1] seminar were all a part of this process. By 1984 two Reform Kibbutzim had been established. It was clear that if the graduates of the youth movement were to have Reform Zionist impact, there had to be preparation for Reform Zionist congregations (as distinct from Diaspora style congregations of ritual worship) in urban areas. A YEAR OF SERVICE AS A NORM ON THE PATH OF SELF REALIZATION (9) was an attempt to recruit High School graduates to live together in the city within a "year of service" framework prior to being mobilized into the army. The purpose was to give them experience living together in the city as distinct from the *Nachal Garin*[2] framework. The problems inherent in maintaining the movement connection within the *Garin* framework are reflected in TO GARIN KAVE ON YOUR DAY OF CELEBRATION (12). The idea of a city group having a Reform Zionist impact on their surroundings never really fully materialized.

Explaining Tzofei Telem

The creation of a new youth movement in Israel was not an every day event. Nor was there any educational tradition within the Reform movement, in Israel or the

---

1. Efal — United Kibbutz Movement seminar center near Tel Aviv.
2. Settlement group within the army framework — classically designated for settlement in a particular kibbutz.

Diaspora, to smooth the way for such an attempt (see Section 5). IT'S NOT EVERY DAY THAT A NEW YOUTH MOVEMENT ARISES (7) was an attempt to explain Tzofei Telem (and to recruit leadership) within the UKM.[1] TELEM NOAR AND THE FUTURE OF POSITIVE, CREATIVE AND RELEVANT JUDAISM IN ISRAEL (8) was written as background to a request for funds from North American sources. The dynamics of internal tensions created by participating in the intense youth movement "pressure cooker" necessitated an attempt to clarify the issues for the benefit of young Americans in A LETTER TO JILL GRONER OF GARIN ARAVA (13).

The circumstances surrounding the dismantling of Tzofei Telem have been dealt with in the Preface.

---

1. United Kibbutz Movement — TAKAM.

Authority in Telem Noar[1]
Telem Noar: The First Educational Council, Kibbutz Yahel

The attempt to establish an independent youth movement within the framework of the Israel Movement for Progressive Judaism (IMPJ) immediately raises an important question: How will this movement determine its educational and Jewish direction, and from where does it draw the authority to make rules for itself? This question naturally relates to the general question of the authority to introduce Tikkun or reforms. An independent youth movement of the IMPJ may be seen as a synthesis of Reform, general Zionist and pioneering elements. Thus Telem Noar has inherited varying and complex traditions on the question of authority.

Telem Noar draws from two ideological traditions, that of the Reform movement and that of pioneering Zionism. Both these traditions are movements for Tikkun that have emerged among the Jewish people in modern times. In different ways, both movements attempted to bring new forms and content to the Jewish people by separating the religious element of Judaism from its social element.

The classical Reform of the early nineteenth century negated Judaism as a national and social entity. However, it accepted the religious element, while attempting to adapt this element in the spirit of the times and the circumstances of "followers of the Mosaic faith" immersed in western culture. The Reform approach to religion was based on the conclusions of historical research showing that Judaism had always developed and changed throughout the generations according to changing social circumstances.[2] As an *a priori* principle, Reform

---

1. April 1980 (translated from Hebrew).
2. A comprehensive summary of the principles of development in Judaism was provided recently in an article by the philosopher Robert Gordis: "A Dynamic Halacha: Principles and Procedures of Jewish Law," *Judaism*, Vol. 28, No. 3, Spring 1979.
   See also: Gil Nativ, "The Tikkun of Tradition in the World of the Sages" in *Tikkun in Jewish Tradition*, colloquium at Kibbutz Yahel, Pesach 5738 (Hebrew), and: Michael Chernick, "Which Halacha" in M. Langer (ed.), *Reform Zionist Perspective: Judaism and Community in the Modern Age*, UAHC Youth Division, New York, p. 356.

Judaism negated the authority of Rabbinical Judaism, seeing its uncompromising positions as one of the reasons for the spread of assimilation, and thus as a threat to the continued existence of the Judaism that many had begun to abandon.

For its part, the pioneering Zionist movement negated the religious element of Judaism, i.e., faith and Halacha, while affirming the national social and communal element (though it demanded far-reaching changes in the social structure of the people).

The main components of the Tikkun advocated by pioneering Zionism were: the return of the Jewish people to its land; the revival of Hebrew language and culture; a communal and cooperative structure; manual labor and agricultural work. For the purpose of our discussion, however, the important point was the negation of the social authority embedded in the alliance between Rabbinical Judaism and the communal leadership that had typified life in the small Jewish towns of Eastern Europe. The pioneering movement also saw these distortions as one of the causes leading many Jews to assimilate in the general humanistic Socialist movements which were opposed on principle to manifestations of Zionist nationalism.

Ideological sources for authority

The question we must ask is: what were the ideological sources used by the movements concerning their authority to introduce Tikkun, and to what extent could these serve to develop a "Halacha" that would be accept as legitimate among the movement?[1]

In the Reform movement, the authority to introduce reforms rested (and to a large extent still rests) with the individual conscience. This was a natural consequence of the fact that the Reform movement constituted an integral part of the bourgeois liberal revolution of the eighteenth century. According to this approach, religion was a matter of the individual's personal conscience. As will be recalled, the separation of religion and state was one of the guiding principles of the liberal revolution that overthrew feudal society. The liberal revolution led to the end of communal life. In Judaism, however, the community had been the social basis and authority for a way of life based on tradition and Halacha. Now each individual was entitled to interpret the sources and observe the commandments as he or she saw fit. It should also be recalled that classic Reform saw itself

---

1. Hanoch Jacobson addresses the question of the sociological criteria require for acceptance of reforms: "Essential Conditions for the Success of Reforms in Religious and Cultural Tradition in Modern Times," *Tikkun in Jewish Tradition*, colloquium at Kibbutz Yahel, Pesach 5738 (Hebrew), Ihud Publishers, 5739.

as integrating in the nation state as a purely religious community. In keeping with this perspective, Reform consciously gave up most aspects of social authority in the community.

The pioneering Zionist movement, by contrast, negated religion and did not even address the question of religious authority. However, as a movement that strove to transform Jewish society, it did address the issue of authority in general. The pioneering movement found itself torn between two approaches to authority prevalent in the Socialist movement as a whole. On the one hand, centralist Socialism (whether democratic or totalitarian) adopted the position that authority rests with a central body such as the state, central committee, etc. On the other hand, decentralized Socialism (or anarchistic Socialism) argued that authority rests with cooperative communities, whether rural or urban. The general meeting in the kibbutzim, as the authority for social reform, can be seen as an expression of the decentralized approach. However, the institutionalization of the Labor Zionist movement, particularly after the movement led Israel to independence, was mainly in the direction of democratic centralized Socialism.

To sum up, the authority for reform in both the Reform movement and the pioneering Zionist movement is based on the democratic principle. However, since the Reform left all decisions to the individual, and Reform communities seeking a comprehensive Reform way of life were not established, the movement's reforming decisions did not have extensive social implications and remained mainly in the field of religious ritual. On the other hand, the social reforms of the Zionist pioneering movement were based on communal democracy and reflected an attempt to develop a comprehensive and distinctive way of life. However, these reforms as a matter of principle ignored the sphere of "religion," and were therefore not of significance in terms of cultural and religious change. In the Zionist pioneering youth movements, the tradition of moral authority developed as the basis of the authority to introduce reforms. This authority was based on an integration between the individual future and the future of society. In other words, the perspective was that personal change within each member of the youth movement community would create change in the future Jewish community. I believe that this perspective has direct ramifications for Telem Noar. This aspect is currently lacking in the other "youth movements" (which are in fact primarily youth organizations rather than movements).[1]

---

1. See Zippora Efrat, "The Youth Movements in Contemporary Israeli Social Reality," *Year Book of the Kibbutz Seminar*, 5739, *Beit Midrash Mamlachti*, Tel Aviv, 1979 (Hebrew).

Authority in Judaism

God's commandments are ostensibly the supreme authority in Judaism. For practical purposes, however, the question is: who are those responsible for interpreting the injunctions embodied in the written and oral Torah in the context of the changing circumstances of each generation? One concept that was certainly absent in the past was individual authority. I believe that this reflected a different social reality: until the modern age, the individual was not a player in the social arena. The basic unit was usually the patriarchal household. The concept that the individual is born free, and has autonomous rights as distinct from the social, communal and affiliative entity to which he or she belongs was not found in any society until 300 years ago.[1] Cases were found where authority rested with a given institution or individual, such as Ezra, the Sanhedrin or the Nesi'im during the Mishnaic period.

In his book *Hebrew Law*,[2] Menachem Eilon stresses that there have always been many sources of Jewish public authority in place of or in addition to the authority of the sages. In general, public authority was derived from the law of the king, who was anointed by God. However, this authority was not always in harmony with the authority of the prophets, who were also emissaries of God. In the ritual sphere the priests also enjoyed authority. Over the course of time, when there were no longer kings, patriarchs (Nesi'im) or other forms of spiritual hegemony accepted by the entire Jewish people, the monarch's authority devolved to the community. In the Middle Ages, communities and associations of communities came together to legislate "communal ordinances," although according to Eilon, "the Talmudic Halacha does not even discuss the concept of the source of authority of the public to enact ordinances."[3] However, Eilon notes that questions of permissions and prohibitions continued to be the sole prerogative of the sages (the rabbis). While it may be possible to produce a forced interpretation of the sources providing a basis for broader, communal and democratic authority, Progressive Judaism (as distinct from the Conservative movement) as a whole cannot accept the path of forced interpretations — and this applies even more so to the youth movement.

Democracy as a value, and its integration in Judaism

As a general rule, Judaism has never been democratic. Moreover, Judaism has not

---

1. On this subject, see Stanley Meron, "The Individual and Society" (Eng.), in Michael Langer, ed., *Reform Zionist Perspective*, UAHC Youth Division, New York, 1977, p. 38.
2. Menachem Eilon, *Hebrew Law*, Magnes Press, Jerusalem, 5733; esp. pp. 42-49, 561-574.
3. Op. cit., p. 561.

acted according to the principle of human equality (many humans were seen as no more than property). This is true despite the fact that one may easily base democratic ideas on the Book of Genesis. We are all descendants of Adam, who was created in God's image. As for equality of the sexes: "And God created man; in God's image he created him; male and female he created them." (Gen. 1:27). Or, for example, take the vision of Hosea (2:18): "And in that day, said the Lord, you shall call me 'my man' (*Ishi*) and you shall no longer call me 'my husband' (*Ba'ali*)."

We must accept that our moral and ethical awareness has developed over the generations and continues to develop and change. Accordingly, there is certainly room in Judaism for the "shedding" of injunctions (the rituals of *Yivum*[1] and *Halitsa*,[2] the annulment of debts, the death penalty). Equally, however, there is room to enrich our Judaism with values from other peoples that may be reconciled with the sources. The equality of the sexes and democracy are two such values. The question is how to interpret the sources in each generation in a manner that draws us closer to the prophetic vision that guides us in interpersonal relationships to maintain "justice, law, loving kindness and mercy" (Hosea 2:21).

Where does this leave us?

1. We must accept the principle of development in Judaism: the right and obligation of each generation to introduce reforms.
2. We must accept the value of democracy as a pan-human value latent in our sources for the first time in human history. It remains to be determined how to realize this in Telem Noar.

The authority for reform in democratic Judaism

As mentioned above, the form of public decision-making in a democracy may be either centralized or decentralized. Centralized authority means that the state, through institutions (such as the Knesset or courts) introduces reforms. This involves the establishment of the mechanisms of a centralized state for the purpose of implementation. Examples of centralized authority in Judaism include the Sanhedrin, the Chief Rabbinate, and the Council of Torah Sages.

Decentralized authority means that communities of various types (rural or urban) make decisions which guide and/or bind only those members who voluntary affiliate to the community. This is direct democracy. The internal

---

1. The requirement in certain cases for a man to marry his deceased brother's wife.
2. The ritual according to which a woman frees a man from the duty to follow the rule of *Yivum*.

political reality of the State of Israel means that cultural and religious reform on the state level is impractical. This is a considerable limitation, particularly in areas such as personal status (marriage, divorce and so on) where it is impractical to reach decisions on the level of a single community or group of communities.

However, the model of decentralized authority applied in the kibbutz community (the general meeting as the body determining the rules of the kibbutz) can operate in most areas of our life. Will this not lead to chaos due to diverse developments in different communities? Not necessarily! Over several generations, what one might see as a kibbutz "Halacha" has developed in the field of social reform. Each kibbutz clearly enjoys a large measure of sovereignty (varying to some extent according to the movement to which it is affiliated). Yet while there are approximately 250 kibbutzim in Israel, and each one differs from the next, they may certainly be identified as a single movement.

The social "Halacha" of the kibbutzim is the product of joint experience and joint discussion of problems. I believe that this should also be the case in the field of cultural and religious reform. As already mentioned, the kibbutz movement for many years negated the Jewish sources as a primary ideological source, and accordingly negated the authority of those who interpreted these sources. Accordingly, the kibbutz movement preferred universalistic theories such as Socialism as the basis for its reforming efforts. This is unacceptable in our case.

On the other hand, we in Telem would be mistaken to attempt to cut ourselves off from the world of thought and practice beyond our own people and state. Even in the past, this could not be maintained on a long-term basis. Jewish history during the Persian and Greek periods is evidence enough of this. However, our interpretative efforts must be directed primarily at our own accumulating sources, which often absorb external influences.

The starting point of the IMPJ, and particularly of comprehensive communities such as our kibbutzim and youth movement, could be similar to that of the kibbutz movement. The kibbutz movement did not set out with a social "Shulchan Arukh" or constitution which was then tested and amended. The principles were built and developed layer by layer according to actual needs. In my opinion, Telem Noar has the social conditions needed in order for reforms to take root. According to Hanoch Jacobson,[1] these conditions are:

1.   In principle willingness on the part of the public to accept reform.
2.   Willingness on the part of the reformers to reform.
        (In the case of Telem Noar and the kibbutz, there is no need to distinguish between these conditions.)

---

1. See note 2 above.

3. Improved "functioning" of tradition; enhancing the "acceptability of the rationale." We may and indeed must ask whether this "works" for us and perhaps even adds to the sense of uniqueness in the movement activities.

In my opinion, the very process itself does indeed enhance our uniqueness and, one might even say, it sanctifies us.

This principled approach is a response to those who claim that we act according to "whatever is convenient for us." We must act according to actual needs in the field; there is no obligation to feel that we must examine in advance each of the 613 commandments. The question of how we are to define our priorities is an extremely important one.

Our starting point is not a community of believers in the 613 commandments who have suddenly decided to introduce far-reaching reforms. For us, the principle of "we shall do and [then] we shall understand" can apply only to such a period and field as we decide in advance[1] — we have taken on the burden of all aspects of our heritage. We see its renewal in a way meaningful to us as our life project. This is our path to personal self-realization. We take on authority as a movement aware that we are responsible to past, present and future. Yet the yardstick must be what we ourselves are willing and able to accept. In this respect, the experience of communal authority on kibbutz is clear: common responsibility is always more binding than personal responsibility. This may already be seen in the decisions made by Kibbutz Yahel regarding Kashrut and regarding driving and smoking on Shabbat. But the priorities regarding the subjects we needed to address were a product of ongoing pressure in our day-to-day work.

One of the complex questions regarding which we will have to develop a tradition is that of *leadership*, including the question of *rabbinical authority*. This question is also far from simple in the kibbutz movement. The Ha'artzi and Meuchad kibbutz movements both have a powerful "historic" leadership (whether formal or informal). In the Ichud movement, by contrast, rotation is a sacred principle.

As for the place of the rabbi, it is interesting to note that in the religious (i.e., Orthodox) kibbutz movement a rabbi with Semicha[2] is not considered an authority — he is simply a member. A religious committee is accountable to the general meeting.

It may be (and this is the view I favor) that the status of the rabbi in Telem

---

1. For example, decisions for the movement to follow a certain format (Garin or youth group tradition) regarding prayer at a given movement stage.
2. Ordination.

Noar is mainly that of teacher and educator. The rabbi as teacher is a familiar concept in Jewish tradition; this implies that the rabbi of a youth movement is an educator and teacher rather than a rule-maker (*Posek*). As a movement, Telem Noar must make its own rules or set its own Halacha. Accordingly, I believe that the authority of the rabbis who work in the movement should be informal and not institutionalized.

Conclusions for Telem Noar

1. Our youth movement must function as a communal and social framework. The participants will come and go, and we must ensure both development and continuity — and, perhaps above all, we must ensure continuing vitality. I believe that no ideological tradition is better prepared than Progressive Judaism to meet this goal. We may succeed where older movements (including kibbutz movements) have slid into various "orthodoxies." In recent generations, we have sadly learned that ideological orthodoxy (whether Socialist or religious) is a sure route to a centralized system whose commitment to democracy will be doubtful at best.
2. The subject of this article, authority, is one of the subjects we must clarify for ourselves as we set out. There are many innovations in the proposed process of democratization.
3. As a movement just setting out on its way, we must be careful in deciding how to prioritize our establishment of movement rules. Movement life must determine these priorities. For example, the subject of Shabbat in the movement is one that demands immediate attention,[1] particularly in the light of our intention to integrate in the Scout movement as an independent unit. Another subject is prayer — many members believe that this also requires urgent discussion.

By way of a conclusion, a word of warning. The challenge facing Telem Noar is considerable. We cannot answer every question at once. We cannot reach solutions of one hundred percent. If we demand immediate perfection of ourselves, we will secure only immediate failure. We must gather up courage, make decisions and act according to them. We must also not be afraid to discuss issues again after a reasonable period of time.

Will we be prepared to move down the difficult way that lies ahead?

---

1. See "Shabbat in Telem Noar," Section 6:2.

Appendix

DECISIONS ON AUTHORITY IN TELEM-NOAR

First Educational Council, Kibbutz Yahel
Ayar 5740 — 17 April 1980

1. The Educational Council will discuss Halacha and norms[1] for Telem Noar members — as individuals and as groups. The decisions will be authoritative for all national activities of Telem-Noar. The decisions will constitute recommendations for the norms of individuals, local youth groups, garinim,[2] etc.

2. The Educational Council will conduct discussions on the basis of the platform of the Israel Movement for Progressive Judaism.[3]

3. The Educational Council will meet twice a year. National Board meetings have authority to convene an additional council (by a two-thirds majority vote of those present).

4. The National Board of Telem-Noar will meet at least once every two months and will constitute the authoritative forum between meetings of the Educational Council.

5. Any member of Telem-Noar, garin, leadership group or Vaadat Higui,[4] has the right to suggest issues for discussion on the National Board and the educational council.

6. The National Board will determine the agenda of the Educational Council and will publicize it at least one month before the council's meeting date.

7. All bodies and individuals participants in the Educational Council are entitled to submit an appeal against the agenda. To this end they must notify all constituent groups two weeks in advance. The appeal will be discussed at the beginning of the Educational Council (one person speaks in favor; one against). The appeal will require a two-thirds majority.

Trans from the Hebrew: Michael Livni.

---

1. "Halacha VeHalichot"
2. Garinim — settlement groups within the army framework.
3. Much of the IMPJ platform was declarative and required interpretation in a given situation.
4. Vaadat Higui — Joint steering committee of the United Kibbutz Movement and the World Union of Progressive Judaism.

Shabbat in Telem[1] Noar[2]

My starting point in discussing the subject of Shabbat in Telem is the element of uniqueness — or sanctity, if you will — that distinguishes Shabbat from the other days of the week. In order to explain the principles behind my approach, I will propose two basic assumptions:

a. In setting apart that which is sacred, we should express the sacred and unique elements of the Jewish people, namely:
    — The People of Israel.
    — The Torah of Israel.
    — The Land of Israel.
b. We must interpret the sources in order to create movement activities and a movement experience that will shape a Shabbat character reflecting the sanctity of these elements.

In relating, as I do above, to the Triple Covenant of People, Torah and Land, a particular value-based direction already begins to emerge. *The guideline is that for the people in its own land, the sanctity of Shabbat, the sanctity of the Land and the sanctity of the sources must be integrated in order for the people to fully express its uniqueness.*

In terms of educational activities, this implies study and experience of Torah study and study and experience of the Land of Israel as an element of equal value to ritual religious worship. I do not want to discuss here in depth the ramifications relating to religious worship and Torah study. I am convinced that it will prove necessary for the subject of religious worship, in the sense of prayer, to be brought before an additional Educational Council in the near future. However, the subject of the study and experience of the Land of Israel does require here some principled comments in terms of my position.

Firstly, I refer to study of the Land of Israel in the widest sense of the word "study" — not merely study of sources relating to this subject. An approach in the spirit of the verse "In all My paths is knowledge" requires study of the principles

---

1. Telem: Tnuah L'Yahadut Mitkademet: The (Israel) Movement for Progressive Judaism.
2. Proceedings, First Education Council, 1980, (translated from Hebrew). The article was published in 1980 but was discussed at Educational Couneils during 1981-1982

dictating what is permitted and what is prohibited on Shabbat. We must interpret our sources in the context of our own reality, and in the context of the educational objectives outlined above.

Telem Noar and Shabbat rules

While this is not the time or place to engage in systematic study of the laws of Shabbat, I must relate to the distinction between *"avoda"* (permitted types of work) and *"melakha"* (types of labor prohibited on Shabbat).

"God finished His work which He had made" (Genesis 2:2).

"Remember the Sabbath day to keep it holy. Six days shall you labor and do all your work, but the seventh day is a Sabbath unto the Lord your God; in it you shall not do any manner of work." (Exodus 20:9).

Even Shoshan's dictionary gives three meanings for the Hebrew word *melakha* (work):

1) Work — manual labor.
2) Craft — the making of various tools.
3) The art of preparing objects from a raw material.

This implies that *melakha* relates above all to the concrete making of some object; to making in order to make a living. To use the terms used by economists, *melakha* is about an action that adds value to the materials involved.

In the Biblical sense, the word also has another meaning, namely: to give a service according to someone's instructions. This is used in the expression *"malekhet avoda"* ("an act of labor"). Here, the work is performed by way of a service (just as the angels — melakhim — are servants of God's will). "You shall have a holy convocation; you shall do no manner of servile work" (Leviticus 23:7). Hertz's English translation, on which the translation here is based, supports the perspective of traditional Judaism in translating *"malekhet avoda"* as "servile work" — i.e., work performed at another's behest. The word "servile" is derived from the Latin word for slave (servus).

I shall not discuss the other express prohibitions here, but I would note that, in my personal opinion, we must attempt to be faithful to express prohibitions such as "You shall kindle no fire" (Exodus 35:3). On the other hand, while the express prohibition against gathering in the harvest (Exodus 34:21) was interpreted by the rabbis as forbidding uprooting and plucking of any kind, I do not believe that this applies in the context of an activity relating to the study of the Land of Israel, which is another form of religious worship. I do not believe it is justified to prohibit the collection of specimens from nature, including the uprooting or plucking of non-protected plants. I do not feel that it is necessary to prohibit hammering on a rock in order to investigate its properties (since in this context, this is not *melakha*). Neither am I sure that in modern-day reality writing constitutes *melakha* (though this is debatable).

Driving is another story altogether. I believe that this should be examined not from the standpoint of "You shall kindle no fire," but rather in terms of performing *melakha* (driving could be seen as *malekhet avoda*). We should note, however, that Shaul Lieberman of the Conservative movement has permitted driving on Shabbat when the purpose is to participate in religious worship in a setting that sanctifies the people.

As a general principle, I do not believe that our starting point can be the traditional definition of 39 types of work prohibited on Shabbat.

We must accept the principle of not performing any *melakha* (adding value), and we must interpret religious worship as including matters relating to the sanctity of the Land of Israel.

The question should be whether an action is intended to serve the sacred work of Shabbat, without infringing a Biblical prohibition, or whether the action is an everyday act of work — i.e., work designed to create a material livelihood, as opposed to work designed to create a spiritual livelihood.

I believe that at Kallot[1] and other discussions, we must develop proposals on the subject of Shabbat in Telem Noar. The needs of the movement must be taken into account in adopting basic positions on these issues.

It is evident that our way is the hardest and least convenient one. We must accept the yoke of the commandments (unlike secular movements) while clarifying and studying our sources, and without confining ourselves to the interpretations and interpretative methods used by the rabbis (as do the "religious" movements). Thus Shabbat in Telem Noar is also a challenge to us in terms of *renewing tradition*. Renewing the tradition in such a key area as Shabbat — a renewal by which we can live and act — will have educational ramifications on wide circles, including many outside our movement.

---

1. Kallah (pl. Kallot): learning seminar.

Telem Noar as a Movement and a Community[1]

Telem Noar currently includes some 350 youngsters and members of *Garinim*.[2] Approximately one quarter of this number are members of *Garinim* who intend to settle on Yahel and Yahel B[3]; they are currently at various stages of the Nachal army track. Another third are in our largest group, in Haifa, and the remainder are members of the smaller groups in Jerusalem, Tel Aviv, Beersheva, the Ben Shemen Youth Village and the Eshel Hanassi Agricultural School.

It was three and a half years ago that Rabbi Tovia Ben Horin, the rabbi of Telem Noar, proposed that all the groups and *Garinim* should be combined in a single movement. The author of this article was recruited from the Ichud kibbutz movement to assist in this task, and to attempt to establish a "real" youth movement beginning from the junior sections. This process include experimental activities in various directions.

Over the past year, our main efforts have been devoted to creating a sense of being a movement and a sense of togetherness without which no real youth movement can function. This was the goal behind the five-day movement-wide camp held on Kibbutz Yahel in the spring — an event we intend to repeat at Hanukkah. In the fall, we held several national conclaves. The summer camp at Kfar Silver also contributed to this goal, particularly for the younger section. Most important of all, we introduced regular educational leadership meetings every two weeks, and we can now note that the movement has a national team of youth leaders.

The youth movement as an autonomous community

It is not enough just to create awareness of our being a movement. We also need to develop a tradition of responsibility on the part of members of the movement for directing work and setting policy. This clearly implies that Telem Noar must be an independent youth movement.

We held two educational councils this year, each attended by approximately

1. *Tlamim* (Newsletter of the IMPJ), Kislev 5741, December 1980 (translated from Hebrew).
2. Settlement groups of men and women within the "Nachal" Army framework where periods of military service alternate with living and working as a group, generally on a kibbutz.
3. Yahel B — the future Kibbutz Lotan.

forty members, representatives of local groups and youth leaders. We may note with satisfaction that a democratic process is emerging at the educational councils for determining the "Halacha" of Telem Noar, at least as far as national events are concerned. This also underscores the responsibility taken on by the youth leaders and the young members. To some extent, a youth movement functions as an independent community. Thus the youth movement could be seen today as an additional community within the IMPJ framework.

We hope that the different activities and experiments in the Telem Noar community will serve to train the future leadership of the IMPJ on the national level, in the congregations in the cities and in the kibbutzim. Perhaps we will even manage to develop additional social models through which Progressive Judaism may be experienced.

The Circle of Friendship[1]

The circle is an ancient
symbol and shape. The properties of
the circle dictate the significance attached to this
symbol. The circle is a geometrical shape in which each
point is at an equal distance from the center — no one comes
first and no one comes last. Every person around a circle is "at the
center" and has equal value. The circle also symbolizes completion —
by definition, a circle must be complete. When a group of people order
themselves in the form of a circle, this can be seen as an expression of a desire
for completeness and togetherness. When we arrange ourselves in a circle, each
individual forms a distinct *unit*, yet together we forge *unity* (note the relationship
between the two words). Thus the way to togetherness and unity is through
cooperation and mutual assistance (hand reaching out to hand around the circle).
Martin Buber claimed that only by living togetherness can we discover the Divine
element within humans. The opposite of the circle is the straight line (ABCD).
This symbolizes action toward a defined goal. The person in a row or line is a
means toward a goal or a symbol. The person in a circle symbolizes the human
within society — not as a means, but as an end in himself/herself within
society. This is why the Circle of Friendship in Tzofei Telem has replaced
drills symbolizing "linear" activity — activity that unites people
toward specific goals (war, etc.) These goals are not always
compatible with the Jewish approach to the role of the human
and the goals of human society. As a reflection of the
desire for completeness, the Circle of
Friendship in Tzofei Telem is a form
of collective prayer.

---

1. *Tlamim* 9 (Newsletter of the IMPJ Youth Movement), Adar II, Nissan 5741, March 1981 (translated from Hebrew).

From 5741 to 5742[1]

What have we been through?

Over the past year we have worked under the pressure of local and national activities, to the point that we may have failed to notice just how far we have come. We have laid the foundations (although so far they are no more than that) for a national youth movement. We have done this through a broad range of movement activities, including fifteen national and regional camps and conclaves.

We have held regular meetings of the National Committee of Telem Noar and the Educational Council. We have published a regular journal, *Tlamim*, and the first song book reflecting our own unique heritage of songs. Above all, the Council of Youth Leaders has worked all year to ensure that the program was implemented. All this in addition to the local activities of each group and age band!

This is the first year when we can say that we have begun to attempt to integrate the ideas of Telem with the framework of the Scout movement. We spoke of a two-year experiment, but the fact is that it has taken us an entire year to get organized for this experiment! It is therefore obviously too soon yet to draw conclusions. In Haifa we are fast approaching a situation where most of the age groups will be integrated in Tzofei Telem. In Jerusalem the Baka/Talpiot troop is beginning to operate, despite a host of problems. We have also worked hard to provide the educational support for this attempt; I believe that our success in this respect has been considerable, though still only partial.

I have no doubt that the consolidation of the younger age groups in Haifa and Jerusalem is dependent on our ability to go into the schools to recruit members. Our integration in the Scout movement makes this possible, but it provides us only with a framework. Within our independent section,[2] we must fill this framework with our own unique content.

By contrast to previous years, we already began at Passover to practice working with the kind of camps movement run. We overcame numerous

---

1. *Tlamim* 11 (Newsletter of the IMPJ Youth Movement), Tishrei 5742, October 1981 (translated from Hebrew).
2. Tzofei Telem constituted an autonomous subsection of the national Scout movement.

technical difficulties in order to implement the Bar Giora camps. But we were innovative in other fields, too. We introduced a "working camp" for the senior groups, and we saw that it is possible to include educational content in these programs. We changed the nature of the Kallah[1] into a training workshop, though we must continue to improve the way this is implemented. For the first time we held a Telem Noar camp focusing on knowledge of Israel. We also ran a number of joint programs together with the Scout movement at the Scout Farm and in Ofer Forest. We will have to discuss the educational ramifications of these activities.

Have we bitten off more than we can chew? There were many snags in the camps due to our inability to implement this plan in full. Despite this, I feel that a movement must always be moving rapidly forward — not necessarily in terms of the numbers of members, but in terms of patterns and content.

As a movement model that attempts to "change the world," we face the question as to whether we are a political movement (not so much in the sense of identification with any political party, but rather in terms of activities intended to achieve specific goals). This is certainly put to a severe test when it comes to our struggle to achieve the means to establish Yahel "B."[2] I do not believe we can do this without political involvement. I also believe that such issues as "Who is a Jew" will oblige us to engage in informational efforts and political action over the coming years.

Where will all this lead us? We cannot tell, and "it is not for us to finish the task..." I wish us all a year of development and growth, as individuals and as a movement.

---

1. Study retreat.
2. The future Kibbutz Lotan.

The (Sixth) Convention of the Israel Movement for Progressive Judaism[1]

On the weekend of October 22-23, 1981 (Parashat Bereshit) the Israel Movement for Progressive Judaism (IMPJ) held its convention at the Remez guest house in Zikhron Yaakov. A delegation of our youth leaders participated in the convention (Tut,[2] Hila Zemer, Rachel Nissim, Meir Azari and myself). A number of members of Telem Noar also participated, but as representatives of Leo Baeck or the congregations (Ramat Hasharon).

Telem Noar or Tzofei Telem is one of the constituent bodies of the umbrella organization known as the IMPJ. The movement also includes all the congregations (synagogues), the Leo Baeck School, the Hebrew Union College, Kibbutz Yahel and the Council of Progressive Rabbis (Maram), in addition to Telem Noar.

Telem Noar has the status of a movement, while Kibbutz Yahel is considered a congregation. Within this umbrella organization, all the constituent bodies are independent, but all share a common question: "How can we promote Progressive Judaism in Israeli society?"

It would be inaccurate to claim that the different bodies are in agreement on the question of how to promote Progressive Judaism.

The main disagreements related to the question of the place of the congregation or synagogue here in Israel. No one doubts that the IMPJ must enable such frameworks to exist in order to meet the needs of those in the cities who seek to come together for religious worship. However, as several speakers noted, this framework of synagogues has not proved itself over the past fifteen years. There are now proposals to open community centers of which the synagogue will form one part. (Motti Rotem from Or Chadash in Haifa and Tovia[3] from Har El in Jerusalem are both interested in this direction.)

After a number of internal discussions (as well as with our friends from Kibbutz Yahel), we reached the conclusion that in the long term what we need is a

---

1. *Tlamim* 12 (Newsletter of the IMPJ Youth Movement), Heshvan 5742, January 1982 (translated from Hebrew).
2. Ron Tutenhauer.
3. Rabbi Tovia Ben Chorin.

greater emphasis on educational systems. Our experience over the past two years shows that we need more schools such as Leo Baeck (i.e., formal education). Such schools provide a convenient base for the complementary education that a *Reform youth movement* can provide. However, there is no infrastructure for this purpose. Above all, we need rabbis who are prepared to be educators and teachers in such schools. It is an open secret that even at Leo Baeck there are *almost no* teachers who personally identify with Progressive Judaism.

At the convention itself, discussion groups were held on four subjects: youth in the IMPJ; the struggle against the religious establishment; the struggle against secularism; and the struggle in the Diaspora. The Telem Noar delegation cooperated with the delegations from Kibbutz Yahel and Leo Baeck School. We allocated members to the different groups in order to try to promote decisions that would emphasize the importance of strengthening a Reform education system and recruiting rabbis and teachers for this system. Almost all the proposals in this vein were accepted, but a number of proposals we submitted relating to the function of rabbis in educational work and in the movement were not discussed. It was promised that these issues would be brought before a forum including Telem Noar in the near future. What is this all about?

There are two reasons why we thought it was important to raise these proposals:

a. Telem Noar as a movement is one of the "consumers" of the rabbinical workers. We are not always able to obtain the help we need at the right time or in the right place.

b. The graduates of Telem Noar will certainly include some people who will be candidates for professional work in the movement. There is a sense that the conditions of employment within the IMPJ require modification.

It is necessary to note that in the work group on the subject of youth in the IMPJ, disagreements surfaced between the representatives of the congregations and Telem Noar. Regretfully, this was exacerbated by the lack of familiarity of the members of the congregations with the conditions "in the field" in which we operate, which prevent our holding regular activities in most of the congregations.

Telem Noar was also active in electing the new Executive of the IMPJ.

This is the first time we have participated so actively in an event of the whole movement. This required several preparatory meetings. The Youth Leaders Council decided that due to pressures relating to the Educational Council, it would be impractical to involve all of Telem Noar in these discussions. However, following the decisions of the Educational Council relating to changing the status of the National (Youth) Board, I believe that we will be better placed to promote effective discussion of key issues on the agenda of the Reform movement in Israel as a whole within the senior sections.

It's Not Every Day That a New Youth Movement Arises[1]
The United Kibbutz Movement Shaliach to Tzofei Telem
Tells us about the Movement

This time there's no doubt: things began with the chicken rather than the egg. The trauma of the Yom Kippur War and the opening up of new ideological horizons seen among some young people following the war was reflected in a number a little-known developments, one of which was the establishment of the first Progressive (Reform) Jewish *Garinim*.[2]

With the help of a handful of enthusiastic Reform rabbis, a small group of 12th graders, only a few of whom had any background in the Reform movement, persuaded the Ichud kibbutz movement to allocate them a site to build a new type of kibbutz, one that would combine social Tikkun (mending) with cultural and spiritual Tikkun. *Garinim* from the IMPJ (the Israel Movement for Progressive Judaism) joined the Nachal;[3] together with a small number of Israel program graduates from the American Reform movement, they established Kibbutz Yahel in 1977.

It soon emerged that without a long movement and educational process allowing for consolidation, this type of *Garinim* would not be able to survive and operate creatively. A healthy "chicken" needs a period of protected and controlled development as a fetus inside the "egg" of the youth movement.

Three years ago, it was decided to extend the cooperation between the Ichud (as it then was) and the World Union of Progressive Judaism by establishing a youth movement in Israel to provide the infrastructure for the Reform movement's settlement program. The intention and hope was that such a movement would develop patterns guiding its graduates in realizing its values. It also seemed that coping with questions of culture and religion could be of benefit to other movements.

---

1. From *Yachad*, the journal of the United Kibbutz Movement (Takam), November 19, 1982, (translated from Hebrew).
2. *Garinim*: settlement groups.
3. *Nachal*: An army framework which enables youth to maintain partial links during their military service with a view to encouraging their continued (joint) projects (e.g. settlement) after their service.

A new educational and movement process began for the first time since the 1930s. Initially there was an attempt to "wed" the youth groups of the Progressive Jewish congregations and the *Garinim* in order to create a single strand of movement. However, it emerged that this was unrealistic given the small size of the Israeli Reform movement.

A number of members of the Takam who were graduates of the *Tzofim*[1] felt that the IMPJ idea could provide a fruitful ideological addition to the Scout concept, and it was decided to establish a number of experimental troops in this spirit.

In October 1980, the first Tzofei Telem ("Telem Scouts") troop was established in Haifa. A year later an additional troop was established in Jerusalem.

What does "a new movement" mean?

The essence of a movement process is that it educates toward the realization of a way of life and an ideological perspective that differ from those of existing society (in this respect, even the kibbutz constitutes a particular version of existing society). In the case of Tzofei Telem, the process was an option within the Scout movement. A separate stream of this nature naturally requires educational autonomy and the existence of a certain organizational basis in order to develop an educational alternative. As Eistenstadt wrote some twenty years ago, the movement is the framework (an educating system) in which the general social future is embodied in the changing personal dimension. The transformation in personal identity reflects the movement's vision of an alternative society. This has been the model employed by the youth movements established from the Third Aliyah onward. Over the last generation, however, the vitality of this process has been eroded, due mainly to the blurring of the vision of an alternative society.

In order to establish an educating system *ex nihilo*, there is a need for senior youth leaders and Army graduates to work with 9th grade boys and girls who are interested in a new idea and a unique social experience. It was necessary to consolidate this group of young activists and prepare them for work with 5th graders (on the assumption that the movement would be able to go into schools to recruit participants — a privilege reserved for movements "recognized" by the Ministry of Education). Yet what this implied was to develop a movement experience that none of the youth leaders had themselves experienced. It was also necessary to develop norms and an educational program for the junior sections, and norms and an ideological and social program for the senior sections. This is a

1. The Israel Scout Movement.

highly complex task; in this sense, as mentioned, no new youth movement had been established since the 1930s.

Tzofei Telem's vision

Tzofei Telem's vision is a particular path and way of life that integrates the idea of social Tikkun with cultural, spiritual and religious Tikkun. The approach is democratic and based on the community — the same approach that has guided the social way of life of the kibbutzim. In Tzofei Telem, however, the rules of democracy also apply to decisions relating to cultural life (of which "religion" forms only a small part). The goals is to evolve cooperative communities (which may not be exclusively rural in nature) that will develop a way of life combining social and religious Tikkun and provide a framework for personal and community self-realization. Moreover, since these communities are part of a world youth movement (Netzer Olami — Reform Zionist Youth), they will influence the entire movement and provide a creative alternative model to the polarization between religion and secularism in Israel. This approach is committed to the Jewish sources but does not accept the authority of the rabbinical and *Halachic* process.

In educational terms, the key to educating children and youth to adopt an open attitude to Jewish tradition is to involve them in open Jewish **experience** free of coercion. Accordingly, Shabbat and the Shabbat experience are a central theme in Tzofei Telem from as early as the 5th grade.

Cultural Zionism

Lastly, it is worth emphasizing some basic ideological assumptions. Is Israel a State of the Jews or is it a Jewish State? Tzofei Telem has a clear position on this question: both! **The idea of a Jewish State "like all the other nations" is meaningless.** The Jewish people in its own homeland will not be able to withstand external and internal pressures if it draws exclusively on political or practical Zionism. Now seems to be an appropriate time to experiment with models of **cultural Zionism** designed to fill the framework of political Zionism with Jewish content.

We believe that secular Zionism is unable to create the commitment needed for the Zionist enterprise to succeed. The Yerida[1] rates (and the proportion of failures in our own efforts in the kibbutz movement to create commitment among the younger generation to continue our enterprise) suggest that some kind of

---

1. Emigration of Jews from Israel.

"vitamin" is lacking in our educational fare. We must develop Jewish ways of life that are capable of preventing cultural assimilation (and, outside Israel, physical assimilation). We are seeking commitment to function as further links in the chain of our people's history and creativity. Tzofei Telem is attempting to educate toward self-realization within communities committed to this path.

Will the attempt to establish a new movement prove successful? Naturally, the results of any educational process may be seen only after several years. In the meantime, this goal provides a challenge for members seeking a field of activity that addresses the underlying questions of the Jewish people as well as the specific problems of the immediate present.

Members (including those participating in a "late Year of Service") who are interested in working as youth leaders in Tzofei Telem (on a full-time or part-time basis) should call 03-245271, Takam House, 27 Soutine St., Tel Aviv.[1]

---

1. Tzofei Telem's address in 1982.

Telem Noar and the Future of Positive, Creative and Relevant Judaism in Israel[1]

Can we educate Israeli youth to make a personal commitment to liberal, democratic and creative Judaism? Is it possible to generate "Chavurot" (fellowships) and "garinim" (community nuclei), with enough social and ideological cohesion to enable them to project a positive and creative Jewish alternative to the either/or secular-orthodox polarity in Israel? Can Israeli youth of divergent socio-economic, religious, cultural and ethnic backgrounds be forged into a dynamic youth movement? These are among the crucial challenges confronting Telem-Noar since its establishment three years ago. The movement is dedicated to developing an innovative approach to Judaism within existing frameworks (e.g., Kibbutz Yahel in the Arava, the Leo Baeck School in Haifa, and in the Bak'a Community Center of Jerusalem), as well as formulating and pioneering additional perhaps original forms of an alternative Jewish community in Israel.

This fledgling movement numbers some 400 members. It organizes the "garinim" to Kibbutz Yahel and the future Yahel Beth.[2] It has recruited youth groups from within existing Progressive congregations but more especially from without — via direct approach to youth from all strata of Israeli society. Three years ago, Rabbi Tovia Ben Chorin initiated the first two-week summer Liberal Jewish camp experience for Israeli youth, thus adding a new educational dimension to work in Israel. Last year, in cooperation with the Israeli Scout Movement (Tzofim), two new scouting troops, one in Haifa (Leo Baeck) and one in Bak'a (Jerusalem) were founded. Bak'a is a disadvantaged section of Jerusalem whose inhabitants are mainly of Afro-Asian background. These scouting groups are called Tzofei Telem. The purpose is to provide the informal educational framework for the above educational aims from Grade 5 on. (Grade 5 is when Israeli youth movements begin activity.)

---

1. Explanatory memo written to raise funds, unpublished, 1982.
2. The future Kibbutz Lotan.

Volunteer Leadership

Telem Noar is almost entirely dependent on a small group (currently fifteen) of full-time volunteer leaders. Initially, part-time students were tried but it was found that *building* a youth movement, as distinct from maintaining an existing one, demands a totally free and flexible time schedule. The volunteer leadership works with a coordinator assigned by the Kibbutz Movement, as well as three part-time rabbinical advisors.

The volunteer leaders, all in their late teens and early twenties, are drawn from various sources: 1) those assigned by their garin to a year of education work in the movement (a garin is a settlement group within the army committed to Kibbutz living, in this case Yahel and Yahel Beth); 2) Kibbutz youth who have chosen Telem Noar as their option for a year of movement service that all kibbutz youth must give to some youth movement or young kibbutz; and 3) graduates of the youth groups who are postponing their College education for a year or two and have volunteered for special service.

Not coincidentally, many are graduates of the Eisendrath International Exchange Program, designed for Israeli high school youth to spend an extended experience of study living with an American Jewish family, and have imbibed something of the National Federation of Temple Youth subculture and spirit. These volunteer leaders are a totally dedicated group. They have literally taken one to two years out of their lives to work in Telem Noar. They have to be dedicated — they get a subsistence allowance of $100 per month plus movement organized communal housing. The volunteer leadership is motivated by the knowledge that without them there would not be a movement and that they are creating something totally new on the Israeli scene.

The volunteer leaders are responsible for the entire gamut of Telem Noar activity. This includes twice-weekly activities for all the age groups on a local level, all conclaves — both regional and national (a dozen a year), staffing summer camps, publications, educational planning. All this is done in the almost complete absence of an institutional infrastructure.

Starting from the Bottom

In Israel, youth movement affiliation begins in Grade 5 at age 10! During the past year, Telem Noar, in cooperation with the Israeli Scout Movement and the Leo Baeck School in Haifa, recruited the first group of 10-year-olds from a select number of elementary schools that feed into the Leo Baeck School. Almost all the children come from completely secular homes. These children formed the basis of the first Tzofei Telem scouting group referred to above.

Prior to recruiting these children, it was necessary to recruit and train 14-year-olds (grade 9) — who now (in Grade 10) are the leaders of these 10-year-olds. Of course the high school leaders have to be counseled as well — that among other things is the task of the volunteer leaders. Next year we shall again recruit a new Grade 5 group in Haifa and hence there will be Grades 5, 6, and Grade 7. This very complicated process has begun in Jerusalem this year in the Bak'a Community Center, and will be introduced next year in the greater Tel Aviv area. A major educational objective is to root the program with an emphasis on experiencing and living Judaism rather than just studying about Judaism.

What does the Youth Movement do programmatically? Activities? Where does it function mainly?

The major centers are Haifa and Jerusalem. Lesser activity in Tel Aviv, Rishon Lezion, Netanya.

The program for age groups 10-13 consists of a "mix" of active play, scout type activity, discussions, singing, story-telling in a liberal Jewish environment. The children are basically secular. Liberal Jewish environment means Kabbalat Shabbat and prayers on Friday night that are "NFTY" style in terms of creative service. This is an innovation within Israeli Judaism and it is simply untrue that this "foreign" subculture is inimical to Israeli youth. In these younger age groups we have initiated a kind of "friendship circle" at the beginning and the end of activities where we formally introduce a small prayer reading or NFTY-type songs. Activities are twice a week and Friday night twice a month.

As described above, we are an autonomous part of the Israeli scout movement whose general programming we adapt to our purposes. But we are educationally *independent*. For example, whereas in the regular Tzofim activities boys and girls have separate programming, in Telem Noar boys and girls are programmed together.

At the Grade 9 level, the program is oriented to crystallizing leadership groups which in Grade 10 will go out and recruit youngsters in Grade 5. Our access to the Grade 5 kids is made possible by being part of the Scouting Movement. Only movements officially recognized by the Ministry of Education can recruit within the school system, and since our movement does not yet have official status, the Scouts provide the necessary framework.

The Grade 9 effort is critical. We have to recruit them almost literally from the street. Judaism is not particularly of major importance to the average high schooler in Israel and hence we have to find youth leaders age 18-20 who can recruit the high schoolers and work with them to the point where they can go into the elementary schools to recruit Grade 5 whom *it is relatively easy* to recruit.

Our next question then becomes: where do we get and how do we motivate youth leaders to do this?

About half of our dozen youth leaders are from the Israel movement and/or have had experiences within our exchange programs. Other leaders have no background. However, all are challenged by the idea that we are *creating* the infrastructure for something radically new — an educational process from Grade 5 up — a youth community which, when it achieves adulthood, will have the motivation and background to create institutions and communities within Israeli society which will embody alternative Judaism as a way of life.

The most critical part of our programming revolves around the activities that these leaders plan and execute — national and local conclaves. The leadership, including democratically elected representatives of the Grade 9-12 groups, determine movement policy. It is an autonomous youth movement (in this sense very different from NFTY) and anything less will not motivate young people to work with us on a semi-voluntary basis. The nearest thing to it in America is the Garin Arava volunteer work via "Merakzei Madrichim" (Coordinators of counsellors). Most of the leaders live together in "Batim" similar to what we initiated in America a number of years ago. (Batim is the plural for Bayit [house], in this case a collective domicile housing the youth leaders. They share expenses.)

A total of 10-12 young adult leaders are responsible for 75 youth in Grades 9-12 (including small garinim each year to Yahel Beth). The Grade 10-11 group in turn is responsible for 200-250 kids in Grades 5-7. However, the young adult leaders have to do all the planning and running of conclaves and summer camps on a national level. All this in addition to running the ongoing local activities, movement newspaper, etc. not only are they running a movement, they are building one. Nearly all the programming has to be created from scratch. It will be easier for those who do the same work five years from now.

The relationship to other institutions and programs of the Progressive Movement

Kibbutz Yahel and Yahel Beth[1] — while the youth movement is not limited to a kibbutz orientation, Yahel nevertheless stands as symbol and ideal, even though we do think that regarding ideological initiative and innovation, the youth movement, even at this nascent stage, is ahead of Yahel. Keep in mind that most of the Israelis in Yahel do not come from a movement background.

Leo Baeck School in Haifa (affiliated with the World Union for Progressive Judaism) — Leo Baeck is a framework and a home in Haifa. We give the supplementary informal education. Rabbi Robert Samuels, principal of the Leo Baeck School, and the Israeli Scouts have opened the doors to all the elementary schools that feed into the Leo Baeck Junior and Senior High School. During the past two years we have developed a growing partnership. After all, the pupils at Leo Baeck School are not necessarily religious or religious liberals — there is merely a potential for making them so.

Synagogues — The youth movement is itself a community. 95% of the participants are not from movement homes. They do not identify with the forms of worship found in the congregations. In this sense the situation is *very* different from America, even though even in America there is sometimes tension between youth activities, NFTY and the Temple.

There is an even greater problem with the congregations conceptually: the congregations service *religious needs* of adult members in a way similar to the Diaspora. This is not where the youth movement is at. The youth movement is concerned with total life style. Children from Grades 5-8 live in specific neighborhoods, have to come to activities by foot (there is no transportation on the Shabbat), and this does not necessarily relate to the location of the congregants. A further problem — the children of congregants (of whom there are not many) are generally involved in other movements and do not constitute by and large a basis for building our own movement.

A major religious question in Israel is the role of the synagogue. Are the synagogue a means or an end in terms of impact on Israeli society — an impact that can change patterns of how Israeli society relates to the creative survival of Jewish tradition. As a means, synagogues have not yet proven themselves. As an end in themselves they do not appear to be able to service more than a very limited clientele.

---

1. The future Kibbutz Lotan.

Camping

We have just gone over from American-style outreach camping to using the camps to build the movement. For the past 2 years the numbers have been constant — about 100 per week for 2 weeks (Grades 5-8) and about 50 for a week (Grades 9-10). But the internal composition has changed. We are servicing movement youngsters now — not giving a subsidized NFTY camp experience to all those interested. So physical facilities have shifted from youth village with dining hall, swimming pool, etc., to tent camps in the Jewish National Fund recreational forest. We put the message of our life style across just as well.

Clearly, in the long run we have to subsidize such camps less than the youth village type camp.

An Autonomous Youth Movement and its meaning for Innovative Judaism in Israel. What is the Significance of this Work?

All the major socially and culturally innovative features of Israeli society have had youth movements as their infrastructure. This includes first and foremost the Kibbutz Movement. One of the critical weaknesses of Yahel is the absence (on the Israeli side in particular) of such a movement. Yahel is going through a serious crisis because the pool from which to draw potential members is insufficient.

This principle of youth movement has also been relevant for such phenomena as Gush Emunim working on the radicalized base of the Bnei Akiva movement. Schools (e.g., Leo Baeck) in and of themselves have not been enough.

Israel is not America and quite clearly, Telem Noar is not NFTY in spite of the influence that NFTY is having on Telem Noar (music, creative worship, etc.). By virtue of including the Kibbutz garinim and (hopefully in the future) students in its membership, Telem Noar extends from the age of 10 through to the early twenties. Telem Noar has to be autonomous in order to be innovative, even though autonomy as such is no guarantee of creativity.

A democratic and autonomous youth movement (as distinct from an adult-operated youth organization) cannot be "run" by professional leadership. Nor are the type of volunteer leaders described above prepared to follow a particular "line" dictated by professionals. The decision making process in Telem Noar is fundamentally democratic. The highest body is the Educational Council which meets semi-annually. It consists of the volunteer leadership; one representative per 10 members of the various groups — from Grade 9 up to and including the garinim — determine policy. (Four or five adults, some of them rabbis, some of them Kibbutz members, and a representative of the Leo Baeck School are ex-officio members of this Educational Council.)

Over a period of a generation (both a very long period of time but nevertheless also a very short period of time in the history of our people) we are hoping that the sense of "shlichut" (mission) of the young people will be passed on to those who continue. The graduates of Telem Noar will be the logical base for the development of a creative Liberal Judaism in Israel irrespective of the organizational and institutional framework within which it may manifest itself.

Can we succeed? It is an open question. No new youth movement has been established since the founding of the State of Israel. None of the present youth movements relates to the unique challenge that Israel presents — utilizing the Jewish heritage to build a Jewish community both independent and interdependent based on freedom of choice.

A Year of Service as a Norm on the Way to Self-Realization[1]

To judge by the reactions of some youth leaders and members, it seems that some points require further elaboration. The proposal I made in principle includes many practical problems, and it can be seen that while some members have objections *in principle*, others have practical reservations. It is important to distinguish between the two. A practical problem which all would agree is a special case is the question of the effect on Lotan (or on Yahel a year later).[2] In reply to Rachel, I can only point out that a stronger movement in qualitative and quantitative terms will above all strengthen the existing frameworks for self-realization. In a more practical and immediate sense, however, the Telem Youth kibbutzim will be doing themselves a disservice if they see Telem Noar as the sole source of help. There is also Netzer Olami, there is the possibility of absorbing individuals, and there is the possibility of establishing frameworks for students. I doubt whether all the potential inherent in these ideas has been properly examined or attempted. No one doubts that Telem Noar is the *central* factor in the future of the kibbutzim. *We must consider how we can lead Telem Noar to a point where it can meet its responsibility toward Yahel and Lotan* in a more appropriate manner. This is also reflected in the responsibility of Yahel and Lotan toward Telem Noar.

In any case, it is certainly worth distinguishing between the question of a *Garin* that defers army service for a year and the question in principle.

The main proposal in my article in the Tishrei (September 1983) edition of *Tlamim* was to establish a year of service as a norm for a *shlichut*[3] on the path to realization — not only for a few educators or "naive altruists" but as a norm, if not for everyone then for the majority. A "norm" is that which is accepted and expected in this society we call Telem Noar. It is true that in any society not everyone conforms to all the norms, but it is certainly permissible to

---

1. *Tlamim* 28 (Newsletter of the IMPJ Youth Movement), Tevet 5744, January 1984 (translated from Hebrew).
2. i.e., the effect of delaying arrival on Kibbutz Lotan and Yahel by a year due to the year of service in the youth movement prior to army service.
3. Shlichut: mission — in the service of an idea or the cause of Tikkun ("world-mending").

educate toward these norms. It is permissible for us to constitute a personal example.

As for the *principle of a one-year shlichut as part of the educational process*, particularly in the movement context, there is nothing here that amounts to a "revolutionary" innovation. This norm has existed in the United Kibbutz Movement for many years — would Avi or Ariel argue that this means that those who took part in such a year of service are doomed to a lifetime career of movement leadership?! Approximately two-thirds of young people in the United Kibbutz Movement comply with this norm, whether in the form of a "13th grade" year of service or a year of service after the army. Were it not for this norm, with all its problems (a 10% drop-out rate), several youth movements would cease to exist. It is valid to ask why we should not ask of Telem Noar graduates the same norm that is asked of the youth in the United Kibbutz Movement.

What right does Telem Noar have to accept this assistance, and many other types of assistance, if it is unwilling to establish a norm of recruiting to help ourselves?

A year of service means just that: a year when individuals devote themselves to a mission that is close to their hearts within the framework to which they are affiliated and the world view of a Zionist stream of self-realization[1] — i.e. a stream that attempts to mend the Jewish people and the world. Since we are talking about 18-year-olds, one may also note that this is a year of self-examination and personal development through the acquisition of life experience. In short, this is a year in which "to build and to be built."

Both in the United Kibbutz Movement and in Telem (despite our short experience) we see that *the individual is indeed built*. He/she becomes more mature, with a clearer world view and an enhanced ability to cope with his/her future path, particularly in the field of *values*. As Telem develops, it is dependent on those members and graduates who are willing to take a year off to devote themselves completely to the process of building. It is very hard for those taking a year of service from the United Kibbutz Movement to work in Telem without being part of a mixed leadership group that also includes graduates of Telem. The little that exists today is thanks to those who devoted all their time to the movement over an entire year (or even longer). Part-time youth leaders can complete the picture and fill in holes here and there, but without those who contributed a year or more there would be no picture to complete and no holes to

---

1. See: "Self-Fulfillment and Self-Realization: Two Terms, Two Outlooks," Kibbutz Trends No. 9, Spring 1993; reprinted in Section 4:2.

fill. Even two or three "Halatnikim"[1] would not be adequate (as we have indeed seen).

The United Kibbutz Movement provides additional channels for a year of service in addition to youth leadership, particularly working on young kibbutzim. We have an additional need, however: the need experiment in the development of a Telem culture and way of life reflecting realizing Progressive Zionism. *Tikkun Am* through building and experiencing communal life together. The "together" will become the future of the people tomorrow. *Tikkun Torah*: the starting point for our way of life — the Jewish sources, and the attempt to forge a constructive integration of this tradition with thd heritage of other peoples. *Tikkun Eretz*: (Tikkun of the Land) in all senses, including the physical.

To look at it another way: *Torah*: ongoing study as part of the way of life and constant renewal of thought patterns and content of the individual and society. *Avoda* — both in the existential sense of labor, and in the special sense ("religious" in all its manifestations). *Acts of loving kindness*: by establishing a just society removing the need for charity. A society in which the individual's need for assistance is seen naturally as the responsibility of society as a whole, not of individuals who do justice and mercy.

The absence of gaining this experience severely restricts us in future development (up to half a generation forward) in terms of the nature of our creativity in frameworks for self-realization.

Naturally any particular form of a year of service has its advantages and disadvantages. However, a *Garin* of those deferring their Army service represents a framework and path enabling the participants to cope with the above-mentioned challenge, as well as meeting the need for leadership and activity in the movement. *It adds a year to the life of the movement that is exclusively movement life.* This is a path by which *everyone* can realize a year of service.

What should we do? Firstly, as a movement, we must establish the norm of a year of service for all our members as part of their personal education and as a pressing movement need. The norm of a year of service will be valid for all possible future directions. Secondly, we must attempt to establish an appropriate specific framework for as many members as possible; the proposal is that this should be a group *Garin* that defers its army service.

Thirdly, we must select the desired timing. This is a matter for coordination with the kibbutzim and with the Army. I hope we will at least reach agreement on the first two questions at the movement Convention. Yet the principle of Tikkun

---

1. "Halatnik" — within a settlement group doing army service, 10% do a year of leadership in the youth movement without remuneration.

Torah (and of "building fences" around the Torah) applies here, too. As I wrote: "No youth movement is free of the need to cope with these questions in an understanding and human manner, each young member according to his/her problems and his/her world."

To be blunt, the Zionist movement of self-realization is based on a recognition that it is not always possible in every matter to "honor your father and mother" when it comes to values and way of life. The significance of value-based education from the senior age groups is that each person being educated becomes aware of the values that distinguish the movement from (existing) social norms. Tensions may arise, but we are at least fortunate to be in Israel (at least physically), so that we are not talking about distances of thousands of kilometers.[1]

By its nature a youth movement advocates new positions that do not tally with a given socio-cultural situation. If a youth movement sees the existing norms as a dead-end for the Jewish People in its homeland, then there will certainly be parents who will see their children's participation in the movement as a threat once it gets "serious." In the previous generation in Eastern Europe extremely difficult human situations arose because of this conflict. We heard how Gidon's grandfather ostracized his father.[2] Yet the ostracized son made sure to bring his father to the Land of Israel before it was too late. One could not find a better true-life story (and there were many such stories) to illustrate Shlonsky's[3] line that "We dared to create from the beginning because we had come to continue the path."

As for professional help, this is certainly desirable — on *one condition*: that the professional help derives from the world view that Telem Noar makes its independent decisions. In this respect the Reform movement in Israel has failed to prove its ability to act in this way in relating to us or to Yahel and Lotan. If there are hints regarding the necessity for "professionalism" in those circles within Telem that have doubts about *shlichut* and self-realization as a way of life, we should be very careful about integrating such circles in educational terms, while yet utilizing their professional and technical assistance.

As for the use of professional adults and rabbis in youth leadership (as experts or as role models), limits should be imposed. Do we really want to adopt the model of the "professional Jew" that can be seen in the Diaspora? I ask this despite my respect for those, particularly in the Diaspora, who have chosen this

---

1. The reference is to youth from the Diaspora and the distance separating them from their families.
2. Gidon (Elad), a veteran kibbutz educator, relating the tension resulting from his father's decision to make Aliyah.
3. A. Shlonsky, 1900-1973, the Hebrew poet of Israel's pioneering movement.

path in preference to commerce, medicine, law, and so on, and who "maintain" American Jewry. But are we to encourage such an approach here in Israel?

Here I would prefer to draw on the path of pioneering self-realization in Zionism. We must learn according to the value-based positions we establish, and help from professionals is desirable, but subject to public criticism. And we must *educate* within an independent youth movement.

Clarification of the Term Rabbinical Adviser[1]

LEADERSHIP COUNCIL MEETINGS
MAY 28, 1984, JULY 10, 1985

Introduction

The distinction in English between Rabbi (referring to a communal rabbi), Rabbinical Director (referring to a centralized and authoritative rabbinical position), and Rabbinical Adviser (referring to an adviser who has rabbinical training, inter alia in youth groups) only partially reflects the nature of this function in the Israeli youth movement.

The function of the Rabbinical Adviser is that of a teacher and tutor (individual work, particularly with youth leaders), and that of an educator accompanying the institutions and endeavors of Tzofei Telem.

Rabbinical Adviser — Tzofei Telem

1) Organizational framework.
   • The IMPJ[2] will allocate one of its rabbis to serve in Tzofei Telem, full-time, for a period of three or four years.
   • The Rabbinical Adviser will be acceptable to Tzofei Telem (the Secretariat) and his candidacy will be brought before the joint steering committee of the United Kibbutz Movement and the Reform movement for ratification.
   • The movement coordinator, the Rabbinical Adviser, and the educational programs coordinator together constitute the leadership staff of Tzofei Telem. This implies a flexible division of functions within the leadership staff. It will be readily understood that in a youth movement there is no sharp distinction between the organizational and educational spheres.
   • The Rabbinical Adviser will coordinate the activities of the regional Telem advisers and will serve as a liaison between Tzofei Telem and the Council of Progressive Rabbis. In organizational terms and in coordination with

---

1. Unpublished memo to the Tzofei Telem Leadership Council, 1984 (translated from Hebrew).
2. Israel Movement for Progressive Judaism — TELEM.

Tzofei Telem he must arrange rabbinical assistance for Tzofei Telem endeavors, including *Nachal Garinim*.[1]

2) Personality and character

The Rabbinical Adviser will be someone who likes to work with young people and to draw them closer to the cultural heritage of the Jewish people.

The Rabbinical Adviser will be someone who sets an example in his practical activities of involvement in both cultural/spiritual and social Tikkun.

Authority

The authority of the Rabbinical Adviser is of an educator and is not defined.

The Adviser works within the framework of a youth movement in which democracy is one of the fundamental values, and in his movement activity he is subject to the decisions of the movement's institutions.

3) Practical activities

a) To accompany the national institutions of Tzofei Telem.

b) To accompany and take part in the work of year leadership groups[2].

c) To accompany and take part in the work of planning conferences and camps.

d) To accompany and participate personally in leadership workshops.

e) To be available to the national leadership for personal advice.

---

1. *Nachal Garinim* — settlement groups within the army framework (men and women) which enables youth to maintain partial links during their army service with a view to encouraging their continued (joint) projects (e.g., settlements) after completing the army period.
2. Each such group determines the program for a particular age group: e.g., all the youth leaders working with youngsters currently in the 7th grade.

A Station on the Road to Ideological Clarification[1] in Tzofei Telem

After the summer activities of 1982 were completed, a number of discussions were held by the Leadership Council and the National Committee of Tzofei Telem in order to evaluate the situation after two years of activities (1980-1982).

The operative conclusion of these discussions was that a small group of youth has been developed who have an emotional bond and commitment to the Telem way of life. However, no adequate answer could be found to the question "what is the movement educating toward?"

It was decided to begin a process of ideological clarification the first stage of which was completed at the Efal Seminar[2] in Nissan 5743 (April 27-29, 1983).

The Efal Seminar: The First Station on the Road to Ideological Clarification

The preparations for the Efal Seminar lasted almost four months. We received substantial help from the Training Center at Efal. A preparatory committee recommended that we present a rationale for the work of the movement, i.e. a system of ideological justifications for our education work. This rationale included articles relating to three spheres:

    a. Social values (the human as a social being, the need for community).

    b. The approach toward the Jewish people and our culture (the question of the Chosen People, our cultural uniqueness, etc.).

    c. The integration of these two spheres in self-realization in our generation.

It soon became clear that there is no ideological consensus in Tzofei Telem. It was evident to the team of youth leaders that the disagreements must constitute one of the main foci of activity in the educational process for the senior age groups.

---

1. Published in *Hamitgageim al Ha'eidah* ("Yearning for Community"), Osnat Elnatan (ed.), Tzofei Telem, 1985.
2. Efal: United Kibbutz Movement Seminar Center just outside Tel Aviv.

The seminar took the form of an exercise in values clarification and in locating the key points of disagreement. Members from the United Kibbutz Movement (UKM) and from Telem took part, as well as Yahel, Lotan, the Youth Leaders Council and young members — almost 50 people in total. The values or principles that were not the subject of disagreements were found suitable to serve as the educational basis in work with the junior sections. These appear here as they were phrased, without elaboration. The order is of no significance, and some values overlap:

1. Communal social life.
2. Openness and tolerance.
3. Study of Jewish sources leading to action.
4. Creativity.
5. Democratic way of life.
6. Grappling with Jewish tradition.
7. Life in a Jewish State in the Land of Israel.
8. Development of a Jewish way of life.
9. Realizing the hidden good.
10. Working to improve society around us.

Some of the phrasing of the areas in disagreement overlapped. During the process the disagreements were ranked in order to enable the movement to concentrate on the main areas of disagreement. Three levels of priority were chosen (the third level includes three subjects all of which received identical scores in the ranking process):

1. Self-realization in communities demands economic cooperation — yes or no?

     (Alternative phrasing: spiritual-cultural cooperation alone, without full economic cooperation, as the initial basis for joint action).

2. Activities in the Scout framework or as an independent movement?
3. a. A life of shlichut[1] or a life of restricted Tikkun?
    b. The framework constituting the destination for self-realization: kibbutz or a variety of other frameworks as destination?
    c. Judaism: A means or an end?

Other subjects of disagreement (not ranked):

1. The junior sections — an area to be emphasized or not?
2. Membership requires belief in God — yes or no?

---

1. Mission — dedicated to Tikkun Olam.

3. Close ties with the IMPJ[1] congregations — yes or no? (and what kind of ties?)
4. Must all activists be shlichim and volunteers, or may there also be paid activists?
5. Institutionalize the "Way of the Heart" or not?
6. Continue as a youth movement or go back to the youth group format?
7. Does the Jewish people have a preferential status or are we like any other nation?
8. Political identification — yes or no? (Party political, etc.)
9. The collective: a means or a goal?
10. Should there be defined obligations for self-realization at each of the senior stages?

It was decided that the 1983 Kallah would attempt to prepare activities on areas identified as the subject of disagreement. Thus the Kallah may be seen as the second station on the road to ideological clarification.

The 1983 Kallah

The Kallah was held in Jerusalem in Av 5743 (July 29-August 7, 1983). Approximately 40 participants attended: young members, youth leaders, and members of Yahel and Lotan. The participants were charged with preparing projects (activities) to clarify the ideological areas that are the subject of disagreement. The idea was that these activities would be held in the senior sections, moving Tzofei Telem toward the next stage of ideological clarification.

It was decided to examine the nature of cooperation in community as the main strand. The projects in the Kallah addressed various sub-issues: interpersonal relationships (I-Thou), economic cooperation, democracy in the community and in the state, equality and liberty, work as a value in community, the community and Tikkun Am and Olam (mending the Jewish people and the world), and the community as a means (for shlichut) and as an end in itself. The educational purpose behind the Kallah was to begin a process within Tzofei Telem of addressing the character of self-realization in community in general, and the road to this goal (the youth movement) in particular.

There is no consensus within Tzofei Telem as to the nature of communal self-realization, whether in the city or in the country. Addressing this issue will eventually have to move from an academic process to experiments in the field, i.e. personal and communal self-realization.

---

1. IMPJ — the (adult) Israel Movement for Progressive Judaism.

The Seventh Movement Council, 7-8 Adar I, 5744 (February 10-11, 1984)

This council was the third station on the road of clarification discussed above. The cumulative conclusion of the Efal Seminar and the Kallah was that it is very difficult to develop an educational movement process that does not include an additional thirteenth year for movement education. It also seemed that a thirteenth year was a vital source of youth leaders to guide the process of ideological clarification from as early as the 9th and 10th grades.

Accordingly it was decided that the theme of **A Year of Service as a Norm in Tzofei Telem** was a practical expression of the need to establish minimum norms of shlichut. It seems that without such norms of commitment, it will be impossible to develop a movement process that will enable young members to develop their own personal values, given the existing disagreements. Such a process is also vital in order to provide a practical manifestation of the self-realization objectives that will be developed in the future for the practical realization of those values that are not the subject of disagreement. For the individual, this is an opportunity for personal grappling — "to build and to be built."

The Eighth Movement Council (Shavuot 5744-1984)

This council reached a decision on the second key question identified at the Efal Seminar: activity in the Scout movement or as an independent movement. An unequivocal decision was taken by Tzofei Telem to constitute one of the foci of movement processes within the Scouts Federation. This is based on the assumption that the autonomy of the Telem educational process within the Scouts Federation will indeed prove possible. This decision certainly demands a greater effort to accelerate this process in the fall of 5746 (1986).

This completes the history of the process of ideological clarification in Tzofei Telem as begun in the fall of 1983. However, an idea (an ideology) is not enough. After all, in a movement — "history must not only be made as history but — how should we define it? — as biography: as the lives of living people." (Alterman,[1] from *Kinneret, Kinneret*).

I hope and pray that Tzofei Telem will prove able to continue along this road.

---

1. Nathan Alterman, Israeli playwright, 1910-1970.

To Garin Kave on Your Day of Celebration[1]

I am sorry that I was unable to be with you at a moment that marks a milestone for each one of you, both personally and as part of the movement (but I promise to visit you on "Shalat"[2]). Any declaration of a new *Garin* is a milestone for the family of Progressive Zionist self-realization — Tzofei Telem, Yahel, Lotan (and we hope the family will continue to grow larger and stronger).

Over the coming years, like any Nachal *Garin*, you will have to cope with the daily grind of everyday life as a *Garin* in the Israel Defense Forces (IDF).

One must serve in the IDF, but a Nachal *Garin* is an opportunity — albeit partial and imperfect — to include an experience of value-based and communal life in this experience, and to reflect your own unique character.

Our experience with Telem *Garinim* shows that this is hard, even very hard. You are well aware that the movement process of which you, as a *Garin*, are an essential product, is one that is still very much in its infancy, and that the practical help that the movement will be able to give you over these years will be minimal relative to the needs as you perceive them.

You are also well aware that in order for us to ensure a process of *Garinim* your group will have to continue to be involved in movement activities. Certainly Tzofei Telem will be unable to do without your involvement in all its considerations regarding the question of the year of service framework.

Be aware that self-realization in the sense of Tikkun Adam, Tikkun Am, and Tikkun Olam — mending the individual, the people, and the world — is a dream, and a complex dream. Even those who believe that they have already realized themselves by actually living physically on Yahel or Lotan, working there diligently, and seeing to the everyday needs of the settlement are merely deluding themselves.

As we approach the first convention of the United Kibbutz Movement (Takam), we can see that the entire kibbutz movement is in a crisis of existence due to a merely physical form of "self-realization."

---

1. *Tlamim* 37 (Newsletter of the IMPJ Youth Movement), Sivan 5745, June 1985 (translated from Hebrew).
2. The kibbutz period of army service during *Garin* (settlement group) army service.

It is emerging that this self-realization is too poor in cultural terms and fails to provide a sense of purpose.

Will you as a *Garin* be able to carry your joint forces beyond the existential level of *Garin* life in order to invest of yourselves to build and be built in your cultural and spiritual dimension in Tzofei Telem and self-realizing Reform Zionism?!

Excerpts from a Letter[1] to Garin Arava[2]

Gesher Haziv, Western Galilee, 22815

January 4, 1986

Jill Groner
Garin Arava
UAHC Youth Division
New York, NY 10021

Copies: Yahel
       Yoav Peck
       Ido Aloni, Steering Committee
       (UKM[3] — Reform Movement)

Dear Jill,

About two months ago I chanced to read your letter in Dapei Yahel[4] as well as Nancy's and Avital's answers to your questions. I noted that you asked a number of questions concerning the relationship of Tzofei Telem to Yahel. Those questions went unanswered — at least in Dapei Yahel. Frankly, I was tempted to write you a letter right then and there but my personal involvement and relationship to the "founding generation" of Garin Arava as well as the leadership of Tzofei Telem made me extremely reticent to put down my thoughts. However, in the last few months events have taken such a turn that my silence may well be a disservice to Garin Arava, Kibbutz Yahel and Tzofei Telem. Clearly, I'm going to be giving you my personal analysis and my personal opinions. They are the cumulative result of my involvement in Reform Zionist educational work during the past decade....

---

1. Unpublished letter to Jill Groner, translated into Hebrew and published in Kibbutz Yahel Newsletter, 1986. The letter has been slightly abridged.
2. From 1975 to 1987, Garin Arava was the American framework for those seeking to explore the idea of life in a Reform kibbutz.
3. United Kibbutz Movement — founded in 1981 by the merger of the Ichud (Ichud Hakvutzot Vehakibbutzim) and HaKibbutz Hameuchad).
4. "Yahel Pages" (Yahel newsletter).

Yahel and Tzofei Telem — background

In order to understand the problem that Yahel has with Tzofei Telem a little background is required. In 1978, after Yahel was founded, the World Union, in consultation with the UKM came to the conclusion that recruiting Israeli Garinim in Israel in their Junior and Senior High School year for a Reform Jewish Kibbutz would not succeed in creating a Reform Zionist kibbutz. A youth movement educating over a period of years would be a necessity. In a sense, this conclusion mirrored the historical experience of the Kibbutz movement itself. Although Degania — the first kibbutz — was established in 1911, it was not until the Nineteen Twenties that the initial Kvutzot realized that youth movements had to be set up worldwide to ensure not only people power, but also the qualitative and ideological component. When Yahel was established — we had the chicken but it had not gone through any adequate embryonic development. So the decision to try and develop "eggs" came after we saw that without a significant number of members undergoing a preparatory process (educationally), tremendous problems would ensue in terms of ongoing ability to contend with the challenge of defining a Reform Zionist way of life and propagating it outside of Yahel. In fact, given the limitations Yahel has done surprisingly well in Reform Zionist terms. Yahel has shaped a Reform Jewish calendar for total living. Yahel has been involved in attempting to confront anachronisms such as selling "chametz" to a non-Jew in the Jewish state. Yahel has attempted to be innovative in new interpretation of Zedaka. Yahel has undertaken to have hundreds of kids come through it every summer — a totally disruptive experience for a small kibbutz in its initial stages. But Kibbutz Yahel today does not relate in a systematic way to its Reform Zionist orientation as it affects the movement as a whole.

It was the fear that the movement character of the Reform kibbutzim would be in question without an Israeli (and world-wide) youth movement that led to my recruitment in order to try and organize an Israeli youth movement. The attempt to create Netzer Olami came somewhat later. Tzofei Telem at this stage is very much an experiment. "The experiment has not yet failed" but Yahel's inability to provide leadership threatens the very continuity of the experiment. However, I'm getting ahead of myself.

The idea of a youth movement for Reform Zionism in Israel sounds natural and simple but in fact for almost 50 years no new youth movement has been established in Israel. Many of the UKM chaverim "in" on the decision to try to initiate a movement came from movements, most of those in the Reform movement did not. But *none of us* had gone through a <u>movement founding</u>

experience. People like that are all in their seventies and eighties or no longer with us. Looking back, I think it would be honest to say that we did not know what we were getting into, even though I'm convinced that we made the right decision — even if we did not realize how complicated it was going to be.

The Psychological Demands of Founding a Movement

It really turned out (turns out) that to *found* a new movement which is a "movement for life" you have to have an emotional mind-set comparable to that which existed at the time of the Second and Third Aliyah.[1] You need people who totally care, who become totally themselves by devoting themselves totally to the "cause." Chalutziut was the reactivation of the prophetic principle in Judaism. Read Achad Ha'am's "Priest and Prophet"[2] for a further understanding of the issue involved. I'm sure that just reading this must create goose-pimples amongst some of you. It sounds so fanatic. It must make some of you nauseous. I know that is the reaction of many in Yahel. But that is what the chalutzim were about. They could not have accomplished what they did otherwise. In Tzofei Telem this is accompanied by powerful emotional bonds between those so involved as well as a high degree of responsibility. It also includes a degree of disdain for those not committed to the same degree.

The Israeli youth movements today (as well as the "classical" Zionist youth movements in the Diaspora such as Habonim or even Young Judea) are really "coasting" and not creating. Hence, they don't provide a real comparison to the experience of a founding movement generation.

In general, the American concept of movement is different. A movement in America is ad hoc, for a particular cause, a particular project. It's a one-shot deal. For Garin Arava it means Aliyah — to a Reform Kibbutz. That's Hagshama (self-realization). After that, build your nest and live happily ever after in a Kibbutz, admittedly with a Reform Jewish life-style, but the movement phase is over.

The Israelis on Yahel are at best in a similar situation. There has been a massive absorption (relative to Yahel's size) of non-movement members. Life on Yahel can be attractive for many because of its location and because of its Jewish cultural orientation. In and of itself this phenomenon has positive aspects — it shows that there are people searching for a type of kibbutz where they can live a

---

1. Second Aliyah — Socialist Zionist immigration to Israel, 1904-1914.
   Third Aliyah — Socialist Zionist (youth) immigration, 1919-1924.
2. "Priest and Prophet" in Leon Simon (ed.), *Selected Essays of Achad Ha'am, 1904-1924*, Jewish Publication Society, Philadelphia, 1962.

more meaningful Jewish way of life, for themselves and for their children. But it does not constitute a basis for movement.

All the above is one of the two main reasons why nearly all the members of Kibbutz Yahel who tried to work in Tzofei Telem have had negative experiences. They were not on the wavelength of total immersion and total commitment necessary for a movement founding generation. Nor could they tolerate the intensity of interpersonal relationships generated by this type of movement experience. They never knew what hit them. In some cases, Yahel sent people to work with Tzofei Telem who were committed members of Yahel but without real Reform Zionist commitment. It was a non-viable situation — for them personally and for Tzofei Telem educationally.

Tzofei Telem, the Kibbutzim and Reform Zionism: Means and Ends

The personal factor, the lack of empathy (emotional wavelength) between much of the leadership of Tzofei Telem and many of the members of Yahel, has tended to obscure the more serious differences in ideological emphases.

Are Kibbutz Yahel and Lotan means — or ends in themselves? Was Tzofei Telem created to provide ongoing recruitment for Yahel and Lotan — or was the idea to create an educational framework which would generate organized Reform Zionist commitment?

Clearly, these contradictory emphases can be reconciled in principle. The individual and his/her personal self-fulfillment must always be at the center of a democratic chalutzic Zionist youth movement. But, in fact, Yahel has over-emphasized its existential concerns of the movement. Reform Zionist impact on Israeli society, on world Reform Judaism is of marginal interest in day to day concerns. As many of you know from your personal experiences, this reflects the general reality in the kibbutz movement as a whole. The kibbutz movement as a whole is going through a major ideological crisis because of this but after all — it does exist, Reform Zionism does not really exist as yet and hence the Reform Zionist kibbutzim cannot afford to follow the problematic pattern which currently characterizes the established kibbutzim.

The rationalization of "once we are more firmly established then we'll undertake to do something" is unacceptable. All the precedents show that there is no correlation between "degree of being established" and preparedness to take on shlichut. Most of the evidence is to the contrary — those communities which were/are permeated with the sense of shlichut generated a more intensive sense of mutual responsibility and were existentially strengthened as a result socially and even economically. The evidence is also that these are the kibbutzim that succeed in holding on to their children. Existentially, Yahel does not need Tzofei Telem. It is easier to absorb individuals, both from Israel and from the Diaspora searching for Kibbutz life with a Reform Jewish commitment. But this does not make for Reform *Zionist* commitment which is a dynamic and ongoing concept. Keep in mind, as Garin Arava functions at present, you are apparently going to be absorbed as individuals — whether in Yahel or Lotan. You have the name "Garin" but you don't really function like one when you get here. I'm not taking a position on this question. Possibly the Garin framework becomes counter-productive at a certain stage. But I'm wondering if you are conscious of all the implications and trade-offs.

The relationship between Yahel and Tzofei Telem (ultimately all of Netzer Olami) has exposed fundamental questions that Kibbutz Yahel and Garin Arava must begin to talk about. Tzofei Telem and to some extent Kibbutz Lotan are further ahead on this score. Perhaps there are those in Yahel who are fearful of initiating frank discussions within Yahel regarding its Reform Zionist responsibility. Those who would brush the question under the carpet are doing themselves and Kibbutz Yahel a disservice. The movement potential is still there even though it may have to express itself preferentially in work with Diaspora youth in the next few years.

The Implications for Garin Arava

Garin Arava would be well advised to put the questions of principle raised in the foregoing paragraphs on its educational agenda for future Kinusim.[1] The subject would be: Reform Zionist shlichut and our kibbutz.

In my opinion, only movement-oriented Reform Zionist kibbutzim have the possibility of providing autonomous leadership (as distinct from professional leadership dependent on some establishment for its economic existence) for Reform Zionism in Israel. Only the Reform kibbutzim have real *political* leverage in Israel by virtue of their being an integral part of the kibbutz movement. Hence, at this time, a Reform Zionist strategy oriented to Israel as a whole must be based on tactically strengthening that small base. Yahel, Lotan and hopefully the third kibbutz presently under discussion constitute that base. The base must provide ongoing meaning and self-fulfillment for those who choose this as their personal *hagshama*. But the base exists for the purpose of outreach to Israeli society as a whole — at present to the kibbutz movement, to the Israeli scouts (via Tzofei

---

1. Conclaves.

Telem) and to the minuscule Reform movement. Via Garin Arava and Netzer Olami this influence will hopefully have an ever greater impact in Reform Judaism — particularly among the youth. Yahel is already a symbol for NFTY.

In Perspective

Pretentious. Immodest. Arrogant. Presumptuous... Maybe.

Eighty years ago a handful of East European and Russian Jewish youth saw themselves as personally taking upon themselves the responsibility for ensuring the continuity and continued creativity of the Jewish people. Today, the descendants of that generation have faltered. Israel has faltered spiritually. Creating a democratic society committed Jewishly against the backdrop of constant external threats and internal tensions has created a backlash of yearning for authoritarian solutions.

Can the task of Reform Zionism be less than the attempt to renew the Zionist building of Israel in the prophetic Jewish and Western democratic tradition? Can Reform Judaism in the Diaspora remain creative without being integrally involved in the struggle for the character of the Jewish National Home? Can the meaning of Garin Arava, Netzer, Tzofei Telem, Yahel and Lotan be less than taking on this personal responsibility as a way of life?

In summary, our kibbutzim and our Aliyah must concern themselves with the ultimate questions. The Jewish Agency and perhaps even the kibbutz movement will be satisfied if you make Aliyah — to the kibbutzim, to the Mitzpe.[1] But Reform Zionism as a movement of personal self-fulfillment and as a movement with a message demands a more total commitment.

All the best for your forthcoming Kinusim. I do believe that in its second decade Garin Arava and Netzer in America can come into their own.

---

1. "Look Out" — refers to Har Chalutz, the community (non-kibbutz) settlement initiated by the Reform movement in the Galilee.

The Idea Behind the Ma'amad[1]

The Function of Religious Worship — Then and Now

The offering of sacrifices during the period of the First Temple and prayer as it developed during the period of the Second Temple served three main functions. Our forefathers were aware of two of them.

1. The attempt to relate to a given state of affairs — whether in terms of a calculated attempt to influence them or whether in terms of the psychological need to express one's felt desires and yearnings before a greater power (Belief in a God that hears one's prayers).
2. A ritual expression of individual and community commitment to live a life focused on the divine purpose — obeying God's commandments (fulfilling Mitzvot) as a means to the end of Tikun Olam — i.e., perfecting the world (Prayer as fulfilling Mitzva).

Religious worship also served an additional function — in particular after the destruction of the Second Temple. *It served as the social focus for ritual activity in which the norms and values of Judaism were subsumed.*

In pre-modern times (before emancipation in terms of Jewish history) the norm of human social organization was a communal unit whose magnitude varied from tens to hundreds. Even cities were made up of communal units. The Jews constituted one community in the pre-modern city. The pre-modern communities — whether urban or rural — were characterized by inter-relationships of mutual responsibility between members which permeated all aspects of daily life.

Generally, the social basis for the community was the extended family, most often some variation of the patriarchal clan or groups of such clans. In the medieval cities the basis for the communal units could also be the guild — a kind of trade union. Carpenters, tailors, blacksmiths, etc., all had their guilds which were often based on family ties as well. Each guild had responsibility for determining standards for its particular vocation as well as maintaining a network of

---

1. In "Met'fila L'Ma'amad," *Tzofei-Telem*, 1982, revised 1987 (translated from the Hebrew).
   Ma'amad can be translated as a ritual including creative prayer and other cultural content.

mutual assistance for its members. In many cases the guild members and their families also worshiped together in the same church.

An integral part of the pre-modern community was its religious culture through which the community symbolically expressed its values. In this sense, the Jewish community in the pre-modern city also constituted a kind of "guild."

In the last few hundred years mass society has emerged to take the place of the social-communal frameworks described above. Mass society is characterized by large numbers of people (masses) — individuals or nuclear families (father, mother, children) — living "together" in the modern city. But the "togetherness" is purely geographical — there is no communal network of mutual responsibility and caring which is the essence of community. To a large extent the culture of the mass society becomes mass culture — modulated by the means of mass communication. Such culture has been antithetical to the existence of a community of mutual responsibility and common life-goals.

It was always the "hidden" purpose of religious worship in Jewish society to constitute the social-communal situation in which spiritual togetherness and the shared sense of ultimate purpose found its daily expression. The passing of the pre-modern social-communal life style has meant the removal of the social basis for this cultural togetherness. The religious culture of Judaism, bereft of a base in communal togetherness, lost much of its vitality and meaning for the individual. This process was catalyzed by the inherent skepticism of modernity regarding traditional forms. Nor did Diaspora Judaism, in the absence of a national homeland, have the ability to partially compensate for this vacuum by substituting an element of national togetherness as a substitute for the lost communal togetherness.

Ma'amad: The Renewal of Religious Worship in Community

The Ma'amad constitutes both a means and an end.

In Tofei Telem the Ma'amad is a form of religious worship which seeks to confront the problem of religious worship and identity that faces Jews who do not have a commitment to Halacha.

1. For some, the Ma'amad takes the place of traditional prayer in the sense that its content and style reflect contemporary language and experiential situations and relates to the vision/s of our generation.

2. As an event, the Ma'amad constitutes the socio-cultural focus of being "together." But the purpose of the Ma'amad is not just to bring movement members together, technically so to speak, in order to worship together.

Rather, the Ma'amad should be understood as both search and expression of the movement and its individual members for a Jewish identity relevant to themselves. Within the context of the present reality, the togetherness of the Ma'amad must also bridge the varieties of belief and commitment among members of the youth movement regarding the nature of God.

3. Within the broader historical context, the Ma'amad symbolizes the attempt to renew Jewish religious creativity within the context of a movement committed to reform in all aspects of Jewish life: ritual, communal and national. Hence one might hope that the content of the Ma'amad will be influenced by the movement's striving to develop and personally be a part of the comprehensive Reform Zionist communities of the future.

The Ma'amad as Symbol and Primary Experience

The Ma'amad is a religious-cultural symbol of the youth movement's commitment to reform and the renewal of a Jewish way of life where spiritual expression and commitmient are congruent with the social content of the everyday life within the community.

But what is the importance of the Ma'amad as a symbol? (What, in general, is the importance of symbols?) Symbols have a direct physical impact on our senses: sight, hearing, smell, taste and touch. Our ability to learn, to absorb ideas, develops gradually. We begin with our senses. It is only in the last few hundred years that we have become relatively cut off from our senses and emotions by the rational and scientific modern world. It has not necessarily made us more human.

The primary grasp of people and things via the senses stands in contrast to (but not necessarily in opposition to) our grasp of things by secondary processes of the intellect. For example, rational and ideological explanations of Judaism and/or movement are all secondary process. A major innovation of pioneering Zionism was the rejection of national experience mediated almost exclusively by secondary process.

A.D. Gordon demanded that the Jewish people return to their historical base of primary experience (Eretz Israel) and to primary occupations (such as agriculture and other fields involving manual labor) as a prerequisite for the renewal of Jewish creativity. Living national culture must have its roots in primary process (Chavaya) as distinct from secondary process (Hakara).

Unfortunately, in their rejection of the orthodox Judaism of Eastern Europe, the Labor Zionist pioneers who founded the Kibbutzim rejected all religious ritual outright. It has only been now, some three generations later, that a particular school of thought and action has developed within Reform Zionism (in itself a newcomer to the Zionist scene) which has seen the necessity of translating synagogue-bound ritual into primary experience within the comprehensive togetherness of existence within community.

Our emotional attachments and beliefs relate first of all to symbols — the rational explanation comes afterwards. An instinctive understanding of this idea as an educational principle is evidenced by the recommendations of Tzofei Telem's Educational Council regarding the setting of the Ma'amad (in a natural setting, in a circle where everyone faces each other and possibly holds hands, with dramatic sketches and even dance). At present the Ma'amad does not fully exploit all of these possibilities.

The idea of the Ma'amad is still too new for us to predict its future. Can the innovation of the youth movement become a norm — not a static norm but one in on-going developmental tension — in the adult Reform Zionist communities that will emerge in the next generation? Only then will we be able to evaluate the significance of the Ma'amad as a phenomenon in Reform Judaism and Cultural Zionism.

Appendix

EXCERPTS FROM THE DECISIONS OF THE EDUCATIONAL COUNCIL OF TZOFEI TELEM

3rd Council, Kibbutz Yahel, Pesach 1981

Discussion on Prayer

Whereas in our opinion the term "t'fila" (prayer) in and of itself is not comprehensive enough, it was decided to introduce the term Ma'amad.

Ma'amad designates any gathering characterized by excerpts from prayer, poems, music prayer-study, individual meditation or any other form of expression by the gathering that emphasizes values.

1. A member of Telem Noar accepts the obligation to be present at the Ma'amadim (of movement events that he/she attends)

2. The Obligation Regarding Prayer at Conclaves
   1. At national conclaves there will be at least two Ma'amadim per day. One of them will be either evening prayer (arvit), morning prayer (shacharit) or afternoon prayer (mincha). The second can be as the first, prayer-study or some other Ma'amad.
   2. In Tzofei-Telem the friendship circle substitutes for scouting drill.[1]

3. On the Nature of the Ma'amad
   • Singing and playing musical instruments are to be emphasized.
   • The Ma'amad is to be held in natural settings as much as possible.
   • It is recommended to have the Ma'amad relate to events and situations reflecting current reality.
   • We view the inclusion of dance, drama and the arts in the Ma'amad with favor on the understanding that the purpose is to reinforce the specialness (holiness) of the Ma'amad.
   • We favor the reasonable balance of the traditional and the creative in the Ma'amad.
   • Regarding the text of prayers we direct:
     1. Changing all negative allusions to women, non-Jews, slaves.
     2. Change passages dealing with revival of the dead.

---

1. See Section 6:4.

3. Elimination of passages referring to Satan.
4. Introduction of the idea of the State of Israel.
5. Sidur: All Sidurim are a possible source for the Ma'amad but we recommend the use of Hebrew Sidurim that reflect the spirit of our decisions regarding text as detailed above.

4th Council, Leo Baeck High School, Haifa, Succot, 1981

The subject of the nature of the Ma'amad was brought up for an additional discussion because it was felt that the guidelines of the previous council were inadequate. The discussion below deals with the Ma'amad which is to have the format of prayer.

Innovation and tradition in the Ma'amad T'fila

1. We recommend that the daily Ma'amad T'fila be built according to the outline of the traditional prayer:

   Shachrit: Morning Blessings, Psalms, the Shema and its Blessings, Amida, Torah Portion if indicated, Aleynu, Kaddish.

   Arvit: The Shema and its blessings, Amida, Aleynu and Kaddish.

   Mincha: Amida, Aleynu, Kaddish plus additions for Chagim.

2. In the Ma'amad T'fila the first Parasha of Kriat Shema is to be included as well as Amida – full or shortened version. All other parts can be substituted for by a creative passage reflecting similar content.

3. Regarding creativity, we recommend that members of Tzofei Telem compose prayers.

Translated: Michael Langer, Sept. 1987

The Reform Kibbutzim

Synopsis of the Section

The fusion of Reform Zionism within the Kibbutz framework, from the Reform point of view and from the Kibbutz point of view, is the subject of this section.

The decision of the Ichud Hakvutzot Vehakibbutzim kibbutz movement and the Reform movement (specifically, the Youth Division of the Union of American Hebrew Congregations under the leadership of Rabbi Stephen Schafer) to establish a Reform Kibbutz led to my personal involvement in what was to become Reform Zionism. The Preface to this book details the organizational path by which I became involved as first *shaliach* (emissary) to the UAHC.

Gidon Elad of Kibbutz Chatzerim replaced me as *shaliach* to the UAHC in 1977-1979. He has recently researched and documented the evolution of the Reform Kibbutz idea within the Reform movement and its implementation in detail.[1]

As *shaliach* to the UAHC from the Kibbutz movement, I had the particular task of formulating a detailed rationale for the Reform Kibbutz. REFORM KIBBUTZ AND RELIGIOUS PIONEERING was a presentation made in June 1976 to a conclave of Garin Arava, the organizational framework established in America for those interested in weighing the possibility of settlement on the planned kibbutz. On the other hand, as a *shaliach* of the kibbutz movement I felt a parallel obligation to explain the idea of the nascent kibbutz to the kibbutz public — PIONEERING ZIONISM AND REFORM JUDAISM: NEW IDEOLOGICAL HORIZONS. These articles reflect the vision of the Seventies.

Much of my writing during the years between my return from America (1977) and my move to Kibbutz Lotan nine years later reflected my opinion that the Reform Kibbutz has a central role to play in Israeli Reform Zionism. This finds particular expression in REFORM ZIONISM: PROBLEMS AND PROGRESS (1983) in Section One. However, SOVEREIGN CHUPA (WEDDING): COMMUNAL AUTHORITY IN CULTURAL ZIONISM stemmed from the specific confrontation between the beliefs of Tzofei Telem graduates and the existing Orthodox Rabbinic monopoly on certain rites of passage such as marriage. Their Reform Kibbutz community, Lotan, became party to this confrontation. The article discusses the possible implications for ritual authority and Rabbinic authority in general in a Reform Kibbutz community.

---

1. Gidon Elad, *A Light in the Arava?: Yahel — A Dialogue and Joint Task Between the Kibbutz Movement and the Reform Movement* (1997), unpublished manuscript in Hebrew.

OUR REFORM KIBBUTZIM attempts to give a balanced perspective of the status of the Reform Kibbutzim at the end of the Twentieth Century. The Vision Statement of the Kibbutz Lotan community is appended as a fitting summary to this section.

Ultimately, the significance of the Reform Kibbutzim depends on the Zionist or non-Zionist nature of the Israel Movement for Progressive Judaism(see Section Two — REFORM JUDAISM AND REFORM ZIONISM IN ISRAEL — 1991). If the IMPJ is merely a federation of congregations of worship then as two isolated, small congregations the kibbutzim are marginal. On the other hand, if the IMPJ is the expression of a Reform Zionism seeking to impact on Israel, then their relevance is as comprehensive communities uniquely able to confront questions of Reform Judaism in both the ritual and the social realm. In addition the kibbutzim can (and do) serve as centers for an immersion experience in Reform living for young people from Israel and the Diaspora. However, the significance of the kibbutzim in this latter context depends on recognition by the Reform movement both in Israel and in the Diaspora that significant educational experiences are vital to creating lasting Zionist impact.

Reform Kibbutz and Religious Pioneering[1]

What is the *potential* of the Reform Kibbutz to engage in religious pioneering by virtue of its being a collective community? I emphasize the word potential, because in actuality, the realization of that potential will be determined by the felt needs of the members of the kibbutz.

Martin Buber was one of the first to see in the kibbutz an expression of religious pioneering. For him, the collective commune based on mutual responsibility between its members, a strong striving for an egalitarian economic ethic, and the conscious commitment to create Jewish community, made it a potential framework for the achievement of dialogue, of the "I-Thou" relationship within a contemporary Jewish setting. Buber asserted in his *Paths to Utopia* that the kibbutz was an experiment that had not yet failed — i.e., the kibbutz had not succeeded in realizing its utopian aims, but it was still, in spite of the exigencies of everyday life, concerned with striving towards this goal. More recently, another kibbutz member, Muki Tsur, has put it succinctly: "The kibbutz is not an ideal society, but it is a society built on ideals."

There are a number of reasons why the kibbutz has been chosen as the framework within which to attempt the realization of a new organic development within liberal Jewish tradition. There are a number of reasons why potentially the structure of the kibbutz as it has developed up to now makes it a possible vehicle for such development. Perhaps the most important reason is that insofar as liberal Judaism strives to evolve new norms and new forms for Judaism in response to the challenge of the modern age, it must have a community within which such a Judaism can be lived. The organic Jewish community within which traditional rabbinic Jewish community was rooted is no more. The basis for "halacha" (law) binding upon the community has disappeared. Without a community with norms binding upon its members there can be no halacha. The kibbutz represents one of the few viable contemporary frameworks of community.

---

1. Third National Conclave, Garin "Arava," 1976, published in *Reform Zionist Perspective*, UAHC Youth Division, 1977. p. 371.

Dialogue in a Liberal Community

The egalitarian nature and the comprehensive collective framework do result in ongoing interaction at various levels within a small community of people. In the social sense, this is an organic community. Interpersonal relationships at work are inextricably bound up with interpersonal relationships outside of work. The principle of job rotation on the kibbutz — in particular insofar as elective office is concerned — tends to negate the formation of a power elite within the kibbutz. One's status depends not on the particular job that one does, but on how well one does one's job, whatever it is. This type of communal environment is far more conducive to the realization of a relationship of dialogue and the observance of mitzvot between man and his fellow man than the fragmented human inter-relationships which constitute the norm in the contemporary urban framework, whether in Tel Aviv or Scarsdale. The Reform Kibbutz will be the first community where a liberal interpretation of Jewish tradition can orient the developments in interpersonal relations.

The concept of mutual responsibility and community extends beyond the confines of the single kibbutz. In actual fact, all the kibbutzim in Israel are organized into networks of movements based on mutual responsibility and self-help among the 250 different kibbutzim. National and regional organizational frameworks exist within Israel to give expression to this principle. The Reform Kibbutz, therefore, by choosing the kibbutz framework, is automatically integrating into a national network of communal institutions based on principles of mutual responsibility and assistance. Moreover, the kibbutz movement sees itself as a movement in the service of the Jewish people. Indeed, every kibbutz is responsible for allocating 5% of its work force to service outside the kibbutz, either in the central institutions of the kibbutz movement, within the state of Israel, or within the framework of the World Zionist Organization. Hence, the kibbutz framework will make it possible for the kibbutz to always release some of its chaverim (members) for work with the World Union for Progressive Judaism (now a constituent member of the WZO). Of course, who and how many are released at any particular time will be the decision of the kibbutz itself. Practical difficulties notwithstanding (especially during the kibbutz's first years), the kibbutz tradition makes it "natural" for the Reform Kibbutz to be available as a resource for liberal Judaism.

The Kibbutz As Potential For Developing Tradition

To what extent can we be certain that the Reform Kibbutz will develop some kind of viable liberal Jewish tradition which can be instructive and perhaps even inspirational to the Jewish State as well as liberal Judaism in the Diaspora? In truth, there can be no such guarantee. It is true that to the extent that a Reform Kibbutz movement arises (i.e., more than just one kibbutz), the possibility for such a development becomes stronger. Nevertheless, it would be relevant to point out that the *potential* for developing such tradition is ultimately dependent on the existence of a viable multi-generational community. Tradition can be an organic outgrowth only if there is a continuity of generations within the same community. After all, the fundamental failure of all the nineteenth century utopias and modern experiments in communes has been their failure to motivate the next generation to carry on with their particular way of life. This, then, is the iron test. Will the Reform Kibbutz be able to propagate itself over a period of generations? Without this there can be no development of organic tradition. Given the social ability to "reproduce" the development of such tradition is not yet guaranteed, but becomes potentially possible.

In general, the kibbutzim, since their establishment some 70 years ago, have succeeded in "reproducing themselves." There are fourth-generation kibbutznikim. There are kibbutz great-grandparents living together with their children, grandchildren, and great-grandchildren in the same community. In a way, the kibbutz, which in fact sees itself as a kind of an extended family framework, has also succeeded in recreating a traditional family framework within the context of a modern economy and society. The development of the nuclear family, the great geographic mobility, the lack of on-going contact with natural surroundings, make it most difficult to develop Jewish tradition meaningfully. The kibbutz as a framework provides these attributes. The community itself constitutes a framework within which norms and traditions develop. The communal sanction ensures that these norms will be observed. Indeed, with the exception of a few islands of ultra-orthodox Judaism, Jewish community in which communal consensus truly determines individual behavior exists nowhere except on the kibbutz. The existence of such a communal framework is surely the pre-requisite for the development of norms and practices (a halacha) by which Judaism can seek to confront the Modern Age.

The rural ecology of the kibbutz (note: the kibbutz is a mixed industrial-agricultural economy today, but significantly, its ecology remains rural) makes possible the development of a cosmic relationship — a relationship to the natural order as perceived in its totality. Here we have the organic-inorganic whole of one's environment as well as the dimension of time through which man and his environment move. Perhaps in this lies the possibility of the kibbutz developing a relationship to the cosmic; for a further development of those laws that have to do with the relationship of the individual and his community to God (*bein ha-adam la'makom*). This is an area in which the majority of the kibbutzim have not yet involved themselves.

The Sacred and the Profane

Only through community can we achieve a heightened sense of the separation of the sacred and everyday (*bein kodesh v'chol*). Only through community can one truly express the weekly cycle of work and Shabbat. Only by relating to the events in the annual cycle as a community — the same community in the same place year after year and generation after generation — can tradition with regard to the observance of holidays and festivals develop organically. The meaning of the significant events in one's life — birth, bar mitzvah, marriage, death — are quite different if they are marked by the same individual in the same community within his or her extended family. The nature of current middle-class Jewish urban existence fractures the underlying unity which, ideally, should link the significant events in the life cycle. The norm is to mark the life cycle events in different communities, with different friends, and in a context of cultural banality. Finally, the potential for a meaningful relationship to the significant events in the national history of the people to which one belongs will likely be greater when this relationship takes place in its historic homeland.

◆ ◆ ◆

In summary, the kibbutz framework has the potential for contributing to the development of a liberal Jewish halacha — in matters of individual and communal observance as well as in the relationships between individuals, their community, and their people. It is for this reason that those seeking to establish the first liberal Jewish community in history chose the kibbutz framework. The young people undertaking this venture hope to make a vital contribution to a creative Judaism. Some of them are apprehensive with regard to their "historic responsibility." There are no real precedents to guide them except one — *naase v'nishma* (we will do and then listen).

Hence the Reform Kibbutz is also one of the most exciting options for Jewish self-realization for young Reform Jews today.

Pioneering Zionism and Reform Judaism: New Ideological Horizons[1]

This year the first kibbutz of the Reform movement (which in Israel is called the Movement for Progressive Judaism) was established. The Telem and Nir settlement groups founded Kibbutz Yahel, some 65 kilometers north of Eilat.

A new pioneering movement would seem to be emerging among Reform Jewry. This article discusses these ideological changes in one of the main Jewish streams in the largest Jewish community in the world.

We are currently witnessing a revolutionary transformation in the Reform movement's attitude to Zionism. An apparently surprising combination is emerging of two antagonistic movements, both of which developed in response to the problems of post-emancipation Judaism. We must understand the historical background to this antagonism, which is now reaching its end.

The understandable emotional rejection of some of the characteristics of Reform Judaism by the Zionist movement prevented a neutral historical examination. Our approach to the history of the Reform movement is highly reminiscent of the "treatment" meted out in earlier generations to the messianic movements (such as that of Shabbtai Zvi) at the hands of the founders of modern Jewish studies (many of whom, interestingly enough, were Reform Jews!).

After the Emancipation brought down the walls of the Jewish ghetto in the West, the communal and social frameworks that had provided the authority for the traditional Halachic approach of Rabbinical Judaism largely disintegrated. In terms of Western history, this was an essential side effect of the elimination of medieval organic and community-based society. Under the influence of the Enlightenment and Liberalism, the European societies lost the traditional patterns based on mutual responsibility that followed from the "natural" affiliation to the community.[2]

---

1. *Shdemot, A Platform for the Kibbutz Movement*, Issue 62, Winter 1977 (translated from Hebrew).
2. See Stanley Meron, *Society and the Individual*, Ihud Hakibbutzim VehaKvutzot, 1966. Also in Michael Langer, ed., *Reform Zionist Perspective*, UAHC Youth Division, New York, 1977, p. 38.

There emerged the nation state, in which "contractual" relations exist both among the citizens and between citizens and state. The state demanded that the Jews abandon their communal autonomy and reduce their Judaism to a purely religious affiliation (analogous to the Protestant faith) and integrate as individuals in the new nations.

The Emergence of Reform

The Reform movement arose in response to this situation, and attempted to prevent the mass exodus from Judaism, particularly in Germany. The response of this movement was as follows:

a) We accept as a given that emancipation and the revolution have brought a new age in human history. Intermediate communal frameworks separating citizens from the authority of the new state are no longer viable. Judaism must adapt to this situation. The Jews must be "citizens of the Mosaic persuasion," loyal to the state. Accordingly, we clearly negate the concept of a distinct Jewish people with an affinity to its historical homeland. The Reform thinker Geiger even stated that a scientific and historical perspective shows that Judaism developed and changed greatly from Mt. Sinai onward. There was a period when there was a need for an autonomous people in order to maintain God's Torah. Now Judaism can forego the material world and function as a purely spiritual element: the carrier of the moral values that underlie Western society as a whole. Judaism carries the universalistic mission to be dispersed among the nations, serving as an example and thus giving new meaning to the expression "to be a light unto the nations."

b) As enlightened moderns, the position of the exponents of Reform Judaism toward the Halacha was that the Torah was as much (if not more) Moses' Law rather than God's Law. In other words, the Written Law and Oral Law were from the outset the joint composition of humans and God. This cooperation must be expressed in new interpretations and even new laws in each generation, according to changing circumstances and as human wisdom develops. There were (and still are) differing views within the Reform movement as to the nature of the cooperation between humans and God, and the nature of the relationship between God and Israel.

In conclusion, Reform Judaism negated the national and communal basis of Judaism as anachronistic in modern times, while affirming the value-based dimension of Judaism. In practice, Reform also affirmed the Halacha as the practical expression of Jewish values, while advocating an ongoing process of Tikkun (Reform) and the right to enact new legislation. The leaders of the movement in the nineteenth century even attempted to formulate new Halachic principles.

Classic Reform *separated the national, group-based element of Judaism from the culture (religion) itself.* The movement negated the ethnic element of Judaism, while affirming the religious element provided that this undergo reforms according to the spirit of modern times.

There were two main weak points in this approach:

1) The Reform rabbis failed to appreciate that a binding Halacha was an impossibility in the absence of a communal framework providing the authority and infrastructure for this Halacha in everyday life.

2) The theory of Liberalism emphasized individual rights and liberty. This approach served as an "ideological passport" for Jewish religious freedom and the integration of the Jews as individuals in general society. In internal Jewish terms, however, the ideological ramification of this was that each person could do as he or she saw fit. The problem was not whether people chose to keep the commandments. The problem was that every Reform Jew, Reform rabbi or Reform community was authorized to develop Halacha. On the basis of the principles of religious freedom and individual rights, it was no longer possible to impose communal authority. It should be noted that to this day there is considerable tension within the Reform movement on the issue of acquiescence to central authority.

Political and Cultural Zionism

Zionism in its modern sense was established two generations later. Its emergence followed the discrediting of the basic political assumptions of Reform Judaism by the rising tide of European nationalism. In order to properly appreciate the ideological connection between Zionism and the Reform movement, we must examine their shared identity as an attempt to meet the challenge posed by the modern era to Judaism as a viable way of life. Such a comparison requires a distinction (however artificial) between the political stream of Zionism and its dimension of cultural renaissance.

Political Zionism was established in response to anti-Semitism, reflecting a feeling that in a world based on the nation state, the Jews would also require their own national framework in order to guarantee their physical existence. In such a world — and it was here that the pessimistic prediction of political Zionism contradicted the optimistic Liberal vision of the Reform movement — there could no longer be a safe place for the Jews anywhere but in their own nation state. In postulating this position, political Zionism was of course established in order to solve the problem of the Jews, rather than the problem of Judaism. It should also be noted that within the Reform movement there was a minority that also saw the need for a Jewish state due to a political assessment that differed from that of the majority (Rabbis Gottheil and Magnes were among the first political Zionists in America at the time of Herzl).

In our opinion, the cultural Zionism of Achad Ha'am provides a better basis for appreciating Zionism as a response to the problem of Judaism. This stream argued that a national Jewish center was needed in order to guarantee the creative existence of the Jewish people *per se*. This argument was based on the assumption that Judaism is the cultural expression of the Jewish people, and that the people and its culture are inseparable. In contrast to political Zionism, this approach reflected the assumption that Diaspora Jewry would continue to exist, and that the function of the Jewish center would be to preserve the quality of this existence.

The practical issues faced by Zionism heightened the contrast between political and cultural Zionism. There were, however, always those who advocated a combination of both approaches (and they would later come to form the majority of the Zionist movement). The Reform and Conservative rabbis who joined the Zionist movement in America mainly emphasized their affinity with cultural Zionism.

The Ideology of the Chalutzim

In the Land of Israel itself, the starting point of the pioneering Zionist movement (the *chalutzim*) was for the most part a particular type of cultural Zionism. The pioneers advocated the revival of Hebrew language and culture. However, the pioneering Zionist movement was far more radical than the cultural Zionism of Achad Ha'am in its analysis of the condition of the Jewish people and of what was needed for its rehabilitation in modern times. The pioneering movement concluded that it was not enough to advocate a Jewish center in the Land of Israel; there was a need to evolve a communal way of life different from that that was gradually deteriorating in Eastern Europe. The social basis for the renaissance of the people in its land must be founded on social justice as embodied in the philosophy of the Prophets and as expressed in modern times by the aspirations of Socialism.

The pioneering Zionists were also more extreme than Achad Ha'am in terms of their attitude toward religion and tradition. Achad Ha'am's secular approach underwent a "metamorphosis" in the pioneering Zionist movement, which came to identify Rabbinical Judaism with the conservative regime of the Jewish ghetto. The revulsion at the social values of the ghetto was due to the perceived alliance between the rabbis and the communal leaders of the East European *Shtetl*.[1] This led many pioneering Zionists to an almost total rejection of the Halachic religious tradition. It seemed that the new Socialist message, based on universalistic values, would provide the ideological content for the new Jewish culture. After all, Socialism itself had emerged under the inspiration of the values of social justice rooted in the writings of the Prophets. This anti-religious tone predominated in the pioneering movement, despite the reservations of such spiritual leaders as A.D. Gordon and Berl Katznelson.

The pioneering Zionist response to repairing the state of the people also had its weak points:

1) The pioneering Zionists ostensibly achieved their immediate goal, at least partially. However, their rejection of Jewish tradition and their total negation of the Diaspora raised serious questions of Jewish identification and the attitude toward Jewish culture among the next generation within the pioneering Zionist endeavor.

2) It now seems that Socialism functioned as an intellectual "crutch" enabling a certain section of Jewish youth in Eastern Europe and Russia to develop their thoughts and actions in the ideological context of that time. Presently the Socialist movement (both the democratic and totalitarian branches) is becoming increasingly sterile. Anarchistic Socialism, perhaps the most promising from our standpoint, has been almost completely eliminated. In the kibbutz movement, official adherence to Socialism as an ideological theory guiding our thoughts is now an anachronism (if not idol worship). The time has come to remove these ideological crutches.

Reform and Chalutziut: The Mirror Image

It should be noted that the classical manifestations of the pioneering Zionist movement (as of the Reform movement) generally distinguished between the national or group-based element of Judaism and the religious and cultural

---

1. Small Jewish town.

element. The pioneering movement broadly rejected religious-cultural tradition, but affirmed the affiliative and group-based element. However, in affirming the group-based and communal element the pioneering Zionist movement demanded extensive changes (reform) in the ecology and social structure of the new Jewish society in the Land of Israel.

Moreover, both movements preferred universalistic values to Jewish values. In Reform Judaism, the universalistic mission of the Jews among the nations replaces the particularistic basis of this mission. For its part, the pioneering Zionist movement replaced Halachic Judaism with one or other of the shades of Socialist ideology.

While these two movements differ profoundly in origin and outlook, each serves as the mirror image of the other. This contradiction contained the latent potential that a natural and creative reconciliation of both approaches might one day emerge. An examination of the courses taken by both movements shows that such a reconciliation could be possible when both movements once again adopted a full perspective of Judaism, no longer advocating separation between the people and the heritage of its generations. Why did it take three generations for the circumstances to emerge that could allow this logical combination of the ideas of Reform Judaism and pioneering Zionism?

The Evolution of Reform

In this context, a number of factors are usually postulated as influencing and eventually "softening" Reform Judaism:

1) The rise of Jews of Eastern European origin to key positions in the Reform movement, in place of the leadership that had its roots in the central European Jewish immigration to America in the mid-nineteenth century. The ethnic basis of Judaism was negated mainly by those who had been through the process of emancipation in Germany.

2) The influence of the philosophy of Mordechai Kaplan (founder of the Reconstructionist movement) among young Reform rabbis in the USA. Kaplan defined Judaism as a developing religious civilization, and saw the Jewish people as the bearer of this civilization. This idea is very similar to that expressed by Geiger seventy years earlier, but now the element of the people became of central importance.

3) The growth of Nazism in the land of Reform Judaism's birth and the absence of a place of refuge for those persecuted by Hitler led Reform

Jewry to accept as early as 1937 an official platform encouraging the development of a Jewish center in the Land of Israel.

4) Following the Holocaust and the struggle surrounding the establishment of Israel, no anti-Zionist element could gain anything more than marginal support (though these marginal groups, such as the American Council for Judaism, were Reform). On the other hand, Reform rabbis such as Abba Hillel Silver and Stephen Wise were among the vanguard of those responsible for recruiting Jewish and general support for political Zionism in America.

Despite this, the Reform movement continued to adopt a relatively reserved approach to the Zionist movement until the mid-1960s. Leading Reform Zionists worked mainly through Zionist organizations, rather than through the institutions of their own movement.

The acceptance of Zionism as an integral part of Reform Judaism began no more than ten years ago. This process was characterized by a situation whereby a small and active minority moved forward, established facts on the basis that there was a "vacuum" and that "there is no decision against this," and then later received official approval. This is a well-known process in Zionist history.

The Reform Rabbinical Seminary (Hebrew Union College) opened a branch in Jerusalem. At first, the center concentrated on Biblical and archeological research, but it was later agreed that every rabbinical student would be required to spend one year in Jerusalem. The headquarters of the World Union of Progressive Judaism were moved to Jerusalem. The Reform movement's Youth Department began to organize annual summer programs in Israel with hundreds of young Reform participants. The influence of Israeli culture was felt in the summer camp experience in America. After two dialogues between Reform educators and rabbis and members of the kibbutz movement, the idea emerged of establishing a Reform kibbutz, ostensibly under the auspices of the World Union of Progressive Judaism, but actually as the initiative of a number of American rabbis in the movement's Youth Department. The author of this article was recruited as the first Shaliach to the Youth Department and the Israel Affairs Committee of the Reform movement in America, in order to develop Zionist educand assist in recruiting a *Garin*[1] to settle the Reform kibbutz.

In 5736 (1976) the World Union of Progressive Judaism joined the World Zionist Federation. After the United Nations passed an anti-Zionist resolution, Rabbi Schindler, President of the Reform movement in America, declared before the biennial conference of Reform congregations that, affirming the eternal

---

1. Settlement group.

covenant between the God of Israel, the People of Israel, and the Land of Israel, "we are all Zionists." Rabbi Schindler was surely referring to Zionism in its cultural sense. In May 1976, however, the Board of the Union of American Hebrew Congregations passed a resolution accepting Aliyah as one of the options for personal Jewish self-realization. The resolution also advocated encouraging individuals and *Garinim* in the spirit of Progressive Judaism. The convention also discussed the role and position of Progressive Judaism in the emerging future of Judaism in Israel. There can be no doubt that the decision about Aliyah was influenced by the facts that were already being established "on the ground."

The growing trend toward Zionism does not imply satisfaction with the State of Israel. It is obvious that the absence of legal and religious recognition of the status of Reform rabbis and institutions in Israel is the source of grave frustration. There are also Reform circles that severely criticize Israel's internal and external policies.

However, the above description of the "Zionization" of the Reform movement relates to no more than some five percent of the one million members of Reform synagogues. The vast majority have too marginal an involvement in Jewish life for any influence to be possible.

What led a small and active minority to move toward practical Zionism as one of the expressions of Reform Judaism? I believe that a number of factors are involved:

1) By the early 1960s the existence of the State of Israel was already an accepted part of reality. However the universalistic and prophetic mission of classical Reform demanded that the practical expression of these ideas for enlightened Jews must be in America. The time was right for such an approach: the struggle for Black rights, the peace movement, and Kennedy's New Frontier all attracted young Reform Jews. They had a wide range of possibilities for expressing their identity as Americans and as Jews. This also expressed a sense of responsibility to help achieve the goal of "America as a Second Zion." On a positive note, it should be stressed that young Reform rabbis who participated in general American movements emphasized their Jewishness, in contrast to the accepted approach in the past.

   However the years of enthusiasm were followed by an awakening to reality. Kennedy's New Frontier and Johnson's Great Society turned sour as the nightmares of Vietnam took over. The trend within the Black rights movement to reject the involvement of any outside bodies in its struggle

("If I am not for myself, who will be for me?") led to considerable discomfort.

2) Just as enthusiasm with social and political activism was waning, the Six Day War occurred. For many Jews, including young activists, this period was a watershed. They began to ask whether another Holocaust might occur while the Jews were busily engaged in universalistic missions such as the peace movements, the struggle for Black liberation, ecological issues, and so on. The equivocal position of the American Administration toward saving European Jewry in the Holocaust had only recently come to light. Accordingly, and without rejecting the traditional Reform mission to all peoples, a trend began to develop of intensifying the practical ties with Zion. This process was only partially conscious. The Yom Kippur War and the UN resolution against Zionism were to intensify this line of development.

Israel: The Search for Jewish Identity

The combination of the Reform religious expression and pioneering Zionist expression also required developments on the Israeli scene. After two generations of almost total devotion to political Zionism, the rehabilitation of cultural Zionism began against the backdrop of the fateful events that Israel had undergone.

The Eichmann trial, the excavations at Masada, the Six Day War and the Yom Kippur War, and the UN decisions condemning Zionism were all milestones in the renaissance of Jewish awareness and Jewish identity among the young generation in Israel. The search for new approaches also opened the door to religious alternatives to Orthodoxy. Moreover, Israel as a Jewish state now came to be a subject that preoccupied the kibbutz movement, as can be seen in almost every issue of *Shdemot*.[1] Following the increasing rejection by other nations of our right to exist as a people in our own land, we were pushed into finding strength in our own spiritual sources.

This process, in which we have been engaged since the early 1960s, prepared us as a movement to cooperate with the Reform movement.

In conclusion, a few guesses as to what may prove to be the ideological ramifications of the combination of Reform Judaism and social pioneering Zionism:

1) As Rabbi Shalom Lilker, a member of Kfar Hamaccabi, notes in his

---

1. The literary quarterly of the kibbutz movement.

doctoral thesis on Judaism in the kibbutz[1] (and see also Ben Chanan, "Marking Holidays in 'Godless' Kibbutzim," *Israel Horizons*, September 1975), a "secular" Halacha has already developed in the kibbutz movement and is implemented by a network of committees and institutions in each kibbutz, each movement and even on the inter-movement level. The authority of this Halacha derives from the communal framework. The scope of this "Halacha" includes relationships between individuals, and between the individual and the community. There is also a growing tendency to develop traditions regarding holidays. Combing Reform Judaism in the kibbutz framework raises the possibility of conscious Halachic development free of the shackles of the Orthodox Halacha and not limited by the processes of change sanctified by that stream (see Yedidia Cohen's article "Can There be Changes in the Halacha?" *Shdemot* 59 [1976]).

2) An increase in the Progressive Jewish stream's strength diversifies the religious and political options available. At present bodies such as Gush Emunim operate almost unchallenged from their foundation in Jewish tradition. I believe that a response to extremist Jewish nationalism is required that draws on Jewish tradition rather than on Socialist ideology.

3) In terms of political activities and the ramifications thereof for the Jewish people as a whole (as distinct from party political activity in the State of Israel), the question will arise regarding the position to be taken on issues of "religion." The entry of the Reform movement into the public Zionist arena may be the harbinger of a new element in Zionist ideological responses. This element will reflect a different approach to the Jewish perspective on everyday issues. The political parties with ideology based on class and economic interests borrowed from other nations will become devoid of meaning.

The liberation of the Zionist movement from the party political system of the State of Israel could serve as a healing agent for Zionism in ideological terms. In the new ideological map of Zionism, it is reasonable to assume that "kibbutz" Zionism and "Reform" Zionism will find a common language on many issues relating to the continued creative existence of the people.

(Gesher Haziv — New York)

---

1. Published as *Kibbutz Judaism: A New Tradition in the Making*, Herzl Press, New York, 1982.

Sovereign Chupa (Wedding): Communal Authority as an Ideology in Cultural Zionism

Appendix: What Does a "Sovereign Wedding" Mean For Us?[1]

The Zionist Movement arose not only to assure a political framework so the Jewish People could be "Like all the Nations." On the contrary, the aim of Zionism is to assure the unique nature of the Jewish People and the continuity of its creative existence — wherever it may be. This is the basic assumption of Cultural Zionism, and today it would seem that without this, Zionism has no meaning.

Cultural Zionism means reshaping the face and format of Jewish Society and its culture. Many of the founders of the Zionist Labor Movement thought that in and of itself, self-realization in a cooperative framework on the soil of Eretz Yisrael constituted an adequate social framework. But a person's culture and his ties to his society are shaped by a world of symbols which repeat themselves throughout the year; symbols which accompany the cycle of the individual's life, and the collective life of the community and the people.

No people more than Israel has known throughout the generations how to maintain a world saturated with religio-symbolic deeds in the social context of its communities. These symbols repeat themselves over and over every day, every week, every month, every year, generation after generation, and thus guard our singularity and identity.

In a sense it was easy to be revolutionary in renewing the face of a People, sovereign in terms of communal authority — *creatio ex nihilo*. There was no weighty tradition of autonomous social-political existence in the land, since the destruction (of the Second Temple). Anything was possible.

On the other hand, the situation regarding cultural reform is different. There we have the accretion of a two-thousand-year tradition and Law shaped by Rabbinic Judaism. Rabbinic Judaism determined forms for the ways of expression in the religio-symbolic realm. This brought about not only the negation of the

---

1. *Shdemot* — Literary Journal of the Kibbutz Movement, No. 102, August 1987, pp. 75-77. Translated from Hebrew by Lea Benami and Michael Langer.

traditional way, in which these symbols were expressed, but also the negation of the symbols themselves as a part of the revolutionary act of rejecting the existing fossilized Jewish society.

During the last generation more and more voices have been raised calling for the renewal of cultural initiative. Certainly *Shdemot* has established a reputation for itself as a forum for these discussions.

But Movement organization arising specifically as a result of a conscious desire and feeling of obligation to an organic total social-cultural reform, is a new phenomenon. Tzofei Telem — which functions as an autonomous movement process within the Israeli scouting movement — is still tiny in numbers. Nevertheless it has established several far-reaching principles in this matter. Its first Educational Council (at Kibbutz Yahel, Passover 1980), in considering the whole question of authority concerning reform, determined: "The Educational Council will discuss Movement norms in matters of Jewish and general conduct (Halacha VeHalichot) both for individuals, and for Movement groups. Its decisions will be binding on national movement activities and will serve as recommendations for a way of life for its members."[1] Here we have the idea of the communal democracy as authority for cultural-religious reform — sovereign democratic communal authority instead of traditional rabbinic authority.

In the years since then various questions have been discussed in Tzofei Telem — the nature of Shabbat, creative prayer (called Ma'amad),[2] and social questions such as the relationship with the Israel Scouting Movement and frameworks for self-realization. Communal authority (in this case the authority of the autonomous Youth Movement) takes the place of Rabbinic authority (including the authority of reform Rabbis). The Rabbi is seen as teacher-educator-advisor, and not as an arbiter of Jewish Law.[3]

This ideological approach finds its clear expression in the reasons adduced by the couple from Kibbutz Lotan for their sovereign chupa.

Up till now communal authority in Yahel and Lotan in matters pertaining to Jewish observance has been exercised only regarding the internal life of the Kibbutz. In 1980 there was an attempt to have a Reform Rabbi officiate at a wedding. There was no follow-up and as a result the Israel Movement for Progressive Judaism appealed to the Supreme Court to grant its right to officiate at and register marriages. No verdict has as yet (May 1988)[4] been handed down.

---

1. See Section 6:1, "Authority in Telem Noar."
2. See Section 6:14.
3. See Section 6:10.
4. A negative verdict was finally handed down by the Israel Supreme Court in 1989.

However it is clear that even a favorable verdict would not satisfy the ideological approach of the Lotan couple.

The sovereign wedding of the Lotan couple (both of them Tzofei Telem graduates) constitutes a precedent because it raises the question: Can new movement norms emerge which constitute a renewal of cultural Zionism and a message for Israeli Society as a whole?

Time will tell.

LETTER TO THE MEMBERS OF LOTAN: WHAT DOES A "SOVEREIGN WEDDING" MEAN FOR US?

To the members, shalom:

We wanted to write to "Babayit"[1] our feelings concerning our wedding. And especially as we relate to the wedding ceremony in a manner different than that of the couples who have wed at Lotan until now, and in our position as "firsts," or singular in our approach, we want to clarify together with you what the significance of the wedding ceremony is for us.

Rabbinic Wedding

For ourselves we cannot even consider a "rabbinic" wedding. From a legal standpoint, there is no possibility in Israel to be registered as married without a religious (orthodox) ceremony — there is no civil marriage in Israel. We believe that, given the present political situation, the way to fight such compulsion is by opposing the institutional authority of the rabbis "within reason" by/while creating meaningful/viable alternatives. To this end, we have written to the group which is trying to help couples who wish to marry in such a manner (they are called "The Secular Service"). We hope to receive from them, and from others as well, legal advice, as needed.

Reform Wedding

For ourselves, a reform wedding might be considered but even it is not exactly in accord with our ideas. (We shall certainly consider it seriously should the movement win its case in the Supreme Court.) We believe that the task of Progressive Judaism in our generation, is to go from a stage of rabbinic authority to one of communal authority. The fact of our life on Lotan expresses this idea. It

---

1. "At Home" — Kibbutz Lotan newsletter.

is important to us to express, in the wedding, the effort (which has not yet been successful and which even has trouble staying alive) to create communal spiritual authority which derives from all of us together. In the process of study which we wish to undertake (together with you) in the coming months, we will try to create the spiritual authority and sanctity of Ma'amad, but not via a rabbi who comes from outside the community, not even a reform rabbi.

What We Value Positively

We want a wedding in which/by way of which we will declare (by the *ketubah*[1] we will write and other expressions) to you and our families our shared life. A Jewish wedding which will express our feeling of obligation to the continuation of the creativity of the life of the Jewish People. A wedding in which the members of the community are full participants in the process.

The Process

We attach great importance to the process of study. We want to learn in the near future as much as possible about the Jewish, legal and intellectual aspects of our feelings, in partnership with you. We hope that "in the end" we will know more exactly what it is we want. What kind of ketubah? Rings — yes or no? Breaking of the glass? Will both partners say "According to the Religion of Moses and Israel" or a different formula, and many other questions.

In any process of learning we hope to share with you in different ways. You are our real witnesses to this experience. (We don't intend to do anything which would not be accepted in the community.) It is very important for us to get from home both emotional and collective support if the need arises. All are welcome to speak with us as much as possible and we will try to have organized opportunities to study together and see where we will get to.

This challenge, to realize the dreams of the Youth Movement and words like "Communal Authority" and "Ma'amad" in the actual lives of grown-up people (more or less) is very attractive, but we need a great deal of support.

Chanan Cohen   Osnat Elnatan

---

1. *Ketubah* — marrige contract.

Our Reform Kibbutzim[1]

November 1995

It is 18 (*Chai*) years since the dedication ceremony of the first of our two Reform Kibbutzim, Yahel, in 1977. By no coincidence, that was also the year that ARZA was founded. Kibbutz Lotan was founded in 1983 — one of the last kibbutzim to be established.

Yahel and Lotan were founded in the very last years that the kibbutz movement still appeared to be a true bastion of pioneering Zionist ideology (with which many Reform Jews who considered themselves to be Zionists had always sympathized). The Reform kibbutzim were a symbolic expression of an alliance between two of the seminal movements of modern Jewish history committed to reviving the prophetic tradition within Judaism — Reform Judaism and Labor Zionism. The common denominator was an activist commitment to social justice and ethical human interrelationships.

A central tenet of Reform Zionism is the development of living communities in Israel which synthesize between religious reform and social reform. Reform Zionism draws on the Cultural Zionist tradition of Achad Ha'am which sees the Jewish National Home as a "pilot plant" for creative modern Judaism and Jewish community. Reform Judaism's pluralistic and democratic traditions preclude a single predetermined form for such community but clearly the Reform kibbutzim are one option. They are grappling with the day to day challenge of realizing a particular and unique option within Cultural Zionism — Reform Zionist community.

The Historic Image of the Kibbutzim

In the past, the kibbutzim were seen (and saw themselves) as the midwives of the State yet in embryo. Before the establishment of the State and throughout its first difficult years the kibbutzim willingly took part in the practical tasks of settling the land under primitive conditions, organizing the mainstream underground opposition to the British Mandate, leading the way in the War of Independence, and confronting initial tasks of state-building.

---

1. Unpublished leaflet of the Educational Tourism Branch of Kibbutz Lotan, 1995.

By their practical achievements, the kibbutz pioneers lent credibility to the claims of political Zionism. In 1947 the United Nations Special Committee on Palestine (UNSCOP) visited the first kibbutzim in the northern Negev and saw the results of the initial efforts in desert agriculture. It was one of the factors in the decision to award the then totally barren Negev to the future Jewish State. Yahel and Lotan have inherited that tradition of desert pioneering.

After the establishment of the State, many kibbutz members accepted the idea that their purpose was now to serve the State as it is. The original premise that the kibbutz was to be a model community exemplifying a particular social vision rooted in prophetic ideals of what the State should be, was shunted aside in the name of practical exigencies.

Today, almost 50 years after the establishment of the State, the kibbutzim are no longer a "practical" necessity for Israel. Those who find the kibbutz way of life personally satisfying and meaningful continue to live on the kibbutz but they are no longer on center-stage as far as the Israeli public is concerned. Many kibbutzim are undergoing a crisis of purpose.

Two small but significant "islands" stand out in today's kibbutz movement. One is a "cultural island" — the orthodox religious kibbutz movement of some 15 kibbutzim whose kibbutz ideology was (and is) based on orthodox Judaism. (The Reform kibbutzim are unacceptable to the orthodox kibbutzim even though some of the latter's individual members have great sympathy for the Reform kibbutzim.)

The other "island" of 10-15 kibbutzim are those far from the center of the country, particularly in the Negev and the Arava — a "geographical island." Ninety-five percent of Israel's population lives north of Beersheva. A mere five percent inhabit the Negev and the Arava which constitute 55% of the country's area.

Yahel and Lotan, de facto, are both cultural and geographical islands. A relevant ideology and the challenge of geography have strengthened their sense of purpose. However, it would be naive to suppose that our kibbutzim have been unaffected by the unprecedented technological, ideological, economic and political changes which Israel and the world have undergone during these years.

Forces Shaping the Reform Kibbutzim

It was quite clear to most of those who opted to settle in Yahel and Lotan that their role in State building was marginal. From the beginning, the rationale of the Reform Kibbutzim was to be a "pilot plant" for Reform and for Cultural (rather than Political) Zionism. There was to be a synthesis of Zionist pioneering with the Reform tradition of creative adaptation of the Jewish heritage to a twentieth century setting.

At a personal level, for many of the founding members of Yahel and Lotan, there was the exhilaration of starting something from the beginning. For all there was the challenge of "making the desert bloom." It was an adventure.

The longer haul has sometimes been less than romantic. As has been the case with other desert kibbutzim, both Yahel and Lotan have found that the economic exigencies, the relative isolation, and the difficult climate have generated special selective pressures. In particular, most members of Yahel and Lotan do not come from personal backgrounds of economic deprivation and the challenge of economic viability in the desert was one for which they were not really prepared. In both kibbutzim, first in Yahel and currently in Lotan, this has been one cause of membership turnover as the founders reach their early thirties and ask themselves "Is this really where I want to invest myself and raise my family?"

A nucleus of those electing to remain are determined and focused people. Amongst a significant number on the Reform kibbutzim that determination is rooted in Reform Zionist commitment. The clearer focus is also reflected in a more realistic absorption policy for each kibbutz. Hard lessons have been learnt. The Reform Kibbutzim are not a refuge for those who can't "make it" outside of the kibbutz.

The Challenge of the Reform Kibbutzim

Outside of Yahel and Lotan there are no Reform congregations anywhere in the world (including in Israel) which constitute total communities as such. If Judaism is to be a way of life, a "Torat Chaim," then our Reform kibbutzim are the unique framework wherein the ideas of Reform Judaism can really be put to the test. There are few partitions in kibbutz community life. The kibbutzim struggle with, among others, questions relating to economic viability, work relationships (including hired labor), Jewish religious education in a secular regional environment, and Jewish ritual and authority in the community.

By virtue of its liberal roots, Reform Judaism is democratic and pluralistic in many matters. The same holds true for Yahel and Lotan. Within the general framework of kibbutz structure both Yahel and Lotan relate differently to many aspects of both religious and secular (social-economic) life.

By their very nature as Reform Zionist kibbutzim, Yahel and Lotan raise basic questions both for Reform Judaism and for Zionism.

Is the purview of Reform Judaism limited to a Diaspora type congregational framework whether in Israel or the Diaspora? What does Reform Judaism have to offer in the way of ideas and practice to Jewish community?

Was the Zionist purpose in establishing Israel primarily to serve as a refuge for Jewish homeless and oppressed? Or was/is Israel also a framework for creatively confronting the challenge of a pluralistic and meaningful Judaism in the twenty-first century?

Reform Zionism is based on the premise that Reform Judaism must innovate forms of Jewish community in order to ensure Jewish continuity. Reform Zionism is also based on the premise that the Zionist purpose of the Jewish National Home is to ensure the continued creative survival of the Jewish people whether in Israel or the Diaspora. There is no doubt that the Reform kibbutzim are pioneers in that endeavor.

The Shlichut of Reform Kibbutzim to the Reform Jewish Community

Above all, it is the sense of Reform Zionist Jewish identity and educational obligation to Reform Jewish youth throughout the world (including Israel) which has given Yahel and Lotan a sense of purpose, of *shlichut* (mission). Such a specific sense of purpose sets Yahel and Lotan off from most other kibbutzim.

The day to day ramifications of undertaking this obligation are many. In particular, it means committing leadership to youth work and it means "flooding" the kibbutz with youth groups. Even when this takes the form of an economic activity (educational tourism) few kibbutzim in the country have the inner motivation to cope with hundreds (even thousands) of young people impacting on a community whose permanent adult population rarely exceeds one hundred.

Given the current quandary of Diaspora Judaism in matters of Jewish education, identity and commitment, one can only assume that a living experience on a Reform kibbutz in Israel will be of ever greater importance to the educational effort of Reform Judaism in the Diaspora. Hopefully, the Reform movement will assist the Reform kibbutzim in acquiring the wherewithal to develop the necessary infrastructure to expand this role.

Although by their nature the Reform kibbutzim are an inspiration to many but the life path of only a few, both Yahel and Lotan add a unique dimension to Reform Judaism's challenge to define meaningful Jewish community.

Appendix

<u>Our Path: A Vision Statement, Kibbutz Lotan</u>

This is where we, the members of Kibbutz Lotan, have chosen to make our home and build our future. Through our commitment to *Am Israel, Torat Israel* and the State of Israel, we are working together to create a community based on Reform Zionist Jewish values:

* **Jewish Renewal:** We work towards creating a progressive expression of Jewish religion and culture in our rituals and day-to-day life, through *mitzvot* in our relationships between each other and with God.

* **Equality:** Our belief in the equal worth of every wo/man is expressed through direct democracy, equality in the work-place, gender equality, and mutual responsibility.

* **Economic Cooperation:** Together we are responsible for our livelihood and share our resources as an expression of our belief in the strength of communal action.

* **Ecology:** We strive to fulfill the biblical ideal "to till the earth and preserve it", in our home, our region, the country and the world. We are working to create ways to live in harmony with our desert environment.

* **I - Thou:** We aspire to openness, communication and mutual respect in order to constantly better relationships with each other.

* **Livelihood:** We strive for economic independence, and aim to support ourselves in ways that are in keeping with our values.

* **Home and Community:** Our commitment to our home and community is expressed through cooperative action in work, education, culture, health, and day-to-day life.

* *Tikkun Olam* --**"Repairing the World":** We work towards the betterment of ourselves, our people and the world. Our home is a community of *shlichut*. Our way of life constitutes the message we wish to impart to those that enter our gates and to those outside of our community with whom we are involved.

This declaration is a living document which requires ongoing involvement and engagement on our part.

> "It is not for you to complete the work
> Neither are you free to desist from it."

(Signed by the members of Kibbutz Lotan, 23/10/97--Simchat Torah 5758)